D0921227

The post-Mao urban reforms of the past decade have physically and psychologically transformed China's cities. *Urban Spaces in Contemporary China* explores how the character of city life changed after political and economic restructuring intensified in 1984, and how this change affected the creation of new physical, economic, and cultural spaces in urban China. The book focuses on the impact of increased commercialization and reduced state power on associations, economics, government, and creativity in urban areas.

The authors draw from a wide range of backgrounds, including anthropology, economics, comparative literature, art history, law, political science, and sociology, and all have lived and worked in a Chinese city for an extended time in the late 1980s or early 1990s. Each brings personal insights to dimensions of Chinese urban life that are often misunderstood: China's large "floating populations," avant-garde art, labor movements, and leisure.

WOODROW WILSON CENTER SERIES

Urban spaces in contemporary China

Other books in the series

Michael J. Lacey, editor, *Religion and Twentieth-Century American Intellectual Life*

Michael J. Lacey, editor, *The Truman Presidency*

Joseph Kruzel and Michael H. Haltzel, editors, *Between the Blocs: Problems and Prospects for Europe's Neutral and Nonaligned States*

William C. Brumfield, editor, *Reshaping Russian Architecture: Western Technology, Utopian Dreams*

Mark N. Katz, editor, *The USSR and Marxist Revolutions in the Third World*

Walter Reich, editor, *Origins of Terrorism: Psychologies, Ideologies, Theologies, States of Mind*

Mary O. Furner and Barry Supple, editors, *The State and Economic Knowledge: The American and British Experiences*

Michael J. Lacey and Knud Haakonssen, editors, *A Culture of Rights: The Bill of Rights in Philosophy, Politics, and Law—1791 and 1991*

Robert J. Donovan and Ray Scherer, *Unsilent Revolution: Television News and American Public Life, 1948–1991*

Nelson Lichtenstein and Howell John Harris, editors, *Industrial Democracy in America: The Ambiguous Promise*

William Craft Brumfield and Blair A. Ruble, editors, *Russian Housing in the Modern Age: Design and Social History*

Michael J. Lacey and Mary O. Furner, editors, *The State and Social Investigation in Britain and the United States*

Hugh Ragsdale, editor and translator, *Imperial Russian Foreign Policy*

Dermot Keogh and Michael H. Haltzel, editors, *Northern Ireland and the Politics of Reconciliation*

Joseph Klaits and Michael H. Haltzel, editors, *The Global Ramifications of the French Revolution*

René Lemarchand, *Burundi: Ethnocide as Discourse and Practice*

James M. Morris, editor, *On Mozart*

James R. Millar and Sharon L. Wolchik, editors, *The Social Legacy of Communism*

Blair A. Ruble, *Money Sings: The Changing Politics of Urban Space in Post-Soviet Yaroslavl*

Urban spaces in contemporary China

The potential for autonomy and community in post-Mao China

Edited by
DEBORAH S. DAVIS, RICHARD KRAUS, BARRY NAUGHTON,
and ELIZABETH J. PERRY

WOODROW WILSON CENTER PRESS

AND

Published by the Press Syndicate of the University of Cambridge
The Pitt Building, Trumpington Street, Cambridge CB2 1RP
40 West 20th Street, New York, NY 10011-4211, USA
10 Stamford Road, Oakleigh, Melbourne 3166, Australia

First published 1995

Printed in the United States of America

Libary of Congress Cataloging-in-Publication Data
Urban spaces in contemporary China: the potential for autonomy and
community in post-Mao China / edited by Deborah S. Davis . . . [et al.].
p. cm. — (Woodrow Wilson Center series)
Includes index.
ISBN 0-521-47410-8.—ISBN 0-521-47943-6 (pbk.)
1. Cities and towns—China. 2. City and town life—China.
3. Urbanization—China. I. Davis, Deborah, 1945–   . II. Series.
HT147.C48U72 1995
307.76'0951—dc20   94-41879
                                    CIP

A catalog record for this book is available from the British Library.

ISBN 0-521-47410-8 hardback
ISBN 0-521-47943-6 paperback

Contents

Acknowledgments

The editors thank all who participated in the conference "City Living, City Life: The Potential for Autonomy and Community in Post-Mao China," which took place at the Woodrow Wilson Center from May 1 to May 4, 1992.

In particular, the editors are indebted to Mary Brown Bullock, director of the Asia Program of the Woodrow Wilson Center, who inspired and led us throughout the endeavor, crafting the first grant proposals, remaining committed when initial efforts failed, and coordinating the publishing process. To her there must be special accolades, for without her unstinting efforts and imagination, this book would never have appeared.

Support for the conference and this volume was provided by the Henry Luce Foundation and the Woodrow Wilson Center's federal conference funds.

1

Introduction:
Urban China

DEBORAH S. DAVIS

CITY LANDSCAPES BEFORE AND AFTER MAO

Chinese urban spaces were transformed during the 1980s. The number of cities multiplied, and the formally registered urban population grew to nearly 240 million.[1] In addition, at least 70 million transients abandoned life in the villages to settle in urban areas. Though officially considered temporary residents and therefore uncounted in government statistics, these rural sojourners became an integral part of city life and dramatically increased both the density and heterogeneity of urban settlements.[2]

Demographic shifts, however, capture only one dimension of the transformation of urban spaces; equally important were changes in the political economy that altered the lines of authority and the flow of

---

[1]The total number of residents officially registered as living in cities and towns is actually rather poorly defined. For example, the total number registered by the government as living in towns and cities grew from 191 million to 301 million between 1980 and 1990, but that number does not accurately measure numbers of urbanites because a looser definition of urban used after 1984 included millions of agricultural households who were not treated as urban residents. If one restricts the definition of urban to include only those in non-agricultural households the total of urbanites between 1980 and 1990 jumped from 168 million to 239 million, and it is this latter number that I assume most closely represents the urban population for the purposes of government services and planning. There are also problems in making comparisons because some reports use end-of-year totals, while others use mid-year figures or do not give month of census. *Zhongguo renkou tongji nianjian 1992* (Chinese population statistics yearbook) (Beijing: Zhongguo tongji chubanshe, 1993), 451; *Zhongguo tongji nianjian 1993* (Chinese statistical yearbook) (hereafter *ZGTJNJ*) (Beijing: Zhongguo tongji chubanshe; 1994), 81; *Renmin ribao* (hereafter *RMRB*), November 30, 1984, 1.

[2]*RMRB*, December 18, 1990, 4; and Roger Chan, "Challenges to Urban Areas," in *China Review 1992* (Hong Kong: Chinese University of Hong Kong Press, 1992), 12.12.

resources between the central government and the municipalities. When the central plan dominated, city economies were directed by Beijing's priorities. City enterprises were cut off from their natural hinterlands and, in a clear departure from earlier Chinese experience, cities developed "hard edges" that segregated rural and urban populations as clearly as any moated city wall. After 1980, the new enthusiasm for markets, decentralization, and foreign investment undermined barriers between urban and rural populations. Cities became economically more autonomous from Beijing and more embedded in their immediate locale; the visual result was an urban-rural sprawl reminiscent of that observed during years of rapid industrialization in Japan, Korea, and Taiwan.

Within urban areas, land use and allocation of space also changed in response to the new economic and political priorities. For example, in the years immediately after 1949, the Chinese Communist Party (CCP) leadership systematically denigrated religious and ritual spaces by either closing them to the public or transforming them for secular use. By the mid-1980s, urban leaders had relaxed this censorship and even deliberately encouraged city bureaus and private citizens to return temples, shrines, and churches to their pre-Communist functions. They also tolerated more diverse and spontaneous uses of parks and sidewalks, and public spaces again became available for a wide range of nonstate—even antistate—activities, which at times antagonized local officials, but which ultimately further accelerated the pace of transformation.

Decentralization and greater reliance on market mechanisms also altered the urban topography environment built within city centers. Between 1950 and 1976, most cities were designed to expand in increments of self-sufficient industrial "cells" (*danwei*), a plan that China copied from the Soviet Union of the 1950s. By contrast cities of the early 1990s grew around specialized nodes of commerce, finance, and trade, and the new construction created skylines that contrasted dramatically with the uniform, gray horizons of the 1960s and 1970s.

These transformations in the material dimensions of urban space had parallels in the social world of Chinese cities. When self-sufficient enterprises typical of the *danwei* system defined boundaries of ownership and control, Chinese citizens spent most of their lives living and working behind gated walls. Every unit had a limited number of entry points; most could be locked, and almost all were staffed by security personnel. After commercial activity returned to the streets, and skyscrapers towered over six-story walk-ups, the walls that had dominated urban terrain could no longer regulate human and material traffic as effectively. Some *danwei* walls were dismantled, and others were breached by newly constructed stores and restaurants that burrowed through the walls into once exclusively *danwei* space. As a result of such architectural reconfigurations, previously protected interiors became more accessible to the general public, and city landscapes throughout China developed more in response to individual taste and market competition than administrative fiat.

PERSONAL AUTONOMY AND EMERGENT COMMUNITIES

In the gated *danwei* of the Maoist era, city residents lived under close scrutiny of neighbors and employers; individuals rarely experienced anonymity, and they enjoyed only a modicum of social autonomy. So extreme was the immobility and absence of privacy that even leisure time was closely regulated. After 1980, the depoliticization of the workplace and deregulation of economic life created very different conditions. There were fewer hours of political study at the workplace, and large portions of each day previously claimed as the domain of the party-state became private, or at least less regulated. In city neighborhoods a wide range of new public premises—billiard parlors, bars, and beauty shops— permitted urbanites to spend a larger percentage of their day congregating with friends, or—equally important—enjoying time alone. Most people continued to work in state-owned enterprises as permanent workers, but the retreat of politics and the new legitimacy of commodification (*shangpinhua*) revolutionized consumption patterns and fostered a new range of individual preferences.[3] Leisure time and leisure choices multiplied, and within the less regulated urban spaces, a vibrant urban (*shimin*) culture evolved in directions too diverse to be controlled by party or government censorship.

The decline in the power and reach of the Maoist party-state and the proliferation of new economic and social organizations unquestionably enlivened city life and opened up new venues for both public and private interaction. Yet the retreat of the state did not create the organizational and legal buffers necessary to sustain open criticism of the regime. Nor

---

[3]In 1980 there were 80 million state employees in an urban labor force of 105 million. By 1990, the state labor force had grown to 106 million in a labor force of 153 million (*ZGTJNJ*, 97).

Table 1.1. *Changing fertility trends*

	CBR	Rural TFR	Urban TFR
1950	37	5.9	5.0
1955	32	6.3	5.6
1960	20	3.9	4.0
1965	37	6.5	3.7
1970	33	6.3	3.2
1975	23	3.9	1.7
1980	18	2.4	1.1
1989	21	2.7	1.4

CBR = Crude birth rate   TFR = Total fertility rate
Note: After 1984 urban TFR included birth in *xiang* government settlements, which previously had been counted as rural.
Sources: For CBR 1965–89, *Zhongguo tongji manjian 1992* (Chinese Statistical Yearbook) (*ZGTJNJ*), p. 78; for CBR 1950–60 and TFR 1950–1980, Judith Banister, *China's Changing Population* (Stanford University Press, 1987), 243; for TFR 1989, *Renmin ribao*, December 18, 1990, 4; *ZGTJNJ 1992*, 78.

had the central government and the CCP renounced their power to intrude coercively into everyday life. Rather, as is evident in the design and subsequent implementation of the one-child family campaign and in the arrests of politically or religiously heterodox individuals, the authoritarian party-state maintained its ability to intervene in the most private areas of urban life or to decimate collective challenges to the CCP's political monopolies.

In the realm of personal life, the 1979 policy decision to limit each woman to one child radically altered the family life of fifty million young urban couples. In rural areas, citizens resisted the official quotas, and by the end of the decade the government was forced to accept a two- or three-child norm for rural families. In urban areas, by contrast, the populace was unable to reject the most draconian birth control policy of the entire post-1949 era. In 1980 the total fertility rate (TFR) of urban women was an extraordinary 1.1; in 1989, when the definition of urban had expanded to include the newly incorporated suburban and township areas, average TFR had risen to only 1.4 (Table 1.1). And in the large metropolitan cities like Shanghai more than 95 percent of all births were first (and only) children.[4]

To some extent urban couples found it easier to comply with the one-child policy because urban parents "needed" children less than their ru-

[4]*RMRB*, December 18, 1990, 4; June 17, 1991, 1.

ral peers. In old age, urban residents—whether employed in state or collective enterprises—were guaranteed a pension, while rural elderly had to rely totally on their adult children, typically a co-resident son. City women remained close to their parents after marriage and provided care and support almost as often as did their brothers. Rural women married "out" of their natal villages, and daughters could not easily substitute for a son either economically or in rituals of honor or mourning. For these reasons, city families could more easily tolerate the risk of an only child, and found the consequences of having only a daughter less problematic than did village families. Nevertheless, it would be a mistake either to deny the opposition to the policy within the cities or to ignore the unrelenting coercion that guaranteed the high levels of compliance over the decade.

In the public realms of politics and organized religion, the persistent power of the Communist party-state is also evident. The pervasive repression of the 1970s was no more, but the retreat of state surveillance was relative and often unpredictable. For example in 1976 it would have been inconceivable for the wife of a man who had already been arrested for—among other things—speaking to foreign reporters subsequently to announce in an interview with the *New York Times* that she was considering suing the government over her husband's arrest. But in July 1993, this is exactly what Li Liping told *New York Times* correspondent Nicholas Kristoff when her husband, Fu Shenqi, was detained.[5] It is also equally true that in 1981 Fu had been arrested for his participation in the Beijing Spring pro-democracy movement and spent the next five and half years of his life in prison.

After 1978 government and party officials altered their relationship to ordinary citizens. They did not control consumer choices as tightly, restrict physical and social mobility, or monitor social relationships as they had in earlier decades. Yet the state (*guojia*) retained substantial, authoritarian powers that sharply limited personal autonomy and denied legitimacy to most nonstate organizations. Even in the realm of commerce, where one might have found the first signs of an emergent public sphere parallel to that mobilized by eighteenth-century European merchants, increased commodification did not serve immediately as a catalyst for social empowerment. Instead, as David Wank and Yves Chevrier discovered in their studies of the new urban business class, the largest

[5]*New York Times*, July 12, 1993.

financial gains often were made by those still deeply embedded in party-state bureaucracy, rather than by those working independently in lightly regulated competitive markets.[6] The "spoiler state" of the high Maoist era was in retreat, but both CCP and government officials continued to exercise such unbridled powers that ordinary urbanites were unable to define the limits of either the possible or the probable without attention to persistent state and party privileges.[7]

Decentralization and deregulation created the physical and social space for individuals to seek personal satisfaction more openly than had been true for several decades. They did not, however, grant the freedom to escape entirely CCP or government supervision and intrusions. Even less did they enable citizens to challenge or resist state monopolies by organizing around antistate or antiparty ideals.

The subordination and powerlessness of ordinary Chinese urbanites during the late 1980s were modest in comparison to the oppression endured by slaves or prisoners. Yet James Scott's study of rebellion and resistance among these two populations suggests one scenario in which the new—if limited—freedoms to escape the narrow political rhetoric of official Maoism may have created the foundation for fundamental realignments of power in urban China.[8] In *Domination and the Arts of Resistance*, Scott focuses on the power of hidden transcripts—both the deeply felt criticisms subordinated groups share when they are away from their overseers, masters, and prison guards and the equally hidden transcripts that circulate among elites when they are not in a socially heterogeneous public space. Scott argues that the persistence of domination rests on an unspoken acceptance of the transcripts' remaining hidden; but when they are suddenly articulated in public, even one act of speech can galvanize power previously checked by the superior resources of the dominant group:

[6]David Wank, "Merchant Entrepreneurs and Development of Civil Society," paper presented at the Annual Meetings of the Association of Asian Studies, April 1991, and Yves Chevrier, "Social Autonomy and Civil Society," paper presented at the Euro-American Symposium: "Society versus the State in Chinese, Japanese, Korean, and Vietnamese Traditions," Paris, May 1991.

[7]Jan T. Gross created this term to describe the soviet state of the Stalinist era, which gained its power and maintained its hegemony in a zero-sum exchange wherein each increment of state power represented an equal evisceration of society. I find it an apt description of the oppressive state of the high Mao era (*Revolution from Abroad* [Princeton: Princeton University Press, 1988]).

[8]James Scott, *Domination and the Arts of Resistance* (New Haven: Yale University Press, 1990).

When the first declaration of the hidden transcript succeeds, its mobilizing capacity as symbolic act is potentially awesome. At the level of tactics and strategy, it is a powerful straw in the wind. It portends a possible turning of the tables. Key symbolic acts are, as one sociologist puts it, "tests of whether or not the whole system of mutual fear will hold up." At the level of political beliefs, anger, and dreams it is a social explosion. That first declaration speaks for countless others, it shouts out what has historically had to be whispered, controlled, stifled, and suppressed. If the results seem like moments of madness, if the politics they engender is tumultuous, frenetic, delirious, and occasionally violent, that is perhaps because the powerless are so rarely on the public stage and have so much to say and do when they finally arrive.[9]

Scott requires that we give serious thought to the power of voluntarism to destroy coercive and enduring institutions; he also directs our attention away from the obvious levers of state power and demands that we consider alternative mechanisms of mobilization. In Scott's historical overview, individuals, even when severely repressed, retain the ability to envision alternative regimes. In this way people become psychologically prepared to act collectively at that moment when one of their number dares to articulate the alternative. Scott employs this scenario to explain the sudden implosion of East European party-states; if he is correct, then it is possible that despite the successful coercion exercised by the Chinese party-state in support of the one-child family and against political dissent, Chinese urbanites may already be psychologically prepared for radical and successful confrontations against CCP hegemony in the near future.

DEFINING QUESTIONS OF THIS VOLUME

During the 1980s Chinese cities became a critical meeting ground for the new traders, investors, brokers, and customers ready to take advantage of the reduced scope of political controls. Cities provided the physical and social space where previously suppressed economic, political, and cultural activities emerged into public view. The new complexity and openness of city life, however, did not create a Habermasian public sphere of "private people coming together as a public to debate the general rules governing relations in the basically privatized but publicly relevant sphere of commodity exchange and social labor."[10] Neverthe-

---

[9]Ibid., 227.

[10]Jürgen Habermas, *The Structural Transformation of the Public Sphere*, trans. Thomas Burger (Cambridge: MIT Press, 1989), 27.

less, the partial retreat of the party-state and the disorder created by irregularly monitored market exchanges permitted residents of Chinese cities to converse publicly and privately about an ever wider range of subjects and with an ever more diverse group of people than at any time since the establishment of the People's Republic. State monopolies of information—the key resource in postindustrial production and trade— were crumbling, and more privatized ownership of the means of production and of capital empowered individuals and social strata whom the Maoist regime had consistently silenced to act on their immediate self-interest. As a result, China was poised for momentous change as its citizens gathered the knowledge and resources with which to nurture new solidarities and ties of reciprocity.[11]

Under such circumstances of material and ideological dislocation, the boundaries between public and private "were rendered problematic" and the urban public began to use its "critical judgment" to reevaluate the legitimate scope of state power and the ideal processes of government in ways not dissimilar to what Habermas described for eighteenth-century European cities.[12] As Margaret Somers has demonstrated in her study of the expansion of citizenship among the English poor, civil society and the public sphere need not emerge well defined or neatly compartmentalized from markets or government institutions. On the contrary, Somers found that in the English case "the public sphere denotes a contested participatory site in which actors with overlapping identities as legal subjects, citizens, economic actors, and family and community members form a public body and engage in negotiatons over political and social life."[13]

Working within Somers's perspective, therefore, an examination of the character of contemporary Chinese city life legitimately—even necessarily—addresses questions about the potential for civil society and the quality of the public sphere.[14] Whether one focuses on individuals like

---

[11]Anita Chan, "Revolution or Corporatism?" *Australian Journal of Chinese Affairs*, no. 29 (January 1993): 31–62; Mayfair Yang, "Between State and Society," *Australian Journal of Chinese Affairs* no. 22 (July 1989): 31–60.

[12]Habermas, *The Structural Transformation*, 24.

[13]Margaret Somers, "Citizenship and the Place of the Public Sphere," *American Sociological Review* 58, no. 5 (1993): 587–620.

[14]Thus in terms of the debate over whether or not West European experience with civil society is relevant to the Chinese case, this volume more consistently agrees with the arguments of Mary Rankin, William Rowe, and David Strand. For an example of this debate, see Symposium in *Modern China* 19, no. 2 (April 1993), and David Strand, "Protest in Beijing," *Problems of Communism* 39, no. 3 (May–June 1990).

Fu Shenqi and Li Liping or on emergent associations such as those in Tiananmen Square during the spring of 1989, one observes urban Chinese from many walks of life debating the ideal form of government, the limits of privacy, and the definition of public responsibility more openly than since the 1940s. Even within the CCP and especially within the government bureaucracy, not only discussion but explicit efforts have taken place to routinize political power and to renegotiate the Maoist boundaries between public and private interests.[15]

After the massacre on June 4, 1989, optimistic predictions about the ability of social forces to redefine the Chinese polity seemed naive, and both within China and without, many postmortems attributed the debacle to the weakness of societal associations and more broadly to the historical absence of a civil society.[16] In most of this post-1989 literature, however, the focus was on the primary political actors. Rather little attention was given to how the transformation of everyday life or organizational innovations in areas not directly drawn into the Beijing confrontation and final military attack had begun to reshape urban society more generally. To my knowledge no one focused on altered roles of cities or attempted an integrated study of urban life in the 1980s comparable to what Martin Whyte and William Parish did for the 1970s.[17] In part, the absence of such a general examination of urban life is explained by the lack of time to reflect on the turbulent decade and the accelerating pace of institutional and ideological change after 1990. Yet as the twentieth anniversary of Mao's death approaches, such broad overviews of the social consequences of the post-Mao reforms should begin. Otherwise, an important opportunity will be lost for understanding how this decade of fundamental social upheaval prepared the way for subsequent events.

In terms of pace of change and numbers of people affected, rural China could claim priority for such a scholarly review. Yet if the focus of interest is the transformation of the boundary between state and society, and more narrowly the emergence of a public sphere, urban spaces and city life have equal claim on our attention. Political power is concentrated in Chinese cities, and it has been urban residents who have

---

[15]See for example the study by Melanie Manion, *Retirement of Revolutionaries in China* (Princeton: Princeton University Press, 1993).

[16]One of the earliest and still most comprehensive discussions of different views is Strand, "Protest in Beijing," 1–19.

[17]Martin Whyte and William Parish, *Urban Life in Contemporary China* (Chicago: University of Chicago Press, 1984).

been most visibly involved in political debate. Moreover, urban society is more accessible to outsiders and the published record is denser and more easily available. For these several reasons, the goal of this volume is to use a broad overview of city life after 1979 to explore the many ways in which shifting boundaries between public and private, and between state and society, have created the conditions for an emergent public sphere.

The contributors first met on the weekend of May 4, 1992. To each participant, the organizers posed two simple questions: In reference to the sphere of contemporary urban life that you know best, where have been the greatest gains for personal autonomy? And if relevant, to what extent did you observe associational ties that signaled emergent urban communities or nonstate institutions? The organization of the volume reflects the priority given to these initial questions. It also reflects the debate and discussion of the conference itself. Thus in addition to the shared focus on questions of individual autonomy and collective associations, there are chapters on the transformation of the physical urban environment, as well as on the creation of distinctive post-Mao urban cultures and identities highlighting the altered relationship between state and society.

Part I, "Urban Space," focusing on the changing allocation and use of physical space, begins with geographer Piper Gaubatz's portrait of the socialist city as seen from the perspective of Chinese city planners. In this chapter, she documents how new market forces as well as greater openness both to the outside world and to China's pre-Communist traditions rapidly undermined the cellular landscape of Maoist cities and created a new urban environment built around functional specialization. In Chapter 3, Barry Naughton, though primarily dealing with the Chinese city as an economic actor, addresses the phenomenon of physical sprawl to illustrate his larger theme of increased integration between urban and rural markets. In Chapter 4, Vivienne Shue also emphasizes "urban sprawl," but in contrast to Naughton, who associates the attendant sprawl with the retreat of the state and the extension of markets, Shue attributes it to the new regulations that control tax revenues and land use. In the final chapter of Part I, Dorothy Solinger analyzes the life chances of the rural immigrants who have transformed street life with their stalls and tarpaulins, as well as staffing the construction teams that have created the new physical environment. Despite their obviously central role and physical presence throughout urban China, Solinger found city leaders unwilling to consider them legitimate urbanites. Without a doubt the party-state's unwillingness to recognize the reality of the new urban society speaks directly to its decreased ability to design and implement its own blueprint for modernization.

Geographer Gaubatz, economist Naughton, and political scientists Shue and Solinger each analyze contemporary urban spaces through their distinctive disciplinary lenses. Yet, read in sequence, these several perspectives capture the centrifugal and centripetal forces that reshaped Chinese cities in the 1980s. In this way, Part I explicitly documents the contested ground on which Chinese citizens challenged preexisting boundaries between state and societal authority. Each author identified elements of the Maoist spoiler state that maintained critical monopolies. The persistence of this powerful authoritarian state is best illustrated in Solinger's discussion of the barriers preventing assimilation of the rural emigrants and in Shue's discussion of the expansion of a new regulatory state. Even when scholarly priorities are not focused on the political or administrative, as is the case for Gaubatz and Naughton, authors discovered that the new autonomy and dynamism within post-Mao cities were constrained by an enduring party-state reluctant to share its administrative and coercive power.

In Part II, "Urban Culture and Identities," the central questions shift from questions about space to those about time. The section begins with a study of ordinary consumers—their enjoyment of home videos, romance novels, and karaoke—and then considers the world of high culture artists. Throughout, the authors share a concern over how participation in the more heterogeneous urban society of the 1980s created identities at variance with those proscribed in the Mao era, and how in turn these identities fostered collective association and activity.

Because of the CCP leadership's repeated use of class struggle and pervasive censorship after 1949, Chinese artists and nonartists *necessarily* took their cues from party and government agendas out of concern for their security—even survival. Public identities were shaped to fit with the official ideals of sacrifice for the collective, hatred of the bourgeois, and, in the extreme version that prevailed during the Cultural Revolution, rejection of all traditional art forms. In private, the tenacious or alienated individual might nourish a counteridentity that celebrated the ethereal, the sensual, or the intensely private. But such pleasures and identities could not be displayed in public. Nor could they provide the link to draw peers together openly into communities of fellow connoisseurs or performers.

As Richard Kraus explains in Chapter 7, however, the situation was not simply one of repression. On the contrary, after 1949, the CCP state greatly expanded the number of those who could work professionally in the world of culture and through the guarantee of lifelong employment, the state provided artists with unprecedented material security. As a result, urban artists and writers—and they were overwhelmingly based in urban places and addressed urban concerns—occupied a paradoxical position in which both resources and audience greatly expanded even as the Communist state exercised pervasive censorship, a paradox that Hungarian critic Miklos Haraszti elegantly captures with the phrase "velvet prison."[18]

After 1980 conditions for the creation and consumption of cultural products radically changed. Overall it was a period marked by a massive liberalization. Previously forbidden subjects, authors, and foreign imports flooded the urban markets. Efforts were made intermittently to punish individual artists or eradicate a particular product, but in terms of individual autonomy and associational ties, the decade produced noticeable gains for both artists and their audiences. Yet openness to the West and reliance on consumer preferences also had negative consequences. After an initial period of rebirth and expansion, some high art and traditional art groups began to falter when they lost state subsidies and failed to develop a mass audience that could pay salaries and cover expenses. No event captures this destructive capacity of post-Mao reform better than the 1993 decision to tear down the old Beijing Opera house on Wangfujing Street to make way for a joint venture mall sponsored by a Hong Kong consortium of real estate investors.

Part II addresses these conflicting trends from several different vantage points. In Chapter 6, Shaoguang Wang reviews the explosive growth in movie and reading publics, and the impact of the VCR revolution in urban China. His primary concern is how the state has loosened rather than lost control over the private sphere of life and as a result redefined the boundaries between public and private life. Autonomy and privacy, not identity, are the central issues. In Chapter 7, political scientist Rich-

---

[18]Miklos Haraszti, *The Velvet Prison: Artists under State Socialism* (New York: Noonday Press, 1989).

ard Kraus shifts the readers' attention to the artists and creators of cultural products, paying particular attention to how the retreat of the CCP party-state—in terms of both its past censorship and financial support—and the advance of various markets created new cleavages among urban intellectuals and artists. In a parallel with the May Fourth intellectual reformers, many contemporary artists and writers felt an obligation to improve and rectify their society through their artistic work. However, such ambitions as often encouraged co-optation by ministerial authority as they fomented critical discourse or antistate mobilization.

Chapters 8, 9, and 10 provide case studies of these dependencies among three different communities of artists. In Chapter 8, Paul Pickowicz discusses the careers of several major film directors who not only have developed complex relations to Chinese authorities, but also have prospered because of their involvement with foreign producers and audiences. In Chapter 9, Julia Andrews and Gao Minglu share their observations of the rise and fall of the Beijing avant-garde. For this group of artists independence from the state was largely guaranteed by their overtly antistate messages. On the other hand, ties to party patrons and official associations sometimes improved their ability to create and perform. In Chapter 10, Su Wei and Wendy Larson trace the evolution of several genres of poetry. In the early years of the reforms, poets played an extraordinarily public role by Western standards. However, as sensibilities changed and old Maoist taboos became trivial, the audience for poetry changed; unfortunately few poets understood the new cultural dynamics. Autonomous and more individualistic, they became less engaged with the larger public and defining events of contemporary urban life.

Part III, "Urban Associations," continues the discussion of the viability and scope of collective action introduced in the chapters in Part II, but here authors focus more narrowly on popular associations that have directly confronted the Maoist institutions of party and government. Through case studies of industrial workers, legal scholars, and university students, the authors in this section focus on questions about organizational transformation and the presence or absence of a public sphere. They also confront the ambiguity and complexity of the binary opposition between state and society that lies at the heart of much contemporary academic debate over the nature of civil society and its relevance for understanding the postsocialist world.[19]

___

[19]Krishan Kumar, "Civil Society: An inquiry into the usefulness of an historical term,"

Whether they focus on activists concerned about wresting power from the Communist party-state or those building legal protection for their membership, the subjects of these three case studies often found it impossible to draw a clear line between themselves and the state. Instead the typical pattern documented in Elizabeth Perry's study of labor leaders (Chapter 11) was one of societal forces internally fragmented both by parochial loyalties and by continuing relationships with different segments of state bureaucracy. As a result, concludes Perry, neither state nor society emerged as a homogenous or coherent actor, and any theoretical paradigm in which state and society are clearly defined becomes misleading when applied to the Chinese experience.

Chapters 12 and 14 pursue Perry's analysis by examining the several ways in which newly emergent associations were defined by their preexisting relationships to state agents. For the legal scholars interviewed by Mark Sidel for Chapter 12, the critical concern during the 1980s was to "establish law and legal institutions as an independent basis for authority separated from the party." In practice, their slow emergence as a protean community of activists rested on patronage. As a result, Sidel concludes that legal innovations followed rather than precipitated expanded market exchanges. The student movement studied by Jeffrey Wasserstrom and Liu Xinyong in Chapter 14 experienced an equally problematic trajectory. For many outside China the emergence of outspoken critics among students of elite universities documented an emergent civil society reminiscent of the early Solidarity movement. Wasserstrom rejects such parallels and concurs with Perry that among university students public and private realms were intertwined and that therefore a symbiotic relationship with the party-state fundamentally defined Chinese student activism.

In Chapter 13, Nancy Chen departs dramatically from the world of student leaders, legal experts, and union cadres and introduces readers to the transcendent world of *qigong*, whose practitioners often use urban parks and other public places for meetings of their holistic healing movement. While obviously in public view, *qigong* practitioners simultaneously mobilize public space to private use. In a radical departure from the oppressive censorship of the late Mao era, *qigong* masters openly flaunt their personal and individual loyalties and involvement. Their as-

British Journal of Sociology 44, no. 3 (September 1993): 375–96; Christopher G. A. Bryant, "Social Self-organization, Civility, and Sociology," *British Journal of Sociology* 44, no. 3 (September 1993): 397–405.

sociational potential is less obviously harnessed to political agendas than the groups studied by Perry, Sidel, and Wasserstrom and Liu. But the cohesion between masters and disciples fosters collective loyalties of immense potential, and to the extent that prolonged adherence to the alternative world of *qigong* socializes ordinary people to strive for alternatives to the status quo, the *qigong* movement manifests the most vivid and complete expression of Scott's hidden transcripts.

CONTEMPORARY URBAN CHINA IN HISTORICAL AND COMPARATIVE PERSPECTIVE

The 1980s have been characterized as a decade when a resurgent Chinese society expanded beyond the limits imposed by the Maoist party-state. But it has also been a decade in which the growth of nonstate activities failed to curb arbitrary use of state police powers. On the other hand, as Shaoguang Wang has shown in his study of CCP fiscal policy, the 1980s witnessed a clear decline in "state capacity," and by the early 1990s political power at the center was clearly weaker than it had been during the late Mao era.[20] The thinning of central state powers, however, was often counterbalanced by a "thickening" at the local level, a phenomenon well illustrated here in Vivienne Shue's analysis of a North China county town (see Chapter 4) and by the enormous growth in the number of state and party cadres.[21] Consequently, although the central state progressively weakened after 1978 and the contradictory and competitive drives of various economic actors—peddlers, "fixers," entrepreneurs, consumers, and investors—created new interest groups that mobilized resources outside state control, no societal association emerged with the moral and institutional power to limit state coercion consistently rather than at intermittent moments of crisis.

This pattern of state sprawl and societal weakness in the contemporary period evokes strong parallels with Pransenjit Duara's argument about the devastating impact of "state involution" on Chinese society during the 1920s and 1930s: when they were unable to maintain a co-

---

[20]Shaoguang Wang, "From Revolution to Involution: State Capacity, Local Power, and Ungovernability in China" (unpublished paper, 1991).

[21]Gilhem Fabre, using estimates from the Chinese press and the research of J. P. Cabestan, calculates in the 1980s there were 30 million new administrative government and party positions created, 10 million in state enterprises, 10 million in government and party organizations, and 10 million in state-run social services ("La Nouvelle 'nouvelle classe' " unpublished paper, June 1993).

herent, effective national program, the Nationalist government and the Kuomintang ceded power over society to rapacious local warlords, organized crime, and feuding factions.[22] Under these conditions, local bullies increased their ability to terrorize rural communities and village-based elites were decimated. Duara substantiates his case for state involution and societal atrophy by using examples from rural areas of North China. Parks Coble's work on Shanghai and Nanjing under the Nationalist government describes a parallel phenomenon in major urban centers, where the Kuomintang leadership devastated the very societal forces that earlier had offered hope for a modern, more pluralistic polity.[23] Unwilling to trust an autonomous bourgeoisie and increasingly dependent on the coercive powers of criminal organizations, the Kuomintang disempowered the urban middle classes as a political force as completely as they had earlier devastated the workers' movement.[24]

In his analysis of urban society during late Imperial China in this volume's Conclusion, David Strand describes how intermittent leadership from the central government fostered vibrant community life by default, with the result that a lively imbricated urban society sustained an embryonic public sphere. Perhaps within contemporary cities, intermittent or inconsistent supervision by the central government may also encourage new forms of public activity and civic independence that can overwhelm the forces within the party-state apparatus hostile to social autonomy. James Scott's work suggests that within the urban population thousands are ready to articulate alternative views of state accountability, and the chapters by Chan, Perry, Sidel, Pickowicz, and Andrews and Gao identify a range of social groups who have successfully created realms of relative autonomy since 1980. Another historical comparison to the events of the 1930s, however, cautions against concluding that a sustainable and independent public sphere is likely to emerge in the near future.[25] Thus Bryna Goodman's study of urban native-place organizations during the 1930s concludes that civic activism under a weakened but still authoritarian regime fosters collaboration, not independence.

[22]*Culture, Power, and the State: Rural North China, 1900–1942* (Stanford: Stanford University Press, 1988).

[23]Parks M. Coble, *The Shanghai Capitalists and the Nationalist Government* (Cambridge, Mass.: Harvard University Press, 1986).

[24]Alain Roux, *Le Shanghai ouvrier des années trente* (Paris: Harmattan, 1993), especially pp. 163–206.

[25]Bryna Goodman, "Creating Civic Ground: Public Maneuvering and the State in the Nanjing Decade," paper presented at the Annual Meetings of the Association for Asian Studies, March 1993.

Chapters in this volume by Perry, Sidel, and Wasserstrom and Liu imply that Goodman's conclusions may be equally relevant to the contemporary world.

A second brake on the evolution of a dynamic and independent public sphere is the bureaucratic corruption (*guandao*) that since 1980 has diverted an ever-increasing percentage of national wealth away from public investment and weakened the authority of the party-state.[26] This seemingly paradoxical need of civil society for a strong national government is not as strange as it might at first seem, and has powerful historical precedents, both in Western Europe and in Asia. Thus, for example, recent scholarship on early modern England has stressed that the evolution toward a strong, coherent central state was as critical for the emergence of the institutions of a civil society as the growth of an ideology of individual rights or the increase of nonstate associations.[27] Marie-Claire Bergère, in her study of the Shanghai bourgeoisie in the early twentieth century, makes a parallel argument for China when she concludes that the weakness of the central state as much as that of the bourgeoisie prevented increased societal and associational autonomy after 1900 from evolving into a viable civil society.[28] In an anarchic environment, just as in a totalitarian one, societal forces cannot mobilize, institutions of civil society remain vestigial, and there is no viable public sphere.[29]

In the 1980s urban China became increasingly volatile and the party-state lost (or renounced) much of its power to dictate societal and personal activity; yet there was relatively little disorder. By the early 1990s, the government had created effective new institutions of civil law, com-

---

[26]In the early years the scope of corruption was modest, small pay-offs to get licenses, elaborate banquets, and souvenirs. By the early 1990s, violations involved millions of yuan and heavy prison sentences. For example in August 1993, Hong Kong's Communist newspaper *Ta kung pao* reported that Sichuan authorities investigated 102 cases in the provincial banking system in the first six months of the year. Six of the cases involved embezzlement of amounts over 100,000 *yuan*; in one city an official had illegally accumulated 25 million (*China News Digest [CND], September 1, 1993*). In the same month, Beijing courts sentenced four officials to death for embezzlement of public funds (*CND*, August 28, 1993). Equally threatening to the integrity of the contemporary state is the scale of the corruption, documented dramatically by the official announcement in January 1994 that one-fifth of all cadres in the province of Anhui had been arrested on charges of corruption (*Far Eastern Economic Review*, January 20, 1994, 15).

[27]Derek Sayer, "A Notable Administration," *American Journal of Sociology* 97, no. 5 (March 1992): 1382–1415.

[28]Marie-Claire Bergère, *The Golden Age of the Chinese Bourgeoisie*, trans. by Janet Lloyd (Cambridge: Cambridge University Press, 1989).

[29]Ibid.

pleted many large-scale infrastructure projects, and translated policy goals for a national system of pensions and unemployment insurance into viable programs.[30] Yet because of the increasing scale and scope of official corruption, the ambitious entrepreneurs and municipal authorities who had played a leading role in revitalizing city economies after 1980 confronted severe obstacles in making subsequent, long-term investments or in mobilizing politically. Bureaucratic corruption also damaged public trust and threatened to divert an ever higher percentage of new wealth exclusively toward private consumption and away from community needs.

When viewed in a broad historical and comparative perspective, the residents of Chinese cities greatly expanded their ability to realize personal and community preferences in the first fifteen years after the death of Mao Zedong. Moreover, unlike the situation facing Chinese urbanites of the 1920s and 1930s, the contemporary trajectory has been toward *less* bureaucratic control and *less* reliance on police and military force. The international environment is also more conducive to robust growth and maturation among nonstate associations. China's national integrity is secure, and the country faces no serious military threat. Urban professionals in the fields of art, film, law, and even labor have constituencies abroad as well as within China that support public associations independent of the party and government. Greatly increased purchasing power in urban households has created new markets for domestic industries, which in turn have responded by mass production of items once considered luxuries for a few.[31] With plentiful, and relatively affordable, consumer durables filling store shelves, urban residents not only share directly in the economic growth of the 1980s, they also perceive themselves to be less dependent on the state for their material welfare.

Rapid economic growth and multifaceted gains in personal and professional autonomy during the post-Mao reforms distinguish the con-

[30]For a summary of the limited progress in this area, see Edward Epstein, "A Matter of Justice," in *China Review 1992* (Hong Kong: Chinese University of Hong Kong Press, 1992), 5.1–5.37. One of the clearest areas of investment has been in electrical energy, which while still falling far below demand has grown exponentially, adding as much capacity between 1987 and 1992 as was created in the nearly three decades between 1950 and 1978 (*China News Analysis*, no. 1498 [December 1, 1993]: 5–7).
   Deborah Davis, "Financial Security of Urban Retirees," *Journal of Cross-Cultural Gerontology* 8 (1993): 179–95; *China News Analysis*, no. 1502 (January 15, 1994).
[31]For example in 1985 only 6 households in 100 owned a refrigerator; by 1992 the ratio was 52 in 100. In 1985 only 17 in 100 owned a color television; by 1992 it was 75 in 100 (*ZGTJNJ* 1993: 289).

temporary situation from that of China in the 1930s and from that of Russia in the 1990s; they also partially blunt the negative consequences of bureaucratic corruption and the continuing hostility of the national leadership to political reform. In the 1990s the challenge for Chinese urban residents, therefore, will be to use their new wealth and autonomy to enlarge the nonstate sphere and to develop organizations able to nurture a nascent civil society. The following chapters analyze the initial efforts made by millions of Chinese citizens toward that ambitious reconfiguration of state and societal power within the urban spaces of contemporary China.

Part I

Urban space

Introduction

●━●

BARRY NAUGHTON

The essays in this section focus on the economic and political forces that structure urban life, and the way those forces produce specific urban landscapes and ways of life. Economic actors "give structures" to the urban landscape in an entirely literal sense, placing buildings, roads, and parks in patterns that shape the interactions of all urban dwellers. In addition, economic and political forces metaphorically give structure to the urban environment by creating regular incentives to behave in certain ways, and by defining the range of what is permissible. Urban space is shaped gradually and cumulatively by these forces working over time at different speeds, and the quality of urban time is shaped by the physical environment in which urban processes unfold. The urban physical environment can be read to provide clues to the nature of urban life. Indeed, not only the present of urban life but also its past can be discerned because the urban landscape changes relatively slowly.

The authors in this section approach their topics from different directions and with different disciplinary backgrounds, yet the general picture of Chinese cities that emerges is fairly consistent. Between 1949 and 1978, forces external to the individual city shaped urban activities and landscapes into a narrowly restricted range. The progress of economic reform since 1978 has weakened those forces substantially. The result has been a trend toward increasing complexity and diversity in urban life, whether in economic activity, the physical structure of the city, or the ways in which urban dwellers allocate their time to different tasks. The trend has by no means run its course: Restrictions on activity inherited from the past remain significant, and Chinese cities are still some distance from the turmoil and creativity of cities in most other parts of the world.

The definition of the city in China is changing. It is true, of course, that the official definitions of what constitutes a city and an urban resident are changing, and this creates constant headaches for demographers and geographers attempting to trace China's urbanization

23

process.[1] But the reality of the city is changing even more rapidly than the administrative definitions. Our authors make clear that new types of activity have become "urban" in at least three ways over the past decade, creating thereby at least three new types of urban resident. Dorothy Solinger's chapter describes an entire new class of temporary urbanites, the so-called floating population; the piece by Vivienne Shue describes the emergence of entirely new urban centers, using an example from the North China plain; and my own chapter argues that urban activities have spilled over into suburban regions to create new districts of undifferentiated urban sprawl. These changes make clear that not only the *how* but also the *what* of urban life differ from the past.

Our authors also show that the pace of change for the existing group of urban residents, fully vested with the privileges of urban life, has been significant. While change has not occurred at the same dizzying pace for these urban dwellers as it has for the formerly peripheral groups, change has nonetheless been substantial. The pace of change differs in different realms: many different types of time coexist in the urban landscape. As Shaoguang Wang demonstrates in Part II, the partial recession of the political apparatus and a modest reduction in the demands of the workplace have left individuals with more leisure time, creating a "space" for greater personal autonomy and autonomous organizations. The richer and more diverse urban cultural life discussed later in this volume is fundamentally based on this expansion of the personal sphere. The same relaxation of controls underpins the increase in rural-to-urban migration discussed by Solinger. Millions of formerly rural residents have entered cities to fill niches in the urban economic structure.

As a result, though perhaps paradoxically, the relaxation of controls over individual activities has created a more complicated urban environment. Urban dwellers—particularly long-term urban dwellers—are likely to feel that their environment has become more crowded and difficult to navigate, so that, despite the increase in their personal leisure time, they may feel that they have less "personal space." Indeed, the urban

[1] Laurence J. C. Ma and Gonghao Cui, "Administrative Changes and Urban Population in China," *Annals of the Association of American Geographers* 77, no.3 (1987): 373–95; Harry X. Wu, "China's Urbanization and Rural-to-Urban Migration," University of Adelaide, Chinese Economy Research Unit, Working Paper No. 91/8 (November 1991); Kam Wing Chan and Xueqiang Xu, "Urban Population Growth and Urbanization in China Since 1949: Reconstructing a Baseline," *China Quarterly*, no. 104 (1985): 583–613; Sidney Goldstein, "Urbanization in China, 1982–1987: Effects of Migration and Reclassification," *Population and Development Review* 16 (1990): 673–701.

landscape of China's biggest cities—such as Shanghai or Tianjin—often struck observers on the eve of the reform process as an artificially preserved environment left over from an earlier era. The largest buildings dated from the 1930s, and the urban fabric seemed to have changed little since then. Similarly, urban life at that time was unusually sheltered. The prohibition of in-migration and the restriction on the range of permissible activities maintained an artificially calm environment. Although urban dwellers had little time to dispose of freely, they operated in an environment that was in many ways simpler and less stressful.

As the character of urban life changes, so do the spatial patterns of urban activities. The chapter by Piper Gaubatz traces the way in which the spatial organization of the city is changing. Gaubatz is concerned primarily with the manner in which the division of the urban space into functionally different types of land use is changing. She finds that Chinese cities are becoming increasingly differentiated. New districts and neighborhoods grow up, and with them new patterns of commuting and residence. Previously, neighborhoods approached an ideal of self-sufficiency, in which all the essential urban activities coexisted in each neighborhood. In principle, an urban resident might never need to leave his neighborhood in the course of a lifetime. Such an organization of space was entirely consistent with the restrictions on personal mobility documented by Solinger.

My own chapter stresses that personal immobility under the prereform economy was closely related to the key role that cities played in extracting revenues for the national government. The apparent self-sufficiency of urban neighborhoods, in other words, was not the result of an economic self-sufficiency or autarchy of the urban neighborhood economy. Quite the contrary: it was precisely because cities were so closely integrated into the national economic system that such tight restrictions on personal mobility were imposed. As urban economies have become less dominated by revenue extraction, and correspondingly the free exchange of goods and services has become more important, the restrictions on mobility of labor and capital have become less essential. The lowering of barriers has permitted both the inflow of new residents into the cities—as described by Solinger—and the outflow of urban-type activities into the suburbs and to new towns of the type described by Shue.

Shue's chapter is particularly valuable in that it provides us with a glimpse of life in a smaller urban center, Xinji City. Most of our authors have experienced and written about life in the biggest Chinese cities. Life in the smaller urban centers is much less well studied. Some suggest that smaller towns are intrinsically more oppressive than large cities: they witness fewer checks on the power of local officials, less anonymity than in the teeming cities, and fewer and lower quality diversions from the daily routine. Whether that is true in general must remain an open question, but it certainly does not seem to be true in Xinji City. Although the city is "gritty," it seems to have a significant cultural life, and comes across as a pleasant and fairly relaxed place to live. Xinji is distinctive in the dynamism and receptiveness of its political elite, and it may be equally unusual in the quality of its public life.

The speed and thoroughness with which the Xinji governing elite are reinterpreting the economic role of the state may also be exceptional, but the general character of the changes they are implementing seems to be reasonably widespread. Xinji's local state apparatus is being recast as a regulatory state, but without turning itself into an arm's-length regulatory authority. This regulatory apparatus is extremely intrusive, stepping in repeatedly to shape the actions of individuals, even while according individuals the right to make most basic economic decisions.

The intrusive regulatory state that leads Shue to speak of "state sprawl" leads us to consider the pace of change in another sense. For while change is occurring rapidly in some respects, many of the basic elements of the intrusive state remain. This emerges perhaps most clearly in Solinger's chapter in which she shows how the continuing effects of national government policies obstruct the integration of the floating population into the urban milieu. Tracing the impact of state intervention through all the various channels that lead to integration in most societies, Solinger demonstrates the pervasiveness of state controls and the harmful effect they have on the life chances of the migrants she describes. More generally, most of the authors find that remnants of the former system are common at the core of urban life, and that change is most rapid at the margins. Physically, around the margins of the cities, the suburban areas are the places where economic change is occurring most rapidly, as traditionally urban activities spill over into space officially classified as "rural." Socially, the margins of urban life are increasingly occupied by transients, hailing originally from rural districts, but increasingly living urban lives, even if they remain less than fully integrated into the urban scene. A sense of the incompleteness of change emerges strongly from these chapters, as indeed from all the essays in this volume.

Of course, cities can change only gradually. As economic and social systems change, the incentives that shape individuals can change rapidly but the urban fabric changes at a much slower pace. As Blair Ruble has stressed in conference discussion, the physical form of cities is the outcome of millions of individual decisions made over many decades. Individuals invest their own resources, and the resources of the state and corporation, in myriad construction, destruction, and renovation projects. The Chinese city today reflects the continuous layering of decisions made under different social and economic contexts, and the city is a patchwork of successive historical periods. Patches of traditional Chinese urban architecture—usually two wooden stories—still survive in many cities. Western-style architecture from the treaty port era dominates the commercial districts of many cities, but has begun to be supplanted by the modern office and hotel towers sprouting among the older buildings. Socialist architecture—not only the wide avenues lined by concrete apartment blocks, but also the Stalinist wedding-cake Palaces of Culture and Minorities—still predominates in many cities. Even where changes in the economic, social, and political system have dramatically changed the incentives for individual action, the totality of the urban environment and experience can only change incrementally. Indeed, this coexistance of different types of time in the urban landscape is part of what gives cities their fascination.

2

Urban transformation in post-Mao China: impacts of the reform era on China's urban form

PIPER RAE GAUBATZ

The social and economic changes in China since Mao's death have fundamentally transformed patterns of industry, housing, transportation, and other aspects of spatial organization in China's large cities. During the Maoist period, large cities were altered from the small-scale neighborhood-oriented traditional form of the Chinese city to uniform, standardized landscapes of mixed industrial and residential compounds, where block after block of three- to five-story brick and concrete structures were used for everything from steel production to residences and kindergartens. Today, Chinese cityscapes are becoming increasingly differentiated (Figure 2.1). High-rise buildings cluster in revitalized downtown districts and outlying housing developments, mirrored towers mark the location of joint-venture luxury hotels and office complexes, shopping districts bustle with new vitality, and new industrial districts ring the cities. New commuter patterns are replacing the close linkages between residence and workplace typical of the Maoist era. Yet amid all this change, a new concern has arisen over preserving and restoring traditional cityscapes. This chapter argues that much of China's recent urban change can be viewed as a product of spatial and functional specialization, in sharp contrast to the generalized urban patterns China sought to establish during the first three decades of the People's Republic (PRC).

Figure 2.1. The monumental Mao-era spire of the Shanghai exhibition center now competes for prominence with newly built skyscrapers. *Photograph by Piper Rae Gaubatz*

CHINESE URBAN DEVELOPMENT DURING THE MAOIST PERIOD

The spatial organization of the Chinese city during the Maoist period was strongly influenced by a "generalized" ideal of urban organization. In spatial terms, each district of the city ideally was to be relatively self-sufficient, offering its residents all or most general functions such as housing, employment, and the provision of subsistence goods and services. The city would consist of many such districts, all relatively indistinguishable from one another. Though never fully achieved, this type of structure became typical of newly developed areas in the large cities of both the Soviet Union and China.[1] In China the generalized form was embodied in the work-unit compound in its ideal form, in which each

---

[1] The geographer R. A. French notes that on the macro scale in large Soviet cities, residential, industrial, and service functions can be found, mixed together, in all parts of the city ("The Individuality of the Soviet City," in R. A. French and F. E. Ian Hamilton, eds., *The Socialist City: Spatial Structure and Urban Policy* [Chichester: John Wiley and Sons, 1979], 94).

work unit (*danwei*, the employer or organization to which a citizen is assigned) would provide a wide range of services for its employees.

The multifunctional compounds built by Chinese work units since 1949 are walled areas somewhat reminiscent of the walled wards of the early traditional Chinese city. But unlike the walled wards, which were primarily residential in function, the work-unit compound became a miniature city within its own walls, offering residents spaces for work and for play, for home life and for neighborhood life. The highly controlled environment of the work-unit compound is entered through a guarded gate, just like many industrial complexes elsewhere in the world. Within the gate, the architecture is utilitarian and regimented. Production facilities and residential facilities are usually housed in separate structures. Orderly rows of residential structures commonly consist of rectangular three- to five-story brick or cement buildings. Dwellings within these buildings are arranged with an entryway and stairwell system, with two to four units on each landing of the stairwell. These units include both apartments for families and dormitories for single workers. Like the residential units, production facilities are housed in large rectangular structures. In spite of this modern form, remnants of traditional Chinese architecture can still be found within the grounds of the post-1949 work-unit compounds. Many work-unit compounds retained and made use of preexisting buildings on their sites. Thus the regimentation of orthogonal brick and concrete is occasionally broken by the now ramshackle sweep of a curved tile roof.

Common areas between the buildings in the work-unit compound serve as bicycle parking lots, children's play areas, recreation places for volleyball and other sports, and green areas. Other facilities within the walled compound vary but ideally include dining halls, provision shops, medical facilities, recreation facilities, meeting rooms, and administrative offices. Thus the work-unit compound serves as the locus for the organization of many facets of life, such as the group-oriented leisure activities identified by Shaoguang Wang in this volume.

The work-unit compound was the principal unit of newly constructed urban space during the Maoist period and urban planning was in many cases limited to grouping certain types of work-unit compounds in certain areas of the city. Under the guidance of state priorities before 1978, as David Buck has observed, "the needs of production units took precedence over considerations for the environment, workers' amenities or the overall plan of a community."[2] Because newly constructed factories and other work-unit compounds took a standardized form, this planning style created functionally and visually homogenous landscapes in the newly developed (post-1949) districts of large Chinese cities.[3] Given the often phenomenal growth of Chinese cities since 1949, this homogenous landscape of low-rise compounds sprawling across vast areas became typical of many Chinese cities.

One of the most significant structural changes in the Chinese city since 1949, then, has been the development of these relatively self-sufficient units combining housing, workplace, and the provision of social services. Although Chinese urban planning was heavily influenced by the Soviet Union during the 1950s, the work-unit compound model ultimately went much further in its attempts to integrate working and living space than did the Soviet model, whose principal urban unit, the *microrayon*, was based on residential districts spatially separate from the workplace. Commutes of up to forty minutes on public transportation were considered acceptable in Soviet planning.[4] In the Soviet Union, it was only the industrial priority established during the Stalinist era that led to the establishment of industry within or near residential areas in spite of urban plans intended to carefully separate these functions.

Of course, the spatial significance of the work-unit compounds should not be overstated. Many Chinese continued to live in housing separated from their workplace, and even to live in housing not provided by their own work-unit. Women in particular needed to commute, as housing assignments were more often associated with husbands than with their wives. And the work-unit compounds were primarily a function of the establishment of *new* workplaces and particularly those built from the mid-1950s through the early 1970s.[5] Those whose residence was not

[2]David D. Buck, "Changes in Chinese Urban Planning Since 1976," *Third World Planning Review* 6 (1984): 7–9.
[3]As Clifton Pannell notes, "A consequence of such planning is the emergence of less distinct functional separation of land uses in Chinese cities" ("The Internal Structure of Chinese Cities: Nanking," in C. K. Leung and Norton Ginsburg, eds., *China: Urbanization and National Development* [Chicago: University of Chicago Department of Geography Research Paper No. 196, 1980], 187–214).
[4]James H. Bater, *The Soviet City: Ideal and Reality* (Beverly Hills, Calif.: Sage Publications, 1980), 28–29.
[5]Given the well-documented slowdown in housing construction between 1961 and 1972, most of this construction can, in fact, be attributed to the 1950s. See, for example, Reeitsu Kojima, *Urbanization and Urban Problems in China* (Tokyo: Institute of Developing Economies Occasional Paper Series No. 22, 1987), 36, and R. J. R. Kirkby, *Urbanization*

within a work-unit compound were often assigned to neighborhood or residential unit committees that served similar social functions by offering a variety of community services and requiring participation by residents. Neighborhood committees sometimes also functioned as work-units. By organizing small production workshops and other neighborhood labor they limited the need for long-distance mobility within the city.

Thus ideals of social and spatial organization were creating distinctly undifferentiated social and functional landscapes during the first decades of the PRC. Coupled with preferences for low-cost, low-rise structures, this resulted in the development of an urban environment with three prominent characteristics: generalized functional organization, low-rise, standardized landscapes, and the persistence of the "walking scale" of the city.

Generalized functional organization. The reorganization of the city around the work-unit compounds resulted in the development of functionally mixed districts within the city. Theoretically, residents could find social services, subsistence goods, recreation, and other needs within their own work-unit or district. Industry and other functions of all scales and sizes were mixed together in close spatial proximity. This also contributed to the increasing homogenization of landscapes by creating ever-decreasing differentiation between districts such as the "central city," "suburbs," and "industrial districts." Moreover, the reorganization of commercial ventures into collective and communal enterprises reduced the functional role of small business districts, though the physical form of these districts in many cases was retained within the context of the reorganization of ownership and management. The most significant districts to escape this generalization of structure were the oldest districts of the cities, whose complete transformation was often too costly or too impractical to be undertaken.

Low-rise standardized development. The reorganization of the city around the work-unit compounds resulted in the creation of landscapes of sprawling, low-rise development. Initially following the Soviet model, multifunctional compounds consisting of three- to five-story structures

in China: Town and Country in a Developing Economy 1949–2000 AD (New York: Columbia University Press, 1985), 173–75.

were built to accommodate rapid urban expansion. The low-rise nature of this style of development requires massive areas of land for construction. Thus Chinese cities have extended far beyond the earlier limits of their built-up areas. Chinese cities today are still characterized by these sprawling developments surrounding or sometimes supplanting comparatively small core areas dating from the pre-1949 era.

In spite of the generalization of functions and homogenization of the physical landscape in these new urban districts, however, the social landscape continued to vary considerably as work-units with differing power and access to resources were able to develop different levels of resources within their compounds and neighborhoods. This social differentiation was manifest during the Maoist period in aspects of life ranging from the quality of housing and medical care to the quality of schools and recreational facilities.

The persistence of the "walking-scale" city. The patterns described above contributed to the persistence of "walking-scale" urban life even though cities were very large. Although most cities, taken in their entirety, are far too large to be described as "walking-scale" cities, nonetheless the style of urban development in 1950s–1970s China promoted the areal extension of the city without the development of high-volume transport infrastructure. Rather, this style of development assumed that most people would have little need to travel beyond walking distance from their homes on a daily basis. The work-unit compound–based city, however, was never realized in its ideal form, and some people in Chinese cities have always commuted to work, such as spouses who work in different units from one another, or members of those families who live in the older housing districts of the central city area but work in newly developed areas. Nonetheless, services were provided for urban residents with the assumption that they would seek goods and services primarily in their own neighborhoods.

STRUCTURAL CHANGES IN POST-MAO URBAN FORM

The social and economic changes in China during the post-Mao era have had a substantial impact on urban form. Several of these have been particularly significant:

1. The transition from communal organization and management of resources and production to the present mixed system of state, collective, and individual management of resources and production
2. Significant changes in the mobility of individuals at all scales from daily intracity movement to rural-urban migration
3. Cumulative and continuing overload of existing infrastructure as a legacy of earlier planning practice
4. An increasing trend toward export-oriented development, including both the development of export-based industries and the development of foreign trade zones

In contrast to the generalized urban form developed during the Maoist period, the post-Mao city is becoming increasingly specialized. Specialized urban forms consist of spatially distinct districts that tend toward functional specialization, such as residential districts, manufacturing areas, or tourist districts. Traditional Chinese urban form was specialized to the extent that distinct neighborhoods, streets, or walled compounds were devoted to different activities such as trade, and some districts were differentiated based on social, economic, and ethnic distinctions.[6] Commercial and administrative functions shaped the specialization of districts. Residences were often located within, rather than separate from, such districts. In contrast to the generalized form developed during the Maoist period, many recent structural changes in Chinese cities either derive from or contribute to the increasing development of specialization in Chinese urban form. This increased specialization is both a return to the traditional specialization of commercial functions and, to some degree, a new type of specialization embodying the separation of residential and nonresidential functions.

Thus large cities in China's post-Mao era are developing increasingly specialized forms at many scales. Not only is the national system of cities in China tending toward increased differentiation and specialization of functions and uneven development among cities, but a high degree of specialization is developing (or reemerging) within individual cities as well.[7] These changes follow from a reduction in the planning power of

[6] Streets differentiated by trade were often differentiated as to the level of the type of trade itself. Cities thus had streets devoted to particular commercial or trade activities such as a street of wine merchants, a street of goldsmiths, or a street of tailors.
[7] See, for example, Yu Luo and Clifton Pannell, "The Changing Pattern of City and Industry in Post-Reform China" in Gregory Veeck, ed., *The Uneven Landscape: Geographical Studies in Post-Reform China* (Baton Rouge: Geoscience and Man Publications vol.

individual work-unit compounds and an increase in overall municipal planning.[8] Such changes can be seen in developing patterns of settlement and transportation, as well as in changes in the spatial distribution of some types of commercial ventures.[9]

SETTLEMENT AND TRANSPORTATION PATTERNS

Two factors dominate the character of recent housing transformation in the PRC: the substantial quantity of new housing stock built during the post-Mao era and the undersupply of housing in China's large cities despite the increase in housing stock. The construction of new housing has promoted both increased separation between housing and the workplace and increased functional specialization in residential districts. In contrast to earlier practices, recent housing construction in China has often been administratively and spatially separate from the construction of new places of employment. The state-sponsored construction of housing in China since 1979 has focused primarily on the construction of large-scale housing projects meant to house workers from several different work-units. This approach differs markedly from new housing construction in the late 1950s through the early 1970s, when housing was planned in conjunction with the construction of the workplaces themselves, and was often spatially linked to the workplace. Spatial linkages with the workplace are becoming less important than the provision of the housing itself. The increasing separation between housing and the workplace contributes to mounting traffic problems in China's large cities.

The separation of home and workplace is taking place for enterprises of all sizes. The recent trend toward the construction of massive new residential areas on the outskirts of the present urban area adds to the increasing separation of housing and workplace for large work-units, which purchase housing in peripherally located developments in order to relieve overcrowding in their more conveniently located but aging

30, 1991); Wu Chuanjun, "The Urban Development in China," *Journal of Chinese Geography* 1, no. 2 (1990): 1–11; Quan Zhangxing, "Urbanization in China," *Urban Studies* 28 (1991): 41–51; and Chen Xiangming, "China's Urban Hierarchy," *Urban Studies* 28, no. 3 (1991): 341–67.

[8] David Buck discusses the decrease in the power of the work-units and the increase in overall municipal planning in Buck, "Changes in Chinese Urban Planning," 6.

[9] Although as any recent visitor to China will be quick to note, the distinctive mark of Maoist urban planning can still be seen.

work-unit compounds. For example, the Fangzhuang development in southeastern Beijing, a large new residential district projected to house 76,000 persons, has already become the home of hundreds of households with family members working in the Ministry of Foreign Affairs and the Public Security Bureau. This complex of 90 high-rise and 82 low-rise residential structures is beginning to function as a "bedroom" suburb of Beijing, with schools and a few stores already built, and parks and recreation centers on the drawing board. No plans have been made to integrate employment and housing in the project. Residents of the community commute to work either in public buses or in shuttle buses provided by work units. Places of employment for most residents are beyond easy bicycle commute range.

The proliferation of small work-units is also contributing to commutation problems. There have always been enterprises in the PRC too small to provide housing physically attached to their production facilities, and these enterprises constitute a growing share of the economy. By 1982, for example, enterprises employing fewer than thirty-three employees accounted for about 60 percent of all industrial enterprises.[10] Such small enterprises do not normally provide their own housing structures for their workers, and are more likely to provide subsidies for workers to occupy housing elsewhere. As Joochul Kim observes, small work-units such as elementary schools, secondary schools, small factories, and relatively small stores often cannot afford to provide housing for their members at all. Apartments built and managed by local governments, which account for 15–20 percent of urban housing, serve both people not affiliated with a work-unit and those whose work-unit cannot provide its own housing.[11] This trend toward the separation of housing from workplace in smaller enterprises continues and is perhaps more pronounced with the development of new enterprises in China. For example, in the development of new industry in Shenzhen, only the largest enterprises are constructing housing for their workers.[12]

[10]Christine P. W. Wong, "Between Plan and Market: the Role of the Local Sector in Post-Mao China," *Asian Economies* 64 (1988): 27.

[11]Joochul Kim, "China's Current Housing Issues and Policies," *Journal of the American Planning Association* 53 (1987): 220–27.

[12]Manuel Castells, Lee Goh, and Reginald Y. W. Kwok, "Economic Development and Housing Policy in the Asian Pacific Rim: A Comparative Study of Hong Kong, Singapore and Shenzhen Special Economic Zone" (Berkeley: Institute of Urban and Regional Development Monograph 37, 1988), 491.

Recent reports on city governments' attempts to cope with the problem of the "rush hour" phenomenon in Chinese cities provide evidence of significant and growing traffic problems associated with the separation of housing and the workplace. Representatives of the Ningbo Communications and Transportation Association report that "employees live in scattered locations" and traffic from all directions converges during rush hours. The municipal government has instituted a "flextime" system there that has resulted in nearly 60,000 workers' having their working hours adjusted.[13] At least one-quarter of the workers in Ningbo's old city district are commuters. Ningbo has also instituted a central-city ban on truck traffic from 7:00 to 8:00 A.M., further underscoring the rush hour problem.[14] Shanghai has instituted "flextime" hours for some workers and has placed restrictions on some vehicle types during peak hours on Nanjing Road, Shanghai's central downtown business street. A report in 1985 indicated that about 400,000 workers were making use of staggered work hours.[15] Nonetheless, Shanghai's roads continue to be overcrowded. More recent efforts to cope with rising levels of commuter traffic in Shanghai include the ongoing construction of the Shanghai subway system and the construction of bridges and a tunnel across the Huangpu River to the newly developing Pudong district.

Nonetheless, preliminary analysis of traffic studies carried out in 1993 by the author in Beijing indicates that vehicular traffic congestion occurs both during the rush hour period and throughout much of the business day. During non–rush hour periods on major Beijing thoroughfares, the number of people traveling in motor vehicles other than public buses has now surpassed the number of people traveling by bicycle. Only during the rush hour crush does the volume of bicycle traffic rival that of motor vehicles.

Another factor in the increasing separation of workplace and home is a re-evaluation of the wisdom of locating large-scale industry and residences immediately adjacent to each other. Both the philosophy of com-

[13]This 60,000 workers amounts to about 24 percent of the old city area's 250,000 jobs, or 11 percent of the total population of the old city area. Dong Zuen and Wu Xianzhi, "Transport Projects Aid Expansion," *China Transport* no. 2 (1988): 79.

[14]Dong and Wu report a figure of 100,000 "person times" of commuters traveling to and from Ningbo each day, but the reference to "person times" is not carefully defined in their text, whereas the reference to the adjustment of job hours seems more clearly correlated with individual jobs (ibid).

[15]Huang Banjung, "Treatment of Shanghai Traffic," *ITE Journal* 55, no. 6. (1985): 58–60.

bining production and residential functions into single units and the Soviet-influenced push to develop industry at all cost during the 1950s contributed to this aspect of the generalized urban structure.[16] As municipal governments develop new understandings of the problems of industrial pollution, heavy industry has been increasingly relocated outside residential areas.[17] Reeitsu Kojima observed that the movement of industry to the outlying areas of Beijing in the early 1980s increased traffic problems as residents began to commute from the central city to the outlying industrial districts.[18] Moreover, many new or reorganized industrial ventures whose workers maintain their central city housing have been established in outlying areas.[19] New development has extended the city into outlying areas to the point that traffic is now heavy both coming and going from the central city areas.

The importance of the work-unit in the management and distribution of housing underscores the continued role of the work-unit in sociospatial differentiation within China's cities. In spite of the increasingly common spatial separation between housing and the workplace, housing is still controlled by employers. For example, in Xi'an in the mid-1980s about 75 percent of the housing stock was managed by production units and other centers of employment. At that time the Xi'an municipal government owned and managed about 15 percent of Xi'an's housing stock, and about 10 percent of the housing stock was privately owned.[20] As Nan Lin and Yanjie Bian observe, work unit–related social differentiation between neighborhoods still remains a strong force in China's cities. They note that "better work units tend to provide better housing and this housing tends to be located in districts where better schools are located."[21] Large, powerful work-units now have access to new devel-

---

[16]In the Soviet Union, where planners' ideals separated housing and industrial functions, the Stalinist attempts to accelerate industrial growth in the 1920s led, in many cases, to the construction of industry adjacent to housing. According to a 1982 Soviet *Literaturnaia gazeta* quoted by Henry Morton, "Ministries and plants literally tore cities to pieces. Each one attempting by all means fair and foul to build 'its own' housing right next to the plant" ("The Contemporary Soviet City," in Henry W. Morton and Robert C. Stuart, eds., *The Contemporary Soviet City* (Armonk, NY: M. E. Sharpe, 1984).

[17]Kim, "China's Current Housing Issues," 224.

[18]Kojima, *Urbanization and Urban Problems*, 76. This problem was relieved somewhat after 1984, when laws prohibiting urban residents from changing their residence to the outlying districts were relaxed.

[19]Ibid.

[20]G. Brent Hall and Ji Dong Zhang, "Xi'an," *Cities* (May 1988): 123–24.

[21]Lin Nan and Bian Yanjie, "Getting Ahead in Urban China," *American Journal of Sociology* 97, no. 3 (1991): 673.

opments, such as the new Fangzhuang residential area in southeastern Beijing, which are beyond the economic or political reach of small businesses. This type of differentiation is likely to become even stronger if Chinese workers continue to gain more ability to choose where and for whom they work.

Increasing collective and private ownership of housing may ultimately have an increased impact on the separation of home and workplace as well. Although still quite limited in scope, housing reforms continue that are designed to promote a private housing market. Nonetheless, the private housing market in China remains extremely limited. Even when housing units are built and put up for sale ("commodity housing"), most such units are still being sold to employers, rather than to individuals. Purchasing housing is beyond the economic reach of most individuals in China. And it is common for people whose employment does not provide housing to reside with a family member (such as a spouse or parent) whose employment does provide housing.

Regardless of the form of housing tenure, the increasing physical separation of housing and the workplace in China may contribute to changes in the role work units play in employees' social activities outside working hours. Although, as Jeffrey Wasserstrom notes in this volume, the organization of many activities still takes places through the venue of the work unit, Nancy Chen's discussion of the development of *qigong* organizations, Vivienne Shue's identification of burgeoning personal freedom that extends to individual decoration of homes, and Shaoguang Wang's discussion of the "demonopolization" of leisure time all suggest that many aspects of Chinese life are now taking place outside the spatial and organizational bounds of the work unit.

A further aspect of recent housing reform and urban development in Chinese cities is the replacement of both older central-city housing stock and early post-1949 development on the urban fringe with new housing developments. Post-1949 development in Chinese cities has always been constrained by preexisting structures and settlements. While newly developed work unit–centered districts embodied many of the ideals of the socialist generalized urban form, the older districts of China's cities remained primarily residential in function. For example, a concerted effort has recently been made in Beijing both to replace some older housing areas and to relocate people out of the downtown residential districts, in order to convert the land either to more "efficient" housing or to nonresidential uses. Thirty-two such projects have started in Beijing since

1990.[22] For example, in the Debao residential renovation project adjacent to the Beijing Exhibition Center older housing units have been razed, and new multistory housing blocks are being built to replace them. This new style of development provides for recreation, shopping, and child-care facilities, but no production facilities are located on the site. The Cuiwei residential area development in southwestern Beijing provides another example. This project was originally planned in 1984 to house eighteen thousand persons but has recently been expanded to be a mixed-use community housing thirty thousand persons in high-rise buildings grouped around a central shopping and recreation area. The newer units are being constructed as commodity housing.[23]

Ideally, new housing developments are expected to provide a variety of social services for their residents in order to maintain "convenience" in the residential system. Chinese architectural journals, such as *The Architect*, focus on examples of planned residential developments that, like their counterparts in the United States and Europe, include infrastructure elements such as shopping and day-care centers to attract residents. Nonetheless, the current trend toward specialization of districts reinforces the need for residents to travel to other districts even for relatively basic services, since few of them achieve the ideals of functional integration expounded in architectural journals.

The nature of retail and commercial enterprises within residential developments is also changing. Retail development is a common component of the more "upscale" housing developments in China, but it is designed to cater to a less comprehensive range of the needs of the residents than did the work-unit compound ideal. The retail and service function near residential districts is being taken up more and more by collective and private ventures opening supermarkets, clothing stores, laundries, and other businesses serving residential needs. On the whole, social and commercial functions are becoming increasingly separated from residential districts.

In spite of the construction of new housing discussed above, the present housing infrastructure suffers from continued and perhaps worsening strain. For example, many adult children live with their parents while

---

[22]Long Xinmin, ed., *Beijing shiyong ciliao daquan* (Encyclopedia of practical information on Beijing) (Beijing: Gaige chubanshe, 1992), 62–64.
[23]Wang Guoquan and Qu Shiyao, eds., *Jianzhu shilu* 3 (Architectural digest) (Beijing: Zhongguo jianzhu gongye chubanshe, 1991), 461–65. The Cuiwei project is far from finished, however. Amenities such as a shopping and residential center are still under construction.

working at other units. Qian Jianhong et al. report the following types of housing occupied by newly married urban couples in China in the mid-1980s:

1. Public housing assigned directly to them, 27.1%
2. Private property (not with parents), 6.7%
3. Public housing assigned to parents, 14.0%
4. Living with husband's parents, 35.0%
5. Living with wife's parents, 7.3%
6. Other, 9.8%[24]

Thus nearly half these young adult families live with their parents and another 14 percent apparently do not occupy housing that has actually been assigned to them. This is but one measure of the extent to which housing supplies continue to be inadequate to meet the needs of the population. It also illustrates that considerable numbers of people are housed in one work unit while working in another.

Another recent strain on China's urban infrastructure is the increasing prevalence of temporary urban residents and transients, whom the Chinese refer to as the "floating population."[25] In contrast to many other developing countries, China has not yet developed large populations of street-dwellers or squatter settlements in cities. This may be attributable, in part, to both the household registration system and the high and comparatively effective level of law enforcement within Chinese cities. Official estimates (which may greatly underestimate the actual numbers) place the increase in the transient population in Beijing, for example, from a daily average of about 300,000 transients in 1982, to about 1,310,000 in 1988.[26] Chinese sources also note that the purpose of transient visits to large cities has changed. Rather than traveling to the city primarily to visit relatives or to stay in the hospital, in recent years nearly three-quarters of the transient population has gone to the cities for economic reasons. The transient population of each of China's large (population over 1 million) cities may average as much as one-sixth to

[24]Qian Jianhong et al., "Marriage-related Consumption by Young People in China's Large and Medium Cities," *Social Sciences in China* (March 1988): 218, as reported in Charles E. Greer, ed., *China: Facts and Figures Annual 1989* (Gulf Breeze, Fla.: Academic International Press, 1989), 135.

[25]Temporary residents are those who do not hold permanent residence permits for the city.

[26]Xu Bingxuan reports numbers of transients in a few other large cities as well, such as Guangzhou in 1987, 1 million; Shanghai in 1986, 1.34 million; and Tianjin in 1987, 860,000. Xu, "Luetan Beijing de liudong renkou ji qi guanli," *Gongan daxue zibao* (Public Security University Journal) (May 1990): 31–33.

one-quarter the size of the total resident population.[27] Temporary migrants to Shanghai and other large cities often find housing by renting from farm families just outside the cities.[28] These migrants also generate significant daily movement in and out of the cities. Yet another substantial portion of the floating population, perhaps as much as 40 percent, resides with relatives and friends within the city itself, further crowding the existing housing and other infrastructure.[29] Dorothy Solinger provides a thoughtful look at the lives and prospects of the floating population in Chapter 5 in this volume.[30]

The presence of the floating populations in Chinese cities represents an increased strain on both transport and housing infrastructure. Although some transients might not require housing or long commutes, others place a strain on the transportation system.[31] Increased mobility between the countryside and the city now pressures intraurban transport systems as transient populations and the development of more varied marketing systems (free markets and street vendors) contribute to increased traffic volumes. A Shanghai traffic study conducted during the mid-1980s, for example, indicated that the floating population was twice as likely to make use of public transit, and about twenty-eight times as likely to use taxis as are permanent residents.[32] Shanghai traffic planners estimated that the nonresident population accounts for about one-quarter of Shanghai's public transport carrying capacity.[33] Moreover, with the changing economy providing a wider variety of jobs, increasing numbers of residents from the outlying rural communities surrounding large cities commute daily into the central city districts to engage in retail and service activities. For example, early morning traffic in the outlying areas of Beijing is filled with cart-vendors bicycling their triwheeled carts

---

[27]Ibid.

[28]Alice Goldstein, Sidney Goldstein, and Guo Shenyang, "Temporary Migrants in Shanghai Households," *Demography* 28 (1991): 278–79.

[29]Ibid.

[30]See also Dorothy Solinger, "Chinese Transients and the State," *Politics and Society* 21, no. 1 (1993): 91–122.

[31]For example, Goldstein, Goldstein, and Guo, "Temporary Migrants in Shanghai Households," observe that many of the persons who work in free markets in cities might live in the stalls or in facilities provided by the markets. Though these particular migrants thus would not need to commute to their city jobs, their very presence puts an increasing strain on city resources and infrastructure.

[32]These figures may be somewhat inflated to the extent that they include hotel guests and other short-term visitors to the city in their definition of floating population.

[33]Chen Shenghong, "Major Issues in Transport Planning of Shanghai," *Chengshi guihua* (China city planning review) 6, no. 3 (1990): 20.

toward choice selling locations near the cities' main intersections, taxi drivers heading their empty taxis toward central-district passengers, and still-sleepy workers crowding onto buses and vans for a long ride into the city.

The substantial strains on urban infrastructure that are developing in light of changes in the structure and distribution of urban jobs and housing are intensified by changing modes of transport within cities. Like their Soviet counterparts, large Chinese cities were expanded in the post–World War II era on the basis of public transportation rather than private automobiles. But while Soviet cities grew along subway and streetcar lines, Chinese cities grew with a unique combination of bus and bicycle transport.[34] Bicycles provide a cheap, clean, and convenient transport alternative in cities of moderate population density, moderate rates of bicycle ownership, and ample roads. Although the predominance of bicycle transportation in China is often admired by Westerners, Chinese planners identify bicycles as one of China's key transportation planning problems from the standpoint of urban planning and development.[35] The proliferation of bicycles and taxis in China's cities contributes to increasing gridlock in China's urban transport system.

Although bicycles are more efficient in terms of road-space than automobiles, they are far less efficient than public buses and other forms of mass transportation. Twelve bicycles carry no more than twenty-four passengers (and legally only twelve passengers), yet they take up as much road space as a one-hundred-passenger bus.[36] Bicycles' share of urban transportation substantially increased as they became more available and common in China's cities during the 1980s. The change from reliance on public bus service in the 1950s and 1960s to the dominance of the bicycle in urban transport started in the late 1970s. Urban residents perceive the bicycle as a faster and more convenient means of transportation than the public buses. By 1980, only one-third of commuters in Beijing commuted by bus, while more than half used bicycles. In Wuhan, the ratio of public bus use to bicycle use was four to six, and in Chengdu this ratio was three to seven. Chinese transport engineers estimate that

---

[34]For a discussion of transport-associated development of Soviet cities, see Blair A. Ruble, *Leningrad, Shaping a Soviet City* (Berkeley: University of California Press, 1990).

[35]Wu Liangyong and Mao Qizhi, "Current Problems in China's City Planning," *Chengshi guihua* (China city planning review) 63, no. 6. (1987): 25.

[36]Qiu En, "Acting in a Way That Defeats One's Own Purpose: Bicycles Act City Transportation's Leading Role," *Changjiang kaifa bao* (Yangtze development news) (November 16, 1990): 4.

70 percent of commuters in China's cities today commute by bicycle,[37] and in some cities, such as Tianjin, more than 80 percent of commuters use bicycles.[38]

Yet more alarming is the increasing proliferation of motorcycles in Guangzhou, and the increasing proliferation of taxis in all large Chinese cities. As more and more Chinese citizens travel through the city, there simply is not enough road space for the number of bicycles and non-public transport vehicles vying for space at ten kilometers per hour on urban China's gridlocked streets.[39]

COMMERCIAL AND INDUSTRIAL VENTURES

During the post-Mao era significant changes have also occurred in the location of commercial and industrial ventures in Chinese cities, with a general trend toward the increased concentration of specialized functions in specialized districts. Both the classic "central city" central business district (CBD) and the peripheral business district that is becoming increasingly common in Western cities are emerging in contemporary Chinese cities. These reemerging commercial and business districts can be seen in the development of downtown shopping districts, downtown office centers, and peripheral development of investment properties for business and industry. In general, the pattern has been for concentrated development of commercial, office, and retail functions in the city centers, and commercial, office, and industrial functions in large peripheral developments.

In central city areas, there has been a revival of retail and office districts supported by state planning and investment. As some Chinese consumers develop the ability to purchase consumer goods, department stores are undergoing renovations and new shops are opening in China's downtowns. In the larger cities, these now include a small number of

---

[37]Ibid. Zhao Shengyang et al. provide a figure of two-thirds of all transit trips by bicycle in Beijing in the mid-1980s (Zhao Shengyang, Nagui M. Rouphail, and Robert E. Paaswell, "Urban Transportation in the People's Republic of China," *ITE Journal* 57, no. 3 [1987]: 26).

[38]Shi Zhongheng, "Subway: A Solution to Urban Transport," *China Transport* No. 1 (1987): 51.

[39]This is not to say that bicycles are not an excellent means of transportation in terms of their ease of operation, lack of pollution, and convenience. But there simply is not the road capacity, nor the potential for the road capacity, to handle the current proliferation of private vehicles in large Chinese cities. As in the case of Beijing, Tianjin, and Shanghai, one of the better solutions to this problem is to introduce subway or light rail systems to handle some of the city's overwhelming traffic volume.

joint-venture retail outlets. At the same time, there has been an increase in the development of some new office and hotel complexes in downtown areas. This type of development usually requires the razing of preexisting structures and relocation of their occupants to other sites.

In China's larger cities, the establishment of high-profile commercial developments and districts has led to increased concentration of functions on the outskirts of the developed area of the cities. This is particularly true in cities that are establishing foreign trade zones, office and industrial parks, hotels catering to foreign business travelers, and apartment complexes for foreigners. Because of the substantial land requirements for these types of projects, much of this new development has taken place just beyond the margin of the built-up area of the city, or in previously "underutilized" areas such as warehouse districts in close proximity to the city center.[40] In Beijing, for example, most of the new hotels and business complexes designed to serve the foreign trade have been built outside or just within the Third Ring Road.

The increase in collective and small private businesses in Chinese cities has also led to the spatial concentration of certain functions. The primary controlling factor has probably been the availability of land and facilities for business. Such specialized districts include, for example, the Haidian district in northwestern Beijing, with its focus on computer retail and wholesale ventures and districts organized around some of the newer large free markets (Figure 2.2). For small ventures it is relatively difficult to obtain land and operating facilities in many areas of Chinese cities, and these opportunities are often spatially limited to areas that the state has declared a priority for planning, or areas temporarily available such as the street frontages of large construction projects (the small businesses must vacate when the construction is complete). Far from operating in a free land or rent market, most small businesses must locate in somewhat limited available space. District specialization is neither happenstance nor controlled by the market, but, rather, is based in both state priority for certain types of development (as is the case in the development of high-technology companies in Beijing's Haidian district) or in a lack of state priority, which sometimes leaves land open for other uses.[41] The relocation and new establishment of enterprises in outlying

[40]There are notable exceptions to this, however, such as the Shanghai Center development, which is located on Nanjing Road in the center of Shanghai.
[41]Although in some cases it seems that some concentration of functions and development has preceded policy. This may be the case in the Haidian district, where the universities

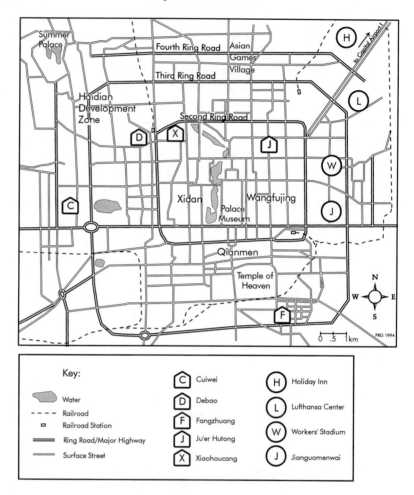

Figure 2.2. Beijing. *Base map adapted from* Beijing Driving Guide *(Beijing: People's Transport Press, 1990) and* Beijing Transport and Tourism Map *(Beijing: Beijing Normal University, 1993)*

areas thus disperses commercial and industrial ventures from the central city and concentrates them in some outlying areas.[42] Whether planning the establishment of new foreign investment zones or developing neigh-

spawned numerous high-tech ventures before the district was declared a special high-technology development zone.
[42]Kim, "China's Current Housing Issues," 224, and Kojima, *Urbanization and Urban Problems,* 76.

borhood shopping centers, the trend of Chinese urban planning and management in recent years has been toward the spatial concentration of commercial and industrial ventures. Identifiable and distinct urban districts are beginning to define the shape of the Chinese city.

THE DEVELOPING STRUCTURE OF THE CONTEMPORARY CHINESE CITY

Specialized districts and emerging neighborhood types. Several specialized districts have emerged or reemerged in the post-Mao era in China's large cities. These identifiable areas cover a wide range of both functions and sizes. Five of the most notable are: downtown retail and business centers, residential districts, targeted development zones, foreign enclaves, and restoration districts. The following discussion draws on examples from Beijing, Shanghai, and Kunming (capital of Yunnan Province) to illustrate the emergence of these districts in recent years.

Downtown retail and business centers. Crowds of shoppers now fill the streets and side alleys in Beijing's Qianmen, Wangfujing, and Xidan areas as the new Chinese consumers and would-be consumers fill their free time with shopping expeditions.[43] Many Chinese cities are experiencing a revival of centralized commercial functions in "downtown" shopping and commercial centers. These reemerging business districts vary in their relationship to prerevolution downtown centers. Some occupy new sites, but the emerging business districts are often developing in the same areas as earlier commercial centers in spite of attempts during the 1950s–1970s to decentralize urban forms.

Many factors influence the location of business and shopping districts, including the existing infrastructure of pre-1949 downtown districts, legacies of Maoist-era planning attempts to relocate the functional centers of cities, and priorities of contemporary development plans. In many cases, the result seems to be a structure involving multiple centers, with few large cities relying on a single downtown center.

For example, Beijing has seen the revival of central business district functions in the pre-1949 downtown shopping districts in the areas of

---

[43]Qianmen is located just south of Beijing's Tiananmen Square. Wangfujing and Xidan are located on the eastern and western sides of Beijing's former imperial palace (the "forbidden city").

Qianmen, Wangfujing, and Xidan.[44] Both local and tourist-oriented
commercial activities in these districts have expanded greatly. According
to Wuyang Yang, a geographer at Beijing University, about two-thirds
of the shoppers on Wangfujing Street are either tourists or rail passengers "passing through" Beijing. Qianmen serves a more local trade, with
a large proportion of the customers from Beijing's agricultural hinterland. Xidan is also a local shopping center, with 70 percent of its customers from the western districts and outlying areas of Beijing.[45] In the
mid-1980s, the Beijing Public Security Bureau reported that about 1.15
million people were going to downtown Beijing every day. This is a
phenomenal increase over the daily average of thirty thousand to sixty
thousand people downtown in 1979.[46] Nonetheless, new centers are also
being developed in Beijing, such as the specialized computer and electronics retail stores in northwestern Beijing's Haidian district (part of
the Experimental Zone for the Development of New Technology Industries) and the joint-venture Lufthansa Center/Landmark Towers area development in northeastern Beijing (Figure 2.3). According to current
urban plans, Beijing will continue to develop a hierarchy of local commercial centers of varying scope and size.[47] Nonetheless, those mentioned above serve as "downtown" centers for the entire city and large
pools of nonresident customers as well.

Although Shanghai's premier commercial downtown center continues
to be Nanjing Road, the commercial core first established during Shanghai's treaty port days in the nineteenth century, Shanghai is establishing
other high-activity downtown centers (Figure 2.4). Considerable development has taken place to the west of Shanghai's Nanjing Road core
area, centered on the Shanghai Exhibition Center–Shanghai Center. This
development is oriented toward foreign trade and business with several
newly built complexes designed to contain business offices, trade services, housing, retail and other services. This development is large enough

[44]Qianmen has been a commercial center off and on since the beginning of the fifteenth
century; Wangfujing developed commercial functions much later—particularly from the
beginning of the twentieth century when Dongjiaomen Road was opened to diplomatic
corps. Yang Wuyang, "The Context of Beijing's Commercial Network—An Empirical
Study on the Central Place Model," *GeoJournal* 21 (1990): 49–55.

[45]Ibid.

[46]*Zhongguo de da dushi*, using figures from 1979, reports about 60,000 visitors per day
to Wangfujing, Xidan, and Qianmen (*Zhongguo de da dushi* [China's great cities] [Hong
Kong: Commercial Press, 1986], 79). *China Daily* reports that about 30,000 persons per
day visited downtown Beijing in 1979 (November 11, 1987, as cited in Greer, ed., *China
Facts & Figures Annual*, 101).

[47]Long, *Beijing shiyong ciliao daquan*, 159–67.

Figure 2.3. Youyi Shopping City, a four-story department store with a super-market in its basement, is the main retail establishment in Beijing's Lufthansa Center development. *Photograph by Piper Rae Gaubatz*

to generate significant employment, support, and service industry op-portunities for local residents. Further retail and business office devel-opment is taking place to the east in the Pudong district on the shores of the Huangpu River just opposite the Nanjing Road core area. Al-though Pudong is focused primarily on manufacturing and business trade, rather than retail, the scale of the development and plans for fu-ture development suggest that retail will soon follow productive enter-prises. And plans and construction are well under way in Pudong for a number of business office complexes.

Concerted attempts have been made in Kunming to establish a new downtown. The development of the eastern half of the city is creating a new center along Beijing Road, which runs north–south along the former eastern boundary of the city (Figure 2.5). Institutions such as the Work-ers' Cultural Palace (a community recreation and social center) and tour-ist-oriented businesses such as hotels have been built along Beijing Road to foster commercial development in the eastern districts of the city. Nonetheless, Kunming's traditional commercial districts remain the bus-iest in the city, and large influxes of private entrepreneurs in these areas

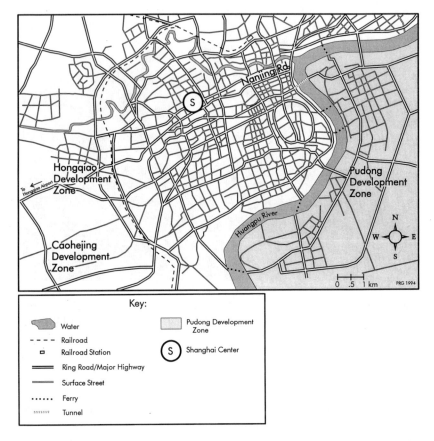

Figure 2.4. Shanghai. *Base map adapted from* Shanghai Economic Zone Tourism Volume *(Shanghai: Academy Press, 1990) and* Shanghai Pudong New Area *(Shanghai: China Cartographic Studies Press, 1992)*

in recent years have served only to reinforce the "downtown" functions of the traditional downtown area.[48]

New residential districts. Districts devoted to primarily residential func- tions are being created in China as a result of two processes: the removal

---

[48]The city of Hohhot provides a counterexample. There post-1949 planning changes have significantly relocated downtown functions even into the present era. Pre-1949 Hohhot consisted of two centers separated from each other: the old Manchu city and the old Han/Mongolian city. Development since 1949 has focused on the space between the two centers, and it is this area that is now functioning as a commercial center.

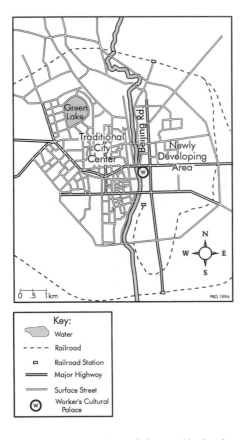

Figure 2.5. Kunming. *Base map adapted from Alfred Schinz,* Cities in China *(Stuttgart: Gebruder Borntraeger, 1989), p. 292*

of industry from established residential areas and the construction of completely new districts on the outskirts of the cities.[49] The new trend is toward housing districts that mix residential, service, and commercial functions, but which do so in a different way from the older work-unit compounds. Heavy industry is conspicuously absent from new or recently renewed residential areas. In large cities such as Beijing and Shanghai, some districts are being transformed from a mixed-use work unit–based structure to more residential uses during the relocation of

[49]"New" in this context means developed during the post-Mao era.

industries from the inner regions to the outlying areas that began in the early 1980s.[50]

Throughout China's large cities, the construction of new housing since 1978 has focused on the development of completely new residential areas. These municipal and state projects differ from housing developed in the 1960s and 1970s in that they are large-scale high-rise developments designed to house employees of many different work-units, whose places of employment are spatially separate from the residential district.

A 1990 report in the *People's Daily*, for example, cited new housing districts under construction in twenty cities.[51] Twenty new residential areas have been established in Beijing alone since the late 1970s, including such districts as Zuojiazhuang (west of the city center), Xibianmen (southwest of the city center), and Fangzhuang (southeast of the city center).[52] In Shanghai, new residential areas ring the city, with the most recent development based in the Pudong development area. And Kunming is focusing the development of new housing in the eastern districts in a continued effort by planners to shift the city center.

Targeted development zones. Another new aspect of recent urban development in China has been the proliferation of targeted development zones. National, provincial, and municipal governments in China have all instituted targeted development programs for new or reorganized urban districts, outlying areas, and satellite towns. Between 1991 and 1993, at least twenty cities established such programs, according to the *People's Daily* and *China Daily*, by designating "high- and new technology development zones," "economic and technological development zones," and "economic development zones." These zones share common features ranging from preferential economic and legal environments, such as tax holidays for investment in business and industry, to promises of extensive future infrastructure development.

The government of the PRC has attempted at times throughout its history to solve urban problems through the establishment of industrial satellite settlements, such as the only partially successful satellite settlements established outside Shanghai during the Maoist period. Efforts to

[50]See, for example, Kojima, *Urbanization and Urban Problems*, 76.
[51]These new housing districts are being constructed in well-known cities such as Beijing, Shanghai, Jinan, Nantong, Suzhou, Wuxi, Hefei, Luoyang, Chengde, Taiyuan, Zhuzhou, Nanning, Xi'an, Chengdu, Shijiazhuang, Kunming, and Harbin ("Twenty Cities Plan New Housing Districts," *People's Daily*, August 12, 1990).
[52]Li Ping, "Progress in Housing Construction," *Beijing Review* (May 13–19, 1991): 22.

relieve population pressure and service demands in the urban core areas include moving industry outside the city proper and establishing planned industrial settlements that will offer a full range of services and urban amenities. Most of these industrial settlements have been planned as expansions of the existing urban area, however, rather than as spatially separate satellite developments. And whereas in early attempts to establish satellite settlements the provision of infrastructure usually preceded the establishment and transfer of industry, the more recent trend has been to move and establish the industry in advance of infrastructure.[53] The pace of employee housing construction often does not match that of the construction of workplaces, and as a result inner-city residents commute to outlying areas. Those employees who relocate to the outlying areas in turn must travel into the city for shopping and social services not yet developed in their new neighborhoods.

The new trends in development zone planning are evident in Shanghai. Shanghai's early industrial satellites, established during the 1950s–1960s, were intended to be industrial communities focused on a single industry, such as machine manufacturing in Minhang, iron and steel in Wusong, the textile industry in Jiading, chemical and building materials in Wujing, and petrochemicals in Jinshan.[54] The new targeted development zones of the 1980s and 1990s, like the earlier satellite settlements, are also designed with strong functional construction. Their business and industrial scope tends to be more broadly defined, however, such as "high-technology development" or "export processing." The largest new development zones, such as Shanghai's Pudong district, encompass a wider variety of functions. The Pudong New Development Zone on the east bank of the Huangpu River is one of the most highly publicized examples of a targeted development zone oriented toward the international economy. Although Pudong resembles the earlier satellite developments to the extent that the districts are planned and designated for specific specialized functions, it differs from the satellite city model to the extent that it is planned as a spatial and functional extension of central Shanghai and is primarily intended for production for the foreign

---

[53]Except, perhaps, in some of the high-profile projects designed to attract foreign investment, where some initial development of infrastructure is necessary to market the project. Shanghai's Caohejing is an example of this, though even in Caohejing, the construction of nearby housing to be rented by employees of the project lags behind the already established industrial and business infrastructure.

[54]L. Yang and R. L. Sterling, "Underground Space Use and Urban Planning in Shanghai," *Journal for Urban Planning and Development* 114 (1988): 35.

market and the utilization of foreign investment funds. This development area, equal in size to the present downtown Shanghai (350 sq. km) is being built as a multifaceted foreign investment and commercial zone. The zone consists of five districts targeted for various specialized activities such as export goods processing, trade and financial services, finance and trade, bonded storage and export processing.[55] This large region has experienced considerable infrastructure development in recent years. Between 1980 and 1990, 4.22 million square meters of apartments were built there. In spite of the massive construction of residential units in Pudong, however, the commute between Shanghai proper and Pudong is lengthy in both directions.

Another example of targeted development is the designation of high-technology zones. China established a formal program to develop high-technology development zones in 1986, focusing on Beijing, Jiangsu (Wuxi and Nanjing), Shanghai (Minhang, Caohejing, and Hongqiao), and Guangdong (Guangzhou, Shenzhen, Zhuhai, Shantou, Foshan, and Jiangmen).[56] Today similar projects are in various stages of development in many other cities, including Chongqing, Dalian, Hangzhou, Ningbo, Wenzhou, Kunshan (Jiangsu), Yixing (Jiangsu), Qinhuangdao, Jimei (Fujian), and Lanzhou.

In northwestern Beijing, state and local planning contributed to a high concentration of state, collective, and private institutions and enterprises devoted to scientific and technological activities in the Zhongguancun area of the Haidian district even before the district was officially declared an experimental zone for the development of new technology industries in 1988.[57] Haidian is devoted largely to research and commercial enterprises associated with high technology. As early as 1984, Chinese sources identified in the area thirty-six institutions of higher learning (5 percent of the national total), eighty research centers affiliated with the Chinese Academy of Sciences, and forty "development companies" (primarily retail businesses selling electronic equipment).[58] The electronic retail businesses were the most significant new aspect of the district, since it

---

[55]Two of the sections of Pudong have not yet been developed. Beicai-Zhangjiang is planned to become a scientific and educational center, and Zhoujiadu-Liuli is planned to be an industrial area similar to Qingningshi-Jinqiao.

[56]Dennis Fred Simon, "Shanghai's Lure for High-Tech Investors," *China Business Review* (March–April 1990): 46–47.

[57]"A Silicon Valley in Haidian?" *Beijing Review* 44 (October 29, 1984): 8–9.

[58]Ibid.

had long had a reputation as a university center. Today the high-technology development in Haidian is even more striking, with high-technology ventures and the businesses that serve them lining Baishiqiao–Haidian Road from the Capital Library to Beijing University. The recent construction of a postmodern office center for the zone and the opening of a Kentucky Fried Chicken restaurant and a Pizza Hut contribute to Haidian's new image.

Shanghai's high-technology and industrial development zones are functionally as well as spatially separate from each other. All three of these, Minhang, Caohejing, and Hongqiao, are south and west of the city core. Heavy industry continues to locate in Minhang, an industrial satellite settlement retooled for high-technology development in 1983.[59] Infrastructural development ranging from road improvement to tree planting continues in Minhang in order to attract foreign investment. Caohejing Park, located in Shanghai's southwestern region, is Shanghai's high-technology and research and development center. Although as of 1994 Caohejing Park still contained many empty lots, large multinational corporations such as the Philips Company, the Foxboro Company, the Raychem Company Ltd., 3M, and France L'Air Liquide had already established manufacturing facilities there. Several research institutes operate near Caohejing Park, and efforts are under way to construct housing in the area for the anticipated influx of workers for the new industrial ventures. The Hongqiao district, on the airport road halfway between downtown Shanghai and Shanghai's international airport, is targeted toward the business, management, and banking functions associated with foreign business operations in Shanghai.[60] Hongqiao is being developed as a showcase convention center, with facilities for foreign consulates, banking, and management functions.

The ultimate success of these high-technology districts remains to be seen. Like the Japanese with their technopolis program, the Chinese are finding it difficult to recreate the extraordinary circumstances surrounding the early success of California's Santa Clara Valley ("Silicon Valley") semiconductor industry and Boston's Route 128 development. The Chi-

---

[59]Minhang is located thirty kilometers southwest of downtown Shanghai on the Huangpu River, and currently accounts for 14 percent of Shanghai's joint ventures. Simon, "Shanghai's Lure for High-Tech Investors," 46.

[60]Ibid. Hongqiao is located near Shanghai's Hongqiao international airport, about six and a half kilometers west of central Shanghai.

nese experiment in high-technology development zones differs from these to the extent that it is highly dependent on foreign investment and stresses production over research and development.

Foreign enclaves. Many of China's large cities are constructing large multifunctional foreign commerce and residential districts to attract foreign businesses. Although difficulties have arisen in establishing and managing such developments in China, they have had increasing success as the business relationships between China and the rest of the world have strengthened in the post-Mao period.[61] Multifunctional foreigner-directed districts are proliferating and starting to compete with one another for the growing market in foreign residence and service provision.

The establishment of foreign enclaves has the dual effect of providing facilities for the conduct of international business and controlling the location of those activities. The necessity for large tracts of land to cater to such needs combined with the desirability, from the Chinese perspective, of spatially isolating foreign activity has led to a relatively high spatial concentration of foreign enterprise development in some districts.

In Beijing, for example, although many businesses and institutions catering to foreign residents and tourists are scattered across the entire city, foreigner-focused enterprises are concentrated in the northeastern quadrant of the city, particularly in those areas bordering on or within the diplomatic neighborhoods of eastern Beijing.[62] These are areas with relatively high concentrations of hotels, exhibition facilities, and office facilities catering to international business people. As infrastructure for foreign business improves in Chinese cities, foreign businesses are moving their offices and foreign employees out of the hotels they occupied during the 1980s and into specialized developments.

One of the best examples of a foreign enclave oriented toward business (rather than diplomacy) is the cluster of housing and services for foreigners adjacent to the Beijing Lufthansa center (Yansha Maoyi Zhongxin). Here in northeastern Beijing, the Great Wall Sheraton Hotel and the Kunlun Hotel, both constructed in the 1980s, are now competing for the foreign residence and office market with the Landmark Towers complex, the Lufthansa center, the Capital City development and

[61]See, for example, Pam Baldinger, "Grinning and Bearing It," *China Business Review* (March–April 1990): 40–43.
[62]These diplomatic areas include Donghuamen, Chaoyangmen, Chaowai, Dongzhimen, and Sanlitun.

Figure 2.6. In Beijing, the recently completed Capital City development (foreground) now dwarfs the Kunlun Hotel (background). *Photograph by Piper Rae Gaubatz*

other multifunctional complexes offering office and apartment space as well as retail, business, and entertainment services (Figure 2.6).[63] The Holiday Inn Lido, the Yanxiang Hotel, and the Grace Hotel, which also serve multiple purposes, are a short two kilometers northeast on the airport road. There are two other major concentrations of foreign business–oriented hotels and office centers in Beijing: the Universe Building, Swissotel Beijing, and the Ramada Asia Hotel just west of the Beijing Workers Stadium, and another, in the vicinity of Jianguomenwai, the road leading east out of Tiananmen Square, including the Asia Pacific Building, the Changfugong Office Building, the Hotel New Otani Chang-fugong, the Gloria Plaza Hotel, the CITIC building, the CVIK Tower and Hotel, the Jianguo Hotel, the Jinglun Hotel, and the China World Trade Center, among others.

Some foreign enclaves (such as the Holiday Inn Lido complex on the airport road in Beijing and the Shanghai Center on Shanghai's Nanjing Road) are being constructed as self-contained "mini-cities." Both the Holiday Inn Lido in Beijing and the Shanghai Center development provide apartments, office space, recreation, restaurants, and shopping malls for their residents. Shanghai is also developing a substantial foreign housing enclave in the Hongqiao development zone near the Hongqiao international airport. The enclave should be nearly self-contained when complete, with a grocery store, banks, apartments, recreation facilities, restaurants, and a park all within easy walking distance.

The foreign enclaves described above are not limited to Beijing, Shanghai, and the Special Economic Zones. As international tourism and business have reached more and more Chinese cities, foreigner's districts are developing in other cities as well. The jobs in foreign-related businesses are often both lucrative and prestigious and employ large numbers of young people who live in their family's home. Thus the establishment of these complexes, whose joint venture firms often offer housing subsidies rather than housing itself, contribute to the increasing commute problem. In cities with fewer foreign trade ventures, however, such as Kunming, foreign enclaves are on a much smaller scale, often consisting of small enterprises clustered around tourist hotels, which in many cases double as foreign offices. This form is similar to the foreign enclaves in Beijing and Shanghai in the early 1980s.

---

[63]All these hotels have wings or floors devoted to business offices for foreign and domestic companies, and all have wings or floors devoted to apartments for foreigners as well.

Restoration districts. Another "new" type of district that has gained some prominence in the post-Mao era is the historic preservation and restoration district. Once discouraged as counterrevolutionary, preser- vation has now become an accepted practice. During the post-Mao era, architects and urban planners throughout China have worked on iden- tifying, maintaining, and restoring examples of past architecture and urban landscapes. This movement has commercial appeal in major tour- ist destinations such as Beijing. It is also being carried out, however, in less well-known districts of more remote places such as Hohhot and Urumqi, which are far off the main tourist routes.

In Beijing, the best-known preservation district is the much publicized Liulichang, a street in Beijing's southwestern quadrant. Liulichang has been reconstructed to appear as a Qing dynasty shopping street devoted to the sale of books, antiques, and supplies for calligraphy and other arts. In other areas of Beijing, attempts have been made to restore the traditional urban landscape while accommodating contemporary housing needs through the construction of new housing with strong architectural refer- ence to traditional courtyard housing. Examples of such neighborhoods include Ju'er Hutong, near central Beijing's Bell and Drum towers, and Xiaohoucang Alley, near Beijing's Xizhimen subway stop.[64]

The restoration of traditional districts has been at the center of a series of debates among Chinese architects and planners over the ultimate goals and articulation of "restoration projects." The primary issue in these debates is the extent to which these restorations are faithful to past forms. Projects such as Beijing's Liulichang, Hohhot's Dazhao neigh- borhood, Chengde's Qing Street, and Kaifeng's Song Street have received both praise and criticism in the Chinese architectural literature.[65] Those faithful to accurate preservation decry these restorations, which tend to restore the neighborhood to a stereotypical period style without rigid adherence to accurate reproduction of individual structures. Others praise the restoration projects' early successes at blending the preserva- tion of cultural heritage with commercial profitability.

Implementation of less high-profile, commercially oriented urban pres- ervation projects can be troublesome when preservation conflicts with

[64]Wu Liangyong, "A Probe into the Organic Renewal of Urban Cells and the New Type Courtyard House," *China City Planning Review* 6, no. 2 (1990): 3–23; Li, "Progress in Housing Construction."

[65]See, for example, Wu Tianzhu, "Comments on the Design of Qingfeng St., Chengde," *Jianzhu xuebao* (Architectural journal) no. 3 (1987): 38–41.

the new drive for economic prosperity. In Kunming in the 1980s, for example, the city government had a difficult time enforcing preservation guidelines for the central city. Retail establishments sought to modernize their buildings as a means of generating greater profits, and city ordinances requiring new structures to be at least three stories tall conflicted with attempts to preserve traditional one- and two-story neighborhood landscapes. Moreover, preservation remains difficult to carry out throughout China in situations without state support. The most widespread "grass-roots" preservation effort in the post-Mao era has been the reconstruction of mosques by many of China's Islamic communities.

CONCLUDING REMARKS

The continued increase in spatial and functional specialization in Chinese cities is strongly tied to increased autonomy and diversity in the social and economic spheres. District specialization and intraurban travel are likely to increase as Chinese individuals and businesses continue to gain increasing control over where they live, work, shop, and gather for recreational activities. This trend is being accentuated by current urban planning tendencies, with urban administrators increasingly emphasizing citywide planning, in which specialized use zones and districts play an increasingly important role.

Whereas the Maoist city was predicated on a static population and a very specific ideal of urban life and space, the post-Mao city is developing in a context of greater socioeconomic and individual mobility and changing and increasingly complex economic organization and urban form. The new districts described in this chapter impose a complex and specialized network on the older forms of the Maoist city and the traditional city. The increasing specialization of districts within Chinese cities is a direct result of China's attempts at reform and redefinition. As the districts identified above continue to develop, and the strains on infrastructure increase, the emerging specialized structure of large Chinese cities will continue to diverge from the generalized model advocated during the Maoist period, and will present increasing challenges to Chinese urban planners, administrators, and residents.

3

Cities in the Chinese economic system:
changing roles and conditions for autonomy

BARRY NAUGHTON

The lives of urban dwellers are shaped by the cities in which they live, and cities themselves are shaped by economic forces that extend well beyond urban boundaries. As economic systems change, the links between cities and national and international economies change, affecting the form of cities and the character of urban life. People cluster in large, dense population units not because they are gregarious but primarily because they can accomplish certain activities more productively in cities. This productivity differential creates the possibility of higher incomes and more rewarding lifestyles, which attracts people to cities in spite of the added costs of urban life. Both the opportunities and the freedom to take advantage of opportunities change during the process of economic reform.

In a socialist economic system, economic planners have enormous control over many economic decisions. Choices of individuals and households are still important, but they are shaped and constricted in significant ways by the choices made by planners. In China, even more than in other socialist countries, planners consistently made choices about the role and function of cities that tended to undervalue the contribution of cities. Particularly between the early 1960s and the late 1970s, planners restricted the growth of cities, and channeled resources away from cities, especially the existing large, often coastal, cities. Despite their antiurban biases, planners were forced to rely on these same cities to achieve their own objectives and to collect the financial resources they needed to run the economic system. Out of this contradictory mixture of neglect and dependence came urban development policies that crucially marked the life choices of urban dwellers, and rural residents

61

as well. Economic planners needed to control city economies, and the economic policies they adopted enforced that control. The needs and actions of economic planners in turn encouraged the adoption of social policies that emphasized social control and severely constricted the autonomy of urban dwellers.

After the initiation of economic reform, and particularly since the mid-1980s, these policies have been relaxed in important respects. Some observers might have supposed that the relaxation of antiurban policies would lead to a resurgence of the traditional urban centers, yet by and large that did not happen during the first decade of reform. In part, this is because some crucial elements of the old policy remained in place, most notably the prohibition against permanent migration to large cities. Even more important, however, is that reform has caused substantial changes in the broader economy within which the role of cities is determined. Those changes have tended to reduce the distance between urban and rural activities and create a more diffuse, sprawly pattern of urban development. As markets have grown, and as cities have tended to spread beyond their initial boundaries, the need for planners to exercise tight control over city economies has become less compelling. Planners have devolved greater power to city governments, and urban dwellers have gained more control over their own lives. The character of cities, and thus of urban life, has been markedly altered.

CITIES IN THE TRADITIONAL ECONOMIC SYSTEM

Chinese urbanization and socialist industrialization strategy. A neglect of the economic importance of cities is deeply rooted in socialist industrialization strategy, and may also have been reinforced by the relatively weak development of cities in China before the revolution. Industrialization strategy in almost all socialist countries has included the desire to achieve industrialization with minimum urbanization costs.[1] This approach reflected a fairly straightforward, if shortsighted, cost-benefit assessment of urbanization. The goal was seen as achievement of industrialization on a nationwide scale, and urbanization was viewed primar-

---

[1]Kam Wing Chan, "Economic Growth Strategy and Urbanization Policies in China, 1949–1982," *International Journal of Urban and Regional Research* 16, no. 2 (June 1992): 275–305; Gyorgy Konrad and Ivan Szelenyi, "Social Conflicts of Underurbanization," in Michael Harloe, ed., *Captive Cities: Studies in the Political Economy of Cities and Regions* (New York: John Wiley, 1977), 157–74.

ily as a cost incurred in the pursuit of industrialization. Cities were costly because urban infrastructure—housing, sewage, and streets—was expensive, and because urban dwellers demanded additional commercial and entertainment facilities. Thus, while a certain amount of urbanization was seen as an inevitable part of the industrialization process, the objective was to minimize those costs to the greatest extent possible. This meant slowing down the urbanization process in general, and in particular redirecting urbanization toward smaller urban centers, where costs were lower.

Moreover, planners attached little importance to the economic institutions that are at the core of city economies in market regimes. Financial institutions, commodity markets, advertising agencies, consulting firms—planners perceived, quite correctly, that the administrative decision-making processes over which they presided were designed to replace these market institutions. In their view, independent institutions of this sort were obsolete, and so cities no longer needed to develop in ways supportive of those institutions. Urbanization was perceived as being one of many spontaneous and disorderly market-driven processes that were to be replaced by the self-conscious activity of the planner acting in the public name. During the 1920s in the Soviet Union, utopian urban planners envisioned both city and countryside disappearing in a reconstructed factory landscape, with rationally organized production spread evenly across the land. These extreme visions faded with the triumph of Stalin, and planners accepted that urbanization was a necessary concomitant of industrialization. Nevertheless, hostility to the largest cities remained one of the central features in urban development theory.[2] A fundamental orthodox tenet in both Soviet and subsequently Chinese urban policy was that the development of large cities should be restricted, and that urban growth should be channeled into medium and small cities.

Such attitudes may have been readily accepted in China because of the country's limited urbanization before 1949. China had no strong tradition of independent cities and limited development of an independent urban culture. Max Weber believed that the lack of urban autonomy was one of the most important reasons that China did not independently initiate a process of modernization and industrialization.[3] Work on the

---

[2]James H. Bater, *The Soviet Scene: A Geographical Perspective* (London: Edward Arnold, 1989), 94–108.
[3]Max Weber, *The Religion of China* (New York: Free Press, 1951), 13–20. Weber argues, "The Chinese city . . . differed decisively from that of the Occident . . . and lacked polit-

Chinese traditional economy has stressed the sophisticated commercial development of China's rural areas and smaller urban centers, suggesting that a "bottom-heavy" economic system existed.[4] China's cities began to play an autonomous and catalytic role only with the arrival of the foreigner. The treaty port cities grew rapidly and—while undeniably creative—they were accompanied by the aura of corruption that came from excessive foreign influence and cooperation with the imperialists. It became reasonable to think of draining cities of the resources that fed this corruption. The Communist revolution achieved its first real successes in the countryside, and finally seized the cities only after the civil war had been won. There was thus a nativist strain of antiurban thought in China, drawing from the rural revolution and the fact that large cities had grown up primarily under foreign aegis.[5] Mao Zedong seems to have had a real aversion to big cities, and his antiurbanism became prominent after the Great Leap Forward (1958–60). The initial draft of the Third Five-Year Plan (in 1964) called for some migration to urban areas, which had been stripped of population in the aftermath of the Great Leap Forward. Mao's comment was: "No way." As late as 1978, urban planners were taking as the guideline Mao's laconic comment: "It's no good if cities are too big" (Chengshi taidale, buhao).

By the 1950s, the period of maximum direct Soviet influence in China, Soviet doctrine on urbanization had been modified from its earlier strictly antiurban stance. As industrialization proceeded, urban planners

ical autonomy. . . . The city as an imperial fortress actually had fewer formal guarantees of self-government than the village. . . . The prosperity of the Chinese city did not primarily depend upon the citizens' enterprising spirit in economic and political ventures but rather upon the imperial administration. . . . [T]hey failed to create a system of guild privileges comparable to that of the West during the Middle Ages . . . this also accounted for the absence of fixed, publicly recognized, formal and reliable legal foundations for a free and cooperatively regulated organization of industry and commerce. . . . These were the legal foundations beneficial to the development of petty capitalism in occidental medieval artisan crafts but in China they were absent because the cities and guilds had no politicomilitary power of their own." This Weberian strain was further developed by Etienne Balazs.

[4] Madeleine Zelin, "The Structure of the Chinese Economy during the Qing Period: Some Thoughts on the 150th Anniversary of the Opium War," in Kenneth Lieberthal, Joyce Kallgren, Roderick MacFarquhar, and Frederic Wakeman, Jr., eds., *Perspectives on Modern China: Four Anniversaries* (Armonk, N.Y.: M.E. Sharpe, 1991).

[5] But see the excellent discussion on this point in R. J. R. Kirkby, *Urbanisation in China: Town and Country in a Developing Economy 1949–2000* (London: Croom Helm), 1–18. Kirkby concludes by stressing that "the purpose of constraining urban concentration in China has been to *enhance*, rather than to curtail, the role of the cities as loci of production." Thus industrialization without urbanization remains the most important explanatory framework.

in the Soviet Union compromised with the demand for cities. Officials of industrial ministries sought to place their projects near the largest cities for reasons of convenience and because they recognized that productivity was higher in those locales. (Thus, the bureaucracy did respond to market forces of a sort.) Beginning in the 1950s, Soviet planners accepted the need for better housing, and allowed resources to be devoted to improving deplorable housing. Planners adapted to these economic forces by accepting increased urbanization but channeling urban growth into distinctive forms. Old center cities were usually left intact, and new growth channeled into the outskirts of the city. New districts (*rayon* in Russian) were constructed that combined factories and high-rise residences, theoretically allowing workers to walk to work. In a sense, while Russian planners accepted increased urbanization, they retained a preference for dispersed development patterns within that urbanization that can perhaps be linked to earlier antiurban attitudes. High-density districts were frequently separated by wide expanses of green or open space, as in garden-city visions. Additional open space was created for symbolic political centers, replicating Moscow's Red Square. Transport corridors were required to connect outlying and traditional centers. These cities required huge amounts of land to accommodate their populations. Moreover, both Moscow and St. Petersburg display the peculiar fact that population densities actually *increase* as one moves away from the center city, in contrast to the opposite pattern that prevails quite consistently in cities in market economies.[6] Such an approach was certainly not a cost-minimizing way to achieve urbanization (particularly if land costs had been taken into account). In fact, significant sums were invested in costly urban improvements, primarily by purchasing open space in inappropriate locations at high prices. The policy shared with the earlier antiurban attitude, though, a hostility to dense and complex development of center cities, and particularly large cities.

During the 1950s, it was this modified version of Soviet doctrine that made the most visible mark on Chinese cities. Existing coastal cities such as Shanghai and Tianjin were starved for resources while investment went to create a new, more dispersed pattern of urban growth. Resources were expended rather lavishly on cities designated

[6]World Bank, *China: Urban Land Management in an Emerging Market Economy* (Washington, D.C.: World Bank, 1993), 2, 38; Bater, *The Soviet Scene*, 111–28.

for key-point development, typically in inland regions of China. To this day, the broad divided boulevards, large squares, and dispersed housing blocks are evident in districts of key-point cities such as Luoyang, Zhengzhou, and Shenyang. Existing cities commonly requisitioned large amounts of land during the 1950s, often doubling or tripling in area. The consequences of this period remain visible in the wide variations in open space and other amenities provided in the 1950s cities compared to the traditional urban centers. Denser older cities such as Shanghai, Tianjin, and Chongqing have only about 3 square meters of open space per resident (including streets, squares, and parks), while Beijing has 10 square meters and Shenyang 8.5, primarily reflecting the 1950s construction.[7] Despite these amenities, of course, most Chinese would prefer to live in the more interesting and productive, crowded but vital traditional centers. What is striking about this period is thus not the underestimation of the benefits of cities overall, but rather the deprecation of the older coastal cities.

After the collapse of the Great Leap Forward, Chinese planners found themselves faced with increasingly serious economic challenges.[8] Unwilling to moderate the pace of industrialization in order to support more rapid growth of living standards, planners found themselves unable to afford the relatively expensive urban development of the 1950s. At this point, the even more radically antiurban strain of socialist industrialization policy became dominant—in a sense, Chinese policy went back to an earlier strand in Soviet industrialization policy, marked by greater hostility to cities and a greater effort to restrain the growth of living standards. In the mid-1960s, Mao Zedong launched an even more extreme policy of dispersing economic activity away from existing urban centers. Mao's Third Front industrialization strategy, carried out between 1965 and 1971, sent industry into the far hinterland in massive proportions. Skilled manpower followed the plants outward.[9] A few new

[7]Zhang Chaozun, *Zhongguo shehuizhuyi tudi jingji wenti* (Questions of land economics in Chinese socialism) (Beijing: People's University, 1991), 244–45; World Bank, *China*, 42–46. The eighteen key-point cities of the First Plan period were Beijing, Chengdu, Luoyang, Zhengzhou, Wuhan, Xi'an, Xuzhou, Shenyang, Anshan, Datong, Shijiazhuang, Qiqihar, Harbin, Jilin, Changchun, Lanzhou, Taiyuan, and Baotou. Not all experienced extensive urban construction.

[8]During the Great Leap Forward itself, urban construction continued at a rapid pace, as cities plunged into grandiose investments. This was the period, for example, when the complex of public buildings around Tiananmen Square in Beijing took shape.

[9]Barry Naughton, "The Third Front: Defense Industrialization in the Chinese Interior," *China Quarterly*, no. 115 (Autumn 1988).

urban centers were created, such as Dukou in Sichuan, site of the Pan-zhihua steel mill. In those cases, the urban model was quite similar to that of the Soviet-inspired planning projects of the 1950s. But more commonly, Third Front projects attempted to dispense with urbanization altogether. Industrial projects were dispersed in mountainous terrain, and workers' dormitories were built alongside the factories. The motivation for these policies was unambiguously military—population dispersion was adopted as a conscious attempt to reduce the vulnerability of the population to strategic attack. The Third Front was an extreme case of industrialization without urbanization.

This period was accompanied by a drastic restriction in the growth of existing urban centers. For most Chinese cities, urban development simply ceased for about a decade, between 1965 and 1978. Beginning around 1967, a policy of rustication of urban youth sent 17 million urban dwellers to the countryside. At the end of the Cultural Revolution, and after the death of Mao, nearly half these youths were still in the countryside. Shanghai, in particular, had a zero population growth rate during most of the 1960s and 1970s as emigration outweighed new births and modest immigration flows. There was even an antiurban model of industrialization advanced: the industrial settlement of the Daqing oil field accommodated several hundred thousand residents in dispersed clusters, each of which was supposed to combine agricultural and industrial production, minimizing settlement costs while maximizing output.[10]

Thus, for about fifteen years, China followed an explicitly antiurban approach that attempted to continue industrialization while minimizing urbanization. This movement occurred while the Soviet Union and other socialist countries were moving in the opposite direction, accepting more urbanization and investing large sums of money in urban housing and infrastructure. Thus, by the late 1970s, China stood out for the extreme lack of attention its urban areas had received; for the degree of neglect evident in its cities; and for the slow pace of urbanization. Yet in spite of this neglect, cities had not become any less important in the Chinese economic system.

Cities as cash cows. In China, as in other command economies, the government has been almost completely dependent on revenues from state-

---

[10]Zhao Xiqing, "A Brief Record of Thirty Years of Urban Planning Work in China," *Chengshi guihua* (City planning review) (January 1984): 45; Kirkby, *Urbanisation in China*, 15–16.

owned industry to fund its activity. The traditional planned economy had no regular taxation system; rather, the taxation system was implicit in the socialist price system. The government maintained low prices for agricultural and mining products, and high prices for manufactured goods. As a result, profits in the manufacturing sector were large, and factories were simply required to turn over those profits to the government. The predominance of state ownership in manufacturing allowed the state to tap into these profits directly in its capacity as owner of the factories. With revenues concentrated in a relatively small number of factories, the state could easily collect revenues, and the government was relieved of the difficult and politically sensitive task of taxing millions of households, farms, and petty traders. Inevitably, most factories were located in urban areas, and cities became the primary collection points for state revenues. The cities were cash cows for the government, and their main role was to be "milked" by the state.

Development of industry around the country did relatively little to reduce the central government's dependence on a few large cities. By 1978, despite years of attempting to disperse industry, 65 percent of total industrial output value was produced in the thirty-eight largest cities.[11] Almost certainly, these large cities produced an even higher percentage of total industrial profits, since state-run urban firms were substantially more profitable than state-run nonurban firms. What these numbers tell us is that the attempt to disperse industry into remote regions of the country was tremendously costly. Productivity was so much lower in the inland exurban sites that production remained concentrated in large cities in spite of the vast investment going to other locales. And since manufacturing production was concentrated in cities, the national government was almost entirely dependent on large cities for budgetary revenues.

Correspondingly, large cities paid an exceptionally large proportion of their national income to the national budget. Table 3.1 summarizes the evolution of the fiscal position of three cities. In 1978 in Shanghai, 69 percent of municipal gross domestic product (GDP) accrued to fiscal authorities, and 86 percent of this was remitted to the central government. Nearly 60 percent of municipal product was turned over to the national government. This had been the case in earlier years as well. The

---

[11]"Develop the Role of Small Towns," *Renmin ribao*, October 20, 1980: 5, translated in *JPRS Economic Affairs* no. 104: 17.

Table 3.1. *Municipal budgets in percent of municipal GDP (percent of budgetary revenues)*

	Total budgetary revenues	Remitted to center	Retained for local expenditure
Shanghai:			
1978	69.0	59.5	9.5
	(100)	(86)	(14)
1985	56.0	46.1	9.9
	(100)	(82)	(18)
1990	37.2	27.1	10.1
	(100)	(73)	(27)
Tianjin:			
1978	52.0	34.4	17.6
	(100)	(66)	(34)
1985	45.7	30.4	15.3
	(100)	(67)	(33)
1990	29.2	15.8	13.4
	(100)	(54)	(46)
Guangzhou:			
1978	31.8	22.6	9.3
	(100)	(71)	(29)
1985	33.6	24.3	9.3
	(100)	(72)	(28)
1990	18.4	11.3	7.1
	(100)	(61)	(39)

Sources: Shanghai Statistical Bureau, ed., *Shanghai Tongji Nianjian* (Shanghai statistical yearbook), Shanghai: Zhongguo Tongji, 1991. 53; Tianjin Statistical Bureau, ed., *Tianjin Tongji Nianjian* (Tianjin statistical yearbook), Tianjin: Zhongguo Tongji, 1991. 267; interviews with Guangzhou Municipal budget officials. Figures include both revenues remitted to the municipal government and revenues generated within the municipality by central and provincial enterprises and remitted directly to central and provincial authorities.

situation in the other cities was similar in character, though not quite as extreme. Tianjin turned over 34 percent of municipal GDP to the national government in 1978, and Guangzhou turned over 23 percent. Tianjin and Guangzhou both retained about a third of fiscal revenues raised, compared with only 14 percent in Shanghai. (Table 3.1 also shows that this fiscal system began to change in the 1980s, and particularly after 1985: this point is discussed below.)

This pattern did not in itself represent extraction of revenues from cities. After all, the cities were able to accumulate such large surpluses in the first place only because state pricing policy made manufacturing such a lucrative activity. The point is simply that the national government was dependent on a fiscal system that used the larger cities as the predominant point of revenue collection. Yet, given the existing tendency to devalue the economic role of cities, it was perhaps inevitable, that planners would look at cities primarily as cash cows and regard them simply as revenue sources to be exploited.

Outcomes of the traditional pattern. In practice, planners did take an essentially exploitative attitude toward existing cities. Cities were milked for revenues and output, while the minimum possible investment went into them. It was not, of course, that urban dwellers were "exploited" in any meaningful sense; quite the contrary, rural dwellers bore a far heavier burden from the state's price and taxation policies. Rather, cities as economic resources were exploited, in the sense that insufficient investments were made to maintain their long-run productivity. The most visible consequence of these policies was the stagnation and relative decline of the traditional urban centers. By the late 1970s, the central districts of Shanghai, Tianjin, and Guangzhou had an almost museumlike character, so little had they apparently changed from the 1930s. Yet actually only the facades had been maintained unchanged. Behind the walls of the old buildings, new activities were occurring: manufacturing and warehousing expanded, crowding out shops and residences. The density of activities, especially industrial activities, increased, even as the density of structures did not. Antagonistic uses were increasingly in proximity, and problems of noise, air, and water pollution became increasingly serious. Urban infrastructure was allowed to deteriorate and became increasingly overburdened.

Stagnation of the physical form of the core cities was an apt metaphor for stagnation of their economic function. The coastal cities gradually began to lose their economic and technological dynamism, and fell further behind world developments. With crucial economic decision-making increasingly in the hands of government administrators, urban economic institutions—finance and information particularly—atrophied. The complex web of services that undergirded urban productivity fell further and further behind growing industry; specific and idiosyncratic skills fell into disuse; and the superior access to information that had once existed gradually evaporated. While cities overall maintained their expected dominance of industrial production, the coastal cities that had led China's industrialization saw a dramatic decline in relative position. Shanghai and Tianjin together had accounted for 26.7 percent of total industrial output in 1952, but by 1978 this had declined to 16.8 percent. The declining share of Shanghai and Tianjin followed inevitably from the development of new inland industrial centers. Nonetheless, such phenomena are unlikely to have been observed if China had pursued a market-led development path. Typically, during the early stages of industrialization, a few primary cities increase their dominant position, and only much later does industry spread to numerous secondary centers. At the early stages of development, growth is constrained by shortages of capital and skilled labor; as a result the largest cities have big advantages in offering a diversified pool of workers, access to capital and information, and connections to world markets. Instead of developing many specialized cities, many different industries cluster in the biggest city or cities. That is what was happening in China before the 1949 revolution.[12] The relative decline of cities such as Shanghai and Tianjin occurred too soon and proceeded too rapidly.

Beyond the obvious implications of physical and economic stagnation, the twin policies of neglect and exploitation of cities led to other consequences that may be somewhat less obvious. The single-minded focus on the extractive role of cities fostered an extreme division of labor between cities and the countryside, as a natural outcome of the Chinese fiscal mechanism. Revenues were raised primarily in the form of profits and taxes on manufacturing. Because manufacturing profitability depended on access to cheap agricultural products used as industrial raw materials, planners had a strong incentive to maintain the state monopoly over agricultural procurement, in order to control supplies and prices. To maintain control over the agricultural surplus, the government insisted that virtually all rural workers should be farmers, since rural handicrafts and factories would merely compete for agricultural raw materials. By the mid-1960s, as documented by Fei Xiaotong and others, the traditional diversified rural economic base had been destroyed, and the rural economy had become overwhelmingly concentrated on agriculture. Chinese statistics show an almost unbelievable 97 percent of the rural labor force engaged in agriculture as of 1965.[13] When rural industry began to grow again, after 1970, it was from this minuscule base,

[12]Andrew Hamer, "Decentralized Urban Development: Stylized Facts and Policy Implications," in Roland Fuchs, Gavin Jones, and Ernesto Pernia, eds., *Urbanization and Urban Policies in Pacific Asia* (Boulder: Westview, 1987), 195–213.
[13]State Statistical Bureau, *Zhongguo laodong gongzi tongji ziliao 1949–1985* (China labor and wage statistical materials 1949–1985) (Beijing: Zhongguo Tongji, 1987), 80.

Table 3.2. *Structure of employment (percent of non–primary
sector employment)*

	Secondary (ind + const.)	Industry	Tertiary (services)
Shanghai 1978	67.3	(60.5)	32.7
Shanghai 1990	67.9	(60.8)	32.1
Tianjin 1985	63.9	(54.9)	36.1
Tianjin 1990	61.7	(53.8)	38.3
Guangzhou 1978	57.1	(—)	42.9
Guangzhou 1990	50.3	(41.9)	49.7

Sources: Shanghai Statistical Bureau, ed., *Shanghai Tongji Nianjian* (Shanghai statistical yearbook), Shanghai: Zhongguo Tongji, 1991. 72–73; Tianjin Statistical Bureau, ed., *Tianjin Tongji Nianjian* (Tianjin statistical yearbook), Tianjin: Zhongguo Tongji, 1991. 185; Guangzhou Statistical Bureau, ed., *Guangzhou Tongji Nianjian* (Guangzhou statistical yearbook), Guangzhou: Zhongguo Tongji, 1991. 340–41.

and with few links to the traditional economies of advanced rural regions.

Conversely, Chinese cities were overwhelmingly specialized in manufacturing. Table 3.2 shows the structure of employment in the three most important coastal cities (agricultural and mining employment has been excluded to eliminate the effects of changing urban boundaries). In all three cities, well over half the urban labor force was employed in industry in 1978. (Equally surprising is the fact that, except in Guangzhou, this structure did not change much in the succeeding twelve years. These employment figures, however, exclude the floating population that provides many of the petty retail services in cities today; they thus understate the degree of change. See Chapter 5 in this volume.) The huge share of manufacturing and the correspondingly small share of services derives naturally from the overall evolution of the urban function. Service employment is low for two reasons. First, in an attempt to economize on industrialization costs, the government systematically starved the urban areas of investment in consumer services and correspondingly sought to expand industrial employment directly. In 1952, there had been one retail sales clerk for every 81 urban dwellers; by 1965, there was a single clerk for every 216 dwellers, a figure virtually unchanged in 1978.[14] Second, service sector employment is low because planners

[14]*Zhongguo tongji nianjian* 1991 (China statistical yearbook), Beijing: Zhongguo Tongji, 1991, 581. Substitution of personnel within the work-unit may account for some of this decline. See Chapter 2 in this volume.

have appropriated many economic coordination functions of cities, which ordinarily generated employment. Thus, in the economy as a whole, service employment was far below what we would anticipate (for countries at comparable levels of development), and the labor force was divided between a rural agricultural labor force and an urban predominantly industrial labor force.

This stark demarcation between the employment opportunities of urban and rural dwellers was followed by severe restrictions on population mobility. Even though policymakers underestimated the importance of cities to the national economy, they granted urban dwellers a privileged place in that economy. Urban incomes were substantially higher than rural incomes. More fundamentally, pricing policy concentrated economic opportunities in the modern sector, itself overwhelmingly concentrated in cities. As a result, returns not only to labor but also to capital and entrepreneurship were potentially much higher in urban areas. In an uncontrolled economic environment, resources, including labor, would relocate to areas where returns were higher.

After the Great Leap Forward disaster, policymakers became acutely conscious of the dangers of uncontrolled flows of resources—particularly labor—from agriculture to urban areas. They imposed strict controls on rural-urban migration. These controls institutionalized and protected the privileged position of urban dwellers. Thus, while cities as economic entities were discriminated against, urban dwellers benefited from the main thrust of economic policy making. The cost, however, was tight controls over labor mobility, and a built-in disequilibrium between urban and rural incomes.

The sharp divide between urban and rural occupations and income also found a physical reflection in the form of cities. Chinese cities, as of the late 1970s, did not sprawl into the countryside. Spatial growth had been effectively limited since the mid-1960s. Cities were relatively compact, given their large populations, and had high densities. A sharp line divided the city from its surrounding agricultural hinterland. Indeed, the average urban dweller, even in Shanghai, the largest metropolis, could easily ride a bicycle to the edge of the city, and then continue out into a countryside that was markedly different from the city itself. The sharp distinction between urban and rural lives was visible in the abrupt end, the "hard edges" of cities. This physical form was only apparently a metaphor for the urban/rural divide; in fact it was the direct physical expression of policies that concentrated economic opportunities in cities and then sharply limited access to those opportunities.

Social consequences of the urbanization pattern. The economic system described here is peculiar in that many of its features implied the need for strong and intrusive social control exerted over city populations. This follows first of all from the basic nature of the planned economic system itself. The traditional hierarchical economic system required direct administrative control over urban production units. In order for the command economy to function, an institutional framework of command had to be in place. Once that structure existed, it was convenient (i.e., economical) to use that structure for provision of benefits, social control, and other functions. Even more important was the need to control the financial revenues raised in cities. In order to ensure a continuing flow of ample budgetary resources to the central government, tight control over urban economies had to be maintained. The delivery by Shanghai of 60 percent of its GDP to the national authorities exemplifies the relationship between cities and their governmental superiors. Since municipal governments were engaged primarily in collecting revenues and handing them over to higher level provincial or national governments, municipal governments had to serve as agents of higher levels and have limited autonomy themselves. And indeed, at the end of the 1970s municipal governments had almost no autonomous financial resources, and precious few financial resources of any kind.[15] Municipal governments did play an important role in managing industrial enterprises—but the resources they controlled remained within the industrial systems, in order to further the goal of industrialization without urbanization.

The drive for social control occasioned by the need to command urban resources was powerfully reinforced by the need to prevent uncontrolled movement by individuals. The disequilibrium between incomes in cities and in the countryside implied a strong latent demand for movement into the city that, in the eyes of planners, had to be contained. Administrative regulations were strengthened to guard the integrity of the two separate economic subsystems, with different relative prices and rules of

---

[15]Nanjing Finance Bureau, "The Role of Urban Finance during the Readjustment Period," *Caimao jingji congkan* (Finance and trade economics digest) 5 (1981): 13–17.

operation. Moreover, with labor mobility between rural and urban areas virtually eliminated, labor mobility among urban work-units also gradually faded away. In sharp contrast to the reality in Soviet workplaces—where labor mobility of blue-collar workers was high—Chinese urban workers gradually lost the ability to change jobs. Restrictions on long-distance migration encouraged the inherent tendency of the system to treat workers as appendages of individual work-units. Workers became permanent members of their work-unit, upon which they were dependant for social services and ration cards, as well as wages. The result was a complicated and dense network of dependencies that kept workers thoroughly enmeshed in relations of obligation and control.[16] The ability of the work-unit to serve as a unit of surveillance and social control was correspondingly enhanced. The work-unit therefore became the basic unit of urban society, increasing the ability of political authorities to control individual behavior, and decreasing the scope for individual autonomy. Tight administrative control of urban areas under the traditional economic system was not accidental, but rather followed from clear economic imperatives. Doubtless, tight social control is a general characteristic of Communist societies, and would have existed in China regardless of the particular way in which cities were integrated into the economic system. But China by the late 1970s was structured such that economic factors strongly reinforced political factors, leading to an urban population that was extraordinarily subject to surveillance and political control, even by the standards of the Communist states.

The other fundamental social consequence of the restrictions on urban growth and immigration was the policy of increasing female labor force participation. In the 1950s, women had difficulty entering the urban labor force, and planners had difficulty providing jobs to all potential workers.[17] But as strict limits on city growth came into effect after the mid-1960s and industrialization continued while many graduates were sent out of the cities, unemployment gradually disappeared, and female labor force participation rates increased steadily. By the late

[16]Andrew Walder, *Communist Neo-traditionalism: Work and Authority in Chinese Industry* (Berkeley: University of California Press, 1986). Walder argues that these outcomes are basically the same in the Soviet Union and in China. However, the absence of labor mobility in China does represent a fundamental difference between the two environments.

[17]Christopher Howe, *Employment and Economic Growth in Urban China, 1949–1957* (Cambridge: Cambridge University Press, 1971).

1970s, almost all urban women entered the labor force after leaving school, and high female labor force participation became an essential characteristic of urban society.

Increased female labor force participation has numerous important implications that cannot be explored here. Note simply that increased female labor participation, combined with a reduction in availability of urban services, greatly reduced the amount of leisure time available to families. (See Chapter 6 in this volume.) Women took on double duties as wage-earners and household workers, and without having any commercialized household or consumer services available for support. Hours were taken up queuing for scarce goods. The urban public social sphere declined in importance as the importance of work-units organized around major employers increased. The external growth of cities was constrained, but the intensity of labor within the cities—like the intensity of land use within the same cities—increased. Here again, the imperatives of the economic decisions made at the top reinforced those of the political decisions made, since this was also the time when personal autonomy and leisure time were sharply restricted by successive political campaigns. Urbanites had little free time.

Not everything about urban daily life was negative. Employment was virtually guaranteed, so life held little economic risk or uncertainty. Lack of commercialization meant that the visual environment was quiet, to the point of being dull. Restrictions on immigration meant that streets were not unduly crowded—at least given the initial high population densities involved—and that there were scarcely any shantytowns or homeless, though many lived in extremely cramped quarters. Thus, although leisure was scarce, life was not particularly stressful. The daily routine was busy but predictable; aspirations were limited, in part because social controls were so pervasive. Outside the immediate family circle, the most dramatic occurrences would have been the political campaigns that occasionally broke from their usual monotony and turned exciting or dangerous.

BEGINNINGS OF REFORM AND EMERGENCE OF A NEW PATTERN OF URBANIZATION

With the beginning of China's reform era, after December 1978, great changes in the economic system began. China's neglect of its coastal urban centers was already obvious to those paying attention. Indeed, even before the beginning of reform, during the mid-1970s, government investment began to shift back toward coastal cities where productivity was higher. Thus, it was reasonable to suppose that one of the effects of economic reform would be the resurgence of China's traditional urban centers, such as Shanghai and Tianjin, particularly since economic reform was accompanied by an opening to the world economy. Yet such a resurgence did not occur. Indeed, through the end of the 1980s, individual cities such as Shanghai and Tianjin continued to experience an erosion in their relative positions.

However, enormous economic dynamism quickly became evident in larger regions extending beyond traditional urban boundaries. Huge increases in output were recorded in large areas around existing cities—labeled rural in Chinese classification, but more accurately considered suburban. The areas where this phenomenon was most obvious were the Pearl River Delta (between Guangzhou and Hong Kong) and the Lower Yangtze, particularly the southern part of Jiangsu Province. This phenomenon provides insight into the changing role of cities in today's China: It shows that, in spite of the failure of traditional cities to take off, the traditional controls over cities and their economies are breaking down. The superior productivity of urban areas is now becoming manifest in larger metropolitan regions, rather than in narrowly defined center cities. As a result, the separation of city and countryside that so strongly marked the traditional economic system is being reduced. These changes are caused by broader changes in the economic system, and present opportunities for increased urban autonomy.

The take-off that didn't happen. By the 1980s, attitudes toward cities were beginning to shift in China. Awareness greatly increased of the importance of cities both as nodes of superior productivity and as centers of regional economic networks. The economist Yu Guangyuan, one of China's most prominent idea men, began arguing for the importance of city-centered economic development regions in 1982. Greater attention to the importance of cities was also manifest in the movement toward city-controlled counties, under which cities (especially smaller and provincial cities) were given administrative authority over suburban or peri-urban counties.[18] Geographers and urban planners began to ac-

[18]Laurence J. C. Ma and Gonghao Cui, "Administrative Changes and Urban Population in China," *Annals of the Association of American Geographers* 77, no. 3 (1987): 373–95.

Table 3.3. *Locally produced exports (billion U.S.$ and percentage of national total)*

	Shanghai share		Tianjin share	
1978	1.29	13.3%	—	
1980	2.08	11.5%	.76	4.2%
1985	2.29	8.4%	.74	2.7%
1986	2.45	7.9%	.79	2.5%
1987	2.80	7.1%	.93	2.4%
1988	3.21	6.8%	1.10	2.3%
1989	3.56	6.8%	1.09	2.1%
1990	3.79	6.1%	1.14	1.8%

Sources: Exports produced within the municipality only—transshipments not included. Calculated from Shanghai Statistical Bureau, ed., *Shanghai Tongji Nianjian* (Shanghai statistical yearbook), Shanghai: Zhongguo Tongji, 1991; Tianjin Statistical Bureau, ed., *Tianjin Tongji Nianjian* (Tianjin statistical yearbook), Tianjin: Zhongguo Tongji, 1991.

knowledge the productivity of big cities, and the need for even the largest cities to grow was again acknowledged.[19]

Yet despite the more favorable attitude toward big cities, an urban take-off, based on reformist policies, never happened. A few numbers can trace the continuing process of decline that was experienced by Shanghai and Tianjin. We noted above that Shanghai and Tianjin's share of national industrial output had declined to 16.8 percent by 1978; this declined further to 10.2 percent by 1990. This picture of relative decline is also reflected in foreign trade performance (Table 3.3). In the early 1980s, planners in Beijing anticipated that Shanghai and other coastal cities would become export powerhouses. A continuing decline in the cities' share of domestic output might have been acceptable, if this were the price paid for success in competitive international markets. In fact,

---

[19]For example, see Zou Deci, "The Review and Prospect of Chinese Urban Planning from 1980s to 1990s," *China City Planning Review* 6, no. 3 (September 1990): 3–16; Zhou Yixing, "Relations Between the Industrial Output and the Size of Cities in China," *China City Planning Review* 5, no. 2 (June 1989): 3–11. The shift of emphasis in China mirrors a similar shift in urban planning circles in the West. In the 1950s, it was common to hear talk of "overurbanization," of unproductive "parasitic cities," and for planners to make serious efforts to restrain the growth of large cities. Such views began to be modified on a wide scale in the 1960s. On one side, programs to restrain large city growth failed with remarkable consistency—attempts to contain Jakarta, Manila, São Paulo, and Mexico City all failed spectacularly. The failure of attempts to limit city growth and redistribute urbanization toward secondary urban centers demonstrated to planners the strength of the economic forces at work in the determination of urban form. On the other side, some planners began to stress the importance of urban diversity and complexity from the 1960s. In the United States, this approach was eloquently exemplified in the works of Jane Jacobs.

existing cities have been outclassed in international markets by newly arising centers of production, most obviously the Pearl River Delta region linked to world markets through Hong Kong entrepreneurs.

Relative decline of traditional urban centers was evident throughout the 1980s. By the late 1980s, government leaders had become concerned about the slow pace of growth within traditional urban centers. Noticing the steady relative decline of Shanghai, the Beijing leadership began to worry that Shanghai might not make it in the new era. Newspaper stories began to appear: "Are Shanghai people losing their traditional pride?" Shanghai was becoming . . . a *backwater!* . . . all the action was in Beijing. Finally, around 1988, policy changed and began to countenance the injection of substantial new resources into Shanghai. In the early 1990s, Shanghai has emerged as a significant beneficiary of central government policy, for perhaps the first time since 1949.[20] Meanwhile, other traditional centers—such as Tianjin and Shenyang—continue to languish. New policies in the 1990s may well reverse the stagnation of the 1980s, but only if they are based on an acceptance of an even broader economic role for China's cities than has heretofore been the case. In order to understand the changing position of Chinese cities, we need to ask why Chinese cities did not take off during the 1980s.

Unbalanced reform implementation. China's cities lagged behind in the 1980s in part because economic reforms achieved earlier and quicker success in rural areas. While rural reforms did not precede urban reforms, they were more thorough and successful at a time, during the early 1980s, when urban reformers were still searching for a workable model.[21] Rural reforms simultaneously released surplus labor from agriculture—by disbanding the agricultural collective system—and opened up new opportunities for that labor by relaxing earlier prohibitions on rural nonagricultural activities. The result was a surge of economic activity that changed the face of the Chinese countryside. In one sense, then, China's cities lagged only in comparison to the dynamic course of reform and economic growth in the countryside. The coexistence in the early 1980s of a vigorous and successful rural reform and

---

[20]This statement depends on our definition of beneficiary. Here I mean simply that the central government treats Shanghai as a priority applicant for resources under central government control.

[21]For a full account, see Barry Naughton, *Growing Out of the Plan: Chinese Economic Reform, 1978–1993* (Cambridge: Cambridge University Press, 1995).

a still floundering urban reform led to one description of the overall Chinese reform strategy as "surrounding the cities from the country-side."[22]

Moreover, even industrial reforms proceeded more slowly in the largest, most productive cities. For example, one of the key provisions of China's industrial reform has been the authority given state-run factories to buy and sell output outside the plan at market prices. The gradual marketization of China's industry has proceeded largely through the steady increase in the proportion of total factory output sold outside the plan. However, the 1985 industrial census showed that the proportion of industrial output sold independently by factories was *lowest* in Shanghai of any province-level unit, 35 percent compared with 54 percent nationwide.[23] Anecdotal evidence suggests that reform proceeded more slowly in Shanghai than other areas precisely because central planners were interested in retaining the revenues generated in Shanghai and the relatively high quality industrial products that only Shanghai could produce. In short, reform proceeded least rapidly in precisely those urban areas that appeared to be most productive and efficient at the outset of reform. As a result, economic growth lagged in the areas that would seem to have had the greatest potential advantage in market competition. The two municipalities of Shanghai and Tianjin, for example, were by far the slowest-growing province-level units throughout the 1980s.

Finally, restrictions on population movement have continued to hamper the growth of the larger cities. After 1980, large cities began to grow again after years of near-zero growth. But while big cities no longer grew less rapidly than medium cities, small cities (population of less than 200,000) grew significantly more rapidly than large or medium cities. An important reason for this differential performance is that restrictions on migration continue to be much more strictly enforced for cities with a population over half a million.[24] These restrictions have contributed

[22]Christopher Findlay and Andrew Watson, "Surrounding the Cities from the Country-side," in R. Garnaut and Liu Guoguang, eds., *Economic Reform and Internationalisation: China and the Pacific Region* (St. Leonards, Australia: Allen and Unwin, 1992), 49–78.

[23]Industrial Census Leading Group, *Summary Volume, 1985 Industrial Census* (Beijing: Zhongguo tongji, 1988), 122–25. The contrast was even greater than the averages indicate, because self-sales ratios were normally higher for light industry and heavy industrial manufactures (61 percent and 68 percent respectively), precisely the kind of industries in which Shanghai specialized.

[24]Zhou Yixing, "The Metropolitan Interlocking Region in China: A Preliminary Hypothesis," in Norton Ginsburg, Bruce Koppel, and T. G. McGee, eds., *The Extended Me-*

to channeling growth into smaller urban centers, including newly emerging small cities such as Xinji (described by Shue in Chapter 4). In addition, since attaining permanent residence in large cities is still nearly impossible, migrants attracted by the economic opportunity in large cities continue to fall into the twilight category of floating population. (See Chapter 5 in this volume.)

Thus, an unbalanced pattern of reform implementation has continued to harm large cities. Even though attitudes toward cities have swung remarkably toward a recognition of their superior productivity, actual policies have continued to disfavor cities, particularly large cities. This shows that earlier policies did not spring merely from "attitudes" toward cities, but rather from serious concerns about controlling output and revenue, and preventing excess urban migration, and that these concerns, while diminished, have not disappeared. Nevertheless, the changing role of cities, and their sluggish revival in the 1980s, cannot be understood solely with reference to the pattern of reform implementation. More profound changes with respect to the relationship between urban and rural areas and the overall progress of economic reform are at work.

Rural industrialization and the urbanized countryside. Of all the changes in the Chinese economy since the beginning of reform, perhaps the most striking has been the rapid growth of industrial production located in rural areas, such that the rural share of total industrial output grew from only 9 percent in 1978 to 27 percent in 1990. While urban industry has also grown rapidly, its growth has been overshadowed by the more spectacular performance of rural industry. Regional growth performance seems to reflect the importance of rural industry more than anything else. During the first half of the 1980s, industrial growth accelerated throughout the country, with no particular pattern, except for the slow growth of Shanghai and Tianjin.[25] However, during the second half of the 1980s, growth became concentrated in coastal areas—but not the existing urban centers. Five coastal provinces emerged as superior per-

tropolis: Settlement Transition in Asia (Honolulu: University of Hawaii Press, 1991), 93, 109.

[25] A strong pattern in the early 1980s is absent because some provinces had been disproportionately burdened by the policies of the Cultural Revolution period. Those provinces experienced recovery growth, while other provinces were accelerating to a new, sustainable high growth path. See David Denny, "Regional Economic Differences during the Decade of Reform," in U.S. Congress, Joint Economic Committee, ed., *China's Economic Dilemmas in the 1990s: The Problem of Reforms, Modernization and Interdependence* (Washington, D.C.: U.S. Government Printing Office, 1991) I: 186–208.

formers: ranked by annual industrial growth rates, they were Guangdong (18.5 percent), Fujian (17.6 percent), Zhejiang (17.5 percent),
Jiangsu (16.4 percent), and Shandong (16.3 percent). The southern coast
became the most dynamic region of the country, with growth radiating
northward through the middle coastal provinces. Here, too, Shanghai
and Tianjin were the two slowest-growing province-level units. The fas-
test-growing provinces were precisely those in which rural industries
were playing a pivotal role in industrial development.

How can we explain this nearly unbelievable explosion of output from
China's rural areas? The key lies in recognizing that the growth of rural
industry is inseparably linked to a change in the economic role of large
cities in the Chinese economy. Although rural industry is diverse, and a
part of it produces goods (such as building materials) primarily for the
local market, the bulk of rural industrialization might best be thought
of as "suburban industrialization." This is especially true of firms that
produce goods for "export" beyond the local community.[26] The most
vigorous regions of rural industrial growth rely largely on the presence
of neighboring cities. Urban areas provide investment, subcontracting
relations, skilled technical and managerial personnel, and information
about market access.[27] Rural industrialization mostly represents the spillover of urban economies from the bounds imposed on them by the command economy. Indeed, there is even a significant outflow of skilled
urban workers to these rural enterprises. Chinese estimates are that 3
million urban people now work in "rural" firms. Four hundred thousand
of these are in Guangdong, but large numbers are also recorded in
Jiangsu and Shandong.[28]

These peri-urban regions are designated as rural by Chinese administrative classification, but few would unambiguously identify these
regions as such. The suburban zones contain some of the most outstanding examples of entrepreneurship in the Chinese economy, as well as

---

[26]Dwight Perkins, "The Influence of Economic Reforms on China's Urbanization," in R.
Y. Kwok, W. Parish, A. Yeh, and Xu Xueqiang, eds., *Chinese Urban Reform: What
Model Now?* (Armonk, N.Y.: M. E. Sharpe, 1990), 91–95. This point has also been
stressed by Bao Yongjiang of the Tianjin Academy of Social Sciences.

[27]Tao Youzhi, *Sunan muoshi yu zhifu zhi dao* (The Southern Jiangsu model and the route
to wealth) (Shanghai shehui kexue yuan, 1988), 90, 99–100.

[28]"Folk from City Flock to Booming Rural Firms," *China Daily*, February 9, 1993. There
were 300,000 in Jiangsu, 200,000 in Shandong, and over 100,000 each in Guangxi,
Hubei, Zhejiang, Liaoning, Sichuan, Anhui, and Fujian. The source also mentions that
many floating population rural residents have returned from sojourning in the cities to
start enterprises in their hometowns, with their urban experiences having provided them
with start-up capital and management and market experience.

some of the wealthiest individuals. In this zone, weak surveillance of economic activity intersects with abundant economic opportunity. At times entrepreneurship goes beyond the bounds of legality, and the suburban zone then becomes the site of China's quasi-legal "hidden economy."[29] In short, it is possible to get things done cheaply and relatively expeditiously in the suburban regions. Urban factories are also attracted by these opportunities: to expand without hiring new permanent workers; to find land to grow on; to cut costs to increase their own bonuses—for all these reasons, city factories sponsor and support rural firms through subcontracting, joint ventures, and investment. The economic influence radiates out from the large cities, whose residents find expansion difficult within their own urban boundaries. Thus, belts of rural industry grow up around existing cities.

The most successful cases of rural industrial development in China are closely related to existing urban centers. The most spectacular example—the Pearl River Delta in Guangdong—owes its vitality not primarily to the city of Guangzhou but to the dynamism of Hong Kong, which by historical accident is separated from its suburban hinterland by a national boundary. Similarly, the lower Yangtze region is heavily dependent on the services provided by Shanghai and other existing urban centers. In terms of speed of growth, two additional emerging regions clearly fit this pattern: Shandong Province, in a belt stretching between Qingdao and Jinan; and the coastal region of Fujian. By level of development, the suburban regions of the Beijing-Tianjin-Tangshan region, and the extended metropolis around Shenyang in Liaoning, also appear to fit this pattern. In all these cases, dynamism in rural industry is closely related to the emergence of a new, more geographically extended urban region centered on an existing urban core.[30]

This pattern should not be surprising when viewed in a comparative Asian context. In most countries, center cities do not contain the bulk of industry. Rather, center cities act as service centers that underpin industrial growth in much larger hinterlands. This tendency, which is found to some extent in all market economies, is if anything stronger in East Asia than elsewhere. Indeed, it has been argued that Asian urbanization, particularly in paddy rice growing areas, tends to take on a distinctive form. These regions—originally densely populated agricul-

---

[29]Huang Weiding, *Zhongguo yinxing jingji* (China's hidden economy) (Beijing: Zhongguo Shangye, 1992), 69 and *passim*.
[30]Zhou Yixing, "The Metropolitan Interlocking Region," 98–108.

tural zones—are transformed under the impact of nearby cities into dense mixtures of agricultural and non-agricultural activities, a kind of urbanized countryside. The phenomenon is common enough that Japanese has a word for that type of landscape (*konjuka*), and it is also highly characteristic of Taiwan, where nearly the entire western plain might be considered an urbanized countryside. Similar stretches are discernible in central Java, Thailand, and the Philippines.[31]

In this type of urbanized countryside, good transportation and communications combine with an initially dense population to spread urban-type activities into the suburban and exurban fringe. These new urban activities do not completely drive out the preexisting agricultural activities, so the two types coexist in a crazy-quilt pattern of activities. Under these conditions, activities apparently do not need to be located within urban boundaries in order to experience the agglomeration economies characteristic of cities. Good transport and cheap agricultural labor are enough, but only if those conditions prevail in close proximity to an existing urban center that can provide essential coordination and service facilities.

Once we take the urbanized countryside as the norm against which Chinese urbanization can be compared, two general patterns immediately become evident. First, Chinese urban development until 1978 was almost the polar opposite of this Asian norm. The sharp "edge" between city and countryside was antithetical to the urbanized countryside. Moreover, despite the publicity given to rural industry in earlier periods, overall the level of nonagricultural activities among rural dwellers was much lower than would be expected for a country at China's level of development.[32] Other Asian experiences would lead us to believe that many profitable opportunities to develop industry were being forgone in the immediate vicinity of large cities. Second, when we examine the rapid growth in these peri-urban areas during the past decade, we find the emergence at breathtaking speed of belts of urbanized countryside

[31]Hsung-Hsiung Tsai, "Population Decentralization Policies: The Experience of Taiwan," in Fuchs et al., eds., *Urbanization and Urban Policies*, 214–29; T. G. McGee, "The Emergence of *Desakota* Regions in Asia: Expanding a Hypothesis," and Norton Ginsburg, "Extended Metropolitan Regions in Asia: A New Spatial Paradigm," both in N. Ginsburg, B. Koppel, and T. G. McGee, eds., *The Extended Metropolis: Settlement Transition in Asia* (Honolulu: University of Hawaii Press, 1991).
[32]Grant Blank and William L. Parish, "Rural Industry and Nonfarm Employment: Comparative Perspectives," in Kwok et al., eds., *Chinese Urban Reform*, 109–39.

concentrated in areas where they can take advantage of neighboring urban centers.

How urban planners have gradually adapted to these changes remains to be examined. The spatial evolution of Shanghai provides a revealing example. Through most of the 1980s, planners had a fairly definite sense of how Shanghai would evolve. Shanghai obviously needed more space, and the accepted plan was for Shanghai to expand along a north–south axis. Urban development would, as was traditional under the socialist model, be led by industrial development. Shanghai would grow to the north to encompass the Baoshan steel mill, and to the south to encompass the Jinshan Petrochemical facility. Ultimately, Shanghai's urban form would resemble a capital "I," with a horizontal bar to the north along the Yangtze, and to the south, along Hangzhou Bay, connected by a north–south axis through the old center city. The areas to the west and to the east (Pudong) would retain their primarily rural nature, and large areas would specialize in growing vegetables. At the heart of this conception, then, was the idea that the sharp edge between urban and rural land uses could be retained to the west and east of the city.[33]

By the late 1980s, though, Shanghai planners began to discover that the actual development of the city was not conforming to the master plan. For a variety of reasons, urban and industrial activities were sprawling into the areas west and east of the city. Despite the attempt of planners to contain the city in a definite shape, it was developing in a direction not too dissimilar from the diffuse, concentric city form common in market economies. New approaches to guiding urban development were tried as planners sought to catch up with a reality that threatened to leave them behind.[34] The development of the area east of Shanghai—Pudong—as a Special Economic Zone follows the logic of accepting a more rapid and more diffuse growth of the Shanghai urban

[33]See Cheng Lu, *Shanghai jingji dili* (An economic geography of Shanghai) (Beijing: Renmin, People's Publishing House 1988); Yang Wanzhong, *Shanghai gongye jiegou yu buju yanjiu* (A Study of Shanghai's Industrial Structure and Layout) (Shanghai: Huadong Shifan Daxue, 1991), 60–70. Chinese planners did not call it an "I," of course, but rather an "inverted *ding*." Even at an early date, some planners were arguing for the expansion of the city east of the Huangpu—i.e., into Pudong—but they were arguing for modest movement of government offices across the Huangpu to relieve pressure on the center city and allow redevelopment. Chen Minzhi, *Shanghai jingji fazhan zhanlue yanjiu* (Studies of Shanghai's Economic Development Strategy) (Shanghai: Shanghai Renmin [Shanghai People's Press], 1985), 30–31.
[34]World Bank, *China*, 100 (Box 4.2).

area. The Pudong Special Economic Zone is not only important as a large zone that provides concessionary terms to foreign investors, and thus opens Shanghai more to the outside world; it is also important as a recognition of the fact that the city will sprawl out, becoming much bigger, somewhat more unruly, extending its economic influence into the countryside in all directions.

Opportunities for greater urban autonomy. The changes in the pattern of Chinese urbanization can stand as an apt metaphor for the broader changes in Chinese society that have occurred in the wake of economic reform. Changes were set in motion that were not in themselves expected to have radical consequences, but which set in motion a process of change that turned out to be of fundamental importance. In this case, the broader process of economic reform has greatly influenced the position of cities. Cities have steadily lost at least a part of their peculiar position in the economic system. The division of labor between city and countryside has become less stark, and the need to control cities has become correspondingly less compelling. Some of these changes are the direct result of reform policies consciously adopted, but others are the unanticipated result of larger processes—including that of rural industrialization—touched off without full awareness of the consequences.

First, a key feature of economic reform has been the shrinkage of the traditional vertically organized economic system. Plans have been virtually fixed in size since 1984, leading the economy to grow out of the plan. As a result, what is still called "the plan" increasingly has come to resemble a set of contractual obligations that state-owned enterprises undertake with regard to the national and local governments. Under these circumstances, the government has far less need to exert direct administrative control over productive enterprises, or over the municipal government bodies that still oversee them. This, then, has been an anticipated component of economic reform.

Shrinkage of the relative size of the state planned economy has, however, had even more powerful indirect effects. Most significant has been the elimination of the prohibition against entry into the profitable manufacturing sector, previously reserved for state-owned firms. This prohibition lay behind the initial sharp division of labor between city and countryside, and its elimination, in 1979, created the conditions for the explosive growth of rural industry. Rapid entry into manufacturing, particularly light consumer goods production, increased demand for raw materials while increasing the supply of finished manufactured goods. Thus, supply of previously overpriced consumer goods increased, while demand for previously underpriced raw materials also increased. These new market forces—combined with administrative price adjustments by the national government—significantly realigned the pricing system. The end result was the steady erosion of the former monopoly profits of the state industrial sector. Manufacturing profitability declined annually every year between 1980 and 1990.[35]

The control of the price system that had previously concentrated revenues in cities like Shanghai eroded. Industry in Shanghai, for example, remained substantially more profitable than the national average. But as profit rates declined everywhere, it became increasingly difficult for Shanghai to turn over 80 percent of its surpluses to the national government. As a result, the net transfer of surplus from cities to the national budget also declined steadily. Correspondingly, the need for the government to guard its cash cows has become less urgent. In Shanghai, Tianjin, and Guangzhou, the share of GDP collected as fiscal revenue shrank by half between 1978 and 1990 (Table 3.1). Particularly striking is the sharp contraction between 1985 and 1988. The manufacturing enterprises located in cities, facing competition from rural enterprises and from start-up state firms in other cities, simply were not as profitable as they had been. As a result, the state's ability to raise huge amounts of revenue from those firms decreased steadily.

At the same time, economic reform coincided with a greater willingness on the part of the central government to give local governments and enterprises control over resources, including financial resources. While the total surplus available to be "harvested" in manufacturing declined, the share of that surplus that could be retained at the local level increased. It is not hard to see why the national government allowed cities to keep a larger share of their resources. As cities were increasingly exposed to the need to become internationally competitive, the dangers of the previous exploitative policies became increasingly clear. Shanghai and Tianjin would never return to vigorous growth if they were not permitted to make substantial investment in their urban infrastructure and other facilities. The result of these trends can be seen in Table 3.1. The three cities now retain a larger share of their fiscal

[35]Barry Naughton, "Implications of the State Monopoly over Industry and Its Relaxation," *Modern China* 18, no. 1 (January 1992).

revenues. Guangzhou now retains 40–45 percent; Tianjin 45–50 percent; and Shanghai about 35 percent of total fiscal revenues. When set against the long-term decline in total fiscal revenues as a share of GDP, the increased retention ratios do not allow the cities a significant increase in total resources (as a share of GDP). Nevertheless, with slightly increased retention and substantially increased autonomy, cities are better able to maneuver and have many more opportunities, to cope with the problems of increased growth. As for the national government, it has less need to exert such tight control over municipal finances. Instead of extracting a majority of urban fiscal revenues, the national government now takes about half, and a significant portion of this comes from the large enterprises that are under direct central government control to begin with. Thus, reduced extraction plus increased recognition of urban needs has added up to greater potential urban autonomy.

The third and final change in the position of cities has come with the rapid growth of income in peri-urban areas. This has combined with increased willingness to tolerate an informal sector in the urban economy. Thus, the local income differentials that fuel rural-urban migration have probably diminished.[36] Here, suburban industrialization has reduced pressure on urban cores by providing employment opportunities to rural residents near their place of residence. Moreover, rapid increases in food supplies during the first half of the 1980s greatly reduced fears about uncontrolled urbanization. As a result, the need to restrict such migration has become less important.

Thus, all three economic motivations for urban control became much weaker during the 1980s. As the economic imperatives of control have become weaker, continued political controls have come to seem more arbitrary, and are more frequently contested by urban residents. In that sense, changes in the economic system might be seen as creating the conditions for a substantial expansion in the autonomy of cities and urban groups.

CONCLUSION

The Chinese failure to anticipate the strength of rural industrial growth may be seen—paradoxically—to spring from much the same roots as

---

[36]The disequilibria between the poorest rural areas and cities is undoubtedly as large as ever. Yet in most countries, migration to cities draws primarily from the cities' extended hinterland, and not from distant regions. Thus, local disequilibria are probably more important in determining the magnitude of migration.

their previous deprecation of the role of existing cities. The extraordinary productivity of large metropolitan regions, creating agglomeration economies and spillover effects, provides an extremely powerful momentum for economic growth. During the 1980s, the Chinese relaxed their control of the economic system enough to bring some of these forces into play. As cities spilled over the economic bounds set on them, much of their economic growth was actually recorded outside their immediate boundaries. But as growth spread outward, it eroded the peculiar position of cities in the old economic system, and this in turn helps to create conditions for increased autonomy in the cities themselves.

Cities, as economic entities, have sprawled out of their previous bounds, squirming out of the control previously exerted over them by the national government. City dwellers have not yet been so successful in defeating the controls placed on them. Nevertheless, their sphere of autonomy has increased. In the economic realm, the rules are far more flexible than they used to be. As a result, city dwellers have more occupational flexibility, and more access to the services provided by others (particularly by temporary migrants to the city—the floating population). City life has become more heterogeneous, with more diversity, but also more crowded and, in some respects, more stressful. Even more important, the economic imperatives that led national authorities to constrict urban development severely have faded in importance. As a result, there are far fewer economic reasons to obstruct continued liberalization of urban life and expansion of an autonomous public sphere. If political conditions develop in such a way as to support such a liberalization, there is no reason to believe that economic conditions will pose significant obstacles. Indeed, the economic changes that have occurred to date support rather than impede a continuing retreat of the sphere of direct state influence. In this sense, the position of cities in the economic system has changed dramatically, and now presents the opportunity for a further expansion in the autonomy of cities and urban dwellers.

4

State sprawl:
the regulatory state and social life
in a small Chinese city

VIVIENNE SHUE

URBAN STATE AND SOCIETY IN FLUX

Urban life in China today—just like rural life, and intellectual life, and political life, and spiritual life—presents a jolting cacophony of possibilities and prospects. Intriguing, unsettling, often contradictory new social truths are found everywhere, for almost everyone to contend with, in the vibrant cities of China in the 1990s. This jostle of options now confronting urban dwellers, some liberating and others intimidating, was neither known nor knowable just a few years ago, when the Chinese people were still held in the thrall of Maoist political and social certitudes. It is not surprising, then, that the suddenly quickened and agitated pace of social choice and change in Chinese cities has proved rapid enough for many urban Chinese to lose their breath, yet slow enough for others to lose heart.

In such newly scrambled circumstances, the shifting realities of urban state-society relations have turned out to be decidedly mixed—a perplexing blend of consciously self-limiting yet reinvigorated state action met by equal measures of avid opportunism and sullen reticence in society. Moreover, the much discussed, and once much heralded, "retreat of the state" under the post-Mao reforms has so far proceeded unevenly, at best, in China's urban environments. State roles, state policies, state actors, the very exertion of state authority itself in city life—all have clearly been subjected to important alteration over the last several years of stop-and-start reform. Along some dimensions of the Chinese urban experience this alteration has yielded, on balance, a diminished profile of state power in daily life and a somewhat expanded scope for non–state-initiated and non–state-directed endeavors. Along other dimensions, however, the state's profile in social life appears to remain as imposingly high as ever, maybe higher.

Scholarly summaries of "emerging" social trends in China, as a result of all this flux and variation, can and often do career into caricature. To avoid contributing to the myths of linear inevitability that still cloud the common understanding of choice and change under reform-socialist-authoritarianism as we address the problem of emerging urban trends, then, we need to examine some different types of urban social settings, and examine them along as many different dimensions of the human experience as possible.

This chapter considers some aspects of state power and social life in Xinji City, on the North China Plain. Unlike the other cases reported in this volume, Xinji is a small city.[1] But thanks in part to its location at the intersection of two of the key rail lines criss-crossing Hebei Province, Xinji has been growing—urbanizing—rapidly in recent years. It is still a basically undistinguished place; an ochre and gray, gritty little town, boasting just one public monument, a handful of ill-lit shops, restaurants, bars, and hotels along its few main streets, and an alarming number of both big and small chemical factories spewing noxious smoke into the air.[2] But I, working with some valued colleagues, have been able to study certain aspects of local state-society relations in Xinji since

[1]Xinji City, about 60 km. east of Shijiazhuang in Hebei Province, was formerly known as Shulu County. The county, with a total population of close to 600,000 people, mostly farmers, was officially designated a city (*shi*) in 1986. It covers an area of over 950 sq. km., of which some 122 sq. km. are designated as "urban" space. (This includes the built-up and more heavily settled areas of the small towns and townships [*zhen* and *xiang*] that comprise the administrative subunits under the city's jurisdiction.) The main urbanized district, however, is concentrated in Xinji Town itself, the old county capital (*xian cheng*). This central city area covers less than 25 sq. km. and has a total population of about 150,000. As of 1990, 82,000 of these central city residents lived in the old county capital proper. (About 35 percent of these people continued to hold rural household registrations [*nongye renkou*], and around 65 percent were classified as urban [*fei nongye renkou*].) The remaining 68,000 or so lived in nearby "suburbs"—i.e., in four former communes adjacent to the old county town, which had been redesignated as part of the new city central district (*chengshi banshichu*). Plans call for this downtown city center not to exceed a population of 200,000 before the year 2000. After that, however, Xinji is slated in the Hebei provincial plan to grow gradually to become a "middle-size city" with a downtown population of 400,000–500,000.

[2]The asphalting of Xinji's downtown streets and main arteries began only in 1983. As of 1990, all roads from the city center to the town and township headquarters in the municipality were paved. Most roads between town and township headquarters and their smaller constituent villages (*cun*) remained unpaved, however, and passable only with difficulty after rain.

1979, and our joint studies suggest that the place may be fairly representative of one kind of urban life experience in China today.[3]

Xinji is an example of that significant minority of small urban places where vigorous local leaders and officials have, both before and after the reforms, managed effectively to foster local economic growth.[4] This growth and accompanying accomplishments in local development have afforded these local leaders, in turn, substantial political legitimacy and a measure of local public trust. Aided by that public trust, they have not hesitated to use the panoply of state powers at their command to elaborate and strengthen the local urban state regulatory apparatus; and in this process of local state-building they have succeeded in attracting to their administrations some of the most dynamic people in their areas. While in some important respects, as explained here, the reform era has brought real and valued new freedoms from state interference to the people of the city, in other equally significant aspects of social life the

[3] I first visited Xinji in the summer of 1979, with Stephen Andors, Phyllis Andors, Mitch Meisner, and Marc Blecher, to conduct extensive but preliminary fieldwork interviews on local government and economy. In 1986 I returned, with Marc Blecher, for a longer stay and more comprehensive interviews. Blecher and I were assisted on that visit by Wang Shaoguang. In the summer of 1990, I returned to Xinji with Marc Blecher again, and with Daniel Kelliher. We three were assisted by Li Ning and by Yue Ming in conducting some two weeks of intensive follow-up interviews on changing local government and economy in the city. With those follow-up interviews completed I stayed on, living for two months in Xinji during the summer and fall of 1990, continuing with the research on local state organization and also investigating other aspects of local social life. Most of the observations in this chapter are based on the 1990 research.

[4] Both Blecher and I, working together but writing separately, have already published preliminary articles that attempt to summarize some of the special characteristics of development in Xinji while contrasting the nature of both the local state structure and the local political leadership and leadership style in Xinji with those in another urbanizing locality, Guanghan County outside Chengdu. See Marc Blecher, "Developmental State, Entrepreneurial State: The Political Economy of Socialist Reform in Xinji Municipality and Guanghan County," in Gordon White, ed., *The Road to Crisis: The Chinese State in the Era of Economic Reform* (London: Macmillan, 1991), 265–91; and Vivienne Shue, "Emerging State-Society Relations in Rural China," in Jorgen Delman, C. S. Ostergaard, and F. Christiansen, eds., *Remaking Peasant China: Problems of Rural Development and Institutions at the Start of the 1990s* (Aarhus, Denmark: Aarhus University Press, 1990), 60–80. Blecher's interpretation, as the title of his article suggests, characterizes the local state in Xinji as "developmental" and that in Guanghan County as "entrepreneurial." My own article, making many similar observations about the differences between the two, characterizes the Xinji local state leadership style as "coordinative," and that of Guanghan County as "competitive." Writing together, Blecher and I will soon publish *Tethered Deer: Government and Economy in a North China County* (Stanford, Calif.: Stanford University Press, in press), which will contain much more detailed data and observations on Xinji's pattern of development during both the Maoist and the post-Maoist periods.

Xinji pattern of local-development-with-urban-sprawl has engendered a kind of local state sprawl as well.

PERSONAL FREEDOMS

In Xinji, as in other towns, the most unambiguous "retreat of the state" seems to have taken place in the realm of the individual's and, to a certain extent, the family's personal life.[5] Here the state's "zone of in-difference," as Tang Tsou once called it, has unmistakably been enlarged. The new freedoms gained may mostly be petty, but they do have a cumulative impact on quality of life. Individual expressions of preference and taste in dress and furnishings are the most important examples in Xinji. With a little more money in hand these days, and with the partial relaxation of the official shame associated with consumption and especially with spending money on oneself, a wider range of popular and individual tastes in fashions and personal accoutrements has become acceptable. Young men in Xinji let their hair grow longer than before, wear leather shoes and leather jackets, and ride around on noisy little motorbikes as fast as they can. Older men and officials generally dress in white shirts and dark pants or cadre suits, and they almost never wear hats. Farmers coming into town wear their traditional loose-fitting padded or broadcloth suits and sometimes still a white towel wrapped around their shaved heads. Young women favor permanent waves or longer hairstyles with ribbons and plastic barrettes. They like to wear shorter skirts and iridescent pink or white plastic sandals in the summer, while older women still prefer long pants with dark-colored cloth shoes and a loose overblouse. Women's dress remains conservative by big-city standards. Lipstick and other makeup are almost never worn. Social pressures barring even the slightest suggestion of promiscuity remain in force. But individuality does have greater scope for expression now through personal adornment and one's deliberate attention or inattention to fashion.

Similarly, the decoration of the homes of Xinji residents shows more scope claimed than before for personal taste and individual interests. Calligraphy scrolls and paintings of various styles and subjects, from the

[5]That is, with the significant exception of the state's high-profile monitoring in the sphere of family planning, of course. The one-child policy for urban residents is pursued and enforced in Xinji as it is in China's larger cities.

garish to the sublime, hang on the walls of private homes now. Scenic calendars, pinup girl photos, folk art papercuts, kitchen god altars, and red paper *duilian* couplets decorate the houses of different families as well. Family members may listen to cassette tapes of rock music or to traditional Chinese opera music, according to taste. In the evenings, male relatives and friends get together to drink beer or *baijiu*, and women gossip and knit as they keep an eye on the children and wave away the moths attracted by the lamps. Summer evenings in Xinji are relaxed. Couples may stroll the streets, but people do not now need to hurry out to mass political meetings or to rallies. Nor do they go out in large organized labor teams to work in the floodlit fields at night, as was common in the 1970s. They watch TV. They watch the neighbors. Private life, that is, family life and the life of the courtyard, holds dominion after work.

Personal freedom to choose where work itself is concerned has also been enlarged slightly in Xinji. Some people seek and find opportunities to work outside the city. Young people, especially, have tried going off to Beijing and other large urban centers, sometimes for years at a time, in search of adventure and fortune. The numbers are not very high. In 1990 just 1,450 people from the whole city were registered as working outside, mostly in construction, transport, and trade.[6] As with most other migrants around the world, many who leave also eventually come back to Xinji. An unmarried waitress at a collectively owned and operated hotel/restaurant in downtown Xinji talked about how, after three years of lonely, hard work at various jobs in Beijing, she finally came to miss her mother and the rest of her family and friends so badly that she decided to move back home to Xinji. The other young women of the restaurant staff manifestly liked and looked up to this young woman, and she was plainly happy in her new waitressing position, even though there was no running water in her dormitory and the traffic noise on the street below interfered with her sleep every night, and even though the enterprise manager (her boss) spent many of his days nervously hid-

---

[6]People from outside also filtered into Xinji, of course, looking for work. Some came with a little capital and set themselves up as petty traders. Others came in circumstances of the most abject poverty and accepted work as agricultural laborers in return for food and shelter. City Labor Bureau officials guessed that more people left Xinji to work outside than came into the city. But they claimed not to be absolutely sure since records on in-migrants were not meticulously kept. Bureau cadres reported being aware of people working in Xinji on a permanent or semi-permanent basis who had come from Shandong, Henan, and as far away as Zhejiang and Sichuan.

ing from his creditors. More personal choice, of course, brings with it more personal risk. And those living in Xinji, by the early 1990s, had taken but a few short steps down that perilous path.

COMMUNITY

Somewhat more space has also been accorded to non–state-defined community life in Xinji. People are encouraged, or at least permitted, to pursue personal hobbies, talents, and interests in concert with others, in a more loosely or more tightly organized way, without necessarily encountering much state regulation or interference. At least this is the case in some fields of endeavor. For example, folk arts and folk culture have experienced a strong revival in Xinji recently. People who are interested get together in groups to paint, to make papercuts, to collect and edit folk legends, stories, ballads, and songs. They organize performances and exhibitions. There are community drum troupes, dance troupes, stilt-walkers, acrobats, kite-makers, embroidery circles, and folk painting associations. The state is by no means totally absent from this realm of activity, but its role is now limited primarily to encouraging and facilitating rather than providing models and dictating restrictions.[7] Pride is now officially expressed in local folk culture and local artistic achievement, even when these are not especially socialist or revolutionary in

[7]There are city government offices charged with supporting folk art activities and others tasked with supporting local fine arts and literary activities. Folk arts come under the Wenhuaju, the Cultural Bureau *xitong* office at the city level of administration. And Xinji's Cultural Bureau has a subdivision called the Xinji Contemporary Folk Painting Academy, for example, which specifically coordinates and promotes folk painting classes, exhibitions, and other activities. Literature and the fine arts, on the other hand, are supported by another local state office, the Wenxue yishujie lianhehui, an artists' and writers' association under the direction of the Xinji City Commission (*shi wei*). (Note that this is a horizontal [*kuai kuai*] state office unlike the Cultural Bureau, which is part of a nationwide vertical system [*tiao tiao*].) As the chairman of the Artists and Writers Association, Li Shufeng explained, a coordinated effort was made between 1986 and 1988 to establish a "creative arts station" in every township and a "creative arts group" in every village in Xinji. Meanwhile, spontaneous groups of interested people formed in many factories and enterprises around the municipality. The result is a "network of official (*guanban*) and popular (*minban*) organizations that all work together as a single body" under the leadership of the Xinji City Commission. The Cultural Bureau tends to stress "popularization" or mass education in its activities, while the Artists and Writers Association stresses raising the quality and artistic level of practicing local creative artists. (The Cultural Bureau has its own network of *wenhuazhan* [cultural stations] in every township also, which operates alongside the Artists and Writers Association network.) Folk arts and fine arts are an unusually important part of local cultural life in Xinji City. Xinji folk paintings, in particular, have achieved a certain reputation in other parts of China and have even been exhibited abroad.

content. And people are permitted to gather regularly—like the one hundred (out of three hundred or so) amateur (fine arts) painters in Xinji who attend monthly meetings of their association—to talk about their art without being subject to heavy political or other guidance of their activities by the party-state.

Beyond the arts, many other types of popular associations contribute to the life of the community. Xinji has a table-tennis club, a martial arts club, an abacus society, a veterinary studies society, a climate and meteorological studies group, a home economics club, and a consumers' association, just to name a few. Their memberships range in size from just ten to over seven hundred. Most of these associations perform voluntary service or consulting roles within the community. They are not specifically organized or run under the supervision of any local state office. But state officials are frequently among the leading members of such associations. And as community organizations they are also explicitly encouraged to maintain regular contact with the Xinji Political Consultative Committee (Zhengxie), which, made up of 169 members from "various walks of life," was chaired in 1990 by a widely respected former mayor of the city. Through its consultations with these popular associations, Zhengxie, which clearly functions as a kind of semi-formal corporatist political structure, aims to learn about community needs and concerns and then to pass these on to municipal officials.[8]

Xinji residents generally are proud of their local community, at least when they talk about it to interested visitors. Even when busy with work and with the relentless to-and-fro of their daily lives, many of them find extra time and sufficient interest to participate in voluntary community associations like these. This constitutes a dimension of city life that is relatively free of direct state penetration and control, although it often works as an adjunct to state policy and to local state legitimacy. It would be an exaggeration to say that the state has adopted an attitude of indifference toward *this* sphere of social life. But it has, at least, backed off in the degree of politicization demanded here; thus a little more space for the evolution of a genuine, popularly based sense of the city as a community may have been created.

---

[8]For more on corporatist-type state-society structures and relations in Xinji City, see my "State Power and Social Organization in China," in Joel S. Migdal, Atul Kohli, and Vivienne Shue, eds., *State Power and Social Forces: Domination and Transformation in the Third World* (Cambridge: Cambridge University Press, 1994).

THE STATE AND REGULATION

The biggest change in the role of the local state to come with the reforms, in Xinji as elsewhere in China, is that more and more economic activity has been permitted to take place *outside* the state plan. This means that the state itself has been directly responsible for a falling proportion of total local investment and receipts. That is not to say that the state plan and the enterprises that operate within it do not still bulk very large in the Xinji local economy. They do.[9] But direct state planning does not account for the recent marked pattern of growth in the local state.

As shown in more detail below, the Xinji local state apparatus has indeed been becoming larger, more complex, and more fully filled out at the bottom—at the precinct level, so to speak. Meanwhile, the actual work of this local state apparatus has been expanding to include numerous new tasks and responsibilities. Finding in Xinji such a conspicuous pattern of local urban state growth and elaboration of local urban state functions in the avowedly "deplannifying" and "marketizing" Deng era may, at first, be thought somewhat ironic. But a review of the evidence collected also plainly reveals that most of the new local state offices, tasks, and responsibilities in this small city are not directive; they are, instead, primarily regulatory in nature.

With a greater proportion of local economic activity permitted to occur outside the scope of direct state planning, the local state has, not surprisingly, been called upon to take a much more active role in monitoring and regulating both the obviously beneficial and also the potentially disruptive activity of this burgeoning nonstate sector. There are several key new or expanding areas of state regulation in Xinji. Most of them involve public goods or other types of market failures, that is, matters in which reliance on markets alone will not necessarily produce the best, or most socially acceptable, distributions or other outcomes. Land use management is one good example.

[9]Nor should this statement about the continuing power of state planning be taken to apply only to industry and commerce. When softer "guidance targets" are not met in agriculture, as they were not met for cotton in 1988, for example, Xinji authorities may use direct planning: They issued sown-area targets for cotton in 1989 that farmers were obliged to meet. For fuller discussion of agricultural target setting, see Marc Blecher and Shaoguang Wang, "The Political Economy of Cropping in Maoist and Dengist China: Hebei Province and Shulu County, 1949–90," *The China Quarterly*, no. 137 (March 1994): 63–98.

Land use. The Xinji Land Management Bureau (Tudiguanliju) was formed in the spring of 1987 when the national land law was passed. The bureau's original staff of ten had already grown to twenty-two by 1990. Like other such offices around the country, the Xinji office is charged with ensuring that land in the city is managed in a unified way (*tongyi guanli tudi*) and that cultivated land is protected (*baohu gengdi*). The very need for such a law and such a bureau, clearly, was provoked by the economic upsurge in rural and in small urban areas that followed the early reforms. The staff of the Xinji Land Management Bureau project an image of vigilance and precision. They carry out surveys and investigations; they distribute questionnaires; and they tear down illegally constructed buildings and fine offenders when unlawful land seizures take place. They closely oversee the construction of new houses by farmers.[10] In Xinji, local regulations stipulate that no household may occupy more than 0.25 *mu* of land. And, generally speaking, no new private housebuilding whatsoever is permitted on land under cultivation.

The Land Management Bureau must also approve all applications for building new factories, workshops, or other enterprises in the city.[11] Those who want a building permit must first go to the appropriate governing office for initial authorization.[12] If that office is in favor of the plan it will, on behalf of the prospective builders, then approach the City Economic Planning Commission (Jihua jingji weiyuanhui) for approval. The commission will not act favorably without concurrent ap-

[10]The process is multilayered and bureaucratic. A farm family wanting to build a new home must first petition the village government committee (*cunmin weiyuanhui*). If the committee approves, the application is then turned over for public discussion and comment by all residents of the village. On the basis of the various opinions expressed, a report is made to the township or town government, and if the request is approved at that level, the application is passed on to the City Land Management Bureau for a final decision. Anyone over the age of eighteen who wishes to set up an independent dwelling may apply. But, if the household (*hu*) this person already belongs to occupies what is regarded as a large plot of land, the application to build on new land may not be approved.

[11]Enterprise building on cultivated land is also forbidden unless a "compensation fee" is paid to the village. This fee is calculated on the basis of the annual output value of the land that is taken over. And the purchase price can range anywhere from ten to twenty times that annual output value figure. The purchasing enterprise pays the full amount of the value of the land to the Land Management Bureau, which transfers it to the village government after taking a 3 percent service fee for itself. In 1990 "compensation fees" were beginning to be charged for farm house-building, and even when the land involved was not originally under cultivation, in townships where land was especially scarce. This was reported to be a rare, but increasing phenomenon in Xinji. In one district near the center of the city, for example, a family with rural household registration might have to pay as much as 1,000 yuan for the 0.20 *mu* it could be allotted to build a new dwelling.

[12]A plan to build a new *xiang* or *zhen* enterprise, for example, first goes to the Township Industries Bureau.

proval from the bureau. If controversy is likely to arise in a specific case, a hearing will be scheduled at which representatives from the Land Management Bureau, the Industry and Commerce Management Bureau, the Economic Commission, the Science Commission, the Agriculture Bank, the Construction Bank, the Commercial Bank, and sometimes the Urban Construction and Environmental Protection Bureau might all be invited to attend and present their views. No building will go forward without a permit from the Land Management Bureau.

The Land Management Bureau also monitors rental transfers of land.[13] Private land transfers (for money) in Xinji are illegal. But when a collective wants to rent out some of its land, it must first have the contract vetted and approved at the city Land Management Bureau. Such transactions are rare in Xinji, though they are beginning to take place in the center city where most residents have full-time non-agricultural occupations and cannot themselves devote enough time to the cultivation of their collective land allotments.

City planning. A second area in which a vigorous regulatory role is undertaken by the local state in Xinji is urban planning and environmental protection. Xinji City has an elaborate urban planning apparatus with a trained staff and an impressive set of plans stretching beyond the year 2000. All building and other developments in the city are expected to conform to the details of the plans generated by the Urban Construction and Environmental Protection Bureau and approved by the City Commission. These plans cover electricity generation, road building, road widening, city districting, lighting, parks and green spaces, vehicular traffic and parking, air and water pollution standards, water treatment facilities, citizens' services, and residential building standards, among others. Bureau officials are modest about their accomplishments; but accomplishments are evident even to the casual eye as one moves about the city surveying the patterns of commercial, public service, and residential building that have taken shape in Xinji since the mid-1980s.

Still, slowed local economic growth rates between 1986 and 1990 did lead to cutting back on some planned projects. And the bureau had to be content with focusing on a pared-down list of priorities. It enforces what it regards as strict pollution controls, fining offenders, and putting

---

[13]All urban land, of course, remains the property of the state, and rural land belongs to village "collectives." Land use rights in Xinji cannot be bought or sold. Use rights can be obtained only in a rental agreement.

pressure on the worst polluters to move their plants and factories further
away from concentrated settlements. Two major plants, a cement factory
and an asphalt factory, have been forced to move. And, beginning in
1983, the bureau was given a budget of some 1.6 million yuan for its
various air pollution control projects. Before 1983 the density of partic-
ulate matter in Xinji's air was measured at 1,000 mg per cubic meter.
By 1990 the readings had been brought down to 700 mg per cubic meter.
Mercury, chrome, lead, and other water pollutants remain a serious challenge in Xinji, however. The bureau routinely deploys its arsenal of
weapons against suspected and convicted offenders—surprise investigations, effluent testing, follow-up visits, fines, and so on. When one bureau official was told that environmental protection standards violators
in the United States had proved both stubborn and cunning and seemed
ultimately hard for the American authorities to control, he claimed that
he had at his command all the power and resources required to meet
the situation. "My job," he said flatly, "is to carry out the law and the
policy of the nation. So, you see, I have a lot of authority behind me.
And anyway, the fine goes up 5 percent a year if you don't comply."
Even so, restraining environmental pollution remains a formidable challenge in Xinji, as in other small cities undergoing rapid growth and
industrialization. The regulatory battle has been joined in Xinji, but it
is far from won. And with prevailing inflation rates well above 5 percent
per year, local fines will have to be made heavier if they are truly to
serve as deterrents to dumping.

Private trade. A final example of the vigorous regulatory roles of the
local state that have grown up in Xinji under the reforms are controls
now aimed at private trade and at private traders by the city government. Encouragement of a larger and more vibrant "free" or "private"
trade sector has, as we know, been a key component of the post-Mao
economic reform program all over China. In Xinji, as in most of the rest
of the country, this sector of the local economy has seen enormous
growth in recent years. The total volume of trade on private or free
markets in Xinji reportedly increased from 3.56 million yuan in 1979
to 63.76 million yuan in 1989. And a short walk down nearly any street
in the city will generally yield the sight of at least a few peddlers, stall-
keepers, or other petty traders going about their work. In response to
this trend of reform, the city government has clearly found it necessary
to become more deeply involved in both the regulation and the pro-

motion of local private trade in recent years. And the City Industry and Commerce Management Bureau, with chief responsibility in this realm, has consequently risen to become one of the most visible local government units, interacting with ordinary citizens in one way or another virtually every hour of every day. Thus, private trade in Xinji has not been developed at the expense of local state power or authority—the two have been rising together.

The local state in Xinji City has, in some respects, made sizable efforts to assist in the expansion of the free trade sector of the economy. Most notably, perhaps, the city government organized and helped capitalize the building of a major marketplace for private trade in the central city.[14] The timely establishment of this massive marketplace, which has attracted traders from all over the country, certainly made a contribution to Xinji's mid-1980s resurgence as a significant trading center on the North China Plain. But several different visits to this market in 1990 revealed many empty stalls and storefronts, a dreary sameness about the wares for sale, and a pace of business that one would have to characterize as sleepy. Discussions with local officials about the life of the marketplace in 1990, dwelling on how to regulate legal commerce and eliminate illegal trade of all kinds, price gouging, shoddy products, tax evasion by merchants, and so on, certainly led to the conclusion that business in the market was not so much "slowing down" from its breakneck pace of growth during the mid-1980s as it was being nearly regulated to death by zealous local commerce cadres.

The crucial turning point came in 1987, when some small firms in the burgeoning private trade sector began to look increasingly threatening as competitors to enterprises in the state and especially in the collective sector of the local economy. At that time, private traders (*geti hu*) were being permitted to buy unlimited inventory directly from factories and other primary producers. In this way, they were starting to encroach on wholesale trade in certain important commodities and products (such as salt, sugar, coal, wine, oil, and chemical fertilizer) that were the specialty of the collective Supply and Marketing Co-op (Gongxiaoshe) trade network in the city. Local restrictions on the scale of *geti hu* operations were introduced following this 1987 scare. "We want the *geti hu* sector to develop," insisted Supply and Marketing Co-op Vice Director Zhao

---

[14]This project has already been described in greater detail in Shue, "Emerging State-Society Relations in Rural China."

in 1990, "but they can't be allowed to become wholesalers." The intention, obviously, was that private trade remain petty trade in Xinji. Anything else, it was apparently believed, might threaten too seriously both
local state-run and collective enterprises and the revenues those enterprises generate for the local state.

The *geti hu* of Xinji were still a pretty heavily regulated lot in 1990.
The Industry and Commerce Management Bureau of the city government has primary responsibility for private sector trade, and this bureau
has clearly applied a rather strenuous hand in guiding local market
growth. The bureau acts as chief market organizer and market ration-
alizer. Both for the central marketplace and for all the other marketplaces in the city, for example, the bureau grants licenses to individual
traders for specific locations, because it wants to help create or reinforce
a clear pattern of specialized markets. In 1990 various such specialized
markets were in operation: three for fur and leather products, six for
vegetables, and others for traditional products, industrial products, and
for textiles and other miscellaneous goods.[15] Working in conjunction
with the urban development plan formulated by the Urban Construction
and Environmental Protection Bureau, the Industry and Commerce
Management Bureau was planning to bring the textile and miscellaneous
goods market, which had been located at the northern end of the city,
and the farmers' market, which had been at the southern end, into closer
proximity, to reduce traffic congestion caused by shoppers moving between them, to make shopping more convenient, and to increase the flow
of customers at both markets. The bureau also was making sure that
fresh vegetable markets were distributed throughout the city, according to a design intended to maximize shopping convenience and reduce
traffic.[16]

---

[15]For example, Nanzhiqiu Zhen has a regular pet bird market, with more than two thousand animals on sale each market day. And on every third day a special market in horse
cart equipment is held at the main city marketplace.

[16]As for the layout and internal organization of these private markets, the bureau (once
again) had a hand in the design. It had built, for example, fixed and temporary canopied
market stalls to accommodate two hundred traders in the farmers' small commodity and
traditional products markets. It charged fees for the use of these stalls, according to the
attractiveness of their location. In 1986 the bureau had plans to introduce electronic
scales and other modern retail equipment into Xinji markets, but by 1990 this had yet
to be accomplished. Still, in 1990, even newer ideas were in the air: more counter space
was a high bureau priority, to reduce the clutter of goods laid out for sale on the ground;
walkie-talkies to make life easier for the bureau's busy market managers; and even TV
monitors to be put up in the main marketplace, not so much to guard against theft (as

The bureau also directly regulates commerce in various other ways besides the physical design and deployment of the marketplaces themselves, of course. It requires all merchants to obtain a business license, which it issues. It also makes sure that food merchants keep their health certificates up to date. It requires that (maximum) prices be publicly displayed, to facilitate its own regulatory work and to protect customers. (Bargaining downward from these maximum prices is, naturally, permitted.) With a total staff of 140 in 1990—up from only 15 or so staff members before 1979—and with offices in every township, the bureau deploys a large army of smartly uniformed market monitors (or market police) who circulate through Xinji's various marketplaces on trading days, checking licenses, monitoring prices, and resolving arguments and public affrays. The bureau's staff has grown so dramatically since 1979 because, according to its director, "the state was putting more emphasis on commercial regulation in these years." At any rate, with all that help at their disposal, bureau officials' claims to have been successful at eliminating black markets in Xinji seemed largely plausible.

Of course, other city government agencies also have a hand in keeping out black-market trade, and in commercial regulation more generally. Vehicles engaged in interregional transport are required to have permits from the Transportation Management Office of the Communications and Transportation Bureau, for example, to help prevent shipment of illegal products. In cooperation with the Transportation Bureau, the Industry and Commerce Management Bureau carries out random inspections of trucks and carts, but as of 1990 it had uncovered little more in the way of illegal trade in Xinji than some pornography in transit and some loads of illegally felled lumber. The Price Bureau is generally little involved in private market price regulation, but it too is called in to enforce price ceilings (called reference prices, *cankaojia*) occasionally, as for pork during the Spring Festival, when demand always skyrockets. Collecting taxes is the affair of the Finance Bureau, and for this purpose private merchants and peddlers are required to report to the bureau on relocations, to keep account books (including information on sources of supply), and to permit these to be inspected by tax authorities. Sometimes state supervision in this realm can indeed be direct and intrusive. In Xincheng Zhen, for example, tax authorities reported that they some-

---

perhaps the merchants might have wished) as to keep track of trade volume, the better to assess the tax liability of petty merchants doing business there.

times spent whole days sitting in the stalls of *geti hu* in order to validate their reported claims about business volume and profits.

In addition to all this, the city government has a political strategy for controlling and perhaps co-opting private traders. In September 1986, the Industry and Commerce Management Bureau established the Individual Household Laborers Association (Geti laodongzhe xiehui)—a local branch of a nationwide organization for private traders. By 1990 the bureau reported that every private merchant in Xinji had joined, certainly casting doubt on the supposed "voluntary" character of membership in the organization, but bringing the official rolls to almost nineteen thousand petty traders in the city. This organization's functions include publicizing market information—also a task of the bureau itself—on bulletin boards, at meetings, and in occasional digests of information from *Shichang bao* (Market News), published by provincial-level bureau offices throughout China. It also facilitates the flow of information to help private enterprises upgrade their operations, by inviting technicians for visits or arranging fieldtrips by local business people. It also—and this seems to be its primary function—explains and clarifies bureau regulatory and other policies to small private merchants. This painstaking propaganda/education work is intended to leave no doubt at all in the minds of traders about which trade practices are legal and permissible locally, and which are not.

The association is supposed to represent the views and interests of the merchants to the bureau as well. But since it shares offices with the bureau itself, is described by bureau officials as "a mass organization under the leadership of the party and the government," and is part of a national association in which the "upper levels give direction to the lower levels," both its democratic and its representative character seem doubtful. The association, in fact, appears to be just another part of a corporatist-paternalist organizing, policing, and regulating stance adopted by the local state toward the private trade sector in Xinji. It is indicative, generally, of how the local state, in the regulatory mode, copes with several of the challenging consequences of economic reform.

Law and order. The coercive functions of the state in Xinji have remained apparently undiminished during the reform era, though their targets have manifestly shifted from political offenders to those whose behavior endangers the public peace and the public welfare. Law and order are vigorously enforced in Xinji. At a national conference convened at Huangshan in 1990, in fact, Xinji was the only small (i.e., *xian*-level) municipality to be named an "advanced city" in legal work. In this sphere, if in few others, Xinji qualifies as a model to be emulated.

The Xinji City Justice Bureau has a staff of just over 30 people. Only 10 of these are accredited lawyers.[17] But this office sits atop an elaborate apparatus, reaching all the way down to every village (*cun*) and every factory shop floor in Xinji; an apparatus charged with both providing legal services and carrying out propaganda/education about the law and the legal system for city residents. More than 21,000 persons are counted as being involved in the propaganda/education effort. More than 130 others scattered around the city work as legal aides, offering counsel and assisting in the mediation of disputes. The Xinji Justice Bureau handles over 150 civil cases a year, considering itself heavily overburdened by this workload. As Bureau Chief He Jinpan expressed it, "Even if we had ten more accredited lawyers, it still wouldn't be enough. We're just going to have to live with a big backlog." Of the 150 or so cases handled at the city office each year, about 100 involve "economic" disputes. (Another 300 or so economic cases are handled each year at lower levels, by the township and town government [*xiang* and *zhen*] justice offices.) An additional 40–50 criminal cases, which must be prosecuted by the city level, are tried in Xinji each year. Xinji lawyers have a reputation for being the best in the district (Shijiazhuang diqu). People from nearby counties regularly come to Xinji seeking expert legal advice and representation. So, on the average, about one-fourth of all cases handled at the City Justice Bureau originate not in Xinji but in other communities.

The Justice Bureau, organized as an office of the city government with just over 30 staff members, is only the smallest part of the full professional legal infrastructure in Xinji, however. The court system (*fayuan*) itself, which is organized under the Standing Committee of the Xinji People's Congress, employs over 100 people to handle legal proceedings—as compared with around 40 court employees in 1979. And the Public Prosecutor's Office (Jiancha yuan), also under the PC Standing Committee, now employs another 70–80 persons, as compared with about 20 staff members in 1979, to process local cases. It could not be determined how many police officers are on duty in the city. But in the

---

[17] Another ten persons who had passed the bar examination were also practicing law on a part-time basis in the city. An additional thirteen were expected to pass the bar in 1990. Once accredited, they would have the option of applying to work either part-time or full-time with the City Bureau.

summer of 1990, four convicted criminals were executed in Xinji, two
for economic crimes and two for crimes of violence. Before facing the
firing squad these four people, along with many others convicted of
lesser crimes, were subjected to public humiliation at an open rally in
the city center. The televised local coverage of the rally revealed an apparently large uniformed police force assembled for the occasion.

The coercive roles of the local state are widely in evidence around the
city. State laws and regulations are posted prominently in public places,
with appended warnings of prosecution for those who fail to comply.
Resort to the law to solve local problems also is becoming more common
and more pronounced. Xinji, for example, has long suffered from water
shortages. The water table in the area has been falling steadily for years.
Yet this shrinking water supply has come under increasingly heavy demand as crop irrigation and industrial water use have expanded. In the
past, public conservation of water was encouraged by mass education
and mass mobilization techniques. By 1990, with the problem becoming
even more acute, legal sanctions had been introduced for those found
guilty of wasting water. Banners and slogans painted on walls around
the city proclaimed the importance of abiding by the new local water
laws and regulations. Some slogans encouraged compliance out of civic-
mindedness. Others clearly carried threats of punishment for those
charged and found guilty of neglecting this civic duty.

GROWTH AND RECONFIGURATION
OF THE LOCAL STATE

The unchallenged and unchallengeable awesomeness of party-state
power in Xinji may have shrunk over the years of Deng's reforms; but
when looked at in terms of its size and complexity, the local state apparatus in this city, as elsewhere in China, has not become smaller or
simpler. Quite the opposite, as detailed in Table 4.1 for the years 1979
to 1989, a steady process of bureaucratic growth, specialization of function, and intensification of activity has been taking place in Xinji. The
major offices and divisions of government administration numbered only
twenty in 1979, for example, but were up to fifty-two in 1990. (See
Table 4.2.) The number of full-time state administrative personnel working in these offices had, not surprisingly, about doubled over the same
period, from around 1,100 in 1979 to more than 2,200 by 1989 (Table
4.1).

Table 4.1. *Total state employees, Xinji, 1979, 1989*

	1979	1989
Total administrative (*xingzheng*):	1,145	2,237
Cadres	945	1,710
Support	200	527
Total institutions and professions (*shiye*):	2,357	4,285
Education	1,698	2,834
Health	306	632
Other	353	819
Total enterprises (*qiye*)	1,036	2,180
State-run	963	1,821
Collective	73	359
Grand total	4,538	8,702

Impressive as these indicators of the recent growth and development of the local state apparatus may be, lists of offices and figures for government administrative personnel alone cannot convey the true scope and presence of the state, as organizer and as employer, in the local context. Employees of two other major categories of state activity have always worked alongside those in state government offices per se: those in state-managed professional (*shiye*) institutions such as hospitals and schools, and those in state-managed enterprises (*qiye*), such as factories and department stores. In Xinji, state employees in these categories have far outnumbered government administrative personnel. Including these other important groups in the picture only confirms that between 1979 and 1989 the generally rapid growth trend prevailing in the strictly administrative sphere of government was matched as well in the other spheres of state-managed activity.

The scope of activity undertaken by the local state bureaucratic apparatus was, thus, steadily elaborated and extended over this decade of reform. And so also was its routine administrative reach extended *beyond* the central urban center to the small towns and villages around the city center. The arresting pattern of growth in state administrative size and density evident at the county (later city) level in Xinji was indeed echoed, though less markedly, at the commune (later, town/township) level as well. A total of just 233 state administrative personnel worked at the commune level in 1979, that is, an average of only 7.5 administrative cadres per commune. By 1989 the figure was 349, up by about

Table 4.2. *Organization and development of local government administration, Xinji, 1979–90*

End 1979	End 1985	1990
County Government Office	County Government Office	Municipality Government Office
Civil Affairs Bureau	Civil Affairs Bureau	Civil Affairs Bureau
	Labor and Personnel Bureau	Labor and Personnel Bureau
	Statistics Bureau	Statistics Bureau
	Price Bureau	Price Bureau
	Industry and Commerce Management Bureau	Industry and Commerce Management Bureau
	Finance Bureau	Finance Bureau
State Commerce Bureau	State Commerce Bureau	State Commerce Bureau
	Grain Bureau	Grain Bureau
	Auditing Bureau	Auditing Bureau
Planning Committee		
Urban Construction Bureau	Urban Construction Bureau	Construction Commission
Industry Bureau	Planning Committee/ Economic Committee	Economic Planning Commission
Transport Bureau	Transport Bureau	Transport Bureau
Culture and Education Bureau	Cultural Affairs Bureau	Cultural Affairs Bureau
	Education Bureau	Education Bureau
Public Health Bureau	Public Health Bureau	Public Health Bureau
Agriculture and Forestry Bureau	Agriculture Bureau	Agriculture Bureau
Water Conservancy Bureau	Water Conservancy Bureau	Water Conservancy Bureau
Animal Husbandry Bureau	Forestry and Animal Husbandry Bureau	Forestry Bureau
		Animal Husbandry Bureau
Science Committee	Science Committee	Science Committee
Sports Committee	Sports Committee	Sports Committee
	Birth Control Committee	Birth Control Committee
	Township Industries Bureau	Township Industries Bureau
	Foreign Affairs Office	Foreign Affairs Office
Public Security Bureau	Public Security Bureau	Public Security Bureau
	Justice Bureau	Justice Bureau

Agricultural Machinery Bureau

Foreign Trade Bureau
Materials Bureau
Second Light Industry Bureau
Hai River Headquarters

Agricultural Machinery Company
Broadcast Affairs Bureau
Earthquake Office
Records Section
Foreign Trade Company
Materials Company
Second Light Co-op Federation

Agricultural Machinery Company
Broadcast and TV Bureau
Earthquake Office
Records Bureau
Foreign Trade Company
Materials Company

Standards and Measures Bureau
External Economic Affairs Committee
Land Bureau
Structural Reform Office
Public Sanitation Office
Investigations Bureau
Nationalities and Religions Bureau
Reception Section
Staffing Office
Real Estate Management Bureau
Local Gazetteer Compiler's Office
Office of Economic Cooperation
Huang-Huai-Hai Development Office
Shenzhen Liaison Station
Machine and Building Materials Company
Chemical Company
Light Industries and Textiles Company
Tobacco Grading, Pricing, and Sales Bureau
Border Region Trade Company

Note that the outline above displays only what might be thought of as the administrative body of the local state bureaucracy. It shows the growth of the administrative apparatus of the local state, but it does not diagram the full array of local government offices as they evolved over the period. It does not show, for example, the organs sitting atop these various bureaus that held chief decision-making and executive authority in Xinji—the Revolutionary County/Municipality Committee in 1979, the County/Municipality Committee thereafter. Nor does it include those offices designed to afford a degree of popular responsiveness (if not direct popular representation) such as the Political Consultative Committee. Nor does it include those offices that actually became subject to electoral selection during the 1980s, such as the local Congress of People's Deputies and the Mayor's Office. And, of course, it does not include the various organs of the Communist Party itself. What this outline shows, therefore, is what could be called the broad bureaucratic-administrative mid-section of the local state. It does not reflect any of the institutions of politics, either grass-roots or national.

Table 4.3. *Zhen government administration, 1990*

Xincheng Zhen government offices	Staff	Year
Civil affairs	1	—
Militia	1	—
Justice	1	—
Police station	3	—
Enterprise office	6	—
Women's association	1	—
Communist youth	1	—
Economic management station	1	1984
Legal services	1	1985
Family planning work station	5	1987
Finance office	6	1988
Land management office	2	1988
Urban construction leading group	2	1988

50 percent. Later, town/township (*zhen/xiang*) governments around Xinji became more complex and differentiated as well. By 1990 many were outfitted with their own branch offices (*suo*) of city administrative bureaus such as the Industry and Commerce Management Bureau, the Township Industries Bureau, the Finance Bureau, the Land Bureau, the Justice Bureau, and the Statistics Bureau.[18] Especially important here, it would seem, was the extension of finance control—in effect a budgetary function—to the town/township level. This gave the town/township governments a strong interest in collecting taxes mandated at higher levels by entitling them to a share of the target and over-target revenues.

In Xinji City's Xincheng Zhen in 1990, for example, the *zhen* government was made up of thirteen administrative offices. The breakdown of offices is shown in Table 4.3, with the number of full-time staff working in those offices in 1990 and with the year each office was established (for those created since the commune period).

Again, this sketch of the administrative structure of government at the *zhen* level does not capture the full picture of the state's local presence. Only 31 people may have been officially working in Xincheng's government administrative offices, but another 5 people were responsible for

---

[18]"Cadres" working at the brigade or village level had always been classified as peasants and had never been on the state payroll. And at that level, interestingly, the trend seems to have been going in the other direction. In 1979, there were some 2,429 such village-level cadres, an average of exactly seven per village. In 1989 this force was down to approximately 2,000. With decollectivization, in Xinji as elsewhere, less work of a purely administrative nature had to be handled in the villages. But much more administration, apparently, needed to be taken care of, one level up, at the town or township government.

party work, another 99 were on the state payroll in state-managed professional institutions (*shiye*) in Xincheng, and 657 more were working in state-run enterprises located in Xincheng. In addition, the local state's profile in the *zhen* was kept quite obtrusive by the existence in Xincheng of numerous branch offices (*fenzhi jigou*) of higher-level state units, including a state grain station (23 employees), an electric power office and transformer station (11), a state cotton purchasing station (9), branches of two state banks (9), a branch tax office (5), a branch office of the court (3), and a materials supply station serving enterprises producing for the state plan (4). Another indication of just how heavy the continuing presence of the state and of state planning was in a common *zhen* like Xincheng is that the *zhen* government Annual Plan for 1990 was a comprehensive, highly specific, classified (*neibu*) document, of some fifty pages in length.

STATE SPRAWL

The data presented here are fragmentary and selective. But the metaphor of state sprawl these data suggest, calling to mind a pattern of rather loose, irregular advance, may hold some heuristic value as we contemplate the processes of urbanization and of changing state-society relations under way in China now.

The post-Mao reforms have sought to deprive the state of some of its former, theoretically unlimited and unchallengeable, direct command authority. This strain of reform has been applied to the urban local state as well as to the central state, but it has not been applied without reservations or exceptions. In Xinji City, local state officials have shown little compunction about issuing direct orders and commands on their own authority when they thought the situation warranted. In some ways, the local state's presence now seems both more selective and more efficacious than before. Still, the beginnings of what may eventually turn out to be a genuine, lasting, and qualitative change in the contemporary Chinese state's claims to and disposition of direct and arbitrary power in society are now becoming visible, and where the local state has been encouraged or obliged to give up its direct command authority, a little space has been created for non–state-initiated social activity. As suggested here for Xinji, the greatest gains in creating such social space have probably been made in the realm of personal and family life—at least this is so if state mandates concerning decisions about procreation are overlooked.

In the uneven, sprawly pattern of non–state-dominated spaces opened up so far by the reforms in China, human activity has frequently remained rather wary; but it has sometimes also turned out to be quite aggressive, even frenetic. This new social activity has often thus, in turn, produced new pressures on public resources and new problems needing common resolution. Rapid economic decontrol and non–state-planned growth, for example, put new pressures on valuable cultivated acreage; they provide opportunities for fraud and sharp trade practices; they encourage theft and certain violent crimes; they endanger the ecology, the environment, and the public health. In response to urgent new social realities such as these, the local state finds its mission again, and it seeks to expand its own personnel resources and its repertoire of controls. Local state authorities move out once more, and in greater force, to apply newly crafted regulatory and administrative-coercive controls in the very social spaces that were so lately liberated from direct state command. The uneven economic growth, social strain, and urban sprawl that characterize development are matched, then, by a not very surprising pattern of local state sprawl, too.

Over the long term, the essential quality of state authority and of state action may be changing as a result of all these unfolding processes of state and social transformation. But for now, the growing local state apparatus and the imprint of its authority are still to be seen just about everywhere in the social life of Xinji City.

5

The floating population in the cities:
chances for assimilation?

DOROTHY J. SOLINGER

INTRODUCTION

The waves of internal migration pulsing through China over the past decade provide us with a window on a major transformation going on. The migration represents one crucial form of the human dimensions of the nation's change from plan to market. This movement of peoples can be both a symbol and a measure of the decline of the Communist regime's institutional structures and of its social system. It also suggests the possibility of the demolition of long-standing barriers erected by the post-1949 government between city and countryside, referred to in Chapter 3 by Barry Naughton, who takes note of the lack of labor mobility before the reform era. Those involved in the movement are members of a new urban grouping, the floating population, chiefly peasants no longer domiciled where they were initially registered to live and estimated in the range of 50 million to 70 million persons.[1]

I acknowledge the Committee on Scholarly Communication with the People's Republic of China and the United States Information Agency for support that made possible two research trips to China (one to Harbin in July 1991 and one to Guangzhou, Nanjing, Wuhan, and Tianjin in May and June 1992). Much of the information in this chapter comes from material collected during those visits. I also wish to thank the Social Science Academies of Heilongjiang, Guangdong, Wuhan, and Tianjin, especially Zhou Lu, Hao Maishou, and Huang Hongyun; the Wuhan City Foreign Affairs Office, especially Yin Guilan; the Johns Hopkins–Nanjing University Center for Chinese and American Studies; and unaffiliated friends who helped me in Wuhan and Nanjing, including (but not limited to) Bernadine Chee, Lu Gang, Lu An, and Shen Yingquan. I was a research associate at the East Asian Institute at Columbia University when I prepared the first draft of this essay, and I appreciate technical assistance I received there and John Smollen's photocopying services. Barry Naughton's and Rick Baum's editorial suggestions were also very useful.

[1]These numbers derive from sample surveys that count as members of the floating population anyone away from home on the day and at the time at which the survey was

Some observers seize on this flow as an emblem of an imminent demise of the party's previous pattern of rule where class structure is concerned. They adopt a positive outlook, alleging that this human tide stands for freedom, for peasants unbound from the sometime shackles of the commune, released from the countryside.[2] Farmers venturing into the cities and towns can hope for the enrichment of their daily lives and for the betterment of their social lot in life, such arguments hold.

But pitted against that view is the fact that the state, by refusing to grant these transients an urban *hukou*—the legal right to household residence in the city and the whole panoply of special privileges and access that that affords (discussed in detail below)—forces them to remain in the "temporary" category. This denial and its accompanying designation, while limiting their total numbers and so reducing somewhat the inevitable pressure on municipalities (recounted in Chapter 2 by Piper Gaubatz in this volume), exclude most of them from normal city life. Thus, as Vivienne Shue makes clear in Chapter 4, the "retreat of the state" is far from complete.

Depending on personal circumstance and skill, the two-thirds or so of the floaters who enter the urban job market (the other third coming for social purposes or for reasons connected with what have been called "urban functions": to visit or stay with family and friends, to attend meetings, to undergo training, for tourism, or to see a doctor) have widely varying ways of life in the city.[3]

According to a major government study of seven of China's biggest municipalities, the largest group of them (about 30 percent) earn their living on construction projects, often bound to specific projects or else to annual contracts; another 22 percent peddle in produce markets, not uncommonly remaining for years on end; some 18.5 percent engage in "household service," many of whom are nursemaids for periods as little

conducted. The majority of the movers are probably moving within the countryside and to medium and small cities and towns. This chapter, by contrast, concentrates on their lives in the big cities, where they often account for one-fifth to one-fourth of the total population. See Cheng Ke, "The Problem of the Floating Population in Large Cities and Countermeasures," *Chengxiang jianshe* (Urban-rural construction) 5 (1988): 18.

[2] As in Keiko Wakabayashi, "Migration from Rural to Urban Areas in China," *Developing Economies* 28, no. 4 (1990): 520; and Alan P. L. Liu, "Economic Reform, Mobility Strategies and National Integration in China," *Asian Survey* 31, no. 5 (1991): 393–408.

[3] Li Mengbai and Hu Xin, eds., *Liudong renkou dui da chengshi fazhan di yingxiang ji duice* (The influence of the floating population on big cities' development and countermeasures) (Beijing: Jingji ribao chubanshe [Economic Daily Publishing Co.], 1991), 9.

as three months; and about 6 percent work in the repair trades (including such activities as shoe, bicycle, pots and pans, and knife repairing).

A catchall category of "other types of hired labor," amounting to 21.7 percent, includes those in state factories (of whom the majority work in textiles) on three- to five-year contracts, day laborers hauling freight, sanitation workers, coal deliverers, and garbage collectors.[4] Other occupations that attract floaters include barbering and tailoring, street performing, fluffing cotton quilts, popping popcorn, bricklaying, restaurant work, and handicrafts and furniture manufacture. Despite real differences, in the eyes of the authorities, as defined by the Fourth National Census, held in 1990, anyone living away from his or her place of legal residence for less than a year is called "floating."

What will be the fate of these displaced persons as the Communist system in its social sense unravels with the progress of market reforms? How much is the state plan, with its coercively mandated residential system, giving way to the market, with its governance purely by economic forces and its purely economically driven status and class categories? How much can the floaters expect to become integrated into the dominant social order (or, put otherwise, to become a part of an incipient social order-in-formation)? Taken a step further, can they venture to imagine not just assimilation for themselves but an actual upward climb for their children, a shot at transferring out of the "peasantry" to a higher social class? Unlike many of the other authors in this book, I am less concerned here with the formation of autonomy, more interested in processes and potential for incorporation.

In the remainder of this chapter, to address these questions I will draw on findings about migration from comparative, historical, and theoretical literature on this subject. I have culled from this material two sets of variables: first, traits that characterize migrant populations; and, second, factors present in receiving societies that determine the life chances of transient peoples. This framework shows that integration for the floating population is blocked, stymied, or distorted because of the stamp of the socialist state and its long-standing social and economic systems. My focus is on the world of the larger metropolises, whose magnetism is most apt to draw migrants from far and wide.

[4]Ibid., 9 and 11.

TRAITS OF THE MIGRANTS THEMSELVES

The traits of the migrants relevant to this inquiry are: their resources (both material and "human capital"); the class characteristics of the migrant community; their family strategies; their "ethnicity" (defined in a special way in the Chinese context, as explained below); their intention to remain in the city; and their subculture. Each of these is conditioned by the residue of the Communist order in ways that affect the integration and mobility chances of the transients and their children. The discussion that follows distinguishes between two groups of migrants: Some of them, undoubtedly a tiny minority, come to town blessed with either the funds or the social connections to enable them to enjoy entrée to at least some of the benefits of the genuine urbanites; others are braving the odds without monetary means or ties to the influential.

Comparative researchers have identified both material and "human capital" resources that can either magnify or limit the chances of migrants in their adjustment to new environments.[5] While material wealth is obvious, relevant forms of human capital for our purposes include special work-related skills, job training and experience, education, and parentage. As for material capital, those with either financial resources or a way of gaining some can hope to use these resources to enter urban society. This they may either do directly by acquiring some of those goods that the Communist system offers free or at a low price to urbanites, or indirectly by bribing the gatekeepers of those goods, thereby obtaining cheap grain, better housing, a good job, or schooling for their young. Often enough money and a "route" (*lu*) are both required, in the words of a Beijing cab driver.

It is not just that variously endowed migrants have different levels of success in their efforts to seek goods reserved by the state system just for urban insiders. Their very chances even to gain the essential material and human capital for seeking these goods in the first place were in the past shaped by that same system. For it is likely that the relevant skills among those who possess them were developed by virtue of their own party membership or by working at jobs in the past in such commune

---

[5]Ewa Morawska, "The Sociology and Historiography of Immigration," in Virginia Yans-McLaughlin, ed., *Immigration Reconsidered: History, Sociology, and Politics* (New York: Oxford University Press, 1990), 198, 201, discusses the components of "human capital" as the following: parental background, schooling and occupational training, work experience, linguistic ability, and length of residence.

enterprises and units as warehouses, supply and marketing cooperatives, and village industries. These are advantages of which only some of the floaters can boast.

As for parentage, all the rural in-migrants start from a more or less common base, cursed by a low-status "peasant" household label. And while their level of schooling admittedly varies, for the most part they have as a group been educated in inferior institutions. Although a portion may have completed senior high school, the nationwide average educational level of peasants is low. According to one sample survey, migrants with a junior high school education represented 20 percent of the sample, those who had only attended primary school were 40 percent, and illiterates and semi-literates accounted for 30 percent.[6]

The second trait, the class characteristics of the migrant community,[7] relates in the comparative literature to whether or not a group of migrants in a given locale creates what is known as an "ethnic enclave," which tends to generate its own "enclave economy."[8] For this not just capital but some individuals with business expertise who are willing to hire compatriots are required. Some of the major theorists in the field of migration have recently pointed to the opportunities that such communities provide for job formation and eventually capital accumulation for co-ethnics—capital that ultimately can become useful in investing in the education and, hence, presumably the upward mobility of the next generation.[9]

---

[6]Li and Hu, *Liudong renkou*, 119, present this data. There is, however, some notable regional variation in this regard, even among the major metropolises. On p. 155 the figures for these categories among Shanghai's transients are, respectively, 43.9, 24.2, and 11.1; on p. 167 it is stated that in Wuhan those with junior high school and primary school education together represent 67 percent while illiterates amount to 9.3 percent; and in Guangzhou, 19.67 have gone to primary school, 68.7 to either junior or senior high school, and only 2.96 percent are illiterate.

[7]Bernard Gallin and Rita S. Gallin, in "The Integration of Village Migrants in Taipei," in Mark Elvin and G. William Skinner, eds., *The Chinese City between Two Worlds* (Stanford, Calif.: Stanford University Press, 1974), 353 and 357 note the importance of class for assimilation among rural migrants in Taiwan. Thanks to Myron Cohen for alerting me to this source.

[8]Michael Peter Smith, Bernadette Tarallo, and George Kagiwada, "Coloring California: New Asian Immigrant Households, Social Networks, and the Local State" (paper presented at the Annual Meeting of the American Political Science Association, San Francisco, August 1990), 20, speak of enclave economies. The concept also appears in Ivan Light and Edna Bonacich, *Immigrant Entrepreneurs: Koreans in Los Angeles, 1965–1982* (Berkeley: University of California Press, 1988). "Ethnic enclaves" is a term used by Alejandro Portes and Ruben G. Rumbaut, *Immigrant America: A Portrait* (Berkeley: University of California Press, 1990), 21.

[9]See, for example, Charles Tilly, "Transplanted Networks," in Yans-McLaughlin, *Immi-

118   *Dorothy J. Solinger*

In the Chinese case, we see again the bifurcation between two groups of in-migrants. Those who have or are in the course of obtaining the capital and the expertise, however, seem less committed to the future careers of their less fortunate co-villagers and more concerned with carving out a point of entry for themselves into the established system.[10] The best examples of this are the once-peasant parvenu construction team bosses (*gongtou*), who gather their fellow locals into a team and lead them to worksites in the city, but whose own time in the city is spent cultivating urban influentials.[11] Also, since a great deal of floating migration is essentially seasonal sojourning,[12] the communities themselves tend to be stable while the individuals who make them up are often on the move, whether back to the villages, to other cities, or to other work or dwelling sites within the same city.[13]

Third is the issue of family strategies, which has several dimensions

gration Reconsidered, 92–93; and Alejandro Portes, "From South of the Border: Hispanic Minorities in the United States," in ibid., 160–84.

[10]Janice E. Perlman, *The Myth of Marginality: Urban Poverty and Politics in Rio de Janeiro* (Berkeley: University of California Press, 1976), 166–67 and 184–85, comments on the propensity of Brazilian migrants' brokers to try to maintain the status quo.

[11]Interviews about *gongtou* with scholars in Guangzhou and with construction team workers in Nanjing in May 1992 gave me this impression.

[12]According to one source, 12 million peasants work in the cities the year around. If this is true, there must be tens of millions of others coming and going. This is reported in U.S. *Foreign Broadcast Information Service China Daily Report* (hereafter *FBIS*), August 26, 1991, 65, from Xinhua, August 23, quoting an article in the Shanghai journal *Shehui* (Society) (hereafter *SH*); Gu Chu, "A Look at the Face of Big Cities' 'Mangliu,' " *SH* 1 (1990): 8, claims that in the late 1980s more than 700,000 peasant workers were permanently living in Beijing, of whom 650,000 were laboring, 60,000 were in commercial work, and 20,000 were nursemaids.

[13]In cities to the far north, such as Harbin, or in the far west, such as Urumqi, there is a great deal of what has been termed "migratory bird" migration. I learned about this in interviews in Harbin in July 1991 and in Yuan Xin and Tang Mingda, "A Preliminary Investigation of Xinjiang's Floating Population," *Renkou yu jingji* (Population and economy) 3 (1990): 46–52. Seasonality is also mentioned in articles on Shanghai and Hubei, however. See Sha Song, "An Analysis of the Characteristics of Robbers Who Come to Shanghai from Outside," *SH* 10 (1990): 10–12; and "Rural Workers Thrive in Urban Workplace," *China Daily* (hereafter *CD*), July 24, 1991, which explains how peasants return to the countryside in the agricultural busy season.

On the other hand, according to Michal Rutkowski, "China's Floating Population and the Labor Market Reforms" (Washington, D.C.: World Bank, December 1991, preliminary draft), 10, one-third stay in the cities they have reached for more than one year (Li and Hu, *Liudong renkou*, 9, cite an average figure across eight cities of 28.67 percent on this), and as early as 1985 scholars writing about Shanghai maintained that seasonality was decreasing among floaters, as "the slack season [for migration] is no longer slack and the busy season is busier." This is in Zheng Guizhen, Guo Shenyang, Zhang Yunfan, and Wang Jufen, "A Preliminary Investigation of Shanghai's City District's Floating Population Problem," *Renkou yanjiu* (Population research) 3 (1985): 4. Also, a writer on Beijing recently said that more and more are tending toward a longer stay there, in *CD*, June 18, 1992, 3.

here. The overwhelming proportion of the transients is male—as high as 87 percent in Beijing and dropping only to 74 percent in Wuhan, according to figures supplied by the Ministry of Construction.[14] Whether they are single or married, this has several implications: since the family, if any, is left in the village, any savings that are garnered are remitted home, and do not go toward building an urban future.[15]

Moreover, these men, if single, find it difficult to find mates in the city, and so are forced to marry rural girls, reducing their commitment to integration into city life.[16] This unbalanced sex ratio, far more skewed than the male-biased ratios that usually issue from the sex selectivity of migration in other societies, obviously makes for uncommon sorts of migrant communities at the place of destination.[17] Men on their own can and will do little to become part of the regular urban scene.[18]

Other features of the floaters that are family-related concern their children. Those brought along end up more often than not as helpers to their fathers in their handicraft trades or businesses, while those who come by themselves have been dispatched by poor rural parents, sometimes after only a few years of primary school, and are sent to toil in joint-venture enterprises under conditions so unsavory and with pay so poor (several sources claim half that given to adults for similar work)[19] that comparisons

[14]Rutkowski, "China's Floating Population," 10; Li and Hu, *Liudong renkou*, 12, have slightly different figures in the summary analysis of their volume, citing 76 percent for Beijing and 61 percent for Wuhan. But elsewhere in the book Beijing's floaters are indeed said to be 87 percent male (p. 128) and Guangzhou's 67.76 percent male (p. 193).

[15]This information can be found in Xu Yingjian, "A General Analysis of the Floating Population in Large Cities and Its Economic Categories," *Wuhan jingji yanjiu* (Wuhan economic research) 2 (1988): 59; dozens of interviews with young transients in four cities yielded the same conclusion.

[16]Ding Jianhua, "Peasant Contract Labor's Wait," *SH* 11 (1989): 18, says of contract workers in the city, "They can only hope to marry a village girl."

[17]Joan M. Nelson, "Sojourners versus New Urbanites: Causes and Consequences of Temporary versus Permanent Cityward Migration in Developing Countries," *Economic Development and Cultural Change* 24, no. 4 (1976): 727, contains a table showing ratios of males to females in major cities of Latin America, Africa, and South and East Asia. In Santiago, Bogotá, Mexico City, Lima, and Caracas males numbered less than 50 percent of migrants; in Nairobi, Tunis, and Cairo the proportion was between 50 and 60 percent; and only in Bombay and Calcutta did it rise to between 66 and 75 percent in the 1960s. See also Lynn Hollen Lees, *Exiles of Erin: Irish Migrants in Victorian London* (Ithaca: Cornell University Press, 1979), which on p. 48 states that the sex ratio was unbalanced among Irish immigrants into London in the late nineteenth century, but on p. 50 mentions that family groups constituted a large segment of the migrants.

[18]Nelson, "Sojourners versus New Urbanites," 754, notes, "The most apathetic group are the young unmarried citizens who are only marginally integrated into their community."

[19]The Chinese government has recently admitted to the presence of 4 million child laborers, according to *Zhengming* (Contend) (Hong Kong) (hereafter *ZM*) 171 (January 1992): 15–16. This is translated in *FBIS*, December 31, 1991, p. 20. A circular issued by the

with nineteenth-century Britain readily leap to mind, if reportage literature out of Guangdong and Shanghai is to be believed.[20]

Also on the subject of offspring, there are allegedly either 10 million or 20 million "black babies" populating the cities.[21] These are those "illegitimate" children born outside the plan whose mothers escaped to the cities to deliver them away from the watchful eyes of village cadres. Born floating, their urban lives are bound to be marked as those of outcasts, unless of course, they or their parents manage to buy or connect their way into the privileges of the settled.

Ethnicity, the fourth trait, takes on a particular connotation among Chinese migrants, given that the great majority of them are, after all, Han like most of the general population.[22] The signs of ethnicity in racially disparate societies include language, dress/costume, custom, facial features, foods, religious practices, and skin color. But "ethnic" division in the eyes of the localistic—and, in response even to their fellow non-local Chinese, one might go so far as to say xenophobic—Chinese, is chiefly defined by place of origin.[23] In these terms certainly extraprovincialites but even rural people from the same province are viewed as foreign.[24]

Ministry of Labor in November 1991 even revealed that the children involved were sometimes younger than twelve, worked up to fourteen hours a day, and were paid just half the adult wage, as reported by this *ZM* article. Cheng Xiaoqi and Huang Jibian, " 'Washed Away' Future," *Nan feng chuang* (South wind window) (Guangzhou) (hereafter *NFC*) 10 (1989): 23, also cite a wage equal to half that of an adult.

[20] Several articles in the *baogao wenxue* (reportage literature) journals *Nan feng chuang* and *SH* in the past two to three years have carried lurid tales on this theme. *ZM* (Hong Kong) is no more explicit or disturbing than these mainland-based magazines. Good examples are Cheng and Huang, " 'Washed Away' Future," 22–24, and Tao Zhiliang and Ding Jiaping, "Homeless Children and Social Environment," *SH* 11 (1990): 19–21.

[21] " 'Black Children' and the 'Floating Population,' " *China News Analysis* 1433 (April 15, 1991): 2, cites ten million; Xiong Yun, "An Analysis of Excess Births among the Floating Population," *Renkou xuekan* (Population bulletin) 1 (1990): 56, states that there was a "black population of twenty million" in 1988 (it is unclear whether the second figure counts only the "illegitimate" children).

[22] For a theoretically stimulating and richly empirical treatment of the relation among ethnicity, native-place identity, and migration in China, see Emily Honig, *Creating Chinese Ethnicity: Subei People in Shanghai, 1850–1980* (New Haven: Yale University Press, 1992).

[23] Here the native-place divisions among urbanites noted by Perry and Strand in this volume become relevant.

[24] For some historical antecedents and discussion of this phenomenon, three good sources are Lawrence W. Crissman, "The Segmentary Structure of Urban Overseas Chinese Communities," *Man* 2, no. 2 (June 1967): 185–204; William T. Rowe, *Hankow: Commerce and Society in a Chinese City, 1796–1889* (Stanford, Calif.: Stanford University Press, 1984), especially 213–14; and Bryna Goodman, "The Native Place and the City: Immi-

With respect to Chinese on the move, local snobbishness may single out the tasteless garb of the bumpkin, or the peasant's sun-darkened skin and, as one urban woman in Wuhan depicted it, his or her "flavor of muddiness." In addition, I was assured by my stylish Harbin host in 1991 (working in the foreign affairs office of the provincial social science academy) that women native to that city were the best-dressed in all China, and that she could therefore tell at a glance a person from outside.[25] But in China language is the most significant source of difference where integration and mobility are concerned.[26] Since many regions of China boast their own dialects, the language barrier people face when transporting themselves to new locales can segregate and subordinate them in relation to their host communities.[27]

This sense of ethnicity is also apparent in the tendency of migrants to dwell separately in the cities, just as sojourners did in Chinese urban places historically, by provincial (or county or village) origin, and sometimes by occupation as well.[28] Scattered journal reports in the past few years and conversations with Chinese people in 1991 and 1992 attested to the presence within many major cities of an array of "villages," such as a "Zhejiang village," a "Jiangsu village," and so forth.[29] Some sources

grant Consciousness and Organization in Shanghai, 1853–1927," Ph.D. dissertation, Stanford University, 1990.

[25]Helen F. Siu, "The Politics of Migration in a Market Town," in Deborah Davis and Ezra F. Vogel, eds., *Chinese Society on the Eve of Tiananmen: The Impact of Reform* (Cambridge, Mass.: Council on East Asian Studies/Harvard University Press, 1990), 63, lists the same marks of "foreignness" in a small southeastern China town.

[26]Kazutsugu Oshima, "The Present Condition of Inter-Regional Movements of the Labor Force in Rural Jiangsu Province, China," *Developing Economies* 28, no. 2 (June 1990): 218.

[27]According to R. J. R. Kirkby, *Urbanisation in China: Town and Country in a Developing Economy 1949–2000* (London: Croom Helm, 1985), 53, n. 62, "migrants to other areas are unable to speak the local dialect even after decades." Similarly, William T. Rowe, *Hankow: Conflict and Community in a Chinese City, 1796–1895* (Stanford; Calif.: Stanford University Press, 1989) (hereafter, Rowe 1989), 49, on nineteenth-century Wuhan.

[28]See, for instance, Pan Li, "Rural Labor Population's Geographic Concentration Effect and Its Geographic Chain Reaction," *SH* 6 (1991): 24–25. Historical accounts of this phenomenon are in Crissman, "The Segmentary Structure," 190; Martin King Whyte and William L. Parish, *Urban Life in Contemporary China* (Chicago: University of Chicago Press, 1984), 11–12; and Goodman, "The Native Place and the City," 3.

[29]Pan, "Rural Labor Population's Geographic Concentration," 25; *FBIS*, February 18, 1982, 59 (from Zhongguo Xinwenshe [Chinese News Service], February 15); Liang Chao, "Controls Urged on Transients," *CD*, June 18, 1992, 3, refers to Zhejiang, Henan, Anhui, and Xinjiang Uygur "villages" in the districts of Beijing; Li and Hu, *Liudong renkou*, 56–58, name specific areas on the outskirts of Beijing, Guangzhou, Tianjin, and Wuhan. In Tianjin's Changqingli Street, supposedly part of a "Zhejiang village," there are also people from Anhui and Sichuan, a stroll there in mid-1992 revealed.

claim that each of these communities is governed by its own special "co-ethnic" chiefs, who mediate the negotiations between their confrères and the local authorities.[30] This segmentation of the city, perhaps a part of the new spatial specialization described in Chapter 2, fragments the migrants as well as cutting them off from the stable urban population. It is thus a force that obstructs integration, and possibly mobility too for the ex-peasant residents of cities.

The fifth migrant trait is intention to remain in the city. According to one migration specialist, whether or not a sojourner eventually does stay on in town, his or her belief that he or she will return to the countryside has a major impact on all sorts of urban behavior, much of it relevant to his or her ultimate prospects for mobility.[31] The person expecting to commit to the urban setting will try to form relevant skills and to build up a reputation, credentials, and contacts there. The reverse, of course, is the case for those who see themselves as only passing through. And in dozens of interviews with floaters I repeatedly encountered either a sense of total aimlessness about the future or else a plan to return home within a short, specified period of time, after accumulating enough cash to build a house or marry in the village. As one young shoe repairman from Zhejiang working in Tianjin told me flippantly when asked about his intentions, "Huo yitian, suan yitian" (Live a day, write off a day).[32]

In general, then, migrants who plan to sink roots at the destination make choices that improve the life chances both of themselves and of their offspring. It is the settled, not the roaming or seasonal migrant, who fits these conditions,[33] but scattered reports offer no clear indication

---

[30]Zeng Jingwei, "Big Cities' 'Trash Collectors,' " *NFC* 1 (1988): 24–25. According to Zeng, there are gangs or factions (*bang, pai*) among trash collectors, from Zhejiang, Subei (North Jiangsu), Anhui, and Shandong, each with their own leaders. The leaders, unlike their subordinate gang members, do not live in the trash heaps.

[31]The article I have in mind is Nelson, "Sojourners versus New Urbanites," 721–57. In particular, the migrant committed to the city will put his or her savings into constructing an urban future, may try to upgrade his or her city dwelling, and may form or join associations that fight to satisfy urban needs.

[32]Jing Yi, "Records from Visits to Donghuang Fire Disaster Victims' Family Members," *ZM* 169 (1991): 25, contains this same information; Oshima, "The Present Condition of Inter-regional Movements," 216, notes that many migrant workers actually hope to return home precisely because of the difficulty of transferring their household registrations.

[33]Rutkowski, "China's Floating Population," ii, puts forward the notion of "two different and increasingly separated pools of floaters: those who stay long, enter the labor market and in terms of way of life become similar to permanent urban residents with a *hukou*, and those who move for various purposes for a short time, usually without changing their labor market status." See also Kirkby, *Urbanisation in China*, 32, who speaks of the transients as "part settled and part floating." See also Yuen-fong Woon, "Rural

of which of these or what proportion of these may be the better endowed as against those who work from a lack of means.[34] Once having made a decision to stay, for those who do so, however, the prospects for integration and mobility should increase somewhat, unless the barriers identified here (and those addressed in the next section) are just too rigid.

The last of our six traits of the migrants is their own subculture. We cannot generalize about these people themselves; indeed, there must be more than one subculture among them.[35] To begin with their underclass, several sources, both oral and documentary, have attested to the docility, obedience, and hardworking habits of many of them, characteristics that link them with other undocumented and migrant laborers around the world.[36]

But this may be just an initial stance, according to a Harbin scholar, replaced with time by feelings of dissatisfaction, small acts of disobedience, and work slowdowns, once the transients have learned of their comparative disadvantage.[37] Such behavior matches the model of the "migrant subculture" depicted by a Harvard psychiatrist, based on data collected in migrant labor camps. In this model, filthy and debilitating conditions, combined with social isolation, extreme poverty, cultural deprivation, and social fragmentation produce a mood of fatalism and antisocial behavior, and result in deliberate wastefulness and the abuse of equipment.[38] Indeed, some of the migrants I visited living on the outskirts of Wuhan and Tianjin were residing in unheated, tentlike shacks

Migrants and Regional Development in the People's Republic of China: The Case of Kaiping County in the Pearl River Delta Region" (Paper prepared for the fiftieth-anniversary meeting of the Association for Asian Studies, New Orleans, April 1991), 31. Woon states, "It is the capitalistic entrepreneurs, not the exploited proletarians, who roam in search of opportunity."

[34]Although Woon, previously cited, claims that it is the wealthy, successful migrants who are on the move, untold ranks of the beggars and stragglers remain at large in the country; one source attests to 10,000 persons' collecting garbage in Shanghai (Tang Xiaotian and Chen Donghu, "Forced Residence and Urban Society Criminals," *SH* 9 [1989]: 19). Also, James McGregor, "Growing Millions of Jobless Peasants Swarm Through China, Rousing Fears of Rural Unrest," *Asian Wall Street Journal Weekly*, May 6, 1991, 5, maintains that "up to three million peasants roam the country in search of work." Thanks to June Dreyer for sending me this last article.

[35]Thanks to Tom Bernstein for alerting me to this distinction.

[36]I discuss this in my article "Chinese Transients and the State: A Case of Civil Society?" *Politics and Society* (March 1993). This is essentially the same paper that was published by the Hong Kong Institute of Asia-Pacific Studies, Chinese University of Hong Kong (USC Series no. 1), 1991.

[37]Author interview in Harbin, July 2, 1991.

[38]This is reported in Robin Cohen, *The New Helots: Migrants in the International Division of Labor* (Aldershot, England: Avebury, 1987), 196–204.

without running water or electricity, or five to six in a room equipped with nothing but two or three beds and several sewing machines at which the occupants labored night and day. That such people have become dispirited should not be surprising.[39]

But despite the strikes at foreign-funded firms in the Pearl River Delta to which Chapter 11 calls attention, such dissatisfaction may not generally find open expression among these transients. Many sources have noted the vulnerable position of such workers and their proclivity either to keep silent, engaging in only covert styles of dissent, or to petition quietly.[40] Surely the allegedly high rates of criminality (much of which may actually substitute for more conventional forms of political association and protest, which Perry's remarks on the lack of unionization for temporary workers and their consequent reliance on criminal gangs suggest) among the transients must bear some relation to such moods of discontent.[41] Whether docile or dissident, these people, who must belong to the unendowed, are not likely to find easy access to the world of the settled urban elite.

Still, this is not the whole picture. Those earning well and building on their *guanxi* (personal relationships) to squeeze into this same world are doubtless cocky and satisfied. But whether they invest their rewards in positive acts to help them become a more permanent part of city society

[39]Ding Jianhua, "Peasant Contract Labor's Wait," 18, writes of contract laborers who "only want to live like regular workers"; Tang and Chen, "Forced Residence," 20, say that peasants who have entered the cities feel "comparatively deprived" and therefore turn to crime; and a *New York Times* reporter quotes a worker as demanding a job from the government (Sheryl WuDunn, "China's Dismal Truth: 100 Million Out of Work," *New York Times*, July 4, 1992, 4).

[40]Wayne Cornelius, "Urbanization and Political Demand Making: Political Participation among the Migrant Poor in Latin American Cities," *American Political Science Review* 68 (1974): 1125–46; Perlman, *The Myth of Marginality*, 187, 243; Josh DeWind, Tom Seidl, and Janet Shenk, "Contract Labor in U.S. Agriculture: The West Indian Cane Cutters in Florida," in Robin Cohen, Peter C. W. Gutkind, and Phyllis Brazier, eds., *Peasants and Proletarians: The Struggles of Third World Workers* (New York: Monthly Review Press, 1979), 380–96; and Martin West and Erin Moore, "Undocumented Workers in the United States and South Africa: A Comparative Study of Changing Control," *Human Organization* 48, no. 1 (Spring 1989): 5, among many others speak of the preference for either quiescence or for pursuing legitimate channels in making demands among those so placed.

[41]As in all other societies where numbers of outsiders are climbing, Chinese authorities have found that over a third of the criminal cases, and up to 40 percent of the arrests, especially in the big cases, involve migrants. Rutkowski, "China's Floating Population," vii, was told that 10 percent of all the migrants were arrested for criminal acts in 1987, a share ten times higher than that among permanent workers. As always, one must question such figures, since the propensity of the police to target and blame outsiders must be high. I discuss this in Solinger, "Chinese Transients and the State."

or return home to bask in the prestige their winnings have gained for them is still an open question.[42]

In summary, migrants reach the cities equipped with a range of resources, strategies, traits, and attitudes. I have presented the plight of these people, where necessary differentiating between the minority who hold or soon acquire the wherewithal to penetrate the realm of privilege, and the bulk of the floaters, who must scrape about the dregs in order to survive. While the odds for integration and then mobility are certainly much greater for the first group, given individuals must still choose whether or not to draw on those odds for the sake of an urban future. Their decision is no doubt colored in part by the factors of the receiving society described below.

FEATURES OF THE RECEIVING SOCIETY

The literature on migration analyzes not just the migrants themselves in attempting to account for the life chances of these people in their destinations. The quality of the community they enter is also determining. Two authors of a recent volume on immigration into America speak of this element under the label "contexts of reception."[43] Under this heading these scholars include the policies of the receiving government, the conditions of the host labor market, and the characteristics of the migrants' own ethnic communities in the new setting. In the Chinese case, governmental policies play an inordinately large role in shaping the entire context in all its aspects.

My choice of features of the receiving society most applicable to today's migrants in Chinese cities, in the context of reception, has been shaped by the comparative literature on migration. They are as follows: the nature of the class structure in the city (clearly a function of state policy in the Chinese case); the pattern of property ownership; the type of labor market; the political system; the patronage networks available to the migrants; the urban educational system and access to it; housing opportunities in the cities; and the attitudes of the receiving community.[44] I will also supply some material on the modes of adaptation that

---

[42]Portes and Rumbaut, writing on migration in general, make the point that most migrants prefer to return home, since it is far easier to win recognition there than in the alien urban environment (*Immigrant America*, 18).

[43]Ibid., 85.

[44]See Zhu Baoshu, Shen Ying, Zhang Jingyue, and Yan Haihua, "The New Trend in the

the transients assume in the cities. True, these features have all come under some degree of assault and have been steadily losing a portion of their power since the reform era got under way. But it is still safe to say that through the early 1990s not a single one of them had become undermined to the point that it ceased to affect in basic ways the options of the newcomers to the towns.

Just as in Latin American cities, in China a closed class structure impedes social mobility for newcomers.[45] The class order of China, however, is clearly a function of governmental policy, as it is still most fundamentally determined by the state-imposed *hukou* system. Indeed, Chinese people are still subject to a finely graded ranking order, which classifies those with a *hukou* in the greatest metropolises at the top, and those with small, isolated rural-township *hukous* at the bottom.[46] It is the urban *hukou* that provides the basis for all the perquisites that urbanites—and only urbanites—enjoy.[47]

Many people with money or the proper sort of *guanxi* can exist rather well without a *hukou*. Still, in July 1991 I was told that the price of one in Harbin was as high as 3,000 yuan; in June 1992 friends in Wuhan and a Beijing cab driver agreed that combined with proper *guanxi* it could run at least as high as 20,000 yuan in Beijing. And journal articles speak of both black-market and official prices with the amounts varying with the prestige of the city.[48] As the *Peasant Daily* noted in mid-1989, "People go on a 'black road' to get an urban *hukou;* those with power

Rural Population's Shift toward Small Cities and Towns and New Problems," *Zhongguo renkou kexue* (Chinese population science) 1 (1991): 54, for a list of the deprivations suffered by peasants as compared to urban *hukou*-holders that has helped me to compile my own list.

[45]See Perlman, *The Myth of Marginality*, 243, on Rio de Janeiro.

[46]See Ding Shuimu, "Household Registration Management and Social Control: Another Opinion on the Present Household Management System," *SH* 3 (1989): 28.

[47]The benefits afforded by the possession of an urban *hukou* are discussed in *Nongmin ribao* (Peasant daily) (hereafter, *NMRB*), November 23, 1988, 3, and May 11, 1989. Thanks to Tom Bernstein for showing me these articles. There is also a discussion of the deprivations experienced by those lacking the urban *hukou* (the inability to receive education, gain employment, or receive health care, to participate in elections, to serve in the army, or to marry; plus ineligibility for state-allocated housing and grain) in Zhang Qingwu, "Basic Facts on the Household Registration System," *Chinese Economic Studies* 22, no. 1 (1988): 8.

[48]See, for instance, "Household Registration Research" Task Group, "The Present Household Registration Management System and Economic System Reform," *Shanghai shehui kexueyuan xueshu jikan* (Shanghai Academy of Social Sciences academic quarterly) 3 (1989): 85; and Ding Shuimu, "A Preliminary View of the Present Household Registration Management System," *SH* 1 (1987): 19.

use power, those with money buy it; those with neither write, [and] run back and forth."[49]

The essentially closed character of this class order is illustrated by the difficulty of marrying across its boundaries, as mentioned briefly above. For the most part city folk are not disposed to wed a "peasant," even a newly urban-based one. Even the official press admits this, quoting a female "peasant" textile worker in a city, who says, "my biggest worry is whether I can become a full-time worker and get an urban residence permit; if I can't, I'll have to find a boyfriend in the countryside and live apart." In the same paper on the same day a commentator states, "Rural workers find it difficult to get to know local young men, let alone marry them."[50] In the typical words of one interviewee in Tianjin, "We wouldn't [*buhuide*] accept them as regular urban people . . . people look down on them as peasants. . . . Tianjin people don't want to marry outsiders."[51]

Researchers tell a plaintive tale of female peasant contract labor in the textile plants of Zhengzhou who "want to find an urban husband, but realize they don't possess the qualifications for this; it's hard to make friends with someone of a higher social position, so the pressure of the marriage problem gets greater and greater."[52] Inquiring of my transient respondents whether they hoped to marry an urbanite, I was met not infrequently with expressions of incredulity or embarrassed laughter.

The role of the pattern of ownership is manifest in the status superiority of the state-owned firms. Their greater prestige was evident into the early 1990s in the preference of many urban youths for remaining unemployed rather than working in nonstate sector jobs. It is well known that some 40 percent of the state-owned factories operate at a loss. Nonetheless, the politicoeconomic order in China not only protects them, it accords them priority treatment. An entire bureaucratic apparatus operates to ensure their survival, with the result that those working in the "private" or "individual" economies may fear that their

---

[49]*NMRB*, May 11, 1989. Thanks to Tom Bernstein for this reference.
[50]*CD*, July 24, 1991, 6.
[51]Interview with a scholar on June 8, 1992. Similarly, on June 16, an official from the city's Labor Bureau told me, "Tianjin people wouldn't look for a man without a *hukou* to marry." On the other hand, many scholars interviewed in Guangzhou thought good-looking peasant women had a pretty good chance of marrying a local man in the growing middle-sized, export-oriented, foreign-invested Pearl River Delta cities, and sometimes in Guangzhou as well. In general, Guangzhou seems more open to allowing outsiders to assimilate than did the other cities I visited.
[52]Li and Hu, *Liudong renkou*, 345.

businesses exist under a cloud of uncertainty. For this reason, it is generally those who have nurtured adequate connections—whether through bribery or otherwise—who feel most confident about their chances of surviving and succeeding as private entrepreneurs to the point of accumulating capital for upward mobility.

The ownership structure also favors the permanent, urban, regular [*guding*] workers in many ways, while housing, eating, and finding a mate become bitter problems for contract labor brought in from the countryside.[53] For instance, an official report on one of Zhengzhou's less profitable textile mills tells of two young peasant girls who had to be sent 20 to 30 yuan each month by their parents because they received insufficient help with living expenses, not to mention welfare benefits, from the plants that employed them.[54]

The fringe benefits that go with work in the state firms offer security only for the regular workers. This is a security for which contract and temporary workers cried out in the Cultural Revolution, as Perry shows in Chapter 11 in this volume; their absence cannot be less painful today.[55] Of all the different types of transients, only peasant contract laborers in profitable state or foreign-funded firms were getting some welfare benefits as of 1992, according to interviews in factories and at labor and textile bureaus in Wuhan and Tianjin in May and June 1992. This variable treatment bolsters Perry's findings of the continuing (but, taking into account the floaters, one should probably say the exacerbated) fragmentation of the labor force in today's China.

The third feature of the receiving community, the urban labor market, holds both advantages and disadvantages for the floating population. Most obviously, there is still enough unmechanized, casual, informal, unskilled labor in the cities to provide a special niche for the transients.[56]

---

[53]A most graphic description is in Ding Jianhua, "Peasant Contract Labor's Wait."

[54]This is reported in Li and Hu, *Liudong renkou*, 344. It should be noted, however, that treatment of peasant contract labor can be quite decent, as in the more lucrative Number One Cotton Mill in Wuhan or Tianjin's Number Three Silk Weaving Factory, both of which I visited.

[55]See, for one discussion of this, Marc Blecher, "Peasant Labour for Urban Industry: Temporary Contract Labour, Urban-Rural Balance and Class Relations in a Chinese County," *World Development* 11, no. 8 (1983): 736; Lynn T. White, III, "Workers' Politics in Shanghai," *Journal of Asian Studies* 36, no. 1 (1986): 108, mentions this problem in the 1950s.

[56]On the importance of such a niche for migrant labor, see John J. DiIulio, Jr., "There but for Fortune: The Homeless, Who They Are, How to Help Them," *The New Republic*,

Much of such work—in construction, and in the textile, chemical, building materials, sanitation, packaging and hauling, and repair trades—is harsh, filthy, and exhausting. It has been disdained by urban young people eligible for more prestigious jobs in the foreign trade sector.[57]

At least in the short run, taking a position in these lines of occupation can have deleterious consequences for assimilation and mobility, they believe. These kinds of jobs as a rule provide no advancement and shunt the transients off into marginality.[58] Consequently, being employed in this way precludes the possibility of achieving what a scholar of the Irish immigration into England of the 1840s called "work-day integration."[59] Like the displaced Irish of that time, many floaters labor in gangs of their fellow villagers or operate on their own.[60] Another negative aspect of this special niche is its suitability for child labor.[61]

One more question about the labor market concerns its degree of competitiveness and the effects this may have on life opportunities for the migrants. The urban Chinese labor market is above all highly segmented. As in all developing countries, there is a dual labor market, with immigrants working in the second, informal sector.[62] Competition for the migrants exists just in the second sector among unskilled workers, and in most cases this means with members of other migrant/minority ethnic groups.

June 24, 1991, 30; and Peter H. Rossi, *Down and Out in America: The Origins of Homelessness* (Chicago: University of Chicago Press, 1989), 21.

[57]Liu Dawei and Wang Qiangzhi, "An Investigation Report on the Problem of the Difficulty of Finding Labor in Beijing City," *Shehui kexue yu shehui diaocha* (Social science and social investigation) 1 (1987): 34–40.

[58]Paul M. Hohenberg and Lynn Hollen Lees, *The Making of Urban Europe 1000–1950* (Cambridge, Mass.: Harvard University Press, 1985), 273, note that as Europe industrialized, skilled workers had far better prospects for upward mobility; David F. Crew, *Town in the Ruhr: A Social History of Bochum, 1860–1914* (New York: Columbia University Press, 1979), 87, found that "manual work . . . constituted an ascribed characteristic" in the late nineteenth-century German city he studied.

[59]Frances Finnegan, *Poverty and Prejudice: A Study of Irish Immigrants in York: 1840–1875* (Cork, Ireland: Cork University Press, 1982), 98.

[60]Rutkowski, "China's Floating Population," 36, found that in Beijing 37 percent of those who were self-employed did not have the local *hukou*.

[61]A suggestive remark on this is in Myron Weiner, *The Child and the State in India: Child Labor and Education Policy in Comparative Perspective* (Princeton: Princeton University Press, 1991), 206: "Employment in India in the nonformal sector is increasing more rapidly than in the modern, factory sector, and it is the former that employs children." For some more information on the situation in China, see note 19 above.

[62]The primary source on this concept is Michael J. Piore, *Birds of Passage: Migrant Labor and Industrial Societies* (Cambridge: Cambridge University Press, 1979).

Several journal articles have commented on the saturation of segments of the second sector in China—in the urban construction market, and, in some places, the crafts labor market as well.[63] The result of this is not hard to guess. As in old Hankow,[64] the unskilled labor market in today's Chinese cities is sectioned off by localized labor gangs, each with its own boss and turf, and brawls over economic opportunity are serious or frequent enough to be treated in the literature.[65]

New "spontaneous labor markets" for unskilled labor sprang up in the 1980s, having no fixed site, involving negotiation in the streets, following no regular procedures, and offering no guarantees. At one I visited as many as two hundred men and women of varying ages were lolling about in mid-afternoon hoping to find employment as nurses, restaurant workers, or painters. Aside from their irregularity and uncertainty, such institutions may sometimes prey on the naïveté of newcomers and encourage criminal and exploitative activities, according to Chinese sociologists who have studied them.[66]

With no way to enter the unions of regular labor, migrants in China cannot dream, at least not under present conditions, of the steady integration into the work force enjoyed by the Irish earlier in this century in London.[67] Only those who through *guanxi* manage to permeate their way into the workplaces of the permanent can begin to upgrade their life chances.

The political system, the fourth feature of the system confronting the cityward sojourner, denies these people any civic, legal, or political status. Even those who have registered as "temporary city dwellers" still lack the urban *hukou* and so remain disenfranchised. Moreover, as noted above, like others of their type around the world, these people are disinclined to protest openly, to organize, mobilize, aggregate

---

[63]Liang Ziming, "On the Use and Management of the Urban Floating Population," *Yangcheng wanbao* (Sheep City [Guangzhou] evening news), March 16, 1988, on construction teams; and "Farmers Lead the New Gold Rush in Beijing," *CD*, July 30, 1991, 6, on the stiff competition among carpenters in the capital.

[64]On this, see Rowe 1989, 198–200 and 232–40.

[65]See, for example, Wang Yanling, Wu Yekang, and Jiang Jianping, "Get Enlightenment from a Bloody Lesson," *SH* 8 (1990): 2–3. I was also told about this problem in an interview in Harbin with a social science researcher on July 25, 1991.

[66]Huang Bicheng, Liu Yong, and Peng Shaoci, "A Report from Changsha's Labor Market," *SH* 3 (1988): 15–17; and Wang et al., ibid., 3.

[67]See Lees, *Exiles of Erin*, especially 239ff. On p. 239 Lees notes, "A more extensive fusion of English and Irish workers' politics did not take place until migrants began to join and to organize trade unions."

demands, or even to lobby; such reticence saps them of political relevance.[68]

In China's authoritarian, one-party system, the absence of any competitive political parties[69] or of legitimate representation for social groups (especially for those on the fringes of the system, such as our floaters), politics is useless.[70] If an outsider could somehow build a bridge that led to party membership, that person could become political in the Chinese context. But such an avenue must be blocked for the masses of migrants. Moreover, these people seem unlikely to have access to the type of alliances with state leaders that Perry's regular workers can call upon.

Fifth is the nature of the patronage networks open to the transients. The issue here is the relation of migrants to the structures of power, status, occupation, and wealth. In this case people with means and those without are clearly demarcated. Migration theory emphasizes the importance for integration and economic success of "ethnic networks." Looking at other societies that do not have the types of barriers erected by the Chinese socialist system, scholars have found that in-migrants may be able to flourish if they can build links to already settled co-ethnics in their new communities who are situated in business or other professional circles, or if they can participate in the community organizations formed by previously settled co-ethnics.[71] Unlike the residents of

[68]There is no hard evidence that floaters (as distinct from unemployed city workers) took part even in the June 1989 demonstrations.

[69]The importance of political parties in Turkey in bargaining for votes in exchange for city services for squatters is discussed in Ayse Gunes-Ayata, "Migrants and Natives: Urban Bases of Social Conflict," in Jeremy Eades, *Migrants, Workers, and the Social Order* (London: Tavistock, 1987), 234–48. See also Cornelius, "Urbanization and Political Demand Making," 1132, on competitive party systems and their pressure on incumbent governments to be responsive to low-income voters in Latin American cities; Hohenberg and Lees, *The Making of Urban Europe*, 317, on suffrage and political relevance in urbanizing Europe; and Lees, *Exiles of Erin*, 233–36, on the significance of the mobilization of the Irish vote in late nineteenth-century Britain for breaking down barriers against the migrants. Nelson, "Sojourners versus New Urbanites," 754, writes theoretically on this issue, and David C. Schak, discussing beggars in Taiwan in *A Chinese Beggars' Den: Poverty and Mobility in an Underclass Community* (Pittsburgh: University of Pittsburgh Press, 1988), 154, mentions the possibilities for using the political support of beggars as a bargaining chip. (Interesting point: What beggars can do in Taiwanese politics honest laborers in China cannot do.)

[70]See Portes, in Yans-McLaughlin, *Immigration Reconsidered*, 171, on the link between political representation and upward mobility.

[71]Portes and Rumbaut, *Immigrant America*, 88, address the value of what they term "ethnic networks" as sources of information, jobs, credit and support, and "from the perspective of ethnic achievement [the importance of] whether they are composed primarily of manual workers or contain significant professional or business element;"

towns like Xinji, described in Chapter 4, our floaters are not apt to be welcome to participate in the types of varied, popular associations Shue found among the permanent residents there.

In China since there are no political parties whose leaders might want migrants' votes or legal associations these people can join, brokers become all-important.[72] But the brokers who serve the underclass are typically tied to the status quo, well aware that any alleviation of the lifestyle difficulties of their charges would only undermine their own power.[73] It is often such brokers, bosses, or community chiefs in Chinese cities who bribe their way into some status for themselves; for their communities their efforts go toward sustaining their people's rights to continue with illicit practices.[74]

The urban educational system is the sixth feature of the municipal environment with which the floating people must cope.[75] The formal prohibition on outsiders attending city schools has led to informal purchase prices for entry for floating children, varying by quality of school and city, as I learned in interviews in Guangzhou, Wuhan, and Tianjin in May and June 1992.[76] A telling piece in a Guangdong journal of reportage literature recounts the inaccessibility of city schools for most of the transients' youngsters.[77] Here are stories of truant twelve-year-olds collecting junk, a carpenter teaching his son his own trade rather

see also Goodman, "The Native Place and the City," 40, and Smith et al., "Coloring California," 23, on the relevance of links with wealthy or acculturated immigrants for the life chances of the less well-off. Leslie Page Moch, *Paths to the City: Regional Migration in Nineteenth-Century France* (Beverly Hills, Calif.: Sage Publications, 1983), 26, also points to the nature of the migrants' connections in the city as helping to determine a group's "concentration in dead-end jobs with no future employment security, higher income or higher status." And Gallin emphasizes the need for forming ties in the city (in Taiwan) with co-village merchants if the efforts of poorer migrants to obtain welfare benefits and credit, legal aid, and protection are to succeed. This is in Bernard Gallin and Rita S. Gallin, "The Integration of Village Migrants into Urban Society: The Case of Taipei, Taiwan," in Robert N. Thomas and John M. Hunter, eds., *Internal Migration Systems in the Developing World with Special Reference to Latin America* (Boston: G. K. Hall and Co., 1980), 170–71.

[72] The leaders of "ethnic" sojourning groups in Chinese cities historically also acted as brokers. See Crissman, "The Segmentary Structure," 202.

[73] See Perlman, *The Myth of Marginality*, 184, on this in Rio de Janeiro.

[74] See Shao Jun, "The Great Army of Migrants is Shaking the Roots of the Public Ownership System," *Zhongguo zhi chun* (China's spring) 8 (1990): 50.

[75] Hohenberg and Lees, *The Making of Urban Europe*, 272; Moch, *Paths to the City*, 200; and Morawska, "Sociology and Historiography," 206–7, all underline the need for education in achieving upward mobility.

[76] See Chaoze Cheng, "Internal Migration in Mainland China: The Impact of Government Policies," *Issues and Studies* 27, no. 8 (1991): 69.

[77] Huang Ruide, "The Next Generation among the Floaters," *NFC* 9 (1989): 20–21.

than leaving him in the village to go to school, and a bean-sprout grower who worried that policy changes might force him and his kind out of the city and therefore did not want to invest his small pot of capital in bribing the teachers. A son helping the "scrap boss" earns 100 yuan a month: "If he went to school his family would lose that source of income and would have to pay school fees besides. School is for the boss's family," explains the author.

The same article also carries the tale of a construction work team leader who could afford whatever the managers of the school of his choice desired as the price for accepting his children; he must be in the minority. The worried writer muses that "shack-village residents will in the future become a 'structure' the large cities 'can't pull down' "; and "After them, we will have one or several 50 million appearing in the cities [of these] low-quality people." Surely the connection between educational opportunity and upward mobility must be one of the best known in any theory of achievement.

Access to housing was "crucial to any social improvement," in the nineteenth-century urbanization of Europe.[78] Given the extraordinary crowding and cramping that even regular city residents suffer in China, one must despair for the fate of the outsiders.[79] Despite "commercialization" of urban housing in the current reforms, the purchase of most apartments still depends on hefty contributions from one's state-owned unit (or upon help from wealthy overseas relatives). Therefore, with no real housing market, almost all urban dwellings being state-allocated and enterprise-owned as explained in Chapter 2, newcomers to the city who lack means are forced to live in a wide range of more or less desperate dwellings.

According to one study,[80] about 40 percent live in residents' homes (which must refer to those who have come to join or camp out in family members' apartments as well as those renting space in peasants' huts along the outskirts of the city).[81] Another 20 percent are in collective unit shelters (this would relate mainly to workers in factory dormitories,

---

[78]Hohenberg and Lees, *The Making of Urban Europe*, 310.
[79]See Kirkby, *Urbanisation in China*, chap. 6 on housing; and Reeitsu Kojima, *Urbanization and Urban Problems in China* (Tokyo: Institute of Developing Economies, 1987), chap. 3, also on housing.
[80]Rutkowski, "China's Floating Population," v.
[81]Li and Hu, *Liudong renkou*, 17, found that 57.45 percent of the floaters of Beijing lived in the city's near suburbs; for Shanghai the figure was 55.66 percent. Some of these must be in peasant homes, some squatting.

but might include those in temporary work shacks at construction sites as well). A further 20 percent stay in hotels (including the many private inns and "underground hotels" that have cropped up everywhere in China today, many of which make ideal residences for peddlers and others in town for relatively brief commercial sojourns),[82] hostels or hospitals.

The remaining 20 percent are in "various other places." According to my research, these "other" places include a wide array of miserable hovels, such as squatter settlements,[83] train stations,[84] on the streets, under the eaves, under bridges, in free markets (a common practice for vegetable and egg peddlers is to lie on a plank under plastic sheeting inside their marketplace), on boats or wharves, in bathhouses, in public toilet stalls, in garbage dumps,[85] on dormitory stairs, or along the river banks.[86]

According to this breakdown some 80 percent of the migrants do have a roof over their heads. But except those residing with family, none of them is situated to become a part of regular city life. Presumably those in the residual category, as well as members of construction teams, are frequently on the move. Even if their housing were more normal, the geographical mobility dictated by looking for work would limit integration.[87] Only those holed up in proper homes and those who are "kings" of the outdoor or construction-team communities have a hope of melting into the mainstream mold.

---

[82]In Heilongjiang half the beds in urban hotels are said to be taken up by various kinds of trading people. This is in Zhongguo renkou zongbianji weiyuanhui (*Chinese population* general editing committee) in *Zhongguo renkou: Heilongjiang fence* (Chinese population: Heilongjiang volume) (Beijing: Zhongguo Caizheng jingji chubanshe, 1989), 168.

[83]On this, see Tang Xiaotian and Chen Donghu, "Forced Residence and Urban Society's Criminals," *SH* 9 (1989): 19–21, 41.

[84]Gu, "A Look at the Big Cities' 'Mangliu,' " 7–9, describes the kinds of people populating the Beijing train station. According to the author, some people actually fall in love, marry, and have children there.

[85]As previously noted, Tang and Chen, "Forced Residence," claim that Shanghai has 10,000 inhabitants surviving by collecting trash (see n. 40); but Gu, ibid., 8, says the number is as large as 30,000. For a fascinating descriptive account of the lives of such individuals, see Zeng, "Big Cities' 'Trash Collectors.' " Even the official *CD* has carried pieces on this kind of community (July 30, 1991, 6). This article specifically mentions Beijing's own "garbage king."

[86]Huang et al., "A Report from Changsha's Labor Market," 16, lists some of these less savory sites. I spoke with a young girl in Nanjing working in a restaurant seventeen hours a day and sleeping on a chair there at night; other restaurant workers I met in Wuhan's outskirts slept on their restaurant's second story, on the floor.

[87]Finnegan, *Poverty and Prejudice*, 7, makes this point for the immigrant Irish.

Localism and xenophobia that shade into overt discrimination, prejudice, and open hostility are the eighth feature of the urban setting that confronts the floaters. As one writer explained:

The floating population sometimes surpass the local people's tolerance level . . . they can't buy transportation tickets, transportation is crowded to the point of *luan* [chaos], amusement areas are crammed, the price of local goods goes up. They often resentfully cry, "Everything is spoiled by outsiders." . . . In brawls, local people get more supporters among the onlookers; there are few dissuaders. The contradiction between local and outside people has now become a social contradiction. . . . They treat outsiders as second-class citizens and see them as the snatchers of local people's interests.[88]

Similarly, a public security officer in Beijing is actually said to have pronounced, "These out-of-towners are no better than animals."[89] These sorts of attitudes among the "host" community cannot but color the reception these transients encounter now and the opportunities they find for social mobility in the near term.[90] Moreover, these attitudes might affect all the migrants alike, since even the successful outsiders could well be a target for resentment among the less fortunate legal urban residents who in their own eyes properly "belong" in the city.

All told, the environment the floaters face runs from chilly to frigid. Granted, many of them may not mind the harsh living conditions if their only motive is to scrape together capital to send back to the farm (either for themselves or for their families). But some untold proportion is camping down in the cities with some measure of permanence, and for them, the closed class order, the biased ownership structure, the irregular labor market, the party-dominated political system, the flimsy patronage networks, the elitist educational system, the barren housing market, and the snobbish urban citizenry are bound to rankle. Even should some of these "foreign" folk manage to crash through or circumvent these several impediments, they too cannot fail to resent the effort called for.

[88]Zhang Youren, "Respecting Outsiders Should Become Social Public Morality," *SH* 6 (1987): 25.

[89]*South China Morning Post*, October 9, 1991, 10, reprinted in *FBIS*, October 10, 1991, 22.

[90]Moch, *Paths to the City*, 26, considers the urban community's attitude to have a bearing on migrants' chances for mobility; Portes and Rumbaut, *Immigrant America*, 87, remind us that "discrimination contributes to confinement to the low-wage segment."

CONCLUSION

This analysis of the fate of China's transients has laid out the paltry attributes they bear to a grim milieu. What does the presence of peasants in the cities—this new, reurbanization of China—help us to see about processes of class and community formation and the potential for a shift in social structure for outsiders in the wake of this country's market reforms?[91] And what does it allow us to conclude about the progress of the market itself in China's reform era and its influence in this arena?

A new two-class structure has been emerging in the cities of China: on the one side, those for whom jobs, housing, education, cheap food, and medical care are an entitlement, and on the other, those who must scramble for these goods or do without.[92] As this chapter has suggested, however, this breakdown is primarily, but not entirely, a matter of urban-*hukou* holders versus those with a rural registration. More precisely, those with an urban *hukou* can command the peak of the status hierarchy and the whole panoply of perquisites.[93]

In addition to them, though, is that minority of rural "outsiders" who lack the *hukou*, but who have somehow managed to acquire either the funds or the social connections to enjoy entrée to at least some of the benefits it provides.[94] One finding of this chapter is that, given all the barriers erected by the socialist system in China, this privileged group among the migrants is small relative to analogous groups in other countries.[95]

On the other side of the divide are those transients who inhabit the cities lacking not only an urban *hukou* but also the material and social wherewithal that could substitute for its absence.[96] For our first un-

---

[91]See Cohen, *The New Helots*, 98, on the notion that social differentiation and class formation arise from the effects of migration.

[92]See Chapter 3 in this volume on the privileged status of urban dwellers.

[93]Given the growing problem of unemployment ("waiting for employment") among urban youths, however, it is no longer strictly accurate to claim that all those with urban registrations receive all the benefits that classification once provided.

[94]One prominent example of such people not discussed here are the returned educated youth, permitted to resume city residence (but often without city registration) after being *xiaxiang*'d (sent down to the countryside) in the 1960s and 1970s.

[95]Thanks to Barry Naughton for noticing this point buried in my analysis.

[96]This group has yet one more distinction: this is the difference between those registered as temporary urban dwellers (they hold a *zhanzhuzheng*, or temporary living certificate) and those who dare to brave the odds and live unprotected without any proper legal label at all. This last group verges on the brink of illegality since its members "violate regulations" (*bu fuhe guiding*) and so are the most vulnerable of all.

hukou'd group, the prospects are reasonably good for climbing the newly modified status hierarchy that now shapes Chinese urban social life; for the second group that procedure promises to be lengthy and tortuous. In fact, the current opportunity structure for most of these folk away from home reflects the class order forged over decades by the Communist system: for the most part, peasants newly resident in the cities retain their old status even as they radically alter their ways of life.

What about the transition from plan to market? If the state is receding, are economic modes of making good replacing mandatory and heredi-tary statuses? The answer to these queries, simply, is no. There has not yet been a full "withdrawal of the state" in this domain (if in any other). What we are witnessing is at once the promise of the market—a force for freedom, for geographic, and perhaps for social mobility—but at the same time a process that very much bears the stamp of the prior state socialist order. That residue of the old state with its passive weight may be distinguished from the measures taken by the active, living, inten-tional state of today. This present state may be less powerful in keeping the floaters out of the cities than are the remnants of the class order long in place in limiting the assimilation and integration of these peoples into current city life.

That old state cannot simply "withdraw" without a trace. For despite the shrinkage of the plan and the drop in the prestige of the party, the institutions and regulations of the state, along with the social relations these structures and rules have fashioned, still linger. Indeed, even those most able to circumvent these institutions and rules must adopt modes of circumvention that themselves are marked by the old system. This refers to the continuing need to develop connections—*guanxi*—with party members and other gatekeepers in order to mediate the acquisition of capital, education, and other essentials necessary for upward mobility. Assimilation and later chances for mobility for all can occur only to the extent that not just market forces overcome and replace these state-defined blockades, but a new political system, accompanied by new class and civic orders, can evolve. What is required is a most complex trans-formation involving fundamental alterations on several fronts simulta-neously.

To judge from the data available, for the majority of the floaters, the probability of real integration and assimilation, based both on what they themselves can bring to bear and on the challenges they face in the

Table 5.1. *Random income statistics on earnings of urban floating-population workers*

Type of Work, City (if given)	Year	Income (yuan)	Other Information
a. Garbage collection	1990	400/month	
Textile worker	1990	220/month	
Self-employed peddler, Beijing	1990	300/month	
Waitress, foreign hotel	1990	500/month	
b. Carpenter, Harbin	1991	20–30/day	I imagine these people can't be assured of daily work
Tailor, Harbin	1991	3,000/month	
c. Hauler	1991	3–4/day	The source said $.64
d. Average	1991	1,000/yr.	This was given for an urban migrant worker
e. New Maids	1989	50/month	
f. Construction worker	1992	7–10/day	Usually one works 7 days/week
g. Restaurant worker	1992	80–150/month	Room and board are free
h. Scrap collector	1992	150/month	

Sources:
[a] "Searching for the Ideal Job," *China Daily*, July 24, 1991, 6.
[b] Interview in Harbin, July 4, 1991.
[c] Sheryl WuDunn, "China's Dismal Truth: 100 Million Out of Work," *New York Times*, July 4, 1992, 4.
[d] Xinhua, August 23, 1991, translated in *FBIS*, August 26, 1991, 65.
[e] Chen Yaohua, "China: Maid Service," *Third World Week*, April 7, 1989, 43. (Thanks to David Strand for the photocopy of this article.)
[f] Interviews at worksites in Guangzhou, Nanjing, and Wuhan.
[g] Interviews in restaurants in Nanjing, Wuhan, and Tianjin.
[h] Interview in Nanjing.

Table 5.2. *Average wages for workers in state/collective and foreign-related firms, 1990*

Type of Work	Income (yuan)
State factory worker[a]	2,140/yr.
Government employee	1,950/yr.
Joint ventures[b]	3,800/yr.

[a] This includes all staff and workers in both state- and collective-sector firms.
[b] The figure here is an average for all types of joint-venture workers.
Source: "Searching for the Ideal Job," *China Daily*, July 24, 1991, 6.

urban setting, is not high. Thus for the "peasant" population drifting into the cities' spaces and floating around them, there has not yet been an essential switch to marketization. Neither has there been any elemental decline in the ability of the Communist structure and its social system to sustain their old barriers against these new urban outcasts.

Part II

Urban culture and identities

Introduction

RICHARD KRAUS

The enormous economic and political changes associated with China's reform program reopen questions about personal and group identity that earlier seemed settled or that political authorities barred as illegitimate subjects. The five chapters in this section examine the changing role of urban culture, especially that of the artists who are its most self-conscious producers.

One of the many things arts "do" in society is provide cues to social identities, offering citizens a focus for questioning and understanding the meaning of their lives. Much art in China is explicitly prescriptive: Both Confucian and Maoist artists present models of good and bad behavior by which audiences may judge their own. While most people do not look on the arts as a set of explicit guidelines for their conduct, most discover that films, novels, or songs speak to them in sometimes unexpectedly personal ways. Even art offered primarily as entertainment may comfort one by addressing, however seriously or lightly, some real issue one faces in daily life.

A Western visitor trying to make sense of the politics of identity in China in the reform era can do worse than take along a copy of Stendhal's *Red and the Black*. Stendhal's postrevolutionary France was a nation of rapid industrialization, expanding commercial networks, and inconsistently authoritarian politics. Indeed, Stendhal's representation of ambition and insecurity in an ambience of uncertain rules and personal greed strikingly resembles the situation faced by urban Chinese at the end of their revolution. The cynicism of political restoration replaced revolutionary idealism in both nations.[1] Stendhal's French citizens, uncertain as to how to behave in the new era, look to art for cues. In fact, Stendhal instructs them to do so: The provincial love affair between

---

[1]Stendhal captures the spirit of restoration in his three basic questions: "When I arrive in a town I always ask: 1. Who are the twelve prettiest women? 2. Who are the twelve richest men? 3. Which man could have me hanged?" (Stendhal, *Memoirs of an Egotist*, trans. David Ellis [New York: Horizon Press, 1975], 131).

Julien Sorel and Madame de Renal might have ended better had they read the latest novels from Paris.

In Paris, Julien's relationship with Mme. de Renal would have been simplified very quickly; but in Paris, love is the child of fiction. The young tutor and his timid mistress would have found their position clarified for them in three or four novels, even in the couplets sung at the Gymnase [a Paris theater]. The novels would have outlined the parts they should play, have shown the model to be imitated; and sooner or later, vanity would have compelled Julien to imitate this model, although with no pleasure and perhaps boggling.[2]

China's leading artists are themselves typically city people, coping in their own lives with the changes their art sometimes explores, and usually reflects. With the major exceptions of peasant folk artists, rural-based amateurs in the elite arts, and some opera companies based in the countryside, the rest of China's artists live in cities. This is where the jobs are, either in the network of state- and party-dominated cultural and educational organizations, or in opportunities to earn money through the new cultural marketplace, which spreads, weblike, over urban China. Even those novels or movies that explore rural themes are likely to have been created by city folk. To talk about Chinese art today is to talk about urban China, the locus for cultural production and consumption.

Chinese cities are often cultural rivals. Beijing and Shanghai perennially compete for leadership. The former enjoys the advantage of being the national headquarters for all important arts bureaucracies, while the latter is simply so large that arts trends there cannot be ignored. In some periods, other cities became noteworthy centers. In the Maoist era, cities such as Shenyang and Xi'an were important centers of leftist arts. Other rivalries can be found in specific arts. The world of painting is centered in cities with major fine arts academies, especially Beijing and Hangzhou, but also Chengdu and Xi'an.

Today, Guangzhou's commercial culture is so popular that Mandarin-speaking performers often say a few words in Cantonese to their audiences just to be trendy. South of Guangzhou is Hong Kong, where the Cantonese culture is even more capitalist, and whose influence spreads rapidly as Hong Kong business extends its investments ever deeper into the People's Republic. The glamor associated with Hong Kong is likely to increase as all Chinese await its integration into China in 1997.

This section opens with Shaoguang Wang's analysis of changing pat-

[2]Stendhal, *The Red and the Black* (New York: New American Library, 1970), 46.

terns of leisure. Wang helps us understand how urban Chinese have enlarged the realm of private time by cutting back unpaid "voluntary" labor. The emergence of commercialized culture and newly available technologies for entertainment have reconfigured the relationship between public and private time, creating space for art and entertainment that is not in the service of state propaganda, even when produced under state auspices.

My own chapter explores the changing relationship between state and market in the arts, and its impact on professional artists. Despite intermittent and increasingly inept periods of repression, state supervision of the arts has clearly diminished as the cultural marketplace has expanded. China's artists can now develop themes much more to their own liking, and the cities are filled with a growing range of cultural products, from both China and abroad. Yet areas of profound discontent remain among professional artists, as they discover some of the market's side effects: vulgarity, job insecurity, and their own diminishing capacity to inspire a desire for political change in their audiences.

Julia Andrews and Gao Minglu examine one response to China's new cultural situation, the emergence of an avant-garde in painting. Cultural bureaucrats did little to aid and much to impede experimental painters, but many brave artists are pained to discover the indifference of commerce to their art. One artist set himself in the middle of an installation at a Beijing show, selling shrimp to viewers, thereby reenacting the commodified relationships of the new cultural market. These radical painters, who consciously rejected China's dominant tradition of realism, were distressed to find that realism, stripped of its former political content, continues to occupy a preeminent position in the market, as it had under a planned cultural order.

Su Wei and Wendy Larson show that in China, as in the contemporary United States, markets generate little demand for poetry. Whether or not one could understand the new poetry became a political question in the literary controversies of the 1980s, as successive schools of increasingly radical poets altered not only the meaning of poetry but also its social position. The writing of poetry once defined China's cultural and political elite; today, poetry has become an activity for specialists, writing for one another without reference to a broader audience.

Poetry and painting were closely joined in traditional elite culture, but little direct contact appears between these two avant-gardes in the reform period. Yet poetry and painting have clear parallels. Each became more stimulating for specialist practitioners, yet more distant from society. Maoists had judged artistic obscurity a crime; it now became a pleasure indulged by artists. Any avant-garde is positioned against society; in urban China, the taunts of these writers and painters helped redefine the position of cultural officials from a stance as "revolutionary" in 1976 to being overtly conservative in the 1990s.

If the mass audience was disregarded by the avant-garde, ordinary citizens did not lack for either lyrics or visual images. But they found them in the new commercial culture, not in elite art forms. For poetry, the words of new popular music, typically inspired or imported from Hong Kong or Taiwan, substituted for elite poetry. Urban residents found new and often arresting visual images in television and its arch rival, film.

Movies are big business in China, which has one of the largest film industries in the world. Yet the industry is embattled from many sides. Audiences are declining from the new threat of television, as in all other nations. One response is to make ever sillier movies, in a losing contest for audiences. Central political authorities also have long identified the film industry as a key point for propaganda. Even with the decline of the Maoist propaganda system, films are more closely regulated than any other art. In his chapter on film, Paul Pickowicz explores two themes: the use by the Chinese state of the international market to make money from bold new films, which until 1992 were little shown inside China, and the ways in which film directors have responded to a new culture of urban individualism. Pickowicz also takes up the "velvet prison" hypothesis. This concept from Eastern Europe suggests that the privileges enjoyed by artists in socialist societies make them complicit in the survival of their regimes.

The increased prosperity of Chinese cities has created new culture consumers, often passive and far removed from the alienated art of the avant-garde. The separation of artist from society is common in complex, market-oriented societies.[3] In China, the emergence of this problem is the more striking because of the vehemence with which the party formerly insisted that artists integrate themselves with workers, peasants, and soldiers. When artists visit factories today, they are more likely to spend time with their new patrons, the owners and managers,

---

[3]On the sociology of avant-gardes, see Diana Crane, *The Transformation of the Avant-Garde: The New York Art World, 1940–1985* (Chicago: University of Chicago Press, 1987).

although most recall years of being "sent down" for long or brief periods to gather party-approved inspiration for their work.

During the revolution, the Communist Party was clear that "works of art were needed primarily to show the people how to act and what to say, and not just to show them who their enemies were."[4] After 1949, the Communists regarded the cities as hostile territory, and made it difficult for artists to express the complexity of urban life. By denying a voice to urban Chinese who were not proletarians, the party disavowed their authenticity. The Maoists froze China sociologically, fearing that a sympathetic art would energize their enemies. Instead, Maoist officials chose to paper over differences of identity with a homogeneous, if false, voice.

When the Maoist aesthetic regime began to disintegrate in the late 1970s, artists and cultural officials agreed to expand the represented social universe of worker-peasant-soldier by adding a fourth category: the intellectual. Armed with eyeglasses and pens, images of intellectuals signaled their rehabilitation after the humiliations of the Cultural Revolution. But there was no subtlety in presentation of this fourth approved social identity. A typical (male) intellectual was engraved on a new fifty-yuan banknote, face in profile alongside the familiar worker and peasant. A popular movie traced the life of China's famous geologist, Li Siguang. But such efforts only reiterated the new official line that intellectuals had become a part of the working class; thus their identity (and only *one* identity was appropriate) was simply that of the urban worker, only maybe a little brainier. The new intellectual was stalwart, eager for change, patriotic, capable of great suffering, and remote from the real-life experiences of most urban Chinese. As Bonnie McDougall described this stereotyping on the eve of market reform, "cultural authorities have insisted on postulating a single, mass, homogeneous audience for cultural products."[5]

The reforms broke the notion of simple prepackaged identities for the urban population to wear, whether they fit or not, like cheap shoes. No longer were artists required to alternate between relentless militancy and cheery optimism. The 1980s systematically unmasked the myth of class

[4]David Holm, *Art and Ideology in Revolutionary China* (Oxford: Oxford University Press, 1991), 94.
[5]Bonnie S. McDougall, "Writers and Performers, Their Works, and Their Audiences in the First Three Decades," in McDougall, *Popular Chinese Literature and Performing Arts in the People's Republic of China 1949–1979* (Berkeley: University of California Press, 1984), 280.

purity, permitting both artists and audiences to revel in a mutual exploration of more human images of urban China, as both producers and consumers of culture tried to keep pace with the economic and social changes that enveloped them.

"All that is solid melts into air," commented Marx and Engels, observing an earlier rush toward market-based industrialization: "all fixed, fast-frozen relations, with their train of ancient and venerable prejudices and opinions, are swept away, all new-formed ones become antiquated before they can ossify."[6] Many Chinese crave understanding of the disorientations of rapidly changing urban life. Novelist Zhang Jie shows her urban characters learning "modern" behavior and language from the arts, much like those of Stendhal: " 'I've never loved anyone else as much as you,' he swore. That is how characters in modern stories, films and TV often talk. Previously such talk was confined to foreign stories, films and TV, but now they talk that way in China too."[7]

Many of China's most sophisticated artists have rejected politics by denying explicitly that their work is *about* anything. Such denials, however, are unlikely to prevent readers, viewers, and audiences from reaching their own conclusions, as ordinary citizens try to comprehend and reconstruct their roles amid the confusion of city life.

[6]Karl Marx and Friedrich Engels, "Manifesto of the Communist Party," in Marx and Engels, *Basic Writings on Politics and Philosophy*, ed. Lewis S. Feuer (Garden City, N.Y.: Anchor, 1959), 10.
[7]Zhang Jie, "What's Wrong with Him?" in *As Long as Nothing Happens, Nothing Will* (London: Virago Press, 1988), 3–4.

6

The politics of private time:
changing leisure patterns in urban China

SHAOGUANG WANG

All complex societies distinguish between public and private, but the definition of the private sphere varies from one society to another, and even within one society it varies over time. This chapter examines the shifting boundary between public and private in contemporary China by reviewing changing leisure patterns in the last forty years.

THE POLITICS OF PRIVATE TIME

The private sphere has two dimensions: spatial and temporal. In discussing the significance of the private sphere, many have focused their attention on private space. What has been neglected is the fact that private time, no less than private space, is an integral part of the private sphere. Both are necessary to the creation and maintenance of the private sphere—a cup of coffee yields little satisfaction if there is no time to drink it.

Even under the most democratic system, work is still tightly disciplined and controlled. However, few question the idea that leisure time should be private time. A universal principle seems to have long been accepted everywhere: "The master's right in the master's time, and the workman's right in his own time."[1] It is in leisure rather than work that individuals see themselves as free to act and develop as they please. That

[1] Quoted from P. Baily, *Leisure and Class in Victorian England* (London: Routledge and Kegan Paul, 1978), 180.

149

is why the overwhelming majority of sociological definitions equate leisure with free time.[2]

Leisure has also been considered essential for human development. Aristotle, for instance, argues: "Nature herself requires that we should be able, not only to work well, but to use leisure well; for . . . the first principle of all action is leisure."[3] Probably no one has attached more importance to leisure than Marx does. According to Marx: "Time is the room of human development. A man who has no free time to dispose of, whose whole lifetime apart from the mere physical interruption of sleep, meals and so forth, is absorbed by his labor for the capitalist, is less than a beast of burden."[4]

For obvious reasons, however, leisure has to be kept within bounds. First of all, it seems necessary to define how much time should be allocated to work and how much to leisure. The historical record shows that this issue has given rise to social conflicts since the beginning of industrialization.[5] More important, free time is open to abuse. The list of leisure abuses is both long and familiar. Free time is often associated with crime, violence, and physical and psychological demoralization. Authoritative voices have long expressed their concern about the possible consequences of unbridled leisure. There have always been voices urging people to use leisure "properly," "correctly," "fruitfully," "wisely," "constructively," and above all "rationally." The problem lies in who has the right to decide which leisure activities are acceptable and which are not. In traditional societies, it was the leaders of "culture" who bore a heavy responsibility for determining correct ways of employing leisure.[6] In modern times, however, the regulation of leisure activities has increasingly involved the exercise of state power. By cultivating or imposing a particular ideal of acceptable leisure activity, the modern state, capitalist and Communist alike, aims to draw all social groups into "rational recreation" to curb the potential dangers of free time.[7]

[2]R. W. Vickerman, "The New Leisure Society: An Economic Analysis," *Futures* 10, no. 3 (1980): 192.

[3]Aristotle, *Politics*, 1337a 31.

[4]Karl Marx, *Selected Works* (London: Lawrence and Wishart, 1968), 219.

[5]For example, see E. P. Thompson, "Time-Work-Discipline and Industrial Capitalism," *Past and Present* 38 (1967): 56–97; and Douglas A. Reids, "The Decline of Saint Monday: 1766–1876," *Past and Present* 78 (1976): 76–101.

[6]W. Sutherland, "A Philosophy of Leisure," *Annals of the American Academy* (September 1957): 136.

[7]For a discussion of the role of the capitalist state, see John Clarke and Chas Critcher,

Thus "free time" is "free" only in the sense that time at one's command is free of duties. Like everything else, the "free" time is more or less regulated. "Bread and Circuses" was already recognized as an effective means of social control in the time of the Roman Empire. Because leisure plays an increasingly important part in people's everyday life today, the state must take notice of leisure activities. In order to maintain the status quo, the state needs to shape a "disciplined" and (physically and psychologically) "healthy" population. To do so, it has to suppress "immoral," "irrational," and "dangerous" activities, on the one hand, and to inculcate "elevated" modes of social and moral behavior, on the other.

The politics of leisure is contained not only in such control efforts on the part of the state but also in the active attempts of the governed to free themselves from restraints imposed by the state.[8] State hegemony is by no means impenetrable. The governed often can "penetrate, neutralize, and negate that hegemony."[9]

Rather than a manifestation of freedom, leisure thus is, more often than not, merely permissible behavior.[10] This is what leisure signifies, and this is why the study of leisure could provide a breach to investigate state-society relations.

The focus of this chapter therefore is not "leisure" as such. Its real aim is to explore what a study of leisure can tell us about the nature of contemporary China. To do so, we first have to answer the following questions: How much breathing time and space do Chinese people enjoy? How does the Chinese Communist state define "healthy" and "unhealthy" leisure? What are the mechanisms through which the state enforces its rules of legitimate and illegitimate pleasure? Have leisure patterns changed over the last forty years? To what extent is the discourse on leisure related to people's daily practice of leisure? Through focusing on the changing structural location of leisure in the overall social, economic, and political context, the vicissitudes of state power in the Chinese society can be revealed.

The Devil Makes Work: Leisure in Capitalist Britain (London: Macmillan, 1985), 122–143.

[8]Chris Rojek, *Capitalism and Leisure Theory* (London: Tavistock Publications, 1985), 180–81.

[9]James Scott, *The Weapons of the Weak* (New Haven: Yale University Press, 1989), 336.

[10]For instance, see Stephen G. Jones, *Workers at Play: A Social and Economic History of Leisure 1918–1939* (London: Routledge and Kegan Paul, 1986); and Rojek, *Capitalism and Leisure Theory*.

LEISURE IN MAO'S CHINA

The control of leisure can generally be achieved in one of three ways or in their combinations: regulating the amount of leisure time, regulating the forms of leisure, and regulating the content of leisure. The Chinese Communist regime tried all three before and during the Cultural Revolution (hereafter, CR).

Regulating the amount of leisure time. In Marx's view, leisure represents a haven from the "dull compulsion of economic relations." He believed that an important measure of wealth in a Communist society is the quantity of leisure time, time that people would be able to spend on the "harmonious development of their personalities."[11] But according to the Maoist interpretation of Marx, leisure is merely the time given to workers for their recuperation. Leisure is meaningful only if people use the time to rest, to reduce stress, or to enhance their physical and mental ability so that they can work more productively later. That is why the following quotation from Lenin was popular during the Maoist era: "Those who don't know how to rest don't know how to work."[12]

Since leisure was supposed to be subordinate to work, it was often sacrificed to boost production. In the 1950s through the 1970s, Chinese planners and managers believed that it was legitimate to cut leisure time so long as it offered workers enough physical restoration. It was not uncommon in those years for people to be asked to work extra hours and even extra shifts with little or no compensation. Moreover, party and Youth League members and political activists were often organized to undertake "voluntary labor" on Sundays and holidays.[13] Such practices were carried to extremes during the Great Leap Forward period, when millions of Chinese were driven so hard that they worked for months without even sufficient time to sleep. Frederick Noisal, a Toronto *Globe and Mail* reporter in Beijing, wrote in 1959 that he had seen on many occasions "the weary workers, the worn-out women, the peasants dead beat with physical fatigue." What he had witnessed led

---

[11]Karl Marx, *Economic and Philosophical Manuscripts of 1844* (London: Lawrence and Wishart, 1970), 737.

[12]Liu Zijiu, "Yishou zhua shengchan, Yishou zhua shenghuo" (Be concerned with production as well as the well-being of the masses), *Chongtian genjin he kexue texin* (Boundless enthusiasm and scientific attitude) (Hong Kong: Shannian Publications, 1959).

[13]Mei Qi, "Yingdang zunzhong bieren di ziyou" (Respect others' freedom), *Zhongguo qingnian* (Chinese youth, hereafter ZGQN) 12 (June 1956): 31.

him to the conclusion that "complete leisure as the Westerner knows it is very rare in China. The endless cycle of life in China today consists of working, studying, eating and sleeping."[14]

People might put up with the weariness for a while but they could not do so forever no matter how loyal they were to the regime. The Chinese leaders quickly realized that the great physical and mental strain being imposed on people might become counterproductive. Between November 1958 and May 1960, the party issued at least two directives requiring that "the masses" be guaranteed eight hours to sleep and a few more hours of "free time."[15] However, here leisure was still considered passive relaxation and restoration of energy for work.[16] More important, the state had no intention of giving up its control over time. The two documents in fact sanctioned that "the masses' time" should be subject to "unitary arrangements."[17]

Regulating the forms of leisure. In Chinese political culture, the public interest had always occupied "a position of sacrosanct priority," and the Communist revolution reinforced this corporate concept of interest.[18] Like everything else, the forms of leisure in the years before and during the CR reflected this tendency. In the name of "collectivism," it became an unwritten rule that leisure activities should take the form of group action. Students and workers were often organized to go to the movies, sporting events, dances, and the like together regardless of their personal preferences. Even reading was often dictated. Party and Youth League branches issued lists of "recommended books," and discussion sessions were often scheduled afterward so that everyone felt compelled to read the assigned books. Those who failed to participate in officially organized leisure activities risked being criticized for "cutting themselves off from the masses" and "lacking collectivist spirit."[19]

[14]Charles Taylor, ed., *China Hands: The Globe and Mail in Peking* (Toronto: McClelland and Stewart, 1984), 26.

[15]Ma Qibin and Chen Wenbin, *Zhongguo gongchandang zhizheng sishinian 1949–1989* (The Chinese Communist Party: Forty years in power, 1949–1989) (Beijing: Zhonggong dangshi ziliao chubanshe, 1989), 185.

[16]See an editorial of *Chinese Youth*, "Laoyi jiehe shi weiliao baozhen chixu dayaojin" (To continue the Great Leap Forward, we have to strike a proper balance between work and rest), ZGQN 12 (June 1960): 30–31.

[17]Ma and Chen, *Zhongguo gongchandang zhizheng sishinian*, 185.

[18]Lowell Dittmer, "Public and Private Interest and the Participatory Ethic in China," in Victor C. Falkenheim, ed., *Citizens and Groups in Contemporary China* (Ann Arbor: Center for Chinese Studies of the University of Michigan, 1987), 17–66.

[19]Mei Qi, "Yingdang Zunzhong bieren di ziyou"; Guo Lin, "Weishenmo yiding yao

Since "collectivism" was highly valued, not surprisingly, team sports such as basketball, soccer, and volleyball were strongly promoted by the government in factories, army units, and schools. Team sports were used to cultivate such desirable personal traits as group loyalty, willingness to cooperate with others, self-sacrifice, and so on.

Regulating the content of leisure. Whereas, in the 1950s, the state had absorbed a great deal of the population's time and started to regulate the ways in which people conducted their leisure activities, in the 1960s and 1970s the regime went further in trying to monopolize people's spare time by specifying the content of permissible leisure activities.

In the early 1960s, the party began to develop a new thesis of leisure: Spare time could not be a "political vacuum"; it was filled by either "proletarian ideas" or "bourgeois ideas." Because of this ideological innovation, leisure became increasingly politicized. By the end of the CR, the politicization of leisure had passed through three stages.

In the first stage (roughly 1960–62), the politicization was relatively mild. People were reminded that it was politically dangerous to enjoy pastimes in a carefree mood. Although they might have been successfully socialized to the Communist ideology, the party thought it necessary to continually reinforce their earlier learning at work as well as in leisure. That was the only way to keep them from slipping into the "mire of bourgeois ideology." In particular, people were advised to be sensitive to "hidden scripts" underlying movies, dramas, music, poems, novels, painting, and the like, especially those imported from abroad and those produced before the liberation. They were also told that sports were not as innocent as they believed. "Cups and medals mania" (*jinbiao zhuyi*), which was said to be still prevalent in China then, was criticized as a manifestation of "magnified individualism" (*fangda di geren zhuyi*). Games were supposed to promote only "collectivism." "Pure leisure" did not exist. Leisure was seen as a "battlefield between the proletariat and the bourgeoisie."[20]

qiangqiu yizhi" (Why do we have to impose rigid uniformity) *ZGQN* 12 (June 1956): 30–31; and Shang Qi, "Guanche ziyuan yuanzhe, gengjia fengfu duocai di kaizhan kewei huodong" (Implement the principle of freedom and develop a more colorful program for extracurricular activities), *ZGQN* 17 (September 1956): 8–9.

[20] Ma Ye, "Kan dianying buneng zhishi weiliao tu qingsong" (Moviegoing is not just for fun), *ZGQN* 15 (August 1960): 24; Ma Xiuyun, "Woman shi zenyang yindao qingnian guohao yeyu shenghuo di" (How do we guide young workers in their leisure activities), *ZGQN* 4 (February 1961): 24.

Whereas during the first stage people had been asked to make personal judgments about what was "right" and what was "wrong" and the party had given a few hints, during the second stage (1963–65) the party began to make judgments for them, probably because it had become disappointed by what had been achieved without explicit direction.

In 1963, two modern dramas, *Never Forget* and *The Young Generation*, were publicized. Each had a negative character, Ding Shaochun in the former and Lin Yusheng in the latter. Ding was criticized for having forgotten his working-class origin partly because he had developed a "bourgeois habit"—hunting. Lin was criticized because he dreamed of marrying a pretty girl and enjoying a "bourgeois lifestyle" together: "Every evening, we may read a novel or poems while listening to music, or we may go to a movie or concert. On Sunday, we may take a walk in the park or visit friends." Both dramas were produced in every major city and eventually were made into movies. Workers and students were organized to watch them. National and local newspapers and journals devoted special columns to them. By presenting the two negative examples, the party hoped to teach people, among other things, what they were not supposed to do in their leisure time.[21] As for what people were supposed to do with their leisure, the answer could be found in the titles of a group of essays appearing in an issue of *Zhongguo qingnian* (Chinese youth) of 1964: "Value Your Spare Time," "Leisure Activity Should Serve One's Work," "You Must Behave Yourself Even in After-Hours," and "Spare Time Must Be Devoted to Studying."[22]

In the mid-1960s, official publications also began to warn people that "pursuing a hobby may sap one's will to make progress" (*wan wu sang zhi*). As a result, fanciers of hunting, fishing, collecting stamps, keeping pet birds, growing flowers, and all kinds of hobbies faced a hard choice: either giving up their avocations or preparing to be criticized for "wallowing in petty bourgeois amusements." Moreover, many movies, plays, and books began to be singled out as "poisonous weeds," which were soon to disappear from the public scene altogether. China thus had become an "unexciting society" even before the CR.

During the CR (1966–76), state intrusion into the daily life of the population reached such a degree that demarcation between "private time" and "public time" became meaningless. Maoist leaders were no

[21]Bai Ye, "Zouchu geren zhuyi xiaotiandi" (Do away with individualism), *ZGQN* 24 (December 1963): 10–11.
[22]*ZGQN* 8–9 (May 1964): 46–47.

longer content with the elimination of "poisonous weeds." They now wanted to saturate people with nothing but Maoist propaganda. The "Smashing the Four Olds" campaign at the beginning of the CR created an unwritten rule that no leisure activities were legitimate unless they were officially sanctioned. Thus, for several years, 800 million Chinese were allowed to watch only eight "revolutionary model plays" and a few dozen carefully selected films. In the later years of the CR, more movies were produced and more books published, but they were largely propaganda in crude artistic forms. They did not even pretend to provide people with relaxation, because the term "leisure" itself by then had become a dirty word.[23]

With the state completing its monopolization of private time (not only the length of private time, but also the ways of spending it), China became a totally dictated society in the late 1960s and the early 1970s.

LEISURE IN DENG'S CHINA

Change in the state's attitude toward leisure. The nature of leisure has dramatically changed since the end of the CR. The 1980s were distinguished from the previous three decades first by a change of official tone. From the 1950s to the 1970s, what the Chinese government had attempted to achieve was to restrain all leisure activities except those harmonious with the state ideology. In the 1980s, however, the pragmatic Deng regime followed a different rule of thumb: people were now allowed to spend their spare time however they pleased so long as those activities posed no threat to the existing social order. It does not follow that the state gave up its control over leisure. In fact, whether or not a certain type of behavior posed a threat to the existing social order was still subject to the regime's discretion. Nevertheless, leisure no longer always had to fit into the schematic straitjacket of the state ideology. After the CR, the party became willing to relinquish its control over leisure partially because it had learned that the monopolization of private time could result in a cheerless society, which was not in its best interests. Moreover, since the party had devalued "collectivism" and no

---

[23]Ironically, in 1967 and 1968 when the CR was at its climax, many Chinese found for the first time in years that they had plenty of free time and that no public authorities existed to impose officially sanctioned leisure patterns. See Shaoguang Wang, *Failure of Charisma: The Chinese Cultural Revolution in Wuhan* (Ph.D. dissertation, Cornell University, 1990), 490–491.

longer "took class struggle as the key link," it made sense for it to recognize relaxation, entertainment, and relatively free choice as valid elements of leisure.

Thus, the demarcation between "public" and "private" time re-emerged, although the boundary line is still ambiguous. As part of the new "social contract," the state developed a new guideline for managing leisure activities: "Encouraging those conducive to the maintenance of the existing social order, allowing those harmless to the existing social order, and suppressing those inimical to the existing social order."[24]

The increase in leisure time. Chinese time-budget surveys generally divide everyday human behavior into four categories: work (including commuting to work), physiological needs, housework, and free time. Time spent on physiological needs (sleeping, eating, and personal hygiene) is obviously the least elastic. Thus the increase of leisure time depends on reducing the amount of time spent on work and housework. Since 1949, the official work week in China has been eight hours a day, forty-eight hours a week.[25] But, as discussed in the previous section, actual hours spent at work were much longer in the first three decades of the People's Republic, if various nonstandard forms of work, such as nonpaid "voluntary" overtime and participation in compulsory and semi-compulsory political activities were included. After the CR, as voluntary work and political study have gradually lost luster, actual working time has been significantly shortened. But, because no time-budget surveys were taken before 1980, it is impossible to document exactly how significant the reduction was.

The housework burden has always been substantial, occupying a large portion of the nonworking time of Chinese households. But thanks to the proliferation of various timesaving machines (refrigerators, washing machines, gas ovens, sewing machines and the like), the improvement of

---

[24]*Zhongguo guangbo dianshi nianjian 1989* (Chinese broadcasting and television yearbook, 1989, hereinafter *DSNJ*) (Beijing: Zhongguo guangbo xueyuan chubanshe, 1989), 336.

[25]Starting in 1994, China has reduced the official work week to forty-four hours. Chinese Statistical Bureau, *Zhongguo shehui tongji ziliao, 1985* (Chinese social statistics yearbook, 1985) (Beijing: Zhongguo tongji chubanshe, 1985), 307–8; *Zhongguo shehui tongji ziliao, 1987,* 281–84; and Qing Nianbing, "Da chengshi zhigong shenghuo shijian fenpai he liyong wenti di chubu yanjiu" (A preliminary research report on the time-budget of Chinese workers living in large cities), *Shehuixue yanjiu* (Research in sociology) 1 (1990): 92–102.

Table 6.1. *Leisure time (in hours and minutes)*

	1980[a]	1982[b]	1984[c]	1986[d]	1988[e]	1991[f]
Free Time	2.21	3.26	3.16	3.59	4.31	4.48

[a]Calculated from Wang Yalin and Li Jinrong, "Chengshi zhigong jiawei laodong yanjiu" (A study of urban residents' housework), *Zhongguo shehui kexui* (Social science in China) 1 (1982): 60.

[b]Calculated from the Chinese Statistical Bureau, *Zhongguo shehui tongji ziliao 1985* (Chinese social statistics, 1985) (Beijing: Zhongguo tongji chubanshe, 1985) 307.

[c]Calculated from the Chinese Statistical Bureau, *Zhongguo shehui tongji ziliao 1987* (Chinese social statistics, 1987) (Beijing: Zhongguo tongji chubanshe, 1987) 281–82.

[d]Qing Nianbing, "Da chengshi zhigong shenghuo shijian fenpai he liyong wenti di chubu yanjiu" (A preliminary research report on time-budget of Chinese residents of big cities), *Shehuixue yanjiu* (Research in sociology) 1 (1990): 92–102.

[e]Calculated from Lu Hanlong, "Laizhi geti di shehui baogao" (A sociological study of individual lifestyles) *Shehuixue yanjiu* (Research in sociology) 1 (1990): 83.

[f]Chinese Statistical Bureau, *Zhongguo shehui fazhan ziliao 1992* (Chinese statistics on social development, 1992) (Beijing: Zhongguo tongji chubanshe, 1992), 114.

commodity supply, the rise of the service sector, and, more important, the growing purchasing power of the average Chinese family, the time spent on housework also drastically declined in the 1980s.[26]

As a result of the reduction of actual working time and housework, the total amount of free time has increased (Table 6.1).[27]

Changes in leisure patterns. The demonopolization of leisure time occurred simultaneously with the advent of tape recording and television in China. On average, China produced only 3,000 black-and-white television sets per annum in the 1960s and 3,000 color television sets per annum in the 1970s. And most of the televisions then belonged to workunits rather than individual households.[28] By the end of the 1980s, however, over 90 percent of urban households owned at least one television

[26]Qing Nianbing, ibid., 95–96, 100–101; and Zhang Jianguo, "Gaige chujing liao zhigong shenghuo fangshi di bianhua" (Reform has resulted in changes in Chinese workers' lifestyle), *Shidai* (Time) 1 (January 1987): 7–10.

[27]Because nationwide time-budget surveys have not been conducted, my estimates about leisure time are based on regional surveys. The comparability of the surveys is, of course, far from perfect. Nevertheless with supporting evidence, I am reasonably confident that the table represents the general trends in China. For instance, in Beijing, the daily amount of free time increased from 3.5 hours to almost 4 hours in the four years between 1982 and 1986. The trend in other cities may be more or less the same. Of course, the situation varies tremendously from place to place and from social group to social group. All statistical data available are too general for us to gauge variations.

[28]*DSNJ 1989*, 331–32.

set.[29] Before 1980, most Chinese had never seen a tape recorder. Now tape recorders have become a common household item in urban China.[30] In the last few years, VCRs, CDs, and karaokes have also become familiar items in Chinese households.

These modern entertainment devices have brought revolutionary changes to the ways in which Chinese spend their leisure time. Before 1980, the dominant free-time activities were probably reading, listening to the radio, moviegoing, socializing with friends (gossiping), and simply doing nothing. In 1985, television audiences for the first time exceeded radio's.[31] A 1987 nationwide survey showed that on average, every urban resident spent 1.5 to 2.0 hours in front of the television each day, which accounted for almost half the time available for leisure.[32] Numerous recent surveys indicate that since 1982 television viewing has become the most popular leisure activity.[33]

The rise of television was accompanied by a great decline in viewing motion pictures. For a typical Chinese urban resident, moviegoing declined from once every two weeks in 1979 to once every four weeks in 1985.[34] Thereafter, movie audiences began to stabilize. In 1990, 4.3 billion urban residents went to movie theaters, which, though representing a 5 billion drop from the record of 1979, shows that going to the movies is still an important form of leisure.[35]

Equally significant in the last few years has been the rise of the VCR,

[29]*DSJN 1988*, 401; Institute of Journalism, Chinese Academy of Social Science, *Zhongguo xinwen nianjian, 1988* (Chinese journalism yearbook 1988, hereinafter *XWNJ*) (Beijing: Zhongguo guangbo chubanshe, 1988), 192.

[30]Chinese Statistical Bureau, *Zhongguo tongji nianjian, 1990* (Chinese statistics yearbook, 1990, hereinafter *TJNJ*) (Beijing: Zhongguo tongji chubanshe, 1990), 294.

[31]*XWNJ 1989*, 217.

[32]Qing Nianbing, "Da Chengshi Zhigong shenghuo" 102; Li Yuanpu and Yen Jinchang, "Tianjin shi jumin yeyu shenghuo chouyang diaocha" (Random samples of Tianjin residents' leisure pattern), *Liaowang* (Outlook) 22 (November 1986): 12; and Deng Tongtong, "Dianshi wenhua shixiang lu" (Reflections on TV culture), *Shehui* (Society) 7 (July 1990): 35.

[33]Zhang Yun, Cai He, and Jiang Shanhe, "Qingnian gongren shenghuo fangshi xianzhuang tedian yanjiu" (Research on new characteristics of young workers' lifestyle), *Shehui kexue zhanxian* (Social science front) 3 (June 1982): 101–8; Mai Jungang, "Qiye gaige yu zhigong xianxia shenghuo fangshi di bianhua" (Enterprise reform and changes in workers' leisure pattern), *Shehui diaocha yu yanjiu* (Social investigation and research) 7 (July 1985): 86–89; and Sun Zaiqing, "Dui zhigong yeyu shenghuo di sanxiang diaocha" (Three investigations on workers' leisure activities), *Qunzhong wenhua* (Mass culture) 11 (November 1986): 11–12.

[34]Chinese Motion Picture Association, *Zhongguo dianying nianjian 1986* (Chinese motion picture yearbook 1986, hereafter *DYNJ*) (Beijing: Zhongguo dianying chubanshe, 1986), 1–5, 11–13.

[35]*Liaowang*, February 18, 1991, 41.

which provides an alternative to both movies and television. Recent estimates have calculated that there are already 60 million to 70 million
VCRs in China, and that the number is rapidly growing. In large cities
like Shanghai and Beijing, at least one out of every five families owns a
VCR, and in Guangzhou the ratio has hit 40 percent.[36] In the early to
mid-1980s, when VCRs were still rare in Chinese cities, many private
entrepreneurs and even state agencies (such as the Workers' Cultural
Palace) found it profitable to open "video rooms." Thus, video rooms
sprang up like mushrooms throughout the country.[37] While the contents
of movies and television are usually subject to relatively strict state control, the government has found it difficult, if not impossible, to monitor
what is being shown in largely profit-driven video rooms. In fact, for
several years, the state simply had no videos to supply. Before 1984,
imports from Hong Kong, Taiwan, and foreign countries had dominated
video rooms. It was estimated in 1985 that about 2,000 "illegal" titles
were circulating in the country.[38] In comparison with tedious Chinese-
made movies and television series, foreign videos were sensually exciting,
which attracted large audiences. Instead of going to movie theaters or
staying home watching television, many, especially young people, became frequent visitors to video rooms.[39]

Apart from watching television, movies, and videos, other popular
leisure activities include listening to radio, listening to records, and playing mahjong, billiards, and video games. The last three items deserve
some attention, for "mahjong fever," "billiards fever," and "video-game
fever" have hit Chinese cities in recent years.

Since 1949, the Chinese government has discouraged mahjong, because playing it was considered a form of gambling. At the beginning
of the CR, mahjong became a target of the "Smashing the Four Olds"
campaign. As a result, mahjong disappeared altogether in China for
more than a decade. The revival of mahjong started in Guangdong in
the early 1980s, and in the last four or five years, "mahjong fever" has
engulfed the entire country. Not only do retirees, housewives, private
business people and workers play mahjong, but government officials,
university professors, college students, and even high school students
also indulge in the game. In Guangzhou, a report suggests, almost every

[36]China News Agency (Beijing), February 12, 1992.
[37]*DSNJ 1988*, 17–70.
[38]*DYNJ 1986*, 1–6.
[39]*DSNJ 1989*, 344.

family has members who play mahjong.[40] Gambling has made a strong comeback in the wake of mahjong's revival, because only with betting is mahjong exciting. For many, gambling provided a new form of diversion and excitement, with the prospect of monetary gain.[41] Although in most cases betting was small in scale, just a few cents or a cigarette a game, concern has been growing that gambling may bring many people to ruin.[42]

If mahjong is popular among all age groups and all social groups, billiards is favored mainly by young workers, and video games by teenagers. Thousands of billiard tables and video game machines have been installed in Chinese cities, big and small. Many Chinese are still living in overcrowded, poorly ventilated, and dimly lit apartments. For those youths who find their homes restrictive, the street is a better place to spend spare time. Thus street corners where billiard tables and video game machines are placed are usually where young people from working-class families like to hang out. Playing billiards or video games not only brings excitement, it also forges an informal collective life for those young people who find the surrounding world increasingly alienating.[43]

Reading has continued to be an important form of leisure.[44] Now Chinese readers have much wider choices than a decade ago. The number of books published rose from fewer than 5,000 in 1970 to 17,000 in 1979 to 88,000 in 1991 (Figure 6.1).[45] Expansion of newspapers has been even more remarkable. Between 1970 and 1989 the number of newspapers grew from 42 (all were national or provincial party organs) to 852 (Figure 6.2). A similar pattern is observable in magazines—the total number increased from 21 in 1970 to 6,500 in 1991 (see Figure 6.3).[46]

[40]China News Agency (Guangzhou), January 1, 1992.

[41]Lu Hanlong, "Laizhi geti di shehui baogao" (A sociological study of individual lifestyles), *Shehuixue yanjiu* 1 (1990): 84.

[42]Wei Yunheng, Liu Yuxun, and Xin Minghua, "Dongbei sansheng dufeng toushi (Gambling crazy in the three northeastern provinces), *Liaowang* 7–8 (February 18, 1991): 19–20; Chen Lu, "Dubo qishi lu" (Reflections on gambling), *Zhongguo zhichun* (China spring) 2 (February 1991): 77–80; and Zhong Shu, "Zhongguo dalu shaoshu getihu di shenghuo baitai" (Private businessmen's lifestyle), *Zhongguo shibao zhoukai* (China time weekly) 3 (January 19–25, 1992): 71.

[43]Yun Lan, "Fangguan jiehe, jiji daoxiang, tuidong wenhua shichang jiankang pengbo fazhai" (Combine "relaxation" and "regulation," actively guide the development of cultural markets), *Qunzhong wenhua* 10 (October 1989): 9–11.

[44]Wang Haiping, "Nanjing qingnian di dushu re" (Reading fever among youth in Nanjing), *Baxiaoshi yiwai* (After eight hours) 3 (March 1987): 11.

[45]New China News Agency (Beijing), December 29, 1991.

[46]*Shijie ribao* (World journal), January 12, 1992.

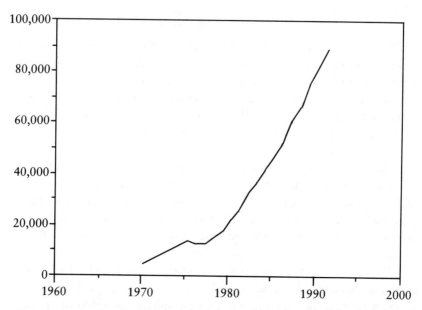

Figure 6.1. Number of books published in China. *Source*: Chinese Statistical Bureau, *Zhongguo tongji nianjian, 1991* (Chinese statistics yearbook, 1991) (Beijing: Zhongguo tongji chubanshe, 1991), 755.

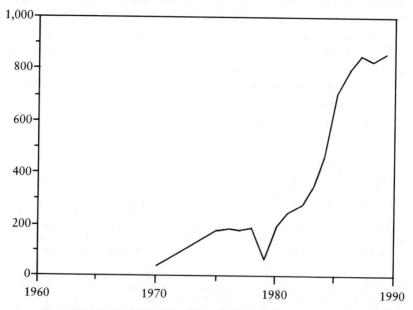

Figure 6.2. Number of newspapers published in China. *Source*: Chinese Statistical Bureau, *Zhongguo tongji nianjian, 1991* (Chinese statistics yearbook, 1991) (Beijing: Zhongguo tongji chubanshe, 1991), 756.

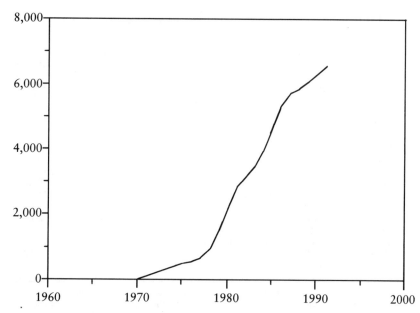

Figure 6.3. Number of journals published in China. *Source*: Chinese Statistical Bureau, *Zhongguo tongji nianjian, 1991* (Chinese statistics yearbook, 1991) (Beijing: Zhongguo tongji chubanshe, 1991), 755.

"Popular" readings account for a large share of the expansion of books, newspapers, and magazines. Among the sixteen magazines with circulation of a million copies or more in 1987, for instance, 13 were "popular" (Table 6.2).[47]

Do those facts suggest that Chinese leisure has been directed more toward distractions and diversions than toward creative recreation? Not necessarily. In fact, minority pursuits have also been on the increase. Take fishing as an example. In May 1983, at the opening ceremony of the First Chinese-Japanese Fishing Contest, a senior leader, Wang Zhen, praised fishing as a "healthy sport." Three months later, the Chinese Fishing Association was founded in Beijing and a special magazine, *Chinese Fishing*, began to be published. By the end of 1988, 24 of the 30 provinces had established fishing associations with a total membership of over 30 million. While sales of many magazines were

[47]The other three, *Honggi* (Red flag), *Banyuetan* (Fortnightly), and *Gongchan dangyuan* (Communists) were subscribed mainly by work-units rather than by private citizens. See *Zhongguo chuban nianjian, 1988* (Chinese publication yearbook, 1988, hereinafter *CBNJ*), 120–21.

Table 6.2. *Sixteen most widely circulated magazines in 1987*
(in tens of thousands)

Magazine	Circulation
1. *Gushihui* (Story-telling session)[a]	494.6
2. *Banyuetan* (Fortnightly)[e]	457.0
3. *Hongqi* (Red flag)[e]	282.0
4. *Jiating* (Family)[b]	255.2
5. *Qingnian yidai* (Young generation)[c]	235.3
6. *Gushi dawang* (Story king)[a]	173.7
7. *Duzhe wenzhai* (Readers' digest)[d]	163.6
8. *Gongchan dangyuan* (Communists)[e]	160.8
9. *Minzhu yu fazhi* (Democracy and rule of law)[d]	159.2
10. *Liaoning qingnian* (Liaoning youth)[c]	150.0
11. *Nongmin wenzhai* (Peasants' digest)[d]	133.4
12. *Zhongguo qingnian* (Chinese youth)[c]	125.5
13. *Zhi ying* (Bosom friends)[c]	116.5
14. *Shanhai jing* (Book of mountains and seas)[a]	109.6
15. *Zhongguo funu* (Chinese women)[b]	107.0
16. *Jingu qiguan* (Eternal wonder)[d]	100.0

[a]Story magazines, [b]Women's magazines, [c]Youth's magazines, [d]Miscellaneous, [e]Propaganda
Source: *Zhongguo chuban nianjian 1988* (Chinese publication yearbook, 1988) (Beijing: Zhongguo shuji chubanshe, 1989), 120–21.

falling, the circulation of *Chinese Fishing* kept growing, topping 130,000 in 1987.[48]

The 1980s also saw increasing numbers of people devote their free time to their fads and fancies. Amateur collecting has attracted more and more people. In Shanghai alone, about 100,000 active amateur collectors amass everything from stamps to maps, from model ships to soft drink cans, and from abacuses to tortoises. Over thirty specialized collectors' associations have been established in the city, with memberships ranging from two dozen to two thousand.[49] Also in the 1980s countless numbers of families started to breed pets. Birds, goldfish, tropical fish, and crickets have their special devotees. It was reported that 500,000–600,000 fish enthusiasts and 500,000 cricket aficionados were in Shanghai in 1990.[50]

Space limitations prevent discussion of the growth of other "fevers" of pastime pursuits, such as "*qigong* fever," "tourism fever," "keep-fit

[48]Dai Banyun, "Fengmi zhongguo di diaoyure" (Fishing fever in China), *Hubei qingnian* (Hubei youth) 8 (August 1989): 20–23.
[49]Sheng Yu, "Shanghai minjian siren shouchang di diaocha" (Private Collections in Shanghai), *Shehui* 8 (August 1990): 16–19.
[50]Zhao Zhenda, "Chongwu chao" (Pet wave) *Shehui* 7 (July 1990): 20–22.

classes fever," "go fever," "dressmaking fever," and the thousand and one other ways in which Chinese people occupied their nonworking hours.[51] (A discussion of "*qigong* fever" can be found in Chapter 13 in this volume.) The vitality or variety of leisure activities is an important indication of how far the state's "indifference zone" has extended.

NEW CHARACTERISTICS OF LEISURE

Depoliticization. During the CR, as discussed above, leisure activities were highly politicized and sometimes even the concept of leisure itself was regarded as an element of "bourgeois ideology." The overpoliticization of social life evoked a strong aversion to anything political among a large segment of the population in the later years of the CR. When reformist leaders came to power, to regain popular support they had somehow to depoliticize social life, redefining the boundary between private time and public time, and allowing greater autonomy for individuals to decide how to spend their private time. The state, of course, has not given up its attempt to control leisure. But the Deng regime's understanding of "control" is different from that of the Maoist regime. For the latter, "control" meant "dictating" or "having everything all my way," while for the former, "control" means "curbing" or "keeping bad things in check." That is why depoliticized leisure is acceptable, or even desirable for the Deng regime. A certain degree of political apathy may be conducive to the regime's stability.

Privatization. One of the results of depoliticizing social life has been the privatization of leisure pursuits. After a decade of weary "class struggle" in the CR, people began to retreat from outside social relationships into the domestic sphere in the late 1970s. This tendency was reinforced by the advent and spread of television, and audio and video equipment in the 1980s. The overwhelming majority of urban residents have become accustomed to staying at home after work. The home thus has become the major site of leisure activities in China, just as has happened in many other countries.[52] Privatization provides an important "out" for many of those who found public life meaningless and alienating, and thus functions like a safety valve for society.

[51]For example, see Yan Jian, "Beijing di weiqi re" (Go fever in Beijing), *Shidai* 1 (January 1988): 55.
[52]Jones, *Workers at Play*, 200–201; and Rojek, *Capitalism and Leisure Theory*, 19–20.

Diversification. As political hindrances to the enjoyment of private time have declined, leisure activities have become increasingly diverse. Indeed, it is only natural that the freeing of private time has led to the expansion of private space. With relative freedom in the area of leisure, people have unleashed previously suppressed emotions, expressed previously hidden desires, and pursued previously disallowed interests. Hence, many previously forbidden avocations (e.g., playing mahjong, reading love stories, breeding birds, etc.) have come out of the closet; and many new leisure activities (e.g., watching television, playing video games, tourism, etc.) have been embraced enthusiastically by millions of Chinese who have long hungered for relaxation, fun, and amusement.

"Westernization." Here "Westernization" refers to influences from the outside world, including Hong Kong and Taiwan. The demonopolization of private time concurred with the introduction of the "open door" policy. In the 1980s, the number of foreign tourists (including visitors from Hong Kong and Taiwan) increased by 500 percent.[53] To accommodate foreign guests, China has built hundreds of luxury hotels in cities all over the country. To entertain foreign guests, those hotels have attached bars, discos, bowling alleys, and in some cases even golf courses.[54] Visitors come and go, but the constant flow of foreign visitors presents vivid examples of how people in other parts of the world spend their leisure time. As a result, bars and dance halls have been proliferating in Chinese cities.

Chinese do not have to go to Westernized bars and dance halls to experience foreign influence. The foreign presence is everywhere. Chinese now listen to the music of Michael Jackson, Deng Lijun (a Taiwanese singer), and Zhang Xueyou (a Hong Kong singer); reading books written by Jin Yong (a Hong Kong writer), Qiong Yao (a Taiwan writer), or translated from American paperbacks; and watching movies, videos, and television programs produced in Hong Kong, Taiwan, and Hollywood.[55] The "open door" policy has widened the cultural aspirations of the Chinese people.

[53]*Zhongguo tongji nianjian* 1990, 658.
[54]Orville Schell, *Discos and Democracy: China in the Throes of Reform* (New York: Pantheon Books, 1988), 349–56.
[55]Ibid., 355.

Commercialization. The changed position of leisure also is manifested in how commerce has intruded into the leisure domain. Instead of regarding leisure as a battlefield between "proletarian" and "bourgeois" ideologies, the Deng regime now considers it a market—a "cultural market." It is accepted that "cultural commodities" such as films, audio and videotapes, books, newspapers, magazines, dance halls, and so forth should be subject to the same economic rules that apply to other commodities. Thus, "cost," "profit," "quantity," "quality," "demand," "supply," "competition," "import," and "export" are no less legitimate concerns for producers and consumers of "cultural commodities" than for their counterparts of other commodities.

Although the government has emphasized that both "economic and social efficacy" are important in "cultural production," the economic reform has in fact driven most, if not all, producers of "cultural commodities" to pursue profits at the expense of "social efficacy." Chapter 7 in this volume provides a detailed discussion of the effects of commercialization on China's cultural industry. The pursuit of profit maximization is part of the reason why Chinese television stations and video studios would rather import programs from abroad than produce their own. It usually costs about 60,000 yuan to purchase broadcasting rights of a twenty-part television series from abroad. But for a television station to make a twenty-part series itself, the cost could go as high as 200,000 yuan.[56] Similar cost-benefit concerns apply to video producers.[57] The result is that Chinese television has become congested with foreign-made programs and the video market has been dominated by imports.

Polarization. The commercialization of leisure implies that purchasing power in terms of income matters. Numerous studies have shown that the gulf between "haves" and "have-nots" has been growing since the early 1980s.[58] One result is the polarization of leisure patterns. At one end, those whose incomes are barely sufficient to maintain the minimum standard of living have not benefited much from the general expansion

[56]Shi Liuzi, "Dianshiju di kewang he kunhuo" (The prospects of TV dramas), *Zhongguo zhichun* 5 (May 1991): 65.
[57]*DSNJ 1989*, 336.
[58]*Tianjin ribao* (Tianjin daily), July 20, 1988; and Zhao Renwei, "Woguo zhuanxingqi zhong shouru fengpai di yixie teshu xianxiang" (Special phenomena in the income distribution of our country during the transition period), *Jingji yanjiu* (Economic research) 1 (January 1992): 53–63.

of commercialized leisure. Many of them have to take second jobs and thus sacrifice hours of leisure to obtain more income.[59]

Most Chinese find that their resources cannot stretch beyond the requirements of basic everyday existence and easily accessible pastimes. For them, the home is the main site of leisure and recreation, and television viewing is the staple leisure activity. Only occasionally do they participate in leisure activities that require not just time but money.

At the other end is a small proportion of the urban population that can afford expensive leisure activities. It is they who are regular customers of Western-style dance halls, bars, and cafés. The new rich includes upstart private business people, employees of foreign companies, cultural elites, and corrupt officials. For those people, especially for private business people, the extravagant pattern of leisure is as much for relaxation and recreation as for flaunting their elite status. With a minimum expenditure of 50 yuan or more per visit, nightlife in dance halls, bars, or cafés is simply too expensive for ordinary Chinese to enjoy.[60] Therefore, there has been a growing sense of inequality of access to leisure.

Formation of voluntary associations. In the first three decades of the People's Republic, the Chinese Communist state did not tolerate the existence of any voluntary groups. This situation began to change in the post-Mao period. The 1980s witnessed "the emergence of avowedly autonomous formal associations."[61] By 1991 there were over 100,000 registered voluntary, semi-voluntary, and quasi-official societies, many of which are recreational groups.[62] The aforementioned national and

---

[59]Contrary to the conventional perception, the "second economy" is not a new phenomenon. At the beginning of the 1980s, 5 percent of state-enterprise employees already had second jobs. The number of state employees who took second jobs has steadily increased in the course of economic reforms. By the late 1980s, about 20 percent of state employees had more than one job. In Shenzhen, the ratio was as high as 35 percent. Lin Guoxing and Yuan Qingshou, "Shehui zhuyi shehui de zhigong yeyu laodong" (Second jobs in socialist society), *Beifang luncong* (Northern tribune) 5 (October 1981): 64–68; Yang Yuan, "Dier zhiye toushi" (Perspectives on second jobs), *Shidai* 11 (November 1988): 17–19; and Zhang Yun, "Shenzhen dier zhiye zhuangkuang kiaocha" (Second jobs in Shenzhen), *Shehuixue yanjiu* 3 (March 1989): 76–85.

[60]Yi Xudong, "Dushi yeshenghou" (Nightlife in metropolises), *Ba xiaoshi zhiwai* (After eight hours) 6 (June 1990): 7–8.

[61]Martin K. Whyte, "Urban China: A Civil Society in the Making?" in Arthur Lewis Rosenbaum, ed., *State and Society in China: The Consequences of Reform* (Boulder: Westview, 1992), 91.

[62]She Dehu, "Youguan woguo shehui tuanti wenti di shikao" (Reflections on voluntary associations of our country), *Qiushi* (Seek truth) 17 (September 1991): 15.

provincial fishing associations are just an example. But national or provincial autonomous organizations are still few and far between. Most of the newly established leisure groups are operating only at the grass roots and at local levels.[63] The folk cultural groups Vivienne Shue finds in her case study of Xinji, Hebei, are typical of popular associations existing in today's China. (See Chapter 4 in this volume.) Such community leisure groups are often sponsored by the official trade unions or Youth League committees in a given unit or a given locality. In theory, they should be subject to the sponsors' supervision. However, in fact those groups have a certain degree of autonomy. In most cases, they are free as long as their activities do not run counter to the sponsors' interests.[64]

To prevent voluntarily organized leisure activities from growing out of control, the state discourages the formation of transunit and transregional recreational organizations.[65] Nevertheless, thousands of such groups have come into existence. In Wenzhou, a medium-sized city, for instance, there were about four hundred transunit leisure organizations, such as poetry societies, art salons, sports clubs, flower-lover associations, and the like in 1987.[66]

For the members of leisure groups, the emphasis is less on the individual home than on the voluntary collective life in the community. Precisely for this reason, the state takes an ambivalent position toward such organizations. On the one hand, home-centered leisure activities, though not harmful, are not as "healthy" as those conducted by voluntary leisure groups, because the former function mainly to kill time rather than to spend spare time in creative ways. On the other hand, however, any autonomous organizations, especially those that transcend administrative boundaries, could become potentially dangerous, even if they initially have no political agenda. After all, groups are not as readily amenable to governmental control as isolated individual households.

[63]Council of Trade Unions, Capital Steel Corporation, "Banhao zhigong wenhua huodong zhongxin, chujin liangge wenming jianshe" (Strengthen employees' cultural centers, promote the construction of two civilizations), *Qunzhong wenhua* 6 (June 1986): 15.

[64]Shao Zhixiong, "Lanzhou lianyou chang zhigong yeyu xinggu huodong kaizhan huoyao" (Pastime activities are brisk at Lanzhou oil refinery), *Qunzhong wenhua* 11 (November 1987): 28–29.

[65]Chen Lu, "Ba qingnian di yeyu wenhua shenhuo zhenzheng huoyao qilai" (Enliven youth pastime activities), *Qunzhong wenhua* 5 (May 1986): 2–3.

[66]Huang Ruigeng, "Wenzhou shi qunzhong wenhua huodong kongqian huoyao" (Pastime activities are brisk in Wenzhou). *Qunzhong wenhua* 10 (October 1987): 16.

INDIVIDUAL PREFERENCES, THE MARKET, AND
STATE CONTROL

When the state demonopolized private time, it intended to *loosen* rather than *lose* its control in this regard. However, in fact, the government's ability to manipulate pastime activities has been significantly impaired in the last decade. This is an unanticipated consequence of the government's initial decision to step back and allow whatever is not "harmful." Once allowed to be expressed through "cultural markets," individual preferences for leisure become a powerful force, so powerful that it is able to "chip away" the state's domination over people's private time. The state is no longer the sole provider of recreational products. Even in those areas in which the state still seems to be the sole provider, its control has become less effective, largely because the reform has transformed many state agents from ideologically motivated propagandists to profit-driven business people. Take book publication as an example.

In the last decade, thousands of printing facilities have been installed by township or village enterprises or even private entrepreneurs. To earn profits, those publishing concerns care more about "market signals" than governmental guidelines. More important, required to assume the sole responsibility for their profits or losses, China's five hundred state presses and six thousand registered journals and magazines have also turned themselves into profit maximizers. As a result, the government has found itself increasingly unable to control what is being printed. The declining state capacity in this regard is best illustrated by its losing battle against "illegal" publications.

Since 1980, Chinese readers' taste has changed in several distinguishable phases: detective stories in 1980, traditional knight errant fiction between 1981 and 1983, modern knight errant fiction between 1984 and 1985, triangular love stories in 1986, pornographic stories after 1987.[67] Accordingly, the content of illegal publications has gone from martial arts to murder, from pornography to obscenity, from feudal superstitions to directly attacking the Chinese Communist Party and the socialist system. The government has tried to discourage publishing houses from printing "unhealthy" and "harmful" material at every turn, but all its attempts

---

[67]Bian Chunguang, "Chong seqing yinhui duwu di chuban suo xiangdao di" (Reflections on the proliferation of pornography), *Chuban gongzuo* (Publication work) 10 (October 1988): 6.

have stopped short of achieving this goal.[68] In the late 1980s, in face of growing competition from hundreds of newly founded pulp magazines, even serious literary journals became more or less corrupted by profit considerations. To respond to "market signals," many of them were forced to cater to readers' tastes for supernatural martial arts, romance, fashion, violence, crime, intrigue, and, above all, sex.[69]

When the state launched its first crackdown against illegal publications in 1987, the target was "underground publishers," namely, unregistered township or village printing houses that did not have permits to publish.[70] However, illegal publications flourished again in 1988. And this time, it was official presses (including ones owned by academic institutions, trade unions, and even the army) that took the lead. Thirty-five state presses received warnings for publishing pornography that year.[71]

But illegal publications were subdued only briefly. The spring of 1989 saw a new wave of pornography. That is part of the reason the Chinese government initiated a more vigorous campaign against illegal publications after the turmoil of 1989. By the end of the year, 31 million books and magazines had been confiscated, 106 pulp magazines, 190 newspapers, and 41 publishing houses closed.[72] Before long, however, illegal publications began to make a comeback. Varieties of "illegal" books and magazines reappeared at bookstalls in 1990.[73] In the winter of 1990 the state started its fourth campaign against illegal publications. In spite of those annual campaigns, illegal publications are still flourishing. Hundreds of "underground networks" are now in operation. Many of them have become highly organized and disciplined. A recently uncovered network, for instance, consisted of 257 editing, publishing, and distributional units that were scattered over eighty-five cities and counties in twenty-seven provinces.[74] In the winter of 1991, China launched a sweep-

---

[68]*Renmin ribao* (People's daily), November 15, 1985; *Zhongguo qingnian bao* (Chinese youth daily), March 16, 1986.

[69]Shen Daran, "Qingchu jingshen wuran, quanli zhengdun shukan yinxiang shichang" (Clean up spiritual pollution, consolidate the markets of books, journals, audios and videos), *Qunzhong wenhua* 10 (October 1989): 7.

[70]*Chuban gongzuo* 8 (August 1987): 6–13.

[71]Cai Bo and Yang Jian, "Huangfeng lueguo Beijing cheng" (Pornography wind sweeping Beijing), *Shidai* 11 (November 1988): 30–31.

[72]Editorial Board, *Zhongguo baoke nianjian, 1990* (China yearbook of newspapers and magazines, 1990) (Beijing: Zhongguo da baike chubanshe, 1990), 145–59.

[73]Yin Jindi, "Xiaochu huangdu, gongzhai qianqiu" (Clean up pornography), *Liaowang* 46 (November 12, 1990): 6–9.

[74]New China News Agency (Zhengjiang), December 25, 1991.

ing new crackdown on illegal publications, the fifth in a row.[75] It curbed illegal publications for the moment. But it is unlikely that the state will win the battle. So long as huge demand for such illegal publications exists, there will be people who are willing to take the risk of violating the law in order to make big profits. When I visited China in 1992 and 1993, illegal publications were on display at almost every bookstall.

CONCLUSION

In the course of China's economic reforms, the legitimacy of private time has been rehabilitated. Along with the changed conception of social time, private space has been enlarged. Chinese people now enjoy a relatively larger private sphere than at any time since 1949.

The expansion of the private sphere is attributable as much to the state's intentional retreat as to societal forces' "nibbling" efforts. The state is willing to retreat because it has learned that, left with little breathing time or breathing space, people are likely to become dispirited and depressed. To arouse the masses' enthusiasm for its Four Modernizations program, the state cannot afford to continue the monopolization and politicization of every minute. But this does not mean that the state will take a laissez-faire attitude toward the ways in which people spend their private time. Although the state's "indifference zone" has been broadened, it still hopes to shape people's leisure pattern so as to channel their excessive energies into activities that it believes are physically healthy, morally correct, socially consolidating, and politically integrative.

The market-oriented reforms, however, have eroded the state's ability to exercise its guidance role. At the same time that leisure has been depoliticized, it has also become increasingly commercialized. Profit has replaced ideology to become the primary concern for most providers of recreational products, including state agencies. To maximize profit, they often ignore official guidelines to respond to "market signals." Individual leisure preferences thus can often be satisfied through "gray" or "black" cultural markets, which effectively expands people's private space.

[75]UPI (Beijing), December 19, 1991.

7

China's artists between plan and market

RICHARD KRAUS

Positioned for more than a decade in the transient, elusive space between plan and market, China's artists are simultaneously liberated, inspired, frustrated, confused, and sometimes even frightened. This "space" is metaphoric, but its consequences are substantive. Two very different sets of institutions organize the arts in China's cities: (1) the administrative system of central planning and (2) the newer mechanisms of the marketplace. The plan is built around a seemingly solid bureaucratic network, while the market dances more lightly across an ever changing web of commerce. The changing relations between plan and market force changes in the lives and visions of China's artists, and in the pleasures offered urban audiences.

This chapter explores what it means to live between plan and market. After looking at the old cultural institutions and a failed effort to restore them after the Cultural Revolution, I review some obviously happy consequences of China's economic reforms. Perhaps more interesting, however, are some perplexing points of ambivalence, such as career insecurity, the search for new patrons, and the coarsening of public life. While the reforms have lightened the political burden on China's artists, they have not removed art from the world of politics. Instead, urban artists now face new and largely unfamiliar conflicts about their ties to society.

A FALSE START IN REFORMING URBAN CULTURE

China has not one cultural bureaucracy but many. The Ministry of Culture administers museums, large arts ensembles, and a nationwide system of municipal and county cultural centers. Parallel to this network stands the Communist Party's Propaganda Department, charged with seeing that China's culture stays in line with party policy. The army has its own elaborate system of arts units, including opera companies, dance troupes, a film studio, and a full complement of novelists and poets, and has operated a major arts school in Beijing since 1960. A fourth bureaucracy is the Federation of Artists, an umbrella organization for bodies representing painters, writers, filmmakers, acrobats, musicians, and other arts professionals. Another, more shadowy presence, is the Ministry of Public Security, which not only arrests artists but oversees their rehabilitation as well; it also must authorize permission for travel outside China, an important privilege for arts professionals.

When the economic reforms began in the late 1970s, this set of cultural bureaucracies was weak, reeling from the sustained shock of the Cultural Revolution. Maoists had rejected the sometimes elitist and highly routinized style of hierarchies such as the Ministry of Culture. Mao's supporters, led by his wife, Jiang Qing, attacked the regular administration of culture undermining the spirit of the Chinese revolution. Radicals pressed for mass campaigns in the arts, demanding that amateurs supplant professionals in order to bring culture closer to the ordinary people. Such populism was neither clearly thought out nor carefully implemented, but it represented an alternative both to the hierarchical bureaucracies that dominated artistic life before the Cultural Revolution and to the less regulated arts of capitalist societies. The Ministry of Culture was effectively closed for several years, reopening only in 1975. Similarly, radicals targeted the party's Propaganda Department as a source of revisionism, and attacked the professional artists' associations even more fiercely. This left only the military arts system, which many performers joined for the personal security provided by the army's unimpeachably leftist politics.[1]

Between Mao's death in 1976 and the political victory of Deng Xiaoping in December 1978, China's arts went through a painful period in which artists and cultural officials dismissed and disgraced during the Cultural Revolution were restored to authority, or were posthumously honored, while Maoists were purged from cultural posts. This process was intended simply to restore the old cultural bureaucracy, as some

---

[1]See my "Arts Policies of the Cultural Revolution: The Rise and Fall of Culture Minister Yu Huiyong," in William Joseph, Christine Wong, and David Zweig, eds., *New Perspectives on the Cultural Revolution* (Cambridge, Mass.: Harvard University Council on East Asian Studies, 1991), 219–41.

leaders hoped to re-create a putative golden age of the 1950s. This was thought to be a system in which the state and the party were gentle patrons, eschewing harsh personal attacks on individual artists, as all worked in harmony to present a vision to China of a modern, yet obtainable future. The 1979 congress of artists, perhaps the culmination of this effort, was the last, brief moment in which it seemed that China's old cultural bureaucracy might easily be reconstructed, but without the excesses of Mao's late years.

Yet such a simple restoration of the pre–Cultural Revolution cultural system was aborted as new commercial relations unexpectedly intruded into what had been a closed bureaucratic world. As the marketplace presented an alternative way of organizing the arts, the authority of Communist officials was steadily eroded, severely diminishing the party's capacity to shape culture. In addition, the uneven decline of the Communist Party's propaganda system loosened once tight political supervision, although censorship and propaganda are periodically reemphasized in campaigns of diminishing credibility.

The reform of Chinese cultural institutions has never been central to the broad reform of politics and the economy that began in 1978. The arts were included almost as an afterthought. For instance, Deng Xiaoping's early assault on Maoists in the party's propaganda apparatus almost inadvertently weakened a major mechanism for controlling the lives and work of artists. Yet economics, not politics, has been the impetus for reforming cultural institutions. The state now demands that arts institutions balance their books as any other enterprise in today's China must.

TWO CHEERS FOR CULTURAL MARKETS

Two consequences of the reform program were widely welcomed: a marked, if uneven, increase in freedom of expression and a dramatic growth in the variety of art.

By the mid-1990s, China's once centrally planned arts world gave way to a partial disengagement of art from politics. No longer are the arts regarded primarily as a tool for mass mobilization, nor are political leaders so deeply involved in the approval of individual works that members of the Political Bureau routinely arbitrate disputes about specific paintings or films.

Reduced authority for the party's propaganda officials was central to the loosening of political controls. Their responsibilities had been to drum up artworks that adhered to the party line, and to discourage or censor those that appeared to challenge it. Unlike the former Communist regimes of Eastern Europe, China has no special corps of professional censors.[2] The party never established a single censorship office in Beijing, but, instead, decentralized censorship functions throughout cultural and propaganda organizations. The highly bureaucratized censorship of the Soviet Union published manuals on how to censor, "telling just which points and phrases are out of bounds; in China the whole responsibility lies with writers, editors, and local officials to read the major pronouncements on cultural policy and divine the direction of the wind for themselves."[3]

Such a system worked well to suppress heterodox ideas when officials throughout the nation believed in (or at least followed) a common cause. But the very informality of China's censorship has made it easier for cultural officials simply to let up their vigilance in a task in which many never found much pleasure. In addition, the rapid expansion of publications in the reform era quickly overloaded the party's control mechanisms.[4]

Concomitantly, professional artists assume increasing responsibility for their own aesthetic choices, while professional organizations (such as the writers', musicians', and fine artists' associations) gained increasing importance as representatives of artists' interests. In the past, these bodies had obviously controlled artists for the party. In the reform decades, the control continues, but now coexists with a sense of professional representation, as the boldest of these organizations buffer some of their members against political criticism. The Ministry of Culture's inability to continue its former generous subsidies to arts organizations forces them to turn to other sources of funds, thereby diminishing the ministry's power.

While the realms of aesthetics and power may still pull further apart, speaking of their "incomplete" separation is inaccurate, as they are not

---

[2]On the Soviet censorship system, see Marianna Tax Choldin and Maurice Friedberg, eds., *The Red Pencil: Artists, Scholars, and Censors in the USSR* (Boston: Unwin Hyman, 1989). China never had any counterpart to the notorious Polish handbook on how to censor, *The Black Book of Polish Censorship*, Jane Leftwich Curry, ed. and trans. (New York: Vintage, 1984).

[3]Perry Link, "The Limits of Cultural Reform in Deng Xiaoping's China," *Modern China* 13, no. 2 (April 1987): 152.

[4]Lowell Dittmer, *China's Continuous Revolution: The Post-Liberation Epoch 1949–1981* (Berkeley and Los Angeles: University of California Press, 1987), 247.

hermetically sealed in any society. At the same time, this movement is neither steady nor unchallenged. In periods of political crisis, as after the Beijing massacre, the public security apparatus continues to play a major role. A painter who wishes to travel abroad, for instance, must obtain an exit permit from the Public Security Bureau; more poignantly, many artists and others who were jailed in 1989 had to pay bribes to gain or keep their freedom. Police informers keep tabs on controversial figures among the urban intelligentsia. Thus, even when some old institutions are in decline, the police can generate fear to induce caution among artists.

Yet the erosion of Communist Party authority is more impressive than the halting efforts to reassert it. Diminished state control is directly associated with the emergence of a cultural market.[5] As art becomes commodified, writers, painters, and singers rely less upon the state's financial support and more upon the sales of stories, paintings, and tickets.[6] The new private arts marketplace is a still inchoate mechanism whose influence is greater in some genres (e.g., painting and popular music in contrast to sculpture and such elite dramatic forms as *qunqu*) and in certain regions (the coastal provinces rather than the interior).

The coexistence of plan and market permits many artists some room to maneuver between two large impersonal forces, enhancing their autonomy and their political boldness. Wang Meng, the writer dismissed as minister of culture after the 1989 Beijing massacre, caused a scandal when he sued a conservative critic who read his story "Hard Porridge" as an allegory about Deng Xiaoping. The courts dismissed his suit, but China's artists all know that before the reform era, Wang Meng had been a "rightist element," who would never have dared challenge his accusers in public.[7]

The market can even shape the role of the arts in expressing political dissent. While some artists seem to fit a model of public resistance suggested by East European dissident figures of the 1980s, many more remain closely tied to the cultural and political establishment, either

[5]See John Fitzgerald, "A New Cultural Revolution: The Commercialization of Culture in China," *Australian Journal of Chinese Affairs*, no. 11 (January 1984): 105–20.

[6]See Colin Mackerras, "Modernization and Contemporary Chinese Theatre: Commercialization and Professionalization," in Constantine Tung and Colin Mackerras, eds., *Drama in the People's Republic of China* (Albany: State University of New York Press, 1987), 183–212.

[7]Timothy Tung, "Porridge and the Law," *Human Rights Tribune* 3, no. 1 (Spring 1992): 9.

supporting the current order or working quietly against it. Yet as the growth of a cultural marketplace steadily erodes party control, it presents opportunities for artists to boost their careers and incomes by taking judiciously critical positions against the status quo. Such steps are clearly risky, especially in unexpected political crackdowns.

A second cause for celebrating the market has been its expansion of the once tightly constricted range of arts and entertainment available in China's cities. An outpouring of new artworks is bringing forth a range of styles and topics that many in China had unsuccessfully sought since the 1949 revolution and before. Some forms have not attracted wide public interest, such as the avant-garde movements in painting and poetry. But the revival of old, previously banned forms of popular urban culture meets broad approval, as does the introduction of such foreign innovations as karaoke and video games.

The more elite arts benefit from China's newly enthusiastic participation in an international arts world. Study abroad and foreign recognition have become important sources of professional validation, and foreign patrons have an impact in some genres, especially painting. Abandoning years of cultural isolation, artists and audiences are becoming increasingly familiar with foreign novels, paintings, and music, as well as foreign aesthetic theories. These new stimuli sometimes arrive in a confusing jumble, as if Freud and Andy Warhol were contemporaries and collaborators, or as if *Falcon Crest* shares some important quality with Stravinsky and Bartok. Some foreign styles are extremely popular, while others (e.g., Soviet models) are declining in influence. Westerners still have only a shadowy notion of the new importance of Hong Kong, Nanyang, and Taiwan artists from Greater China, even after the 1989 crackdown. These other centers of Chinese culture play a critical role in mediating the arts of China and the West. The massacre also intensified the development of exiled communities of artists, now working in foreign settings, but still involved with China's arts scene through personal ties and their new works.

Diversity coupled with diminished political control has freed space for a newly autonomous aesthetic domain in which artists explore the implications of an art separated from politics. As the party slowly relinquishes its claim to dictate aesthetic standards, artists and critics have engaged in serious debates about what constitutes beauty for the first time since 1949. As artists reduce their dependence upon the state, their works have tended to become less social and more personal explorations of the once-restricted terrain of emotion, sexuality, and psychology.[8]

THE MODERNIZING MISSION OF COSMOPOLITAN CULTURE

With Maoist populism in retreat, the 1980s brought a revival of the May Fourth program by which culture must modernize the nation. This doctrine has taken many forms, but at its heart stands the belief that traditional Chinese culture is fundamentally feudal and must be radically reconstructed, typically by adapting foreign models. From Hu Shi and Chen Duxiu through Fang Lizhi, the goal of outward-looking, reformist intellectuals is to use the levers of political power to design and implement a modern culture, which will transform China into a modern state.[9]

In many respects, Chinese politics for the past hundred years has been about reforming culture. Episodes as diverse as the Tongzhi restoration, the May Fourth and New Life movements, the Yanan rectification, the propagation of the Soviet model in the 1950s, the Cultural Revolution, and Deng Xiaoping's reforms have sought to cure China's ills by using political power to transform first culture, and then China. No matter that this approach has not been notably successful, nor that it rests upon a model of cultural change that privileges urban intellectuals over other classes, and ideas over material forces.

Early in its history, the Communist Party joined others in pressing for forced modernization by replacing feudalism with cosmopolitan culture. But at Yanan, Mao Zedong forced urban intellectuals to honor workers, peasants, and soldiers by developing "national forms," even when they would have preferred to disdain them.[10] Isolated in the countryside of the Northwest, the party could not attract peasant supporters if it continued to dismiss their culture as feudal. Some radical cosmopolitans were optimistic that their May Fourth approach would be revived after

---

[8]For a rich sample, see Gérémie Barmé and John Minford, eds., *Seeds of Fire: Chinese Voices of Conscience* (New York: Farrar, Straus and Giroux, 1989); and Gérémie Barmé and Linda Jaivin, eds., *New Ghosts, Old Dreams: Chinese Rebel Voices* (New York: Times Books, 1992).

[9]See Leo Ou-fan Lee, "The Crisis of Culture," in Anthony J. Kane, ed., *China Briefing, 1990* (Boulder: Westview, 1990), 83–105.

[10]See Paul G. Pickowicz, *Marxist Literary Thought in China. The Influence of Ch'u Ch'iu-pai* (Berkeley: University of California Press, 1981); David Holm, *Art and Ideology in Revolutionary China* (Oxford: Oxford University Press, 1991).

the establishment of the People's Republic, but the purge of Hu Feng and his supporters suppressed such ideals until the 1980s.[11] The party promoted its own idealized vision of a modern China through its arts and propaganda, but the imposition of Soviet cultural models upon nativist material was falsely homogeneous, and always strained.

The new cultural politics rejects the party's claim to have the sole choice over what kind of art to promote in China. The May Fourth mission for cosmopolitan culture has returned in new and prominent manifestations, such as the *River Elegy* television series, the introduction of Western abstract styles of painting and music, and in the new vitality of a literary modernism that rejects the realism imposed over several decades.[12]

The new cosmopolitans are modern, yet frankly reminiscent of Confucian instincts for intellectuals to rectify their nation's thought. Both reformers and conservatives are typically "establishment intellectuals," comfortably assuming that they, as sophisticates, are entitled to some power. Timothy Cheek argues that they are in transition from "priests" in the service of a cosmic Confucian, then Leninist state, to salaried professionals in an increasingly bourgeois society.[13] Others link this more professional stance to the growing intellectual autonomy made possible in the 1980s, when the state apparatus was weakening in the face of new social forces.[14]

Reformers who want to use culture to reform the nation find themselves in conflict with conservatives who see old-fashioned Marxism as a last defense against chaos. More practically, many conservatives regard reformers in the arts as a threat to their livelihoods. The reforming editor Bao Zunxin is said to have felt that the " 'cultural front' had to be occupied by the intellectuals in an unambiguous fashion."[15] One of the criticisms against Bao Tong, Zhao Ziyang's imprisoned secretary, was that he blocked the publication of *Deng Xiaoping on Literature and Art*,

---

[11]I discuss the trajectory of cultural cosmopolitanism in *Pianos and Politics in China: Middle-Class Ambitions and the Struggle over Western Music* (New York: Columbia University Press, 1989).

[12]See Su Xiaokang and Wang Luxiang, *Deathsong of the River: A Reader's Guide to the Chinese TV Series Heshang* (Ithaca: Cornell University East Asia Program, 1991).

[13]Timothy Cheek, "From Priests to Professionals: Intellectuals and the State Under the CCP," in *Popular Protest and Political Culture in Modern China* (Boulder: Westview, 1992), 124–45.

[14]Michel Boninn and Yves Chèvrier, "The Intellectual and the State: Social Dynamics of Intellectual Autonomy During the Post-Mao Era," *China Quarterly*, no. 127 (September 1991): 569–93.

[15]Ibid., 583.

on the grounds that this anthology of Deng's speeches was about politics, not art. Bao Tong may have done China an aesthetic service, but his act drew the resentment of conservative cultural figures.[16]

Journalism exemplifies the complexity of Chinese intellectuals' relationship to the state. A field often dismissed by foreigners as the mouthpiece of the regime became more professional and more autonomous in the 1980s, with advanced training at the Academy of Social Sciences, and a new list of journalist heroes such as Liu Binyan and Dai Qing. One account of the 1989 crisis at *Renmin ribao* (People's daily) describes "how editors and reporters at the very pinnacle of the official news apparatus defied, fought and circumvented government suppression in their efforts to promote the cause of the demonstrators and express their own aspirations for greater democracy."[17]

"Cumulatively, the evidence shows that the state's most important propaganda tool emerged as a virtual flagship of rebellion during this period."[18] Like their counterparts in Eastern Europe, many of these presumed house intellectuals changed radically and quickly. When they did change course, many revived the call to overthrow feudal culture by applying foreign models to China.

CULTURAL MARKETS AND POLITICAL POWER: ARTISTS AGAINST THE WORLD BANK?

As the reform program got under way, party leaders showed their kinship with earlier cosmopolitan reformers. In 1982, General Secretary Hu Yaobang hoped to use culture to soften the rougher aspects of new economic markets. "Socialist spiritual civilization [party code for its version of culture] not only gives a tremendous impetus to the building of material civilization, but also guarantees that it will develop according to a correct orientation."[19] Cosmopolitan artists, denigrated for decades, took hope that they would be restored to a central place in China's cultural politics.

[16]Ma Weian, "*Deng Xiaoping Lun Wenyi* de bianji yu chuban" (Editing and publishing *Deng Xiaoping Discusses the Arts), Zhongguo wenhua bao* (China culture news), February 11, 1990.
[17]Frank Tan, "The *People's Daily*: Politics and Popular Will: Journalistic Defiance in China during the Spring of 1989," *Pacific Affairs* 63, no. 2 (Summer 1990): 151.
[18]Ibid., 152.
[19]Quoted in Stuart R. Schram, " 'Economics in Command?' Ideology and Policy since the Third Plenum, 1978–1984," *China Quarterly*, no. 99 (September 1984): 433.

Table 7.1. *The arts*

	Elite art	Popular art
Traditional	ink painting	New Year's paintings
	opera [e.g. *qunqu*]	opera [Beijing opera]
	classical poetry	novels [e.g. *Three Kingdoms*]
	calligraphy	New Year's couplets
	seal-carving	handicrafts
Contemporary	oil painting	pin-ups
	symphonies	Hong Kong pop music
	literary novels	sex and violence potboilers
	ballet	disco
	spoken drama	television and film
	avant-garde poetry	karaoke

But the actual process of reforming Chinese culture is more complex, and perhaps less appealing to professional artists. While many artists are sympathetic to or enthusiastic about reform for the greater freedom it permits them in their personal lives and work, their attitudes toward cultural markets are less straightforward.

Market reforms seem likely to impede, rather than enhance, the ability of cosmopolitan artists to advance a May Fourth agenda. Ironically, this happens at precisely the moment when China is becoming most firmly linked to the outside world through massively increased foreign investment and trade. World Bank officials do not, in fact, press China for reforms intended to frustrate cultural cosmopolitans, but this is the apparent consequence of steady pressures to attract new foreign factories and to increase exports.

Commercialization has a profound but uneven impact on all of Chinese culture. One oversimplified but useful alternative to the state's categories for classifying art is to distinguish elite from popular art, and traditional arts from those adopted in China in this century (Table 7.1).

The contemporary/popular quadrant is the heart of the active new urban arts market, where demand for new products is highest, where potential rewards for artistic entrepreneurs are greatest. But the home base for cosmopolitan cultural reformers is the contemporary/elite quadrant, which is perhaps almost as disadvantaged by the market as the traditional/popular one.

The extension of economic reforms to cultural organizations has eroded state subsidies for precisely those arts held most dear by cosmopolitans. High-minded novelists now have more difficulty finding publishers; ballet and spoken drama troupes and symphony orchestras are forced to cut their payrolls, as well as to find ways of earning additional funds. A two-track system is planned to preserve subsidies for ensembles and institutions that the Ministry of Culture regards as the nation's artistic jewels, but the effect on lesser arts groups is demoralizing. Ironically, these subsidized arts so beloved by cosmopolitan intellectuals first won their subsidies when the Soviet planning model was in vogue.[20]

Perry Link reminds us that Chinese intellectuals ache for their traditional social standing, wanting "a world in which they enjoy respect from the populace and have the ear of the governing authorities."[21] Many reform-minded artists, eager to use their talents to promote their progressive ideals for China's future, find their capacity to do so limited by the impact of the cultural market. Cultural engineering is difficult to sustain in today's China, whether by reforming artists or by their adversaries in the party Propaganda Department.

DOUBTS ABOUT THE MARKET

Resistance to reform from old-line Maoists and others who favor central planning is well known.[22] Less known are cautions about reforms from those thought to be their greatest beneficiaries—intellectuals and artists.

Many cultural pursuits despised by cosmopolitan artists are thriving. Pop singers, especially those influenced by Hong Kong and Taiwan styles, can enjoy extremely high incomes. Chinese flock to small, privately run video parlors to watch tapes of flashy Hong Kong movies, while writers of serious fiction are appalled to discover that ordinary urban Chinese enjoy books as full of sex and violence as their counterparts in other nations. After many years of defending the seriousness of their art against a suspicious state, many artists are profoundly depressed to discover that pornography and vulgarity outsell works of high qual-

---

[20]On the relationship between Soviet culture and China's cosmopolitans, see my "Eastern Europe as an Alternate West for China's Middle Class," *Studies in Comparative Communism* 22, no. 4 (Winter 1989): 323–36.

[21]Perry Link, *Evening Chats in Beijing: Probing China's Predicament* (New York: W. W. Norton, 1992), 174.

[22]See especially Lawrence R. Sullivan, "Assault on the Reforms: Conservative Criticism of Political and Economic Liberalization in China, 1985–86," *China Quarterly*, no. 114 (June 1988): 198–222.

ity.[23] Many older intellectuals share a traditional disdain for selling art works at all. The cultural market reinforces their conviction that beauty and commerce do not mix.[24]

Some have resisted the temptations of economic relief offered by the market. The Central Philharmonic Orchestra declined to change its name to celebrate a potential financial backer. Novelist Ba Jin criticized the new bonds between business and writers: "I am still of the old view that it is readers who sustain me as a writer, not entrepreneurs."[25]

Ba Jin does not need the market, but less celebrated figures have less room to maneuver, and are often unhappy to discover that the market exposes them to new strains, including the threat of unemployment, as the state continues its assaults on job security in almost all sectors of the economy. In China, as in the United States, most intellectuals are simply not very entrepreneurial and are unlikely to become great economic successes when tossed into the marketplace.

Tang Xiaobing describes how the rush of the market "left many writers, who had reached their maturity by taking writing assignments, at a well-nigh total loss. All of a sudden, the reading public was to be entertained rather than educated; it took on the role of a choosy customer rather than a faithful, only less cultivated, fellow comrade."[26]

The case of Cao Hua is a depressing reminder that business skills are not innate. Cao Hua organized a private Jiangxi folk music troupe in Nanchang, the first of its kind, in October 1988, with funding from Taiwanese investors. A student of art theory, Cao's previous job with the provincial Artists Association did not prepare him to be an entrepreneur. Cao killed himself when his thirty-member troupe failed to make money and he could not make payments on his Taiwanese loan. A Jiangxi official "said he feared that Cao's suicide would discourage the hundreds of cultural and art cadres in the province who had already

[23]Much information in this section comes from interviews in Fujian Province in 1985, 1989, and 1992.

[24]I discuss the traditional literati aversion to commerce in art in *Brushes with Power: Modern Politics and the Chinese Art of Calligraphy* (Berkeley and Los Angeles: University of California Press, 1991).

[25]"Zuojia bu neng kao qiyejia yanghuo" (Writers cannot depend upon entrepreneurs for their livelihood), *Fuzhou wanbao* (Fuzhou evening news), March 30, 1989.

[26]Xiaobing Tang, "The Function of New Theory: What Does It Mean to Talk about Postmodernism in China?" in Lin Kang and Xiaobing Tang, eds., *Politics, Ideology and Literary Discourse in Modern China: Theoretical Intervention and Cultural Critiques* (Durham, N.C.: Duke University Press, 1993), 285–86.

abandoned the security of 'iron rice bowl' jobs to take up independent enterprises."[27]

Private patronage permits the introduction of a new coarseness into public life that embarrasses many urban intellectuals. For instance in 1989, Fuzhou's Huafu Hotel set up a nightclub staffed by singing dwarfs. Six singing and dancing waiters eventually found a seventh, thus permitting a Snow White act; many customers came only to see the dwarfs. Offering a salary of 300 yuan per month, plus a special car to pick them up for work, the manager received requests for employment from dwarfs all over China. A public debate ensued: was the nightclub helping the disabled or was it exploiting them?[28]

Less striking examples of vulgarity include simple fraud, as in a commercial exhibition in a Fuzhou park in 1989 that claimed to show costumes of historical dynasties. In fact, the show contained only half a dozen costumes, all historically inaccurate and displayed without variation on mannequins arrayed as a mock pageant of Chinese history.

Cultural markets operate with uncertainties and speculation, which have introduced new jealousies and insecurities of commerce, just as the more obvious problems of political pressure have abated. Politics once made it difficult for artists to speak and act as one group; now their material interests increasingly diverge.

The market magnifies previously minor economic disparities among artistic genres. In the past poets and pop singers had comparable incomes, as did painters and pianists. In interviews with artists in 1989 and 1992, I found practitioners of each genre quick to tell me how *other* artists were enriching themselves. Oil painters assured me that calligraphers could work more quickly and produce many works to sell, while calligraphers were envious of musicians, who could simply perform in an additional ensemble. Their tone was not bitter, but their anxieties were real.

In fact, celebrity artists within each genre had opportunities to earn high incomes, but their less well-known colleagues continued to struggle with inflation. Li Kuzhan sold one painting to an overseas Chinese from the Philippines for $15,000, and painter Fan Zeng is so popular with

[27]Duan Bayi, "Late Payment Due, Art Troupe Head Kills Himself," *China Daily*, February 27, 1989.
[28]Huang Yihua, "You ren xiang ban 'zhuru jiuba' " (Plans to open a "dwarf bar"), *Fuzhou wanbao*, March 10, 1989; Chen Cao, "Lin Dachun he tade qige xiao airen" (Lin Dachun and his seven dwarfs), *Fuzhou wanbao*, June 23, 1989, and subsequent reports.

Japanese collectors that one museum has a permanent display with eighty of his works.[29] Fan has donated over one million yuan to the arts department he heads at Nankai University.[30] But few painters can match these successes.

Inflation in the price of newsprint hits writers indirectly, but hard. In 1989 national publications were forced to increase subscription fees by an average 80 percent, with a resulting one-third drop in orders for both magazines and newspapers.[31] This followed a year in which inflation for periodicals was 97 percent.[32] Publication in Hong Kong assured a few well-known figures additional income. Other writers in Guangdong and Fujian fought inflation by writing pseudonymous scripts for Hong Kong television. Recently, Fujian writers have been able to publish articles in Taiwan publications. Writers further from the prosperous coast may be driven to more reckless measures. A *Henan Daily* reporter was arrested for blackmailing noted calligrapher Pang Zhonghua. The reporter threatened to publish evidence of tax evasion unless paid hush money of 20,000 yuan.[33]

Tax evasion by artists is not a trivial issue, under new laws introduced in 1987.[34] Two years later, Mao Amin, China's biggest pop star, was caught lying to the *Beijing Evening News* about under-the-table payments for performances in Harbin. In the ensuing scandal, she was fined 34,000 yuan and forced to pay 15,000 yuan in back taxes.[35]

But most artists are far from the fast-track glamour of tax evasion. Their apartments are crowded, their incomes are pressed by inflation, and their anxieties are magnified by the market's destruction of a world in which they knew where they and their fellow artists stood.[36]

[29]*Fujian ribao*, May 13, 1989.

[30]Zhang Wei, "Painter Fan Zeng—Talented and Diligent," *Beijing Review* 30, no. 29 (July 20, 1987): 30.

[31]Chan Wei, "Dangbao guanbao huapo, faxing jin you kaizhan" (Landslide in party and official newspapers, subscription war begins), *Jing bao*, no. 146 (September 1989): 44–45.

[32]Wang Xiyou, "Beijing dang'an" (Beijing file), *Jiushi niandai* (The nineties), no. 246 (July 1990): 87.

[33]"Reporter arrested for blackmail," *China Daily*, November 6, 1989.

[34]"Yanyuan yanchu shouru ying yifa nashui" (Performers' stage income must be taxed according to law), *Fuzhou wanbao*, March 30, 1989.

[35]Chen Kechang, "Mao Amin san bu gai" (Three ought-nots for Mao Amin), *Fuzhou wanbao*, May 14, 1989; Hu Min, "Mao Amin chehuang zhuihui moji" (Mao Amin retracts her false story and repents), *Fuzhou wanbao*, May 4, 1989; "Mao Amin toulou shui bei fakuan sanwan duo yuan" (Mao Amin fined over thirty thousand yuan for tax evasion), *Fujian ribao*, May 31, 1989.

[36]On the tense livelihood of urban intellectuals, see Perry Link, *Evening Chats in Beijing*, 90–122.

The reforms intensified regional disparities in material support for culture.[37] Arts organizations in Guangdong, Zhejiang, and Fujian enjoyed opportunities for sponsorship by overseas Chinese, by private business, and by vigorous state enterprises. Arts organizations themselves also have plunged into the commercial economy as entrepreneurs. Fujian Television hired a new business manager to oversee its new restaurant, and to expand its nontelevision income. The Fujian Writers Association runs a factory that manufactures puppet heads and masks, and it operates both a hotel and an advertising agency in Xiamen. These enterprises are intended to make profits, but also to provide employment for artists and their family members. The hotel also houses visiting literati.

From these activities and from private donations, the Fujian Writers Association has set up a small foundation to finance activities without state support. These included twenty scholarships for young writers, an annual two-week retreat for ten writers, subventions to publishers for Fujian writers, and subsidies to employers to free writers to devote more time to their art. The foundation also helped the association compensate for the erosions of inflation in the state budget, enabling Fujian to host a delegation of Italian writers, whose trip was otherwise restricted by a national budget that allocated an unrealistic 25 yuan per night for lodging.[38]

Fuzhou's Cangshan Cultural Center receives 30,000–40,000 yuan from the Cangshan district government each year, in addition to supplementary allocations for special activities on the big national holidays. But in prosperous Fuzhou, this center also raises 120,000 yuan from its own activities, including ticket sales, dances, pool halls, and video games.

However, the drive toward self-sufficiency meant greater poverty for cultural organizations in the interior. Poorer communities will no longer even finance public schools, enlarging the gap between sophisticates and the uneducated. Twelve county libraries in Hunan in 1988 could not afford to purchase any books; one canceled all periodical subscriptions except *Hunan Radio and Television News*.[39] The national press has pub-

---

[37]This discussion draws upon my article, "Four Trends in the Politics of Chinese Culture," in Bih-jao Lin and James T. Meyers, eds., *Forces for Change in Contemporary China* (Taipei: Institute of International Relations, 1992), 213–24.

[38]*Haineiwai wenxuejia qiyejia bao* (News of writers and entrepreneurs at home and abroad), May 22, 1989.

[39]"Ren chi shu" (People eat books), *Fuzhou wanbao*, April 13, 1989; see also Luo Rujia, "Gongchandangren de 'renge fenlie'" (The "split in the moral quality" of Communist Party members), *Dongxiang*, no. 56 (September 1989): 36.

lished many articles praising Shenzhen and other coastal cities as a new model for Chinese culture; but these were as irrelevant to rural Shanxi's real needs as the Dazhai agricultural model was remote from the reality of Guangzhou in the 1970s.

China's professional artists are no more consistent, and no less human, than their counterparts in the United States who desire public recognition and influence even as they want public subsidies for their work, without political controls on its content. In China, cosmopolitan artists may well resist further market reform in culture, preferring that the reforms stop with loosened political supervision, while retaining subsidies for their art and security for their families.

CHINA'S NEW PATRONS

New patrons of the arts are appearing in China's cities. Rather than simply intensifying the dependence of artists on the market, these successful entrepreneurs and managers of state firms can sometimes help cushion artists from the unfamiliar perils of commerce.

The phrase "cultural market" evokes an image of millions of citizens, each backing his or her artistic preferences as sovereign consumers. Rapidly rising personal income has meant that consumers enjoy more cultural choice. Purchases of televisions, for instance, have had a strong impact on the market for movies. For some arts, such as writing, individual consumers are obviously important. Yet even here, in the eyes of most novelists the real patron is likely to be a publishing house or an editor of a magazine. The new patrons are less likely to be anonymous participants in a mass cultural marketplace than individuals and organizations with concentrated economic power.

Artists seek new patronage in the face of inflation and declining public subsidies. But why should businesses give money to artists? One Chengde wine company supported a local spoken drama troupe when it made a television play glorifying the history of its wine. An engineering-supplies company in Zhejiang that provided travel expenses to enable an amateur playwright to accept a prize publicized its philanthropy to enhance its reputation.[40] In Guangdong, the popular Jianlibao health tonic sponsors a Jianlibao Cantonese Opera Troupe and a Jianlibao

---

[40]Zhang Zuomin, "Women weishenma zhichi huaji shiye?" (Why do we support the activities of spoken drama troupes?), *Zhongguo wenhua bao* (China culture news), January 29, 1989.

Light Orchestra, providing a fairly light-handed bit of advertising, somewhat like Texaco sponsorship of the Metropolitan Opera broadcasts.[41]

Many of China's new class of entrepreneurs, seeking public attention and praise, are now able to purchase both. *Xiaoshuo xuankan* (Selections from fiction), a major journal that reprints new fiction from China's legion of literary magazines, prints advertising of a most flattering sort. Its May 1987 back cover featured the Liaodong County Paper Factory of Liaoning. Manager Wang Qingfu appears in four of the five color photos. On the inside back cover are still more photos of Wang Qingfu, under the caption "The Labor and Life of an Entrepreneur." The photos show Wang talking to a reporter, offering a toast to the president of Liaoning University, watching a former provincial governor write a poem while visiting his paper factory, and making a speech to the mayor of Shenyang. A few months later, the same spot was occupied by photos showing the manager of a refrigerator factory on his travels to Venice and Japan, accompanied by a suitably inspirational quotation from Balzac.[42]

More formal commercial links have developed between companies and cultural organizations. In 1987 the Xiamen Arts Association gave partial control of *Xiamen wenxue* (Xiamen literature) magazine to the Xiamen Chinese Medicine Factory. In exchange for financial support, the factory appointed two members to the editorial board, including a deputy editor to take charge of the magazine's finances. The magazine promised to publish articles that "penetrate deeply the life of the Xiamen Chinese Medicine Factory; through their poetry, essays, and reportage they will reflect this factory's new people, new things, and new style. Moreover, the back cover of each issue will print an advertisement of the factory's outstanding products."[43]

The unpleasant job of fawning after wealthy individuals and flourishing enterprises is sometimes worth its cost precisely because it allows artists to avoid even greater dependence on the box office. Arts groups in the United States are quite familiar with this strategy. Foshan, a famous and prosperous city near Guangzhou, established its own Cultural Enterprises Foundation early in 1989. Both overseas Chinese and local

---

[41]Luo Weinian, Zhan Songsheng, and Tian Naiqi, *Shiyong gonggong guanxi 88 li* (Eighty-eight rules of practical public relations) (Guangzhou: Kexue Puji Chubanshe Guangzhou Fenshe, 1988), 124.

[42]*Xiaoshuo Xuankan* (Fiction selections), May and November 1987.

[43]"*Xiamen wenxue* gaiwei lianhe chuban" (*Xiamen literature* becomes a joint publication), *Fujian zuoxie bao* (Fujian Writers Association news) no. 12 (May 15, 1987): 3.

enterprises contribute to a fund to support Foshan's cultural activities through arts prizes, training courses, and new facilities.[44]

Poorer provinces have greater problems. An opera conference in Hebei concluded that its economic dilemmas could be solved only by selling more tickets, appealing more effectively to the tastes of the audience.[45] Arts foundations diminish reliance on both party and box office, permitting artists some autonomy in which they can escape from slavishly following Beijing's instructions or ever more desperate efforts to enlarge their audience at once.

Jeffrey C. Goldfarb contrasted Polish and American artists before the collapse of East European Communist regimes. The game for Western artists was to subvert the market, "avoiding mass-market demands by creating specialized markets or nonmarket supports through state, foundation, corporate, or individual patronage. The politics of culture in the East was about using or avoiding the party-state for artistic purposes."[46]

China's artists are beginning to learn how to play by both state and market rules. Their dissatisfactions with the market are unlikely to lead to demands for its abolition, but may increase calls for the state to ameliorate its effects, and for alternate patrons to buffer them from its harshest impact.

CONCLUSION

The perspective employed here, which emphasizes the new place of marketized commodified relationships in China's cultural politics, breaks with earlier approaches that focused more simply on tensions between artists and the state. Many such conflicts still continue, and others will assuredly arise. But a stark dichotomy between virtuous artists and an oppressive state no longer goes very far in explaining the multiple stresses to which China's artists must respond.

Situated between plan and market, artists occupy an urban space that is daily losing specificity as the peculiar placelessness of the market overcomes the often suffocating solidity of bureaucratic work units. Earlier

---

[44]"Guangdong sheng di yige wenhua shiye jijinghui zai Foshanshi chengli" (Guangdong's first cultural enterprise foundation established in Foshan), *Zhongguo wenhua bao*, March 20, 1989.

[45]Zhou Jianguang, "Jiaqiang dui guanzhong shenmei xuqiu de yanjiu" (Strengthen research into the masses' demands for beauty), *Zhonggou wenhua bao*, March 22, 1989.

[46]Jeffrey C. Goldfarb, *After the Fall: The Pursuit of Democracy in Central Europe* (New York: Basic Books, 1992), 231–32.

chapters in this volume by Gaubatz, Naughton, and Shue emphasize the urban sprawl and constantly rebuilt physical environment of urban China in the reform era. The realm of culture is somewhat different; here the market frees artists from their formerly captive dependence on specific bureaucratic locations, as it similarly loosens the obligations of institutions to support their work.

The attitudes and actions of artists are often complex reactions to highly specific situations that may shift with the next wave of reform. Consider the young writer, progressive in his politics, who told me with quiet pride that he found a certain professional utility in the party's old system of restricted (*neibu*) publications, despite the obnoxious character of magazines that could be read only by those within a certain bureaucracy or at a certain rank in the hierarchy. This writer explained his apparent inconsistency by talking about how badly the reform era's inflation eroded the paycheck he received from his regular office job. Because restricted publications are secret, even from one another's editors and readers, he could publish variants of the same piece, collecting manuscript fees from multiple publications without anyone being the wiser. How can we locate this writer within an uncomplicated scheme of state-flatterer or state-dissident? Happy with loosened political controls, he nonetheless seeks refuge from the market's economic uncertainties in his ability to manipulate familiar bureaucracies.

As China's economy becomes more capitalist, the situation of urban artists sometimes comes to resemble our own. Both China and the United States cut public arts support in the name of efficiency, forcing artists into new and often uncomfortable roles. When we think about China's cultural politics, we might bear in mind that half the budget of the Berkeley Symphony comes from running a weekly bingo game.[47]

A commodity culture encourages passive arts consumers, not mobilized activists. The party has essentially abandoned its former goal of arts that mobilize, discovering in the 1980s that commercial culture offered "bread and circuses" as an alternative. Party leaders lurched, with uncertain success, toward a new kind of legitimacy, surrendering hegemony in the hope of gaining popularity through cultural diversity. The party now witnesses a wider range of cultural choices than it ever imagined, but finds it difficult to restore its old system of subsidy and control. As artists of all stripes explore, embrace, and resist the metamorphosis

---

[47]Interview with Berkeley Symphony violist Marta Tobey, March 28, 1990.

of culture into commodity, their personal ability to maneuver will often grow, as will their ability to spin images and visions of present and future for their audiences. Many will be pained that no one particularly wants to pay attention, and that it may become ever harder to inspire action through art.

8

Velvet prisons and the political economy of Chinese filmmaking

PAUL G. PICKOWICZ

In the 1980s and earlier, late state socialist regimes in Eastern Europe loosened their Stalinist grip on society in order to address serious economic problems. The retreat of the state was especially apparent in the concessions that were made to market forces in the economy and in the sprouting (or resprouting) of relatively autonomous social groups both inside and outside the state sector. At the same time, the state also largely abandoned Stalinist strategies of cultural and ideological control. Although the reforms were designed to breathe new life into the state socialist project, the outcome was exactly the opposite. By the late 1980s, these regimes simply collapsed without much warning. The new market, social, and cultural forces let loose by the state indubitably played a part in undermining its long-term stability. But important questions remain: How extensive was the role of these forces? Do reform initiatives inevitably lead to the demise of such states?[1]

The Soviet bloc is gone, but it still makes sense for China specialists to continue to ask questions about the experiences of those regimes in

[1]By referring to the experiences of the former Soviet bloc I do not mean to suggest that the retreat of the state was a one-way street. Retreats in one sector were sometimes followed by advances in another. Similarly, by mentioning the appearance of relatively autonomous groups I do not mean to imply that such groups enjoyed total autonomy from the state. I am only asserting that certain sectors, especially the urban cultural sector, enjoyed more autonomy than they did during the heyday of state socialism. By raising questions about the role played by comparatively autonomous social groups and by quasi-autonomous individuals in the undermining of late state socialist regimes, I am not asking whether such people played the *leading* role in the demise of state socialism. I doubt that they did. Finally, I am not posing questions about whether quasi-autonomous cultural actors did anything in the late state socialist era that might contribute to the construction of democratic alternatives in the future. That is a separate issue.

the late state socialist phase of their development.[2] It would be a mistake to assume that, just because the Communist Party survived the Tiananmen crisis and is still in power in the mid-1990s, no meaningful historical connections link China to the failed regimes of the former Soviet bloc, China is somehow a unique case, or China need only be studied with reference to itself. Not only do such Chinese thinkers as Liu Binyan tell us to comprehend the things that connect China to Eastern Europe and the Soviet Union, so too do the writings of Eastern Europeans. Hence, when we explore a complex subject like the crisis of Chinese filmmaking in the post–Cultural Revolution reform era, analysis in terms of the cultural criticisms formulated by someone like Miklos Haraszti in Hungary can be useful.

Haraszti's brilliant discussion, entitled *The Velvet Prison: Artists Under State Socialism*, a work that mentions China several times, was first published in France in 1983 under the title *L'Artiste d'état* and then clandestinely in Hungary in 1986 as *A cenzura esztetikaja*.[3] An extraordinarily pessimistic work written well before the unexpected collapse of state socialism throughout Europe, the book solemnly concluded that, despite all appearances, a totalizing and hegemonic culture of state socialism was even more deeply rooted in post-Stalinist regimes than it was in the Stalin era.

Haraszti acknowledged that state cultural planners overhauled the socialist cultural arena in the post-Stalin era. Their reforms were discussed in the West under the headings of "thaw," "liberalization," and "openness," all of which were supposed to contribute to the articulation of "private" rather than "public" expressions, and humanistic rather than class interests. After these regimes had achieved consolidation by using time-honored Stalinist tactics, cultural bureaucrats at the state center no longer needed to resort to arrests, show trials, and strong-arm methods.

The cultural strategy of the more mature and self-confident state socialist regime (plagued with economic problems) amounted to gently placing artists in a comfortable "velvet prison." It was more efficient for the state to flatter and bribe artists by offering them perquisites and a

[2] I make an effort to do this in a recent essay entitled "Huang Jianxin and the Notion of Postsocialism," in Nick Browne, Paul G. Pickowicz, Vivian Sobchack, and Esther Yau, eds., *New Chinese Cinemas: Forms, Identities, Politics* (Cambridge: Cambridge University Press, 1994), 57–87.

[3] Miklos Haraszti, *The Velvet Prison: Artists under State Socialism* (New York: Noonday Press, 1989).

chance to wield a bit of power than to continue to bludgeon them with the familiar instruments of crude censorship. Artists were no longer restricted to doing agitprop work; they could travel abroad and could even obtain approval to recycle the outmoded cultural refuse of contemporary capitalist societies. All that was required was their loyalty (passive or active) to the state. Expressions of a non-Marxist mentality were acceptable: anti-Marxism was not. An advantage of the system was that the state had the option to revert, however briefly, to Stalinist modes of control and assimilation.

Heraszti argued passionately that the new plan worked. Artists sold out to the state in droves and deceived themselves by calling it progress. Some even convinced themselves that they had achieved independence or autonomy. In reality, they enjoyed the power and the comforts, and were unlikely to do anything to jeopardize their new status. Although few admitted it, the vast majority of artists collaborated with the socialist state in the post-Stalin era. Their art was an art of complicity that legitimized and perpetuated the hegemony of the state. All artists were on the state payroll. If they were not on the state payroll, by definition they were not artists. As loyal professionals, artists benefited from lavish state funding for the arts. Indeed, they became addicted to state funding and privately shuddered at the plight of artists in nonsocialist states who, unable to count on a regular state paycheck, were required to navigate the treacherous waters of the capitalist marketplace. Socialism was not so bad after all.

Observers outside the Soviet bloc invariably interpreted this thaw or retreat as a manifestation of the weakening of state power. The wider scope of artistic creativity seemed to suggest greater independence and autonomy for the artist. Apparent criticisms of the state, especially those that Haraszti said were being communicated "between the lines," could easily be interpreted as examples of an emerging civil or independent artistic culture. In reality, he insisted, the state was all too pleased to provide space for loyal critics. It was all part of the subtle cultural construction known as the velvet prison. In brief, Heraszti argued that cultural reforms that brought the apparent retreat of the state, liberalization, thaw, opening, individualism, market reform, and even criticism did not engender artistic autonomy or the emergence of civil society. Under the ingenious velvet prison arrangement of post-Stalinism, the state counted upon artists to engage in self-censorship and self-mutilation.

THE RETREAT OF THE STATE IN
THE POST-MAO FILM INDUSTRY

By the standards of the Cultural Revolution, the Chinese state retreated substantially from the world of filmmaking after the death of Mao.[4] Indeed, if one thinks of Haraszti's conceptualizations, it is clear that the post-Mao state sought to do what the post-Stalin regimes of the Soviet bloc attempted to do as early as the 1960s, that is, convert to the less heavy-handed, more nuanced velvet prison mode of cultural control.

The state apologized to film professionals, almost all of whom had been brutalized in one fashion or another by the profoundly anti-intellectual policies of the Cultural Revolution decade. Like the post-Stalinist leadership of the USSR, the post-Mao Chinese leadership had everything to gain in the short run by allowing film workers to denounce the "abuses of the past." The same thing happened throughout the Soviet bloc. It was cathartic and consistent with party policy. The new leadership piously admitted that it should have been obvious all along that the state could not survive without intellectuals in its bureaucratic apparatus. (Haraszti argued that artists in the Soviet bloc actually liked the idea of being politely invited to work in the service of the state.) The Chinese, of course, refined the idea of intellectual elites serving the state many centuries ago, thus it was relatively easy to restore them to their "rightful" and "natural" position after 1976.

Along with the new power and prestige came better housing, higher incomes, access to slush funds and special stores, drivers, banquets, foreign travel, foreign friends, restricted publications, restricted foreign films, and special opportunities for children. The now famous 1978 entering class of the elite Beijing Film Institute (Beijing dianying xueyuan), the most prestigious art school in China, was said to have been recruited entirely by competitive examination; in fact its ranks included many of the offspring of well-known film professionals and cultural dignitaries (including Bai Yang's daughter, Chen Huaikai's son, Zhao Dan's son, Hua Junwu's son, Ai Qing's son, and Tian Fang's son). Like other intellectuals, filmmakers understood that benefits derived from institution-

---

[4]On the post-Mao thaw in the film industry, see Paul Clark, *Chinese Cinema: Culture and Politics since 1949* (Cambridge: Cambridge University Press, 1987), 154–84, and Paul G. Pickowicz, "Popular Cinema and Political Thought in Post-Mao China: Reflections on Official Pronouncements, Film, and the Film Audience," in Perry Link, Richard Madsen, and Paul G. Pickowicz, eds., *Unofficial China: Popular Culture and Thought in the People's Republic* (Boulder, Colo.: Westview Press, 1989), 37–53.

alized bureaucratic corruption had always been a dividend enjoyed by those who worked in the service of the state. It should come as no surprise that virtually all Chinese filmmakers were attracted to the velvet prison.

The retreat of the state also brought some welcome changes in the structure of the film industry, all analogous to changes made in the Soviet bloc much earlier. China's film studios, which grew in number from ten in 1979 to nearly thirty in 1983, were given almost complete authority to determine which films they wanted to make. Film professionals, after all, were tired of making militant class struggle sagas. The films of the early 1980s featured attacks on the Cultural Revolution and other Maoist campaigns, love stories, accounts of famous historical events and people, folk legends, tales of crime detection, and martial arts adventures.[5] From 1979 to 1989 an average of well over 100 feature films were produced each year. Foreign and domestic observers (including myself), numbed by the narrowness of Cultural Revolution productions, were impressed by the diversity of the content of many post–Cultural Revolution films. Of particular interest was the new priority filmmakers gave to exploring the complexities of "private" and "individual" life in the urban sphere.

The new diversity of content, including the attention given to private life, was closely related to elementary economic reforms carried out in the film industry. Studios had to balance their budgets as state subsidies were phased out. Forced to make profitable pictures, filmmakers had to worry for the first time since the late 1940s about audience tastes.[6] Thus, the idea of a single, integrated national audience was abandoned. Studies of market conditions revealed that there were many popular audiences, some of which had more to spend on entertainment than others. Under these circumstances filmmaking took on a more distinctively urban orientation. Some filmmakers raided the rich treasure house of late imperial and early Republican urban popular culture, while others revived such time-tested genres as martial arts adventures and family melodramas.[7]

---

[5]On the various trends of the 1980s, see Browne et al., eds., *New Chinese Cinemas*, 1–113.

[6]See Chris Berry, "Market Forces: China's 'Fifth Generation' Faces the Bottom Line," in Chris Berry, ed., *Perspectives on Chinese Cinema* (London: British Film Institute, 1991), 114–25.

[7]On post-Mao interest in Republican era melodramatic formats see Paul G. Pickowicz, "Melodramatic Representation and the 'May Fourth' Tradition of Chinese Filmmaking," in Ellen Widmer and David Der-wei Wang, eds., *From May Fourth to June Fourth: Fiction*

Veteran directors sought to re-establish contact with the heritage of May Fourth literature by making films based on Republican era fiction. Young directors were eager to incorporate foreign currents to reassure a weary post–Cultural Revolution urban audience that Chinese city life was "modernizing" in ways that were consistent with "modernity" in "advanced" foreign nations. Relatively few films were made about rural China; and those that were set in the countryside often involved more than a bit of peasant bashing. In brief, they were not really being made for peasants. The heavy hand of Cultural Revolution and pre–Cultural Revolution state censorship was also lifted. Some filmmakers even began working political criticism into their movies, especially implied criticism that was conveyed at subtextual levels.

The response of the starved film audience was extraordinary. Although it is difficult to be confident about statistical estimates, it appears that film attendance in China set a record of approximately 29 billion viewers in 1979. Urban film fans especially appreciated the revival of the "star" system. Such actresses as Siqin Gaowa, Chen Chong, Liu Shaoqing, Pan Hong, Zhang Yu, and Gong Li became household names. Glossy film magazines like *Dazhong dianying* (Popular cinema), featuring images of young starlets in sexy poses and gossipy "news" about the private lives of film personalities, were snapped up by fashion-conscious urbanites. Filmmakers' new concerns about the tastes of the audience and the dynamics of the marketplace were intensified by the television revolution, which exploded on the scene in the late 1970s. The film studios regarded the television studios as powerful adversaries; the two competed for the same audience. Television was bound to rob the film industry of a share of its audience, and filmmakers were panicking in the mid-1980s. But according to the well-known director Wu Tianming, by 1988 the movie audience still numbered around 18 billion.

POST-MAO "URBAN" CINEMA: TWO CASE STUDIES

One of the most striking developments of the 1980s was the emergence of a new-style cinema that probed the contours of the emerging culture of urban individualism. Of special interest were the works of young

and Film in Twentieth-Century China (Cambridge, Mass.: Harvard University Press, 1993), 295–326.

filmmakers who dwelled on the mood of alienation and disaffection that prevailed in major cities. Space limitations prevent a comprehensive overview of the new urban cinema, but a brief discussion of a couple of representative titles provides some sense of its remarkable range.

For example, the profound cynicism of post-Mao urban youth was captured rather well in *The Trouble-Shooters* (Wan zhu, d. Mi Jiashan, 1988), a stylish black comedy released on the eve of the Tiananmen crisis. A postsocialist cross between *Ghostbusters* (d. Ivan Rietman, 1984) and *Easy Rider* (d. Dennis Hopper, 1969), this film tells the story of three enterprising young men in Beijing who launch a popular, new-age private firm called the Triple T Company. These likable con artists earn money by solving the problems of bewildered urban dwellers who are struggling with personal difficulties in the brave new world forged by Deng Xiaoping. One client is a frustrated and deservedly obscure young writer who desparately wants to win a literary prize. The company stages a lavish award gala to make him feel important. Another customer is an angry and unhappily married housewife who wants to heap verbal abuse on her husband, but he is never home. For a price Triple T is more than happy to assign someone to play the part of the missing husband and take all the tongue lashings the woman can dish out. Another poor soul is having problems with unwanted seminal emissions. He is advised not to go to bed too early, not to wear tight underwear, and not to look at pictures of pinup models. An unattractive young man with a thick Shanghai accent is disgusted by his bedridden mother, a veteran revolutionary (hence, "the mother of us all") who now does little more than "shit in her bed" every day. He hires Triple T to clean up the mess (Figure 8.1).

The most remarkable segment of the film is a bizarre sequence about the "Triple T Award Ceremony" that has been staged for the benefit of the talentless young writer. To fund the event, tickets are sold to hundreds of people who feel lucky to be able to witness such a glamorous event. Not only does the audience get to hear high-sounding speeches about the stunning accomplishments of the various award winners (all of whom are fakes), they also get to see a group of sleek and beautifully dressed fashion models who parade around a brightly lit boardwalk. In a surprise development, however, the models are suddenly joined on stage by characters dressed in Beijing opera costumes, followed by female bodybuilders wearing skimpy bikinis, People's Liberation Army soldiers, Qing aristocrats, public security officers, Kuomintang generals,

Figure 8.1. Yu Guan (left), a Triple T partner, has been hired to tell a woman that her boyfriend no longer loves her, in *The Trouble-Shooters* (Wan zhu, d. Mi Jiashan, 1988, Emei Film Studio). *Photograph by China Film Import and Export, Los Angeles*

warlords, Red Guards, rustic peasants, and muscular factory workers. The audience is familiar with all these stock characters, but knows they are strangely out of place when they interact with good cheer on the same stage. At the end of the performance, all the characters begin dancing with one another to the thumping sound of contemporary popular music; the Red Guards cavort with the slinky Western-style models, and the Qing elites frolic with the brawny and oily-skinned female bodybuilders (Figure 8.2).

The Trouble-Shooters, co-written by the immensely popular Wang Shuo, is about young urbanites who have no connection to the revolution, and who find themselves lost in the postsocialist city.[8] The film opens to the heavy metal music of rock star Cui Jian, who shouts:

[8]For an interesting discussion of Wang Shuo, see Gérémie Barmé, "Wang Shuo and *Liumang* ('Hooligan') Culture," *Australian Journal of Chinese Affairs,* no. 28 (July 1992): 23–64.

Figure 8.2. Triple T partner Yu Guan sleeps over in his girlfriend's apartment whenever he wants, in *The Trouble-Shooters* (Wan zhu, d. Mi Jiashan, 1988, Emei Film Studio). *Photograph by China Film Import and Export, Los Angeles*

> Dreamed 'bout livin' in modern city space;
> Now it's hard to explain what I face;
> Skyscrapers poppin' up one by one;
> But let me tell ya, life here's no fun.

The lives of the urban youth portrayed in this film are directionless and devoid of much meaning. Beijing is a vast stage occupied by masked players who are performing in a never-ending theater of the absurd.

A film that captured a very different thrust of the new-style urban cinema of the late 1980s was *Obsession* (Fengkuang de daijia, d. Zhou Xiaowen, 1988). Unlike *The Trouble-Shooters,* a cleverly written and genuinely humorous work that consciously sought to document the phenomena of a generation gap and youth alienation, *Obsession* is an escapist adventure designed to make money by providing spectacular "modern-style" entertainment. In short, *Obsession* is an example of new urban exploitation films that pandered to the curiosities of a restless and bored urban film audience.

Figure 8.3. Trashy magazines poison the minds of Chinese youth, in *Obsession*
(Fengkuang de daijia, d. Zhou Xiaowen, 1988, Xi'an Film Studio). *Photograph
by China Film Import and Export, Los Angeles*

For example, the title sequence is set in a women's public shower and
contains extensive frontal nudity. The camera dwells voyeuristically on
a group of young women who are helping each another wash. The
youngest bather suddenly experiences menstruation for the first time.
Several scenes later this innocent teenager is kidnapped, brutally raped,
and beaten senseless by a muscle-bound thug who spends most of his
time reading pornographic magazines imported from Hong Kong and
Taiwan (Figure 8.3). His room is decorated with posters of Sylvester
Stallone and Bruce Springsteen. When the police interview the victim,
the camera gratuitously zooms in on her tattered and bloody underwear,
which is displayed on a nearby table.

Obsession is a Chinese version of *The French Connection* (d. William
Friedkin, 1971). The victim's elder sister, Qingqing, teams up with Zhao,
a nonconformist, Gene Hackman–like retired policeman, to track down
the rapist. In the end a spectacular car chase is followed by a wild shoot-

Figure 8.4. Zhao, a nonconformist police officer, uses a hostage to capture a rapist, in *Obsession* (Fengkuang de daijia, d. Zhou Xiaowen, 1988, Xi'an Film Studio). *Photograph by China Film Import and Export, Los Angeles*

out and the arrest of the culprit. In a surprise ending, Qingqing avenges her sister's rape by suddenly pushing the suspect off a tall building.

Obsession is an interesting example of the globalization of Chinese urban culture in the post-Mao period. The narrative, flattened and generic in quality, could have unfolded anywhere. In sharp contrast to *The Trouble-Shooters,* this film simply dispensed with meaningful references to Chinese history and culture. The film was unsettling in the sense that it delivered bad news: China is a mess. At the same time it was reassuring: China may be in bad shape, but in that respect it is no different from the rest of the world. Unlike *The Trouble-Shooters, Obsession* does not convey muted political criticisms, but like *The Trouble-Shooters* it left the strong impression that modernity is chaotic and unstable (Figure 8.4).

Compared to *Obsession,* films like *The Trouble-Shooters* are much more conscious of their Chineseness. Repeated references are made to China's socialist past and present. But the allusions are so scrambled and confused that the viewer cannot get a clear picture of the sources of contemporary problems. The purpose of the references is to mock the revolutionary legacy. *The Trouble-Shooters* reveals much more about the late state socialist context of China than a work like *Obsession,* but like almost all the post-Mao urban movies, it gives no indication of how the alienation of urban youth will work itself out. Perhaps that is why films on the theme of urban restlessness and disaffection usually end on a depressing note.

THE STRUCTURE OF THE CHINESE VELVET PRISON

New urban films like *The Trouble-Shooters* and *Obsession* seemed path-breaking when they first appeared, but now, especially in the light of the Tiananmen crisis, it appears that their significance was exaggerated. In the 1980s many foreign and Chinese observers, impressed by the new developments brought by the reforms, failed to appreciate the impor-tance of many underlying and partially hidden structural and psycho-logical dimensions of the Chinese film world that blocked progress. It is here that Haraszti's gloomy conceptual framework can help explain as-pects of cultural conditions in urban China that were ignored when the international spotlight focused almost exclusively on sparkling new films like *The Trouble-Shooters.*

Haraszti would readily concede that the post-Mao state retreated on many cultural and ideological fronts. But he would also argue that the result was nothing like an independent or autonomous film industry. Filmmakers were flattered, empowered, bribed, and co-opted just as their Soviet bloc counterparts had been ten or twenty years earlier. In exchange for comfort, privilege, greater freedom, and access to foreign culture and the storehouse of presocialist Chinese culture, artists had to agree to play by the rules. This meant policing their own industry, know-ing the limits, and engaging in self-censorship, in brief, collaborating with the socialist project in ways that were designed to perpetuate and legitimize state control of society.

In the West many observers, including myself, got very excited about the startling rise of the vibrant Fifth Generation film directors in the 1984–88 period. The remarkable works by Chen Kaige, Zhang Yimou, Tian Zhuangzhuang, Wu Ziniu, and others were exceptionally striking in visual terms. They seemed to be the Chinese equivalents to the late state socialist films of Milos Forman, Jan Kadar, Elmar Klos, and Jiri Menzel produced in Czechoslovakia before 1968. And like most of the

Czech films, they could be interpreted as expressions of individual criticisms of the current regime.

While virtually all of us enjoyed wrestling with the multilayered "meanings" of these challenging and aesthetically pleasing films (works like *Yellow Earth* [Huang tudi, d. Chen Kaige, 1985], *Horse Thief* [Dao ma zei, d. Tian Zhuangzhuang, 1986], etc.), one of the great ironies of their production—an irony not lost on the directors themselves—is that these spellbinding experiments in "fine art cinema" could not have been made without massive state subsidies. Many of the most experimental films, especially those set in the Republican era, had small audiences and lost money for the studios that produced them. Filmmakers, including irreverent young upstarts, knew well that huge subsidies for experimental works were one of the prized fringe benefits for those who willingly worked in the velvet prison. No Fifth Generation artist ever turned down funds provided by the state. Indeed, they, and all other filmmakers, were totally dependent on the state for funding. All filmmakers remained on the state payroll.

Young filmmakers like Mi Jiashan, who insisted on making new-style films like *The Trouble-Shooters* set in a present-day socialist city, were no different from their colleagues who set their work in earlier times. Although they were alienated from the socialist state, they had to include material that gave official reviewers a "way out," that is, a way to proclaim that the work was, after all, a loyal, patriotic, and constructive elucidation of "social problems" whose correction would serve to stabilize the drive for socialist modernization.

When the reform of the film industry deepened in the late 1980s, and the state was openly encouraging the production of lightweight "entertainment films" (*yule pian*), that is, films with higher profit margins, it was the young "pure art" directors (just as Haraszti's framework suggests) who protested the loudest. With profits in command as never before since 1949, the individual studios were no longer inclined to sustain the losses associated with experimental productions, unless, of course, the state was willing to provide special subsidies.

The content and artistic forms of both the new-style films and the films of older directors was certainly more varied than anything that had been produced in the 1949–76 period. Many of the most interesting works (stamped with the seal of state approval) did indeed explore the heretofore ignored realm of individual and private life. Of special note were works like *The Trouble-Shooters* and *Obsession* that treated such problems as social fragmentation, alienation, and youth crime. But there is agreement now that none of these works, including all the new-style productions, amounted to a dissident, independent, or autonomous cinema. It is not even clear whether these films should be regarded as indications of the "true" state of mind of their creators. Private conversations with filmmakers invariably revealed that even the best of these works fell far short of what film artists really wanted to do. The works we see, however controversial they may seem, should not be regarded as examples of the best these artists can do. In reality, no one, including the filmmakers themselves, knows what their best work would look like if the motion picture industry were independent of the state. Few, if any, filmmakers saw themselves as collaborators, but almost all were conscious of the fact that they engaged in self-censorship virtually every day. In the late 1980s the alternative to self-censorship and voluntary participation in the velvet prison was silence and inactivity.

In a formal sense none of the remarkable films of the 1980s era can be viewed as manifestations of unofficial or dissident culture. They are official in the sense that they were all produced in state-run film studios. The state retreated in some important ways from the film industry, but the retreat did not result in an autonomous or independent film world in prelude to the Tiananmen incident.

THE POLITICAL ECONOMY OF FILMMAKING IN THE REFORM ERA

If the state center gave up direct control over what is produced by the film studios, if screenwriters and directors were encouraged to treat themes related to "private space" and the culture of individualism, and if filmmakers were permitted to take into account the tastes of ordinary consumers in the market, then why did the reforms of the 1980s fail to produce an independent or autonomous film culture?

The most obvious answer is that the state never really gave up control. A more detailed answer would involve the unique complexities of the organization of film production in the 1980s. The state never reformed the vast bureaucratic structure of the socialist "film world." The state-controlled Chinese Filmworkers Association (Zhongguo dianyingjia xiehui) continued to function as the uncontested professional (party-controlled) union for all film workers. The dominant publisher of books related to cinema continued to be the state-owned China Film Press

(Zhongguo dianying chubanshe). The many film magazines and journals continued to be owned and published by the state. The powerful Film Bureau (Dianying ju), presided over by the broadminded, but loyal, Shi Fangyu in the mid-1980s, and by the insufferably bureaucratic Teng Jinxian in the late 1980s, was a department in the Ministry of Culture until the late 1980s, when it was shifted to the new Ministry of Radio, Film, and Television. The individual film studios could decide what they wanted to make, but the final product had to be submitted to the Film Bureau for censorship review. Moreover, central state "planners" still dictated the number of films a single studio could produce in one year. State organs controlled the various high-profile award programs, such as the Hundred Flowers (Bai hua) and Golden Rooster (Jin ji) competitions. All film workers (a vast community estimated to include more than 17,000 people in the late 1980s) were on the state payroll, and all studios remained state-owned. The studios continued to be laid out and organized like small socialist walled cities: housing and dining facilities were provided by the studio, welfare and retirement benefits were administered by the studio, and permanent employment was virtually guaranteed.

The nature of film production itself facilitated ongoing state control in the early post-Mao era. Many intellectuals, including novelists, poets, essayists, and visual artists, worked alone at home, and the cost of their basic materials was often quite modest. Independence from the state was easier to achieve for solitary artists who worked beyond the scrutiny of the state. For a variety of practical and logistical reasons their works were more likely to circulate outside China.

Film production was quite different and, thus, far easier to control. According to Wu Tianming, the average cost of making a film was 400,000–500,000 yuan in the mid-1980s and jumped to 800,000 yuan by 1988.[9] Under the reforms the studios themselves did not have the money to fund such projects and had to rely on bank loans that were not available to individuals to finance new work. Private investment in film production was virtually unheard of in the 1980s. Production equipment was expensive, and production staffs were enormous. Represen-

---

[9]Most of the information on the film distribution system presented here is contained in an important unpublished manuscript by Wu Tianming, "Bing shu qiantou wan mu chun: lun Zhongguo dianying faxing tizhi gaige" (A sick tree looks forward to spring: on the reform of the Chinese film distribution system), 1990. Unless otherwise noted, the statistics given in this section are based on Wu's calculations.

tatives of the state were aware of what was going on almost every step of the way. No private entrepreneurs, or *geti hu*, were making commercial films.

But more than anything else, the Chinese film industry, even in its velvet prison configuration, was controlled by the almost totally unreformed iron-grip workings of a poorly understood distribution system. A tightly organized state monopoly, the China Film Distribution Corporation (Zhongguo dianying faxing gongsi), settled almost all matters related to film distribution from its headquarters in Beijing. In the late 1980s its general manager was Hu Jian. Nothing got screened above ground in China without the corporation's approval. Because all films were the property of the state, they had to be handed over to this state monopoly after they were completed by the studios. Only the corporation had the distribution rights. This system was borrowed in its entirety from the Soviet Union, surviving both the apocalyptic surges of Maoism and the market reforms of Deng Xiaoping.[10] Even if a film passed censorship screening in the Film Bureau, it could not be seen if the corporation did not order and distribute copies. The corporation could decide not to order copies or to order only a few copies if it found a new film politically offensive or (as was increasingly the case) lacking a popular market. If few or no copies were ordered, the film studio sustained staggering financial losses.

The corporation's various branch offices (more than 50 provincial and municipal offices, 2,000 county-level companies, and 3,700 village stations) made direct and exclusive contact with the extraordinary number of 161,777 state-owned projection units.[11] No film projection units were privately owned (although in urban settings in the late 1980s thousands of privately run video parlors showed Hong Kong and Taiwan *gongfu* and romance tapes). Altogether approximately 500,000 workers were on the state payroll in the distribution and projection monopolies at that time, all of whom had to be housed, guaranteed permanent jobs, and provided with pensions.[12]

Wu Tianming, the former head of the Xi'an Film Studio, living in exile in Los Angeles in the early 1990s, complained that the distribution

---

[10]For a brief account of the early distribution system, see Clark, *Chinese Cinema*, 34–38.
[11]Hu Jian, "On the Long Road into the Future," *China Screen* no. 3 (1991): 34.
[12]For a brief history of the development of the distribution system, see Mei Chen, "1949–1989 China Film Distribution and Exhibition," *China Screen*, no. 3 (1990): 26–27.

system denied the state studios and, thus, the individual filmmakers employed by the studios, any meaningful control of their destiny.[13] In brief, the studios took most of the risks and were deprived of most of the rewards.

The system worked in the following way. The corporation decided how many prints of a film it would need. It then sold the prints to its provincial and municipal branch agencies for the set price of 10,500 yuan each, regardless of the quality of the film or the studio's cost of production. For a fee the branch agencies then arranged distribution of the film to various projection units in their regions. The local projection units had no control over which titles were offered or when they were offered. If they refused to show the films offered to them by the branch agencies, they would not be able to show anything. Income from screenings was adversely affected by both the high cost of a single screening (from 51 yuan in Shanghai for a single screening in 1983 to 99 yuan in 1988) and the extremely low cost of tickets (between 20 and 25 fen). Throughout the 1980s, the state's Price Control Bureau refused to consider price increases even though the cost of production and distribution of films had increased. Thus, after expenses, very few projection units showed a profit and theaters that were already uncomfortable and unattractive declined even further.

The funds collected by the regional agencies of the corporation were used to pay their costs, most of which involved salaries and benefits for their heavily bloated staffs. Because provincial and municipal governments controlled personnel appointments in the regional agencies of the corporation, the agencies were commonly used by local governments as dumping grounds for their own unwanted bureaucrats. One particularly notorious county-level agency had eleven vice managers.

The cycle was completed when the regional agencies turned over their after-expense profits to the main office in Beijing. The profits were then divided: approximately 29 percent went to the studios that actually made the films, and 71 percent to the corporation itself. If the individual studios showed any profit after meeting their expenses (including the repayment of bank loans), the state imposed a gargantuan 55 percent industrial tax. Not surprisingly, under such a system of distribution only two or three studios were able to turn a profit each year during the

---

[13]Wu, "Bing shu qiantou wan mu chun."

1980s. Consequently, the technical infrastructures of the studios steadily declined.

The overall impact of state control over distribution is reflected in the statistics for 1987. The Film Distribution Corporation reported that the total income for all film screenings was 516 million yuan. Of this the provincial and municipal agencies got 250 million yuan, while the main office in Beijing got 158 million yuan. Presumably the projection units retained 108 million yuan. But the parent corporation claimed its expenses for the year were 183 million yuan (including the payment of distribution rights to the studios); thus it claimed a loss of 30 million yuan.

Some of the consequences of such a system are less apparent than others. The corporation did not really care if the studios made high-quality and experimental "art" films that have a small audience. It simply failed to buy many copies. *Yellow Earth*, *Horse Thief*, *Evening Bell* (Wan zhong, d. Wu Ziniu, 1988), and *King of the Children* (Haizi wang, d. Chen Kaige, 1987), all of which won international awards, were distributed in amounts of fifteen or fewer copies in China. If studios wanted to absorb the huge losses of making such films (while simultaneously trying to balance their own budgets), that was up to them.

But was it not possible in the late 1980s for studios to make money on "art" films in the foreign market? Filmmakers knew that foreigners loved such films and devoted large amounts of time to analyzing them. The problem was that export profits could not be reaped by the studios. The corporation also ran the China Film Import and Export Corporation (Zhongguo dianying jin chu kou youxian gongsi), which opened a branch office on Wilshire Boulevard in Los Angeles. The corporation alone could sell the rights (for sums sometimes amounting to hundreds of thousands of dollars) to foreign buyers. The studio got only 14 percent from the corporation.

On the eve of the Tiananmen political crisis the studios really had no choice about what kind of films to make. Popular "entertainment" films that featured violence and romance were produced in large numbers because that is what the corporation believed urban consumers wanted to see and, therefore, that was what the corporation was willing to distribute. In Wu Tianming's words, the studios were thus cornered into working as prostitutes for the corporation. Films that lost money, namely, crude political propaganda films and experimental art house films, were out.

DEVELOPMENTS SINCE TIANANMEN: THE DEEPENING OF A CRISIS

The harsh political crackdown that followed the massacres of June 1989 revealed all the flaws in the velvet prison construct. The first instinct of the state was to revert to the crude Stalinist mode of control. It cracked down by mobilizing the conservative Filmworkers Association, the Film Bureau, and, of course, the Film Distribution Corporation.[14] Controversial films of the 1980s, including *The Trouble-Shooters*, *Obsession*, and most Fifth Generation works were effectively banned when the corporation simply stopped distributing them. (The corporation continued, nevertheless, to distribute many of these films abroad in order to earn hard currency.) At the same time, the Film Bureau ordered the studios to produce a small flood of films on contemporary and historical topics that praised the army, the party, and the police, while condemning the polluted ways of foreign cultures. Given the nature of the distribution system, these films, and only these films, were guaranteed to be shown throughout the nation. Schools required students to attend free, mass screenings of such works. Most filmmakers faced the difficult choice of making these "command" films or making nothing at all.

Interestingly, however, the freeze did not last long. Films of the 1980s began to be screened once again, the state quickly reassembled the Chinese velvet prison, and leading artists just as quickly returned to work. But, not surprisingly, tensions related to issues of autonomy and control continued to mount. The post-Tiananmen film world was a jumble of contradictions.

At one level, the production of several visually stunning films in the early 1990s, including Zhang Yimou's *Judou* (Judou, 1990), *Raise the Red Lantern* (Da hong denglong gaogao gua, 1991), and *The Story of Qiu Ju* (Qiu Ju da guan si, 1992), and Chen Kaige's *Farewell My Concubine* (Bawang bie ji, 1993) appeared to indicate that the political crisis of 1989 did not have much of a lasting impact on the film world. *Judou* and *Raise the Red Lantern* were nominated for Oscars, *The Story of Qiu Ju* won the grand prize in Venice, and *Farewell My Concubine* took the Palme d'Or in Cannes and was nominated for an Oscar in 1994.

Foreign writers in particular heaped praise on these works for their considerable artistic merits and for what was often interpreted as their

[14]Teng Jinxian, "Teng Jinxian Expounds China's Film Policy," *China Screen* no. 3 (1989): 10.

politically critical subtexts. Films like *Judou* and *Raise the Red Lantern,* set in the 1920s and 1930s, were read as indictments of the dark side of Chinese culture. The legacy of oppressiveness and brutality criticized by iconoclastic New Culture and May Fourth intellectuals in the 'teens, Zhang Yimou and the others seemed to be saying, never really gave way and remains deeply rooted in Chinese culture today. The Communist Party is the heir to this dubious heritage. Its undemocratic, bureaucratic, and brutish ways are symptomatic of a long-term cultural infirmity. When Zhang and other young directors bashed the traditions of the Chinese patriarchy, it was said, they were bashing the decrepit male autocrats who controlled China and oppressed its people. Given the harshness of the post-Tiananmen crackdown, the appearance of these films was a pleasant surprise. They were so fresh that it was difficult at first to figure out their connection to the culture of the velvet prison.

Actually, the making of these works was closely related to issues that had surfaced well before Tiananmen, namely, the need to find sources of funding for serious "art" films. On the eve of Tiananmen it was clear that the state was no longer willing to subsidize movies of this sort. But it was agreed that filmmakers could try to raise money outside China for coproductions or productions entirely financed by foreign capital. *Judou* was funded largely by Japanese interests, and *Raise the Red Lantern* was funded entirely by Taiwan investors who channeled their money through Hong Kong. The producer of *Raise the Red Lantern* was openly acknowledged in the film's credits as Hou Hsiao-hsien (Hou Xiaoxian), the famous Taiwan director. The astounding sound technology used in the film was the responsibility of a cutting-edge Japanese firm.

Because Zhang Yimou, Chen Kaige, and other young post-Mao directors sometimes got into trouble with state authorities in the early 1990s, they are often viewed by foreign critics as quasi-dissident filmmakers. Actually, these artists are highly privileged insiders who are closely connected to and enjoy good working relations with the cultural establishment. It is precisely because they are so well connected and so well funded by foreign sources that they can do what other filmmakers cannot: make finely textured art movies for an international audience.

It is true that *Judou* and *Raise the Red Lantern* were banned in China until mid-1992 and received no awards in China at the time of their completion. The bans fueled the idea that Zhang Yimou is some sort of dissident. Zhang, Chen Kaige, and others actively cultivate the notion that they are political renegades, in part because this is what their foreign audience wants to hear. Actually, the reason why *Judou* and *Raise the Red Lantern* were not released for a time, and why *Farewell My Concubine* was heavily edited before its release in mid-1993, has more to do with what might be called their "reverse" Orientalism. In a word, these trendy new works, funded by foreign sources and made primarily for foreign audiences, reveal the exotic and erotic Chinese world that foreigners like to see rather than a Chinese world that is recognizable to the Chinese themselves. As one particularly unkind critic stated privately, "Zhang Yimou makes his living by pulling down his mother's pants so foreigners can get a good look at her ass." But by mid-1992, Zhang and the authorities had come to terms again. His banned films were finally screened publicly, and Zhang made a new Hong Kong–financed movie, *The Story of Qiu Ju,* that had fewer Orientalist implications and portrayed China's feared Public Security forces in a surprisingly favorable way. In late 1993 Zhang was even allowed to win a couple of highly coveted domestic film awards.

The banning of *Judou* and *Raise the Red Lantern* had more to do with the issues of bureaucratic control and money-making than dissident politics. The post-Tiananmen state permitted directors to raise money abroad, but it reserved the right to determine which films can bear the "made in China" label, and it insisted on getting its fair share of foreign earnings. Foreign interests could invest in Chinese filmmaking, but the state intended to stay in control. Thus the state claimed that Hollywood had no right to nominate *Judou* for an Oscar without its approval; the state protested again when *Raise the Red Lantern* was nominated for an Oscar as a "Hong Kong" film. Only the Chinese state had the right to decide whether it was a "Hong Kong" or a "China" title. The primary issues were not Zhang Yimou's politics or the content of these particular films; the problem was that the state did not want to see the realms of filmmaking, film distribution, and foreign marketing spin beyond its control. In short, the state wanted to find a way to make the velvet prison arrangement work in the newly emerging multinational global economy.

For this system to work, directors and screenwriters have to be willing to engage in velvet prison–type self-regulation. Minor indiscretions can be forgiven, but basic loyalty must be maintained. Regardless of how a film is funded, the shooting script and the final product must be approved by the state. Zhang Yimou and others who produce primarily for the foreign market often base their stories on works of fiction published in the People's Republic, works that have already been through the censorship process once. Directors sometimes try to manipulate the censorship process, and thereby win small concessions, by submitting one script for official approval and making up another when they are actually shooting the film. Needless to say, the state reserves the right to limit the screening of such works in China on the assumption that films designed for foreign market conditions may not be suitable for domestic audiences.

Foreign investors involve themselves in the process to make money. The case of *Raise the Red Lantern,* funded by Taiwan concerns, is particularly illustrative of the complex (postmodern?) regional financial and marketing arrangements that are playing an increasingly important role in Chinese filmmaking in the 1990s. Investors suspected that the film would not be shown widely in China. It could not be screened in Taiwan because it features lead actors and actresses who reside on the mainland. But, laser disks, the technology of choice of the large and growing Taiwan middle class, could be marketed in Taiwan. Incredible as it seems, investors in Taiwan suspected even before the film was produced that they could make a profit by marketing laser disks in Taiwan and by selling the international screening rights and videotape rights in North America and Europe. When multinational financing and marketing are involved, the behavior of consumers in the People's Republic is of secondary importance. In the new era, foreign investors who are willing to spend money promoting artists like Zhang Yimou and Chen Kaige can profit even when domestic distribution of their work is restricted.

Just as interesting is the case of the Zhang Yimou–like film *Five Girls and a Rope* (Wuge nuren he yi gen shengzi) made in 1991 by Taiwan director Yeh Hung-wei (Ye Hongwei). This powerful film, about the collective, ritual suicide of five rural women during the Republican era, was funded, produced, and directed by the Taiwan side. The director shot on location entirely in the People's Republic, made almost exclusive use of (low-cost) mainland actors and actresses, and had virtually all postproduction work done on the mainland. The film was not screened widely in the People's Republic, and, because of its use of mainland players, was not screened widely in Taiwan. (One consideration here is that Taiwan actors and actresses do not want to be driven out of their trade by the existence of cheap labor in the People's Republic.) Still, the film's investors, who put up the equivalent of nearly one million yuan, made money by selling laser disks and by marketing the film in Europe and North America. State leaders in socialist China go along with such arrangements because they provide employment for film workers, generate hard currency income, and appear to pose no domestic political threats. In brief, China's landscapes, processing and editing labs, actors and actresses, film studios, and production crews are all available for rent. Chen Kaige's *Farewell My Concubine* is only the first of several films he has contracted to do on this basis for the Taiwan-linked Tomson Film Company in Hong Kong.

The political economy of Chinese filmmaking underwent some fascinating shifts in the immediate post-Tiananmen period, but critics should not lose sight of the fact that the activities of Zhang Yimou and Chen Kaige were not perceived as posing any fundamental challenges to the velvet prison arrangement. In the mid-1990s the state continued to view these artists as loyal (if highly privileged) insiders.

IS HARASZTI RIGHT OR WRONG ABOUT ARTISTS UNDER LATE STATE SOCIALISM?

The utility of the Haraszti conceptualization of artists under state socialism is hard to deny. I fully agree with such scholars as Gérémie Barmé who believe that it is important to try to understand the realities of state socialism in China within the larger context of state socialist regimes in general, and that the pre-1989 writings of Haraszti, Vaclav Havel, and other East Europeans shed a great deal of light on contemporary China.[15] Two notions associated with the Eastern European and Soviet experiences are particularly important. One is the idea that state socialist regimes can jettison the heavy-handed Stalinist approach to cultural control without sacrificing control itself. This is precisely what the Chinese state sought to do to the film industry after 1976.

The other (and more unsettling) idea is that we should not feel too sorry for artists in late state socialist regimes, artists who work within the framework of the velvet prison. That is, we should be more critical than we are of their active and willing collaboration with the culturally "liberalizing" regime.[16] Virtually all their activities legitimize and thus

---

[15] Gérémie Barmé, "The Chinese Velvet Prison: Culture in the 'New Age,' 1976–89," *Issues and Studies* 25, no. 8 (August 1989): 54–79.
[16] For a critique of Chinese intellectuals, see Timothy Cheek, "From Priests to Professionals: Intellectuals and the State Under the CCP," in Jeffrey Wasserstrom and Elizabeth J. Perry,

help perpetuate the regime. Of course, this is a very sensitive issue. No self-respecting artist in China is likely to admit to playing a collaborative role; on the contrary, in their private utterances, they protest the inhumanities of life under state socialism. The fact is, however, that the artists engage in self-censorship and self-mutilation on a regular basis. Very few have arrived at the position articulated so eloquently by Havel before 1989, that is, the idea that they should stop placing all the blame on the faceless bureaucratic state for everything that ails the nation and people.[17] Artists should not be viewed simply as helpless victims of oppression; all along they have participated in their own oppression; they are partly responsible for constructing and maintaining the system that prevails.[18]

If we follow Haraszti's logic, we would have to conclude that in the realm of Chinese filmmaking nothing that happened in the wake of the state's retreat in the 1980s resulted in real independence or autonomy for this type of art creation. At best, what one finds is indirect and implicit criticism buried between the lines of what can only be regarded as "official" texts. But, as Haraszti pointed out, the velvet prison mode allows for such individual expressions, provided that they can be interpreted as loyal and constructive.

Still, one cannot help feeling that, for all the light Haraszti's work sheds on the situation in China, he was, in the end, wrong. He was wrong about his native Hungary, he was wrong about the Soviet Union, and he is probably wrong about China.

The problem with his gloomy and pessimistic account, written at a time of apparent hopelessness in 1983, is that it argued that the battle is over and state socialism has won. The culture of state socialism, he said, is entrenched in large part because intellectuals have been co-opted by the velvet prison framework. There is a profound finality to his work. Absolutely nothing in his writings anticipated or prepared us for the defeat of state socialism. At precisely the moment he was declaring its permanence, it suddenly collapsed. The reader is left wondering how that could have happened if his brilliant analysis had been correct.

In a hastily written afterword prepared in 1987 for the English edition

eds., *Popular Protest and Political Culture in Modern China: Learning from 1989* (Boulder, Colo.: Westview Press, 1992), 124–45.
[17]See Vaclav Havel, *Living in Truth* (London: Faber and Faber, 1990).
[18]The best recent discussion of the relationship between Chinese intellectuals and the state is Perry Link, *Evening Chats in Beijing: Probing China's Predicament* (New York: W. W. Norton, 1992).

of *The Velvet Prison*, Haraszti acknowledged the apparent contradiction between his thesis and the enormous significance of the Solidarity movement in Poland.[19] Writing in an uncharacteristically defensive manner, he was willing to hold out the possibility (however remote) that at some point in the future places like Poland and Hungary that were on the "western coast" of the state socialist empire and whose communism was not "sui generis" might be able to support a truly independent resistance to state power. "Dissent, however feeble," he stated, "can at least draw upon a democratic past that is altogether absent in the Soviet Union and in China."[20] Still, he was totally unprepared for the sudden collapse of state socialism even in his own homeland, never mind in the Soviet Union. "It might well be that my most pessimistic message is the seemingly good news of the spreading of the Hungarian model . . . the Hungarian model might well represent a more rational, more normative, and more enduring version of directed culture. Mr. Gorbachev understands that in order to have a truly successful society with a modern economy he must boost the intelligentsia's sagging morale by giving it a stake in administering the future. But in Hungary we know very well the cost of such liberating collaboration."[21] Thus, as late as March 1987 Haraszti clung stubbornly to a velvet prison paradigm that ruled out the emergence of critical and "nondirected" culture in places like the Soviet Union and China.

It is in this connection that I came to disagree with Gérémie Barmé in 1991. Barmé, to his credit, takes the velvet prison conceptualization very seriously. This, I suspect, is why he took strong exception to my suggestion that even a thoroughly establishment figure like Xie Jin, who is able to work comfortably in both Stalinist and velvet prison environments and whose amazingly popular films must be regarded as "official culture," gives highly dramatic expression to popular and unofficial discontent with the Communist party-state.[22] Xie Jin is not a dissident; he is not operating in an independent or autonomous realm. Much of what he does legitimizes and perpetuates the dominance of state socialism. However, the many ways in which his works chip away at the foundation of state socialism should not be dismissed.

Barmé and I undoubtedly agree that, personally, we appreciate the

[19]Haraszti, *The Velvet Prison*, 160–62.
[20]Ibid., 160.
[21]Ibid., 162.
[22]Gérémie Barmé, "Outsiders," *Far Eastern Economic Review*, February 21, 1991.

works of the younger directors much more. Still, we must admit that the remarkable films of Chen Kaige, Huang Jianxin, Zhang Yimou, Tian Zhuangzhuang, and others are no less official than Xie Jin's, and that as individuals they enjoy the benefits of the velvet prison arrangement. It is not untrue to say that they also collaborate with the state, that their work also legitimizes and perpetuates the dominance of state socialism. They also engage in self-censorship and self-mutilation. But, just as in the case of Xie Jin and other old school melodramatists, it would be a mistake to refuse to see the many ways in which their work, even that set in the presocialist era, undermines state socialism and exacerbates the problem of popular alienation, especially among urban youths.

It is important for us to understand how the works of Xie Jin and the works of the new-style artists subvert state socialism and erode public confidence in the system. Of course, it would be wrong to exaggerate the significance of their ability to subvert. This would cause us to underestimate the regime's staying power. But so, too, would it be wrong to hold rigidly to the powerful Haraszti model and dismiss too quickly the surprisingly wide range of criticism that emanates from the velvet prison.[23] To do so would be to overestimate the state's staying power, which is exactly what Haraszti did.

If our definition of autonomy requires the existence of *communities* of artists who are independent of the state, then we can surely conclude that filmmakers do not enjoy (in the way they did in the prewar 1930s and postwar 1940s) autonomy from the state. If, on the other hand, we take into account *individual* acts of subversion, even when they are carried out well within the framework of the velvet prison arrangement, we can safely speak of artistic activity that, despite the smug confidence of cultural bureaucrats, is beyond the control of the state. Haraszti and Barmé take the self-confidence of the state too seriously. In the 1980s and early 1990s, the interests of the state were being undermined in this way every day. The state believes that it has control of culture, especially in an industry like filmmaking that seems so easy to control. But in fact, with the deepening of the reform era, much is permanently out of control.

In 1993, for example, the film bureaucracy was enraged by the production of unauthorized "underground" films, including *Beijing Bastards* (Beijing zazhong, d. Zhang Yuan), *Red Beads* (Xuan lian, d. He

---

[23]Barmé, "The Chinese Velvet Prison," 75.

Yi), and *The Days* (Dong chun de rizi, d. Wang Xiaoshuai) that sketched grim and depressing pictures of life in urban China. In fact, the films were not underground productions. They were shot quite openly on the streets of Beijing and elsewhere. They were attacked by officialdom because, unlike all the work produced by the Fifth Generation, these "Sixth Generation" films were independent and relatively low budget productions funded by the filmmakers themselves with help from backers in Hong Kong. These defiant filmmakers were not working in conjunction with any state studio, and they consulted with neither the Film Bureau nor the Film Distribution Corporation. One of the films, *Beijing Bastards,* won the Critics Circle award at the 1993 Lucarno Film Festival. In the fall of 1993 the official Chinese delegation to the Tokyo Film Festival stormed out in protest when it learned that *Beijing Bastards* had been entered in the competition. Later the state tried to take legal action against Zhang Yuan for shooting the film and distributing it abroad without state approval. In a word, Zhang and the others were the first to pursue the idea of the privatization of film culture to its logical end.

And Fifth Generation insiders continued to get into trouble for violating velvet prison norms. Officials in the Ministry of Radio, Film, and Television alleged that Tian Zhuangzhuang's 1993 film *The Blue Kite* (Lan fengzheng), financed by the Hong Kong–based Longwick Production Company, was shot without state approval and then "smuggled" abroad, where it won top honors at the Tokyo Film Festival. It is hard to believe that an artist as well-connected as Tian Zhuangzhuang will experience difficulties for very long, but his problems with *The Blue Kite* highlight the stresses and strains that are constantly reconfiguring the velvet prison. Skeptics might argue that films like *Beijing Bastards* and *The Blue Kite* will have no long-lasting impact so long as the state continues to monopolize film distribution. But in late 1993, film scholars in China were predicting that another wave of change would hit the film world in the mid-1990s. The Film Distribution Corporation, it was said, would soon be broken down into many competing provincial and municipal organizations. Film studios and filmmakers would soon be doing business directly with the regions rather than with the center. Moreover, industry specialists also insisted that privately owned movie theaters will be a reality in the near future.

Of course, it is too early to know precisely how the crisis of the post-Mao film industry will be resolved. The point is that periodic efforts to reactivate the Stalinist mode of cultural control can only be temporary.

Haraszti was wrong when he said that criticism expressed by those who are on the state payroll is hopelessly compromised. That is one of the reasons he failed to anticipate the collapse of state socialism in Hungary and the Soviet Union.

The socialist state in China knows what it is talking about when it rails against "peaceful evolution." The problem is that the state can now do very little about it. The cultural realm is out of control largely because no one, least of all those who are party members, believes in socialism. One of the ironies of late state socialist China is that even a hard-core propaganda film like *Mao Zedong and His Son* (Mao Zedong he tade erzi, d. Zhang Jinbiao, 1991), ordered up by the state immediately after Tiananmen, is unable to play its proper reactionary role. The film was popular for the wrong reasons. Images of a perfect Mao, no matter how unconvincing, only served to remind the audience of the moral failings of the current leadership. In late state socialist China, even crude propaganda works subvert state power.

Perhaps, then, we are asking the wrong question about the future of the socialist state. Does it matter whether fully autonomous and independent social groups in China are chipping away at the state's hegemony when so many quasi-autonomous groups and individuals, all of them heirs to the cultural legacy of late state socialism in the former Soviet bloc, are already doing the job in a "peaceful and evolutionary" way?

9

The avant-garde's challenge to official art

JULIA F. ANDREWS and GAO MINGLU

With the greater degree of personal freedom possible in the 1980s, we might have expected an explosion of new forms of visual art in China. Surprisingly, a significant result of a decade of reform in the Chinese art world was the successful promotion of a widely practiced official style of oil painting only slightly more varied than the one required ten or fifteen years before.[1] The reason for this is simple: Realism is acceptable to people in almost all ideological camps. Thus, although Western styles connected with modernism and postmodernism were suppressed during each of the leftist movements, specifically the anti–Spiritual Pollution movement of 1982–83 and the anti–bourgeois liberalism campaigns of 1987 and 1990–92, realist painters and the critics who supported them continued to exhibit and publish with little interference.

REALISM AS AN OFFICIAL STYLE

The painting that we might define as the official style of the 1980s is characterized by a high degree of realism and extreme technical finesse. Its theoretical foundations may be found in a formalistic nationalism that lays claim to a uniquely Chinese form of beauty best rendered in a realistic manner. The great achievements of Chinese realism were lauded, for example, by the aged critic and bureaucrat Cai Ruohong in an article published in October 1991. He traced the achievements of Chinese re-

---

[1] A survey of 1991 and 1992 issues of China's official art magazine, *Meishu* (Art) (hereafter *MS*), makes this quite clear. The more recent Second Oil Painting Exhibition of the Oil Painting Art Committee, Chinese Artists Association, held in April and May 1994, exhibited some abstract paintings by retired socialist realists, but was still largely dominated by a limited range of realist themes and subjects. See *Zhongguo youhua* (Chinese oil painting), no. 2, 1994, special issue.

alism under Communist Party sponsorship as far back as 1926 and claimed that, since 1949, it had been threatened only twice. The first occasion was in the mid-1960s, presumably the Red Guard period, when, according to Cai, realism was interpreted far too narrowly. The second occurred in the mid-1980s, under the influence of Western bourgeois liberalism, and may be identified with the avant-garde movement, which began in 1985.[2]

This chapter contrasts the ongoing development of official art with the rise and fall of an internationally oriented avant-garde in the 1980s.[3] The avant-garde movement can be viewed from many angles. In the mid-1980s, it was clearly made possible by the partial "retreat of the state." It involved occasional political dissidence. Perhaps most important, particularly between 1985 and 1989, was its role as a challenge to the power and aesthetics of a self-perpetuating official establishment by younger and more outward-looking artists and critics. This ultimately unsuccessful effort was less an assault on the art world from without than an effort to change its direction from within.

Chinese critics have referred to this phenomenon by means of a variety of terms, ranging from "modernist" to "avant-garde." Each of these terms is laden with art-historical meanings in its Western context that may not correspond with the Chinese situation. For convenience, the term avant-garde is adopted here, as used in the title of the retrospective exhibition held in February 1989, "China/Avant-Garde."

The Chinese avant-garde peaked in the mid- to late 1980s and, at least temporarily, changed the comparative relationships within the power structure of contemporary Chinese art. It was as though the Chinese art world were a tripod. The first leg, traditional Chinese painting, was claimed to develop from ancient literati painting. Because landscape painting and bird-and-flower painting were frequently criticized during the Cultural Revolution as "art for art's sake," after the Cultural Revolution this style was allowed to develop even more freely.

The second leg of the tripod we may, somewhat ironically, call neo-traditionalist art. It is based on three related official styles of the pre–Cultural Revolution period, China's so-called glorious revolutionary artistic tradition. It consists of art developed from the realistic styles pro-

---

[2]*MS*, no. 10 (1991): 4.
[3]A detailed account of the avant-garde movement from the viewpoint of critics closely involved with it may be found in Gao Minglu et al., *Zhongguo dangdai meishu shi, 1985–1986* (A history of contemporary Chinese art) (Shanghai: Shanghai People's Press, 1991).

moted by Xu Beihong in the early and mid-twentieth century; the revolutionary realism of the Yanan liberated areas; and Soviet socialist realism. After the Cultural Revolution this manner continued to develop as the official academic style, but revolutionary subject matter was replaced by concern for realism of form. The third style of the late 1980s was the avant-garde. It developed in the context of the conflict between the old and new traditions and in a situation of suppression.

Realism, or "neotraditionalism," has unquestionably comprised China's official style since the 1950s, and has been the dominant mode of Western-style art. The failure of the Chinese art world in the 1980s and 1990s to adopt a truly pluralistic stance and the persistence of a rather narrow view of Western-style art is related to the power structure of the Chinese art world and may raise broader issues regarding the nature and pace of China's "opening to the outside." This chapter describes this phenomenon and addresses some of the reasons behind it.

BACKGROUND: REALIST PAINTING, 1949–1979

One of the fundamental tenets of Chinese art theory since 1949 has been that art and artists should provide political service to the nation. Most periods have witnessed more than one official style, or variations within an official style, but the need to create, refine, and propagate such a manner has formed the foundation of the Communist art education system and of its major official activities, most particularly exhibitions and art criticism. Most important, since the early 1950s, realism has been at the core of official art.

Soviet influence on the Chinese art world in the 1950s, during the period of intensive cultural and technical links between China and the USSR, led to emulation of the Soviet art educational system in China's major art academies. By the mid-1950s, oil painting on the Russian or Soviet model had become the most prestigious form of official painting in China.[4] A standard for art during this period was that pictures tell

---

[4] Discussion of some artistic exchanges with the Soviet Union and of the changes in the art educational system can be found in Julia F. Andrews, *Painting and Politics in the People's Republic of China, 1949–1979* (Berkeley and Los Angeles: University of California Press, 1994), chaps. 2 and 3. Many such paintings are referred to as "socialist realist" or "Soviet," even though they might derive their styles from pre-Soviet Russian realist works, particularly those of the Wanderers. We are indebted to Marian Mazzone for her seminar paper "China's Nationalization of Oil Painting in the 1950s: Searching Beyond the Soviet Paradigm," Ohio State University, March 1992.

uplifting patriotic stories and must, therefore, be figurative and realistic. An undercurrent of nationalism permeated the work and teaching of some academic painters, however, leading to the theory that Chinese oil painting could be "nationalized" (*minzuhua*), or sinicized.[5]

The general emphasis on Russian and Soviet modes of painting was reinforced by the availability of government patronage in the 1950s and 1960s. The major oil painting commissions of this period were issued by Beijing's newly established museums in several intensive campaigns. The earliest group of paintings were commissioned for the Museum of Revolutionary History, then occupying part of the old imperial palace, in 1951 and 1952. Subsequent campaigns, begun in 1958, 1961, and 1964, filled the newly constructed Museum of Revolutionary History, Military Affairs Museum, and Great Hall of the People with history paintings, portraits, propaganda, and nationalistic decorations.[6]

One typical image is *Mao Zedong at the December Conference* (Figure 9.1), painted by Jin Shangyi in 1961, a monumental portrait of the young Mao.[7] Quan Shanshi's *Death Before Surrender* (Figure 9.2), of the same year, is more colorful than Jin's work and is, like the work of other Soviet-trained artists, constructed of large, blunt dabs of paint.[8] Such pictorial conventions as the fierce facial expressions of the heroic soldiers and the sharply tilted ground plan are closely related to Soviet socialist realism of the period. For most artists, then and in the 1980s, the depiction of Chinese themes was sufficient for the "nationalization" of oil painting.

Intensive debates about the value of traditional Chinese painting (*guohua*) had culminated during the anti-Rightist campaign of 1957, after

---

[5] The best-known exemplar of this trend is Dong Xiwen (1914–73), a professor at the Central Academy of Fine Arts. His standard work is *The Founding of the Nation*, in the collection of the Chinese Museum of Revolutionary History, Beijing. See Andrews, *Painters and Politics*, chaps. 2 and 3.

[6] For more detailed descriptions of these commissions see Andrews, *Painting and Politics*, chap. 5. Another important source of patronage, the official agencies charged with organizing the national art exhibitions, is discussed by Ellen Johnston Laing, *The Winking Owl, Art in the People's Republic of China* (Berkeley and Los Angeles: University of California Press, 1988).

[7] Jin, who held the post of director of the Central Academy of Fine Arts beginning in the mid-1980s, studied with the Russian expert Konstantin Maksimov between 1955 and 1957. For a study of Maksimov, see I. I. Kup't'sov, *Konstantin Mefed'evich Maksimov* (Leningrad: Khudozhnik RSFSR, 1984). Jin Shangyi's portrait style is close in many ways to the work of I. I. Brodski, best known for his portraits of Lenin.

[8] Quan was trained at the art academy in Hangzhou (called the Zhejiang Academy of Fine Arts between 1958 and 1994 and now the China National Art Academy) and more importantly, at the Repin Art Institute in Leningrad (St. Petersburg). Quan Shanshi's classmate in Leningrad, Xiao Feng, was, at the time of this writing, director of the academy in Hangzhou, where Quan himself was dean of studies.

Figure 9.1. Jin Shangyi, *Mao Zedong at the December Conference*, 1961. Oil on canvas, 155 × 140 cm. *Chinese Museum of Revolutionary History*

which the authorities accepted a rather generalized nationalism as a sufficiently useful purpose for art.[9] As a result, *guohua* paintings were com-

[9] Julia F. Andrews, "Traditional Painting in New China: *Guohua* and the Anti-Rightist Campaign," *Journal of Asian Studies* 49, no. 3 (August 1990): 555–86.

Figure 9.2. Quan Shanshi, *Death before Surrender*, 1961. Oil on canvas, 233 × 127 cm. *Chinese Museum of Revolutionary History*

missioned by the State Council in 1959 as decorations for the newly constructed Great Hall of the People.[10] We will not discuss the influence of this development on art of the 1980s, but if we were to do so we would find the dynamics of *guohua*'s official status parallel in many ways to that

[10]The largest and most important commission, by Fu Baoshi and Guan Shanyue, illustrated Mao's poem *Ode to Snow* with a patriotic panorama of the whole expanse of China's territory. This work has been discussed by Ellen Johnston Laing, *The Winking Owl,* 36, and by Andrews, *Painters and Politics,* 229–31.

of realist oil painting.[11] The official *guohua* paintings of the late 1950s and early 1960s were significant because they defined China's physical beauty as an appropriately patriotic subject for painting.

Another important form of official art is the form of realism promoted during the Cultural Revolution. Its standards were in place between about 1967 and 1979, and were particularly associated with the national exhibitions. Perversely, Jiang Qing's revolution against the academic curriculum promoted styles of realistic oil painting that validated Soviet educational practices and aesthetic standards.

Selection criteria for the exhibitions of 1972 through 1976 involved both theme and style. The paintings lauded the accomplishments of the Cultural Revolution and included images of happy young people laboring among the workers, peasants, and soldiers; portraits of Mao; and renderings of Cultural Revolution heroes. Equally significant, in the long run, was the creation of a homogenized style, in which brightly lit, monumental figures were rendered in rich colors (Figure 9.3). Such works, with their slick surfaces and theatrical illumination, were later referred to, derisively, as "red, bright, and luminous" (*hong guang liang*), even though key aspects of their stylistic and thematic approach may be traced to painting of the 1950s. Standards of the 1970s influenced a generation of young artists, many of whom entered the reopened art academies after 1979, and form the foundation of realism in the 1980s.

THE EVOLUTION OF REALISTIC STYLES AFTER THE CULTURAL REVOLUTION

Most people outside China might think that the first thing artists would have wished to do at the end of the Cultural Revolution would be to overthrow the standards imposed by Jiang Qing. Because her aesthetic was simply an extreme version of the socialist realistic art of the 1950s, however, and not completely unique to the Cultural Revolution, stylistic changes were slow to appear.

[11]Between 1958 and 1966, practitioners of two or three primary types of official painting, namely, oil painting, *guohua* (literally, national painting, i.e., painting in the traditional media), and woodblock prints, coexisted without great bitterness. Most of the oil painters were employed by the national art academies, the army, or the publishing houses, and painted primarily historical paintings and portraits. The patriotic *guohua* painters, mainly employed by newly established Institutes of Chinese Painting, by the Chinese Artists Association (CAA), or by Wenshiguan (Literature and History Halls), rendered images of the physical beauties of the new China. A third type of art, realist woodcuts, emerged from propaganda publishing houses and the CAA.

Figure 9.3. Tang Xiaohe and Cheng Li, *Follow Closely One Great Leader, Chairman Mao; Ride the Wind; Cleave the Waves; Fearlessly Forge Ahead*, ca. 1972. Oil on canvas, dimensions unavailable. *Collection the artists*

The reopening of the art schools in 1979 was one of the most important artistic events of the early post–Cultural Revolution era. Many of the new graduate students were former Red Guard artists who had excelled at painting in the official Cultural Revolution style. This is not surprising, since the entrance examinations still placed great value on the artist's ability to develop a composition based on a political theme. Graduation works from the academy, if no longer propagandistic, were often thematic, with historical or literary subjects of contemporary relevance particularly popular.

Two realist movements with slightly more challenging subject matter emerged during the same period. The first, consisting mainly of paintings by young art students, has been labeled "Scar" painting, after the literary movement of the same name. The works depict the senseless violence of the Cultural Revolution, thus using realist means for essentially critical ends (Figure 9.4). Their basically negative tone was new, and in the context of the Communist period, was a striking use of realist techniques. This trend was quickly followed by one that has been labeled "rustic realism."[12] Works of this type depict ordinary citizens, particu-

[12]This term, widely used throughout the late 1980s, may have been coined by Shui Tian-

Figure 9.4. Chen Yiming, Liu Yulian, Li Bing, *Maple*, 1979. Illustration after a short story by Zheng Yi, published in *Lianhuanhuabao*, no. 8 (1979): 1

larly herders, peasants, or minority people, the type of people encountered by the young artists during their years spent working in the countryside (Figure 9.5). The unidealized and often rather melancholy

zhong, who used it in his "Guanyu xiangtu xieshi huihua de sikao" (Thoughts on rustic realist painting), *MS*, no. 12 (1984): 55–57.

Figure 9.5. He Douling, *Spring Breeze Has Awakened*, 1982. Oil on canvas, 95 × 129 cm. *Chinese National Art Gallery*

view of the subjects may be linked with concern for the humanistic ideas that swept China's intellectuals during the early 1980s. Like the Scar painters, rustic realists used their technical skills for socially critical purposes. While these artists' paintings are different from those exhibited during the Cultural Revolution, their work, which dwells on themes taken from everyday life and on special characteristics of China's people, had clear links to previous forms of Chinese realism in both style and political connotations.

The only challenge to the stylistic and thematic conservatism of such paintings, that of the amateur Stars group,[13] was an exception, because several of the Stars works were overtly satirical in intent (Figure 9.6) and many had strong modernist or abstract tendencies. Their work had little immediate artistic impact, however, for it was not taken seriously

[13]Their first exhibition was held between November 23 and December 2, 1979 (*MS*, nos. 3 and 12 [1980]). A history of the Stars may be found in the exhibition catalogue, *The Stars: Ten Years* (Hong Kong: Hanart 2 Gallery, 1989).

Figure 9.6. Wang Keping, *Idol*, 1978. Wood. *Collection the artist*

by many young professional painters. By the time their work was published in the official journal *Meishu* (Art), a year after their first exhibition in 1979, many of the artists had made plans to leave the country.

The Chinese government began, in the mid-1980s, requiring arts institutions to become more self-supporting. The Chinese Artists Association initially responded to the new economic policies by formalizing official channels for the sale of art.[14] Officials turned their attention to the foreign art market and encouraged painting that they believed had an easily accessible market, thereby abandoning overt political propaganda in the name of national economic progress. Serving as an inspiration to the newly market-oriented artists, Shanghai-born émigré artist Chen Yifei had abandoned the political themes of his early career in China to begin selling lyrical landscapes and figure paintings in New York, Hong Kong, and elsewhere. A large oil painting of five Chinese beauties was sold at Christie's in 1991 to an Asian buyer for $176,282, a record price for a Chinese oil painting at auction. Works of the rustic realists and their emulators, particularly those who painted plaintive peasant girls and sweet rural children in an Andrew Wyeth–like style, sold well in the late 1980s and early 1990s. The portraitist Jin Shangyi developed an effective combination of nationalism and commercial appeal with images of dreamy urban girls set against distinctively Chinese backgrounds (Figure 9.7).

A new commercial standard has replaced previous political demands on the themes and styles of official art. Indeed, many official critics have adopted success at overseas sales as the primary criterion in judging a Chinese oil painter. The leftist trend in cultural policy of the late 1980s and early 1990s encouraged realism for ideological reasons; the art market, which has created a rather strange niche for these works, reinforced domestic trends with the cachet of international validation. The reasons

[14]One such arrangement led to exhibition and sale of Chinese oil paintings by the Hefner Gallery in New York between 1987 and 1989. Artists who showed in the gallery were often invited to visit the United States. They returned with stories about their experiences that tended to confirm the opinions of the Chinese art establishment. One view that became popular in this period is that Chinese realists are the only true inheritors of the best traditions of classical European oil painting. In their view, this fact can be confirmed by visits to American galleries and to major American museums, which are filled with technically inadequate modern work. Some of the artists who came to the United States while the gallery, which was devoted primarily to Chinese realism, operated in New York, spent their time in Oklahoma, and even during their stays in New York they do not seem to have explored much of the New York gallery scene. Those whose works were sold went home in glory, their wealth viewed as testimony to the importance of realist painting on the international market.

Figure 9.7. Jin Shangyi, *Portrait*, ca. 1987. Oil on canvas, dimensions unavailable. *Collection the artist*

Asian buyers of the period paid such high prices for realist Chinese oil paintings remain a mystery to most Western and some Chinese critics, but the result of this intense commercialization of the Chinese art world has been the maintenance of a gulf between the Chinese critical community and that of the West.[15]

THE AVANT-GARDE MOVEMENT

The avant-garde movement differs from the realist movement in several significant ways. It has no links with the official art of the Cultural Revolution and was developed in opposition to official styles. It was, at least until recently, unconcerned with commercial trends, but instead sought critical recognition, first, within China and, now, abroad. Its artists and critics generally considered artistic values and commercial values unrelated. As part of their rebellion against official art, they promoted creative freedom and individual human freedom.

Nevertheless, the avant-garde developed in a context of official and commercial domination of the art world. Some artists and critics have used both kinds of power for their own purposes, and the official and commercial worlds have, on occasion, tried to co-opt avant-garde artists and critics. The temptations of the official and commercial worlds are a threat to those artists, since much of the power of the avant-garde, at its inception, came from its independent and oppositional stance.

THE POLITICAL AND CULTURAL BACKGROUND OF THE CHINESE AVANT-GARDE

Modernist Chinese art appeared as early as the 1930s, when some artists and groups of artists tried to synthesize contemporary Western styles with Chinese subject matter.[16] Such styles were considered heretical by the Chinese government during the 1950s, however, and modernist work ceased. Not until two years after the 1976 conclusion of the Cultural Revolution did such activity reappear in the Chinese art world. Public

---

[15]A brief, but well-balanced article by Joyce Barnathan and Bruce Einhorn (*Business Week*, October 12, 1992, 80) quotes enthusiastic dealers and buyers on the one hand and dismayed critics on the other.

[16]Little study of these artists has yet been conducted. One notable group was the Juelan she (Storm society), active in Shanghai. See Ralph Croizier, "Post-Impressionists in Pre-War Shanghai: The Juelan she ('Storm Society') and the Fate of Modernism in Republican China," in John Clark, ed., *Modernity in Asian Art* (University of Sydney East Asian series, no. 7, 135–54).

commissions from 1977 and 1978 continue the legacy of the Cultural Revolution and simply substitute icons of China's new leaders for those of the old.[17] Following this post-Cultural Revolutionist (*hon wenge*) period, in 1979, long-suppressed modernist trends reappeared.

The Developmental period of the Avant-Garde, 1979–1984. The Chinese avant-garde could appear only after changes in the Chinese political situation. In 1978, Beijing held a national congress to consider the mistakes made by the Cultural Revolution and Mao Zedong. The policy of opening to the West followed, along with the slogan "Seek Truth from Facts." These circumstances allowed people to express their long-suppressed desire to criticize society and their demand for democracy.

In 1979 and 1980, a total of sixteen exhibitions of work in avant-garde styles were held in Beijing, Shanghai, and Xi'an. Most appeared spontaneously, without official organization. Of these, the most controversial were the two exhibitions of a group called the Stars. Their two shows exhibited 163 works by twenty-three amateur artists. They advocated criticism of society and called for the awakening of human nature. The exhibition motto was "Picasso is our banner; Kollwitz is our model." Wang Keping's sculpture (Figure 9.6), for example, reflects the people's need for freedom and democracy and opposes dictatorship. This exhibition, however, was soon criticized by the authorities.

Simultaneously, as we have already seen, two types of socially critical work that used realistic techniques appeared: Scar painting, which principally described the calamities and spiritual wounds caused by the Cultural Revolution; and rustic realism, which sought to express a humanistic feeling by depicting ordinary herders and peasants.

Trends in art developed along with those in other areas of intellectual activity. Between 1978 and 1980, newspapers and magazines published many articles on Deng Xiaoping's slogan "practice is the only measure of truth." The idea that truth is no more than validated practical reality caused Chinese who were disillusioned by the Cultural Revolution to shift their values to pragmatism and individualism. Beginning in about 1981, the world of philosophy began discussing questions of humanism and alienation.[18] This discussion was initiated by renewed research on

[17]See Gao et al., *Zhongguo dangdai meishu shi*, 26.
[18]This theme is also noted by Bill Brugger and David Kelly, *Chinese Marxism in the Post-Mao Era* (Stanford: Stanford University Press, 1990), chap. 6, "The Importance of Humanism."

Marx's *1844 Manuscript on Economics and Philosophy*. It used the young Marx's theory, which criticized alienation and emphasized humanism, indirectly to criticize the suppression of human nature by contemporary society. This discussion reached a climax in 1983; it touched on human value, human position, human dignity, human rights, and human freedom. It awakened Chinese people to a desire for human liberation and democracy.

Conservatives within the Communist Party immediately counterattacked by initiating the anti–Spiritual Pollution political movement of 1983. In the art world, a movement was launched to criticize self-expression and modern Western abstract art. From the point of view of modernist art, the year 1984 was contemporary Chinese art's most dismal time. Not only was the Sixth National Art Exhibition very backward-looking, there was only one avant-garde exhibition, held in Lanzhou, Gansu Province, in 1984.

The avant-garde's apogee, 1985–1989. A renewal of official support for intellectual interchange with the West began in early 1985. This period was characterized by the most intense discussion of culture since the early twentieth century. Many works of Western philosophy, history, aesthetics, and psychology appeared in translation. All sorts of scholarly conferences were held, one after the other. Chinese scholars, both in China and abroad, involved themselves in the debate. At the same time, ancient Chinese philosophy, history, culture, and religion were reevaluated, criticized, or accepted according to contemporary standards. The discussion proceeded in three stages, as in the early twentieth century: first, analysis of similarities and differences between China and the West; second, comparisons of the respective merits and flaws of Chinese and Western culture; and third, discussion of the future of Chinese and Western culture. In the art world, the struggle between traditionalism and antitraditionalism focused on the questions of whether or not tradition requires modernization, what is modernism in contemporary art, and on Chinese attitudes toward and evaluations of Western contemporary art.

This battle was made more acute by the rather sudden appearance of a new avant-garde movement in early 1985. In the two years 1985 and 1986, more than eighty self-organized avant-garde art groups, spread over twenty-six different provinces, cities, and autonomous regions, and including more than 2,250 of the nation's young artists, emerged to organize exhibitions, to hold conferences, and to write manifestos and articles about their art.

Why did many young artists choose to participate in such groups? The groups had two primary functions. The first was defensive. The dangers of a solitary artist creating avant-garde art, and thus attacking society, or even criticizing the art establishment, are obvious. In the face of past governmental suppression, the artists saw the need to form a stronger united force. When criticism or castigation struck the group, for example, the group naturally felt an obligation to protect every member and not to let the individual artist bear his or her hardship alone. For this reason, most controversial artistic activity since the late 1970s has been conducted by groups. For example, the two exhibitions of the Stars group in 1979 and 1980 were strongly criticized by the government, but no individual artist was singled out for particularly strict punishment. The "Ten-Man Exhibition" of 1983, held in Shanghai, was closed by the government after three days and criticized in *Jiefang ribao* (Liberation daily), but none of the artists were individually punished. An exhibition in Hangzhou entitled "The '86 Final Show," held by six artists of the Zhejiang Academy, was closed by the Zhejiang provincial propaganda bureau three hours after it opened. Although the exhibition received intense criticism, none of the artists were punished.[19]

A second function of such groups was that an artist could find individual value from his group.[20] Usually one thinks of groups as suppressing the identity of the individual, but in the special circumstances of China during the 1980s they provided individuals with opportunities to vent the instincts that would otherwise be suppressed. Because members of a group felt less concern for reputation than each might alone, the structure permitted them to overcome their artistic and social inhibitions. The united group became more powerful than the individual, moreover, as its members came to believe that they could collectively overcome any failure. Perhaps more significantly, the risks of failure were unimportant, for the group sheltered its members from a sense of individual responsibility for a negative result. In the China/Avant-Garde Exhibition of

[19]On this exhibition, see Gao et al., *Zhongguo dangdai meishu shi*, 360–64.

[20]Some of this analysis is inspired by Chinese translations of Sigmund Freud's *Group Psychology and the Analysis of the Ego*, especially chap. 2, "Le Bon's Description of the Group Mind." For an English version see James Strachey, trans. (New York: Liveright Publishers Corporation, 5th imp., 1949).

1989, for example, many performance artists attacked society with a vehemence impossible for an artist acting as an individual, knowing that the organizers of the exhibition, not the artists themselves, would be held responsible for any governmental response.

A third important element was the economic situation. Because the avant-garde groups were organized by the artists themselves, not by the government, and had no commercial foundation, they bore the burden of renting exhibition space, purchasing materials, and paying for transportation. A group was better able to raise such funds than an individual.

The most important activity of the avant-garde groups was organizing exhibitions. The significance of this function cannot be underestimated, because it was almost impossible for a young artist working through official channels to have a solo exhibition in China. Even though some avant-garde exhibitions were closed by the authorities within a few hours of their opening, the group identity gave the avant-garde artists needed visibility. For example, the first show of the "Three-step Studio" in Taiyuan, Shanxi, originally scheduled to last for two weeks, was open for only one day. Nevertheless, when some exhibited works were published by a sympathetic editor of *Meishu*, they attained a legitimacy that could not be withdrawn, even after the provincial art association accused *Meishu* of supporting bourgeois liberalism.[21]

"The Art Field" exhibition, held by the Luoyang Modern Art Study Group, was similarly closed a day after its opening. As part of the exhibition, the group publicized a preface in which it stated its expectation of suppression: "As an exhibition, it will be closed, but as art it will not be concluded."[22] After shutting down the exhibition, the provincial government asked the group to submit all its written material and photographs of the exhibition in order to organize a criticism meeting. Interestingly, none of the art experts or scholars who were contacted for the purpose of criticizing the exhibition consented to appear at the meeting, so attempts to castigate the artists failed.

Many similar examples can be found for the latter half of the 1980s. An important factor in the failure of leftist authorities to suppress the young artists, of course, was the changed political situation of the period and the relatively open attitudes of many members of the art establishment about

---

[21]For information on this exhibition, see Gao et al., *Zhongguo dangdai meishu shi*, 364–69. It appeared in *MS*, no. 2 (1987).
[22]For some background on this exhibition, see Gao et al., *Zhongguo dangdai meishu shi*, 371–74. The text of the exhibition preface appears on p. 374.

creative freedom. However, the group identity helped, as well, by giving the artists the confidence to persist in the face of obstacles and by giving them better visibility for critics and sympathetic cultural leaders.

Between 1986 and the cultural crackdowns following the Tiananmen Square massacre of 1989, one of the most important stimuli in the development of the avant-garde was the process of organizing the China/ Avant-Garde Exhibition. In July 1986, the first large-scale conference about the " '85 Art Movement" was held in Zhuhai, Guangdong. Representatives from avant-garde art groups and critics from all over China attended the event. They discussed the nature and characteristics of avant-garde art as well as the direction in which the " '85 Art Movement" would go. They also viewed 1,300 slides of avant-garde art works that were sent from all over China. At the meeting, it was decided to organize a large-scale exhibition of Chinese avant-garde art, and afterward, a small group of critics began actively working to organize the exhibition. They also established a new group of critics called the Chinese Modern (Avant-Garde) Art Research Association.

In January 1987 the first exhibition planning meeting was held under extremely difficult circumstances in Beijing. During the three-day event, the meeting site was moved from place to place, with participants even assembling outdoors on one winter day in a cluttered courtyard used primarily for storage. These logistical problems were the result of the anti-bourgeois liberalism campaign, a hard-line political movement that followed the student demonstrations in several of China's major cities in late 1986. Soon thereafter, the general secretary of the Communist Party, Hu Yaobang, was dismissed. In April 1987, the Propaganda Department of the Central Committee of the Communist Party issued a document prohibiting professional associations from holding scholarly activities of national scope. In response, the Chinese Artists Association immediately stopped preparations for the national exhibition and broke up the Chinese Modern Art Research Association. The result was that the Chinese Modern Art Exhibition, scheduled for July 1987, was aborted.

In mid-1988 the political situation eased. With the intense efforts of critics who supported it, the political, economic, and organizational difficulties were surmounted, and the China/Avant-Garde Exhibition finally opened at the Chinese National Art Gallery in Beijing on February 5, 1989 (Figure 9.8–9.10). It exhibited 297 works by 186 artists. Some of the works in the exhibition, particularly performance pieces, caused the Public Security Bureau to close the exhibition twice (Figure 9.10). Sub-

Figure 9.8. View of the opening of "China/Avant-Garde," February 1989

sequently, the exhibition was repeatedly attacked, most notably as an important manifestation of the evils of bourgeois liberalism. Moreover, the exhibition was referred to by some hard-liners as the Tiananmen Square of the art world.

Development of the avant-garde after Tiananmen. Two months after the China/Avant-Garde Exhibition, the Beijing student demonstrations broke out. After the democracy movement was suppressed on June 4, 1989, the political situation and cultural policies became progressively more difficult. Normal scholarly research and artistic exchange in the art world became impossible. Critics who supported the avant-garde were attacked in the press. Several important art magazines, because they had supported avant-garde art, were either closed down or strongly criticized, while the staff of *Meishu* was completely replaced. These circumstances had a strong effect on avant-garde circles, for the removal of their venues for publication closed off their most important access to the audiences for their art.

Even under these circumstances, some Chinese avant-garde artists still produced new works. Among new developments, the most important

Figure 9.9. Logo for "China/Avant-Garde," February 1989. Design by Yang Zhilin

is "political pop," which is discussed in detail farther on. During the winter of 1991–92, three solo exhibitions by avant-garde artists were closed by the Public Security Bureau. The practice of holding avant-garde art exhibitions temporarily ceased.

THE ARTISTIC CONCEPTIONS AND STYLES OF THE AVANT-GARDE

For several decades, the Chinese people have experienced the suppression of individual human value. Humanity and humanism were

Figure 9.10. Plain-clothes police arrive at the National Art Gallery, February 5, 1989. *Photograph by Azhen*

regarded as bourgeois and thus criticized.[23] After the Cultural Revolution, artists began using artworks to express aspirations, including the desire for freedom. The Stars group and the Scar painters, mentioned earlier, first expressed such desires. About 1985, a group of works appeared that express humanism even more strongly.

The forms of Chinese avant-garde art are often very close to those of Western modern art. The influence of surrealism, expressionism, conceptual art, performance art, and pop art are especially noticeable. However, the subjects, contents, and values all have strong indigenous qualities. Three major types of avant-garde work are related to the question of humanism. The first we call rationalist painting; the second we call the "Current of Life" school; and the third is performance art. The themes of the first two groups have a somewhat nationalistic tone, but

---

[23]Such criticisms appear in Mao's *Yanan Talks,* for example. In the early 1980s, some groups of intellectuals in China began debating the concept of humanism as the term was used in Marx's writings. They tended to use the term "humanism" to refer to concepts of individual value, human nature, and human freedom. This use of the term is not meaningful to most Western readers. When artists use the term humanism in their writing, they usually mean something like individualism. Here, in order to avoid complication, we continue to use the term as Chinese artists and intellectuals do.

they aim to establish a cultural power different from both traditional culture and Communist culture.

Rationalist Painting. The first group, rationalist painters, expressed their ideas in a cold, severe tone, so as to create a new, tightly controlled structure in which emotions play little role. In 1985, a group of recent art school graduates executed some works on the theme of awakening. One example is Zhang Qun and Meng Luding's *Adam and Eve's Revelation in the New Age* (Figure 9.11). They use the biblical story of Adam and Eve's tasting the forbidden apple as a metaphor for China's youth, which had already begun to awaken. In an article entitled "Awakening in the New Era," the artists advocate a reevaluation of the past and of reality in the context of the reformist, or open, period.[24] They state that Adam and Eve represent the youth of China, that is, people in the same situation as the artists. They clearly differentiate their own background from that of the preceding generation of artists, namely the rustic realists, who emerged from a rural environment. In a rather unorthodox interpretation of the biblical story, the artists imply that Eden represents the old Communist society, God represents the Communist authorities, and the process of coming to self-awareness and leaving the garden is a process of awakening from ignorance.

Yuan Qingyi's *Spring Has Come* (Figure 9.12) has a similar implication of youthful enlightenment, chiefly by virtue of its title. The student depicted in the painting, who turns to look at an apple and a book on his spartan desk, resembles the artist himself. The artist wrote that he sought to express the existentialist thought of Sartre in this painting.[25]

Some artists who worked in China's Northeast made the rather extreme claim that the culture of the temperate zone was dying, and must be replaced by a new contemporary culture from the frigid zone. This trend exemplifies a kind of nationalism or regionalism. In their case, they claimed authority based upon the masculine strength believed to be inherent in the northern Chinese people and culture as opposed to the comparative weakness of traditional culture, which they associated with Jiangnan. They sought an imagery to express the strength and atmosphere of the frigid zone, a cold silence and purity. As a result, they adopted a style derived from surrealism to create a rational order and a feeling of the sublime.

---

[24]"Xin shidai de qishi," *MS*, no. 7 (1985).
[25]" 'Wo' he 'wo' yi ji . . ." *Zhongguo meishu bao* (Fine arts in China), no. 15 (1985).

Figure 9.11. Zhang Qun and Meng Luding, *Adam and Eve's Revelation in the New Age*, 1985. Oil on canvas, 197 × 165 cm. *Collection the artists*

Many of their ostensible subjects were sacrificial, such as the Pietà, or heroic, such as Wang Guangyi's *Postclassical Series: The Death of Marat* (Figure 9.13). Shu Qun's *Absolute Principle* (Figure 9.14) used Christian iconography to establish a rationalistic order that the artist considered capable of creating a sublime realm to purify reality. Both assumed that their paintings could serve as images for a new social order.

In the face of their environment and reality, other painters, such as

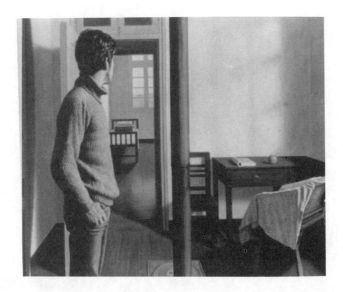

Figure 9.12. Yuan Qingyi, *Spring Has Come*, 1985. Oil on canvas, 200 × 200 cm. *Collection Li Luming*

Ding Fang, liked to express nationalistic themes more directly, by means of natural imagery. Ding took the yellow loess plateau to symbolize the power of the Chinese and their call for self-strengthening (Figure 9.15).[26] Ding used a comparatively romantic, expressionistic style to express the sorrow and struggles of the Chinese.

Other works, including those of Geng Jianyi and Zhang Peili, criticize society by means of scorning reality or self-mockery, with a kind of "gray humor" (Figures 9.16–9.17). Generally speaking, rationalist painting was strongly influenced by the styles of surrealism, but the subjects of rationalist painting are not taken from dreams or the subconscious, as they are in surrealism, but directly from the experience of real life or the artist's psychological reality.

Current of Life school. Every group in the Current of Life school[27] addresses the question of the nature of life in order to explore the

---

[26]Ding's subject matter is rather similar to that of nationalistic film directors of the period such as Chen Kaige and Zhang Yimou.

[27]Lauk'ung Chan (Kong Chang'an), in "Ten Years of the Chinese Avant-Garde: Waiting for the Curtain to Fall," *FlashArt*, vol. xxv, no. 162 (Jan-Feb 1992), 111, translates this term as "vital" expressionism.

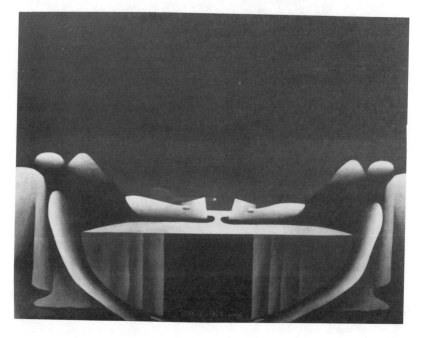

Figure 9.13. Wang Guangyi, *Post-classical Series: The Death of Marat*, 1985. Oil on canvas, dimensions unavailable. *Collection Tang Yujing*

value of humanity. The primary difference between their artistic goals and those of the rationalist painters is that the Current of Life painters express their opinions about the nature of life by means of venting their own individual emotions or expressing their own life situations.

Different artistic groups within this school have different ideas about both the nature of life and the nature of art. Some groups emphasize that life is instinct, while some emphasize the idea that life is accommodation. Usually the process of artistic expression starts as a venting of the individual's emotions, but it can evolve to express social meaning, as well. After expressing their individual feelings, these artists sometimes find that their problems stem from society. The artist Xia Xiaowan, for example, in *Old Infants* (Figure 9.18), conveys a disturbed, morbid, and twisted psychological state. In his early work, Mao Xuhui was interested in pure instinct. He wrote, in about 1985, "When I put the things in life that disturb people, that are irrational, that are disorderly, that strongly

Figure 9.14. Shu Qun, *Absolute Principle*, 1985. Oil on canvas, 150 × 120 cm. *Collection the artist*

exist even though they are unclear, into the magic bucket that is artistic form, then I feel delight."[28] A slightly later work, Mao Xuhui's *Patriarch*, deals with the relationships within individual families and within the Chinese social system as a whole (Figure 9.19).

These artists attack the human distortion their society causes by glorifying a primitive and simple life. A typical example, Zhang Xiaogang's *Eternal Life*, which depicts primitive people surrounded by animals, symbolizes the purity of rustic life (Figure 9.20). This kind of imagery, often based on experiences in Tibet or other remote areas, appeared frequently in the late 1980s. Some of these works, however, imply a conflict between the primitive life and modern civilization. This conflict is basic to the psychology of the artists, and is particularly acute in contemporary urban China. On the one hand, the artists wished to op-

[28]"Yishu biji" (Notes on art), unpublished article, as cited in Gao et al., *Zhongguo dangdai meishu shi*, 254.

Figure 9.15. Ding Fang, *Summons and Birth*, 1987. Oil on canvas, 125 × 180 cm. *Collection Song Wei*

pose the modern society that suppressed human nature, thus their praise for the pure and simple life; on the other hand, they also thought that the people who lived the primitive life in remote areas lacked the desires that push people to necessary reforms of nature and society. The praise for primitivism and naturalness in the works of these artists, which they themselves called nature-consciousness, was not only glorification of the primitive, but also criticism of contemporary culture.

Praise for the "original life" is also reflected in the rise of sex as a prominent subject for other artists. The issue of sex has been a sensitive social and artistic problem in China since the Cultural Revolution. Leftists think that any artistic reference to sex is a bourgeois Western phenomenon, so they strongly criticize such images. In the early 1980s the widespread struggle in the Chinese art world was about nudity in art. This phenomenon came to a head in the late 1980s with the extremely controversial Chinese Nude Oils Exhibition. It attracted a great deal of public attention to what had previously been a professional question within the art world itself.[29]

[29]The Chinese Nude Oils Exhibition was held by the Central Academy of Fine Arts in the

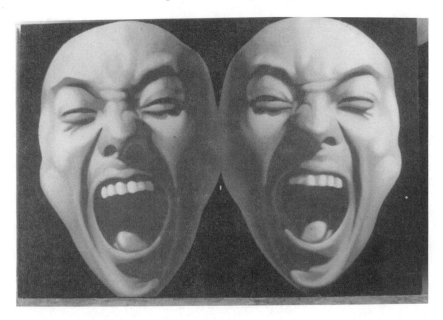

Figure 9.16. Geng Jianyi, *Second Situation*, 1987. Oil on canvas, 145 × 200 cm. *Collection Song Wei*

By the mid- or late 1980s, however, many artists considered sex itself a natural, even scientific subject, and certainly one appropriate to artistic expression. Moreover, the avant-garde artists used the human body or similar symbolic forms as vehicles for attacking the ways in which society suppressed humanity. The popularity of this theme shows a popular hunger for sexual liberation, but expresses little concern for the cause of their suppression.

Avant-garde artists thought more about the cause of this desire than about its immediate effects. Some avant-garde artists directly related the sexual suppression of contemporary society with a lack of what they referred to as masculine strength (*yanggang*). This failing, as mentioned above, was interpreted not only literally but also figuratively, to represent weakness of the national power and national spirit.

National Art Gallery in early 1989. According to the catalogue's preface, written by Wu Guanzhong, this exhibition was intended to explore the beauty of the human body and demonstrate the results of China's "open door" policy. Wu acknowledges that sex is a part of the aesthetic beauty of the human body and argues that the feelings behind such work are not pornographic (*huangse*).

Figure 9.17. Zhang Peili, *X?*, 1987. Oil on canvas, 180 × 200 cm (each). Installation, "China/Avant-Garde," February 1989

The installation *Inflatism* (*Chongqi zhuyi*, Figure 9.21), while stylistically atypical of the group, is thematically similar in that it refers literally to the reproductive functions of the human body. The artists wrote a statement to accompany the piece that praises masculine power as a quality that the Chinese people need. The artists value sex, usually conceived in male terms, as a way to demonstrate their hope that their ancient race should revive its vigorous power of life. This nationalistic and primitivistic cultural and psychological attitude is commonly seen in the literature and arts of this period.[30]

Both the rationalist and the Current of Life schools question human nature and the value of human nature in the social structure. They think human nature is the most important value of the new culture in contemporary China, but the way they express themselves is very differ-

---

[30]Most such work caused controversy at the time, however. *Liangchong ni de shetai* (Stick out your tongue), a 1987 novel by Ma Jian set in Tibet, has many sex scenes. After publication, Lu Xinwu, the editor of the journal that published it, *Renmin wenxue* (People's literature), was fired. A similar situation appeared with publication of the very frank novel *Half of Man Is Woman* by Zhang Xianliang in 1985. The concern of this novel with the loss of masculinity parallels the artists' criticism of China's lack of strength.

Figure 9.18. Xia Xiaowan, *Old Infants*, 1989. Oil on canvas, 30 × 20 cm. *Collection the artist*

ent. Usually the rationalist painters like to emphasize construction, with art representing a kind of ideal or conceptualized philosophical structure. Their tone is usually cool and grim. The Current of Life painters like to emphasize destruction. The atmosphere of the work is emotionally intense, even terrifying.

Performance art. Chinese performance art was concentrated in the second half of the 1980s. Although the amount of performance art was not great in 1985, its extreme forms began to attract attention and controversy. Performance art is not unusual in the West, but the differences between Chinese performance art and that of the West is that the basic goal of the former is less to express an artistic concept than to call for the liberation of human nature.

Before the China/Avant-Garde Exhibition of 1989, performances mostly expressed individual moods of oppression through public or pri-

Figure 9.19. Mao Xuhui, *Patriarch*, 1989. Oil on canvas, 100 × 81 cm. *Collection the artist*

Figure 9.20. Zhang Xiaogang, *Eternal Life*, 1989. Oil on canvas, 130 × 300 cm (triptych). *Private collections*

vate events. This behavior was often expressed in masochistic or sadistic forms. *Stretcher Series* takes the frames used to stretch canvases as the cangues used to restrain criminals in ancient China (Figure 9.22). In *Ceremony*, the naked artist was forced into a wooden restraint by two fellow performers and then beaten with willow branches and clamped by the instrument of torture until he collapsed, along with the cangue, onto the stage. *Violence, Shanghai Street Cloth Sculpture* (Figure 9.23), and such works were all masochistic in some way. Any sort of wrapping, binding, hanging, or beating that one can imagine was performed. This sort of wild behavior, intentionally or not, revealed the sorrow and disturbances hidden in the artist's soul.

By 1989, with the general social unease of the period, some extreme forms of performance art appeared. The China/Avant-Garde Exhibition was viewed by some artists as the best possible opportunity to make a strong social statement or a shocking artistic demonstration. For many, the urge to vent their frustrations was primarily destructive, even aimless, but others saw an unprecedented opportunity to make a name for themselves in the art world. The exhibition venue, the National Art Gallery, had previously been the most important site for exhibitions of official art. Those who attacked the artistic or social system at this site thus felt an exciting sense of sacrilege.

The contract between the gallery and the curators had expressly forbidden performance art, but some artists organized performance activities anyway. The artists felt relatively free, perhaps, because the organizers of

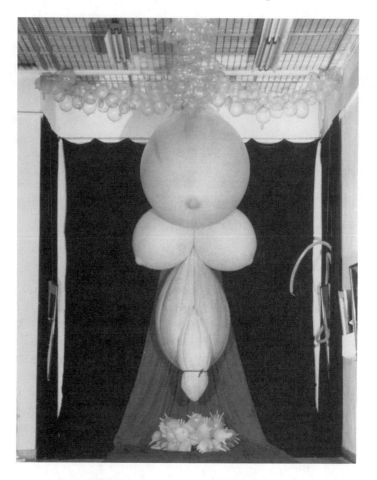

Figure 9.21. Gao Shen, Gao Qiang, and Li Qun, *Inflatism*, February 1989. Installation, "China/Avant-Garde"

the exhibition were ultimately responsible for paying the fines and other penalties levied by the authorities for breaches of contract. These performances went beyond previous examples, which commonly expressed the moods of the individual, and possessed a greater social meaning.

Three hours after the opening of the exhibition, Xiao Lu and Tang Song converted their installation, *Dialogue*, into a performance piece by firing two shots at it (Figure 9.24). Public Security Bureau personnel who were on the spot immediately seized Tang Song. Xiao Lu ran away but

Figure 9.22. Li Han in *Stretcher Series*, July 1987, performance by the Black and White Alliance in Keze, Shandong

Figure 9.23. Zhang Guoliang, Ding Yi, and Qin Yifeng, *Violence, Shanghai Street Cloth Sculpture*, in October 12–13, 1986, performance in Shanghai

later turned herself over to the authorities. After being detained for two and a half days, and with substantial assistance from high-ranking family members, the pair were released, but the exhibition was closed for three days. The artists claimed, in a manifesto given to the curators and later published in *Beijing qingnian bao* (Beijing youth news), that they had no political intentions but had simply felt an urge to complete their work.[31] Their action was both a bid for notoriety and a challenge to the art bureaucracy, but there is no evidence that it was intended as a criticism of the Communist system as a whole, a system that had provided them personally with substantial privileges. Indeed, the ambiguous status of artistic activity in the legal structure of the period made it possible to claim that, within the bounds of the art gallery, an otherwise serious crime might not be illegal. In any case, events developed in ways the artists probably did not foresee. Although the *People's Daily* initially reported the closing of the gallery as straight news, with no criticism of the artists, the authorities acted as though this event were a political

[31]Gao Minglu has preserved the original manifesto. The published version is based on a tape recording of Gao reading the manifesto at the China/Avant-Garde convention held at the National Gallery during the exhibition.

Figure 9.24. Xiao Lu and Tang Song, *Dialogue*, February 1989. Installation, "China/Avant-Garde"

affair.[32] Perhaps more important, most of the foreign news media reported it as a case of political suppression of the arts. Indeed, subsequent left-wing attacks on the avant-garde movement metaphorically described these shots as the first to be fired in the events of 1989.

[32]*Renmin ribao* (People's daily), February 6, 1989.

Figure 9.25. Wu Shanzhuan, *Shrimp Stand*, February 1989. Installation, "China/ Avant-Garde"

From the point of view of the curators, the artists in the exhibition were something like terrorist bombs, with forbidden performances exploding in unpredictable places, magnitudes, and times. Wu Shanzhuan brought several kilograms of fresh shrimp from the place where he lived, a fishing island in Zhejiang Province. Instead of installing his planned piece, he simply wrote the price of the shrimp on a blackboard and began selling them (Figure 9.25). The work, he claimed, demonstrated that modern art and modern society are big business.

Another artist sat down in the corner of the gallery to hatch eggs (Figure 9.26). In his manifesto, which hung across his chest, he wrote: "During the incubation period, I will not discuss theoretical questions with anyone, to avoid harming the younger generation." Li Shan, after completing his installation, which included a wash basin decorated with portrait images of Ronald Reagan, seated himself and began washing his feet. Wang Deren, an hour after the opening, threw more than a thousand condoms from the stairwell into all three floors of the gallery. This performance art

Figure 9.26. Zhang Nian, *Hatching Eggs*, February 1989. Performance, "China/Avant-Garde"

reflected, from different angles, the artists' opinions about art and society. Both its content and its forms provoked a great deal of controversy. After June 4, performance art, which was the primary reason for the two closings of the exhibition by the authorities, was attacked as representative of the exhibition. Although this view is inaccurate from an art historical or critical point of view, the public psychology represented by these artists and their extreme means of venting their professional and social frustrations may be seen as related to events that would develop in Beijing in the months between February and June 1989.

Synthesis of Oriental cultural spirit and Occidental modern art ideas. The Chinese avant-garde is a movement that seeks to attack and destroy the traditional order in the art world, with the ultimate goal of attaining artistic freedom. A few artists, however, take a longer-term view, attempting to build a new art in China at the same time that they destroy the old. As they think about how to do this, they leave behind the thinking that limits their concerns to social problems. Much of their work has a highly conceptual or philosophical foundation.

Although these artists have no explicit program of criticizing the government, they have found Western ideas and forms of art most appealing. Because these forms have been frequent targets of government attack in China, the artists have involved themselves, intentionally or not, in social struggles based on questions of freedom of artistic expression, artistic independence in the face of a patriarchal bureaucracy, and so forth. All five artists discussed in this section have been punished within their own work-units for their artistic activity, even though they have never directly attacked the senior administrators of their institutions. To them, however, the future is more important than the present. To strengthen contemporary Chinese culture, they feel, they must build, not merely destroy. Ironically, all but one of these artists finds himself currently living outside China.[33]

Why have young artists in China, with their ancient traditional culture, so liked modernist Western art? This is a complicated question. To respond simply, the revolutionary aspects of modernist Western art are suitable to the values behind the radical changes in contemporary Chinese society and art. On the other hand, they found some factors similar

---

[33]For further information on Gu Wenda, Huang Yangping, Wu Shanzhuan, and Xu Bing, see Julia F. Andrews and Gao Minglu, *Fragmented Memory: The Chinese Avant-Garde in Exile* (Columbus: Wexner Center for the Arts, The Ohio State University, 1993).

Figure 9.27. Gu Wenda, *Composure Begets Inspiration*, 1986. Installation. *Collection the artist*

to the traditional Chinese cultural spirit in Western modernism. For example, many avant-garde Chinese artists like to use Chan (Zen) Buddhism or other traditional philosophical ideas to explain their works. Gu Wenda, Xu Bing, Huang Yongping, Wu Shanzhuan, and Ren Jian are most prominent in this regard.

Gu Wenda, a painter with technical facility in traditional Chinese painting, tried in the past to use modern Western forms to remold traditional Chinese ink painting. Although he himself has largely abandoned traditional painting, this phase of his career has influenced a generation of younger artists, creating a new school of ink painting referred to as the "Universal Flow." Thereafter, he applied his efforts to installation art. His installation "Composure Begets Inspiration" is constructed from bamboo, hemp, Chinese paper, and such native materials; it uses the forms of Chinese seals and calligraphy to express the solemn and quiet spirit of Eastern philosophies (Figure 9.27). *Words: Right and Reversed* seems to question not only the meaning of language but the tradition from which it comes (Figure 9.28). In the Avant-Garde Chinese art exhibition held in Fukuoka, Japan, his highly conceptual work *Vanishing 36 Golden Section Pigments*, which involved massive excavations,

Figure 9.28. Gu Wenda, *Words: Right and Reversed*, 1985–86. Installation, Hangzhou

aimed to explicate the relationship between Eastern and Western laws of form (Figure 9.29).

Wu Shanzhuan's early work takes Chinese characters as the images in his art (Figure 9.30). He believes that Chinese characters in themselves are a form of visual art. Not only are characters perfect in form but, more important, they are completely filled with historical and cultural meaning. They are independent of man's subjective meaning. Therefore, Wu Shanzhuan's selection of characters as the images in his art is random (Figure 9.31). With this attitude, he puts political jargon, urban language, commercial advertisements, ancient poems, announcements, and all sorts of completely unrelated words together (Figure 9.32). But the basic meaning of the words, which are often juxtaposed in quirky or startling ways, gives his work an ironic quality. This kind of humor accords with his cynical attitude toward society. The serious forms of Cultural Revolution big-character posters and the red, black, and white

Figure 9.29. Gu Wenda, *Vanishing 36 Golden Section Pigment*, 1991. Earthwork, Fukuoka, Japan

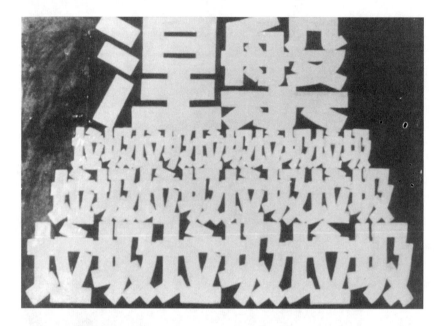

Figure 9.30. Wu Shanzhuan et al., *Nirvana and Garbage*, 1986. Mixed media. From the installation *70% Red 25% White 5% Black*

color of traditional China are all diluted by the humorous phrases he uses. Wu's Chan Buddhist–like quick wit plunges the viewer into an oddly compelling reality.

Huang Yongping is a thoroughly Chan Buddhist artist. He seeks complete randomness, a randomness founded on the concept of nothingness, and believes that artists should not subjectively incorporate meaning into their work. Some of his paintings are made according to the instructions of a spinning wheel, incorporating chance as though it were a roulette wheel or castings from the *Book of Changes* (Figure 9.33). He considers the work of art itself to be meaningless; what is important is the artist's thought process as he creates it. Finally, he considers art history meaningless because it causes what he calls art wars, which damage the natural process of artistic thought. For the China/Avant-Garde Exhibition he washed Herbert Read's *Short History of Modern Painting* and Wang Bomin's *A History of Chinese Painting* together in a washing machine (Figure 9.34). His outdoor works, created for shows in France and Japan in 1992 (Figure 9.35), connected images and ideas with the *Book of*

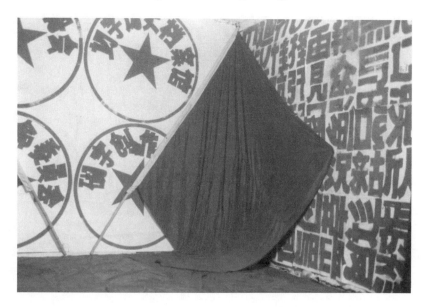

Figure 9.31. Wu Shanzhuan, *Red Seals*, 1987. Installation, *Second Red Humor* series

Changes and Chan Buddhism. Although he was strongly influenced by Dada, he tries to explain Dada by means of Chan Buddhism.

Xu Bing, like Huang Yongping, emphasizes process. He often uses extraordinarily tedious and difficult means to create magnificent works of art. For example, he fabricated more than two thousand characters that no one could read, and then used traditional printing techniques to produce long scrolls and books (Figure 9.36). In another work, he used full-sized ink rubbings of the Great Wall to make an installation, which included a mound of dirt that resembles an ancient tomb (Figure 9.37). The viewer, when he or she sees the former work, will associate it with the determination behind its creation, and the latter with the sweat and blood of the Great Wall's construction.[34] What Xu Bing wishes to express, however, is this difficult, laborious process itself. In Xu Bing's mind, this is simply a process similar to the mindless diligence of Chan Buddhist labor. Thus, this gigantic work reveals to viewers a nihilist, absurdist, and tragic

[34]The exhibition is documented in *Three Installations by Xu Bing: Ghosts Pounding the Wall, A Book from the Sky, Five Series of Repetitions* (Madison: Elvehem Museum of Art, University of Wisconsin, 1991) with an excellent explanatory essay by Britta Erickson.

Figure 9.32. Wu Shanzhuan, *Red Characters*, 1987. Installation, *Third Red Humor* series

Figure 9.33. Huang Yongping creates paintings in response to his fortune telling: *Roulette Wheel*, in performance ca. 1985

Figure 9.34. Huang Yongping, *Concise History of Modern Painting* and *A History of Chinese Art*, "Washed Together in a Machine for Five Minutes." Installation, "China/Avant-Garde," February 1989

Figure 9.35. Huang Yongping, *Fire Ritual*, 1989–90. Installation, Mont Sainte-Victoire, Aix-en-Provence, France

feeling. The artistic concepts of Xu Bing and Huang Yongping present a contrast similar to that between the Northern and Southern schools of Chan Buddhism. The Northern school emphasizes gradual enlightenment, whereas the Southern school emphasizes sudden enlightenment, but they share a basic idea similar to the *wu*, nonbeing, of Daoist philosophy.

Ren Jian believes that art does not exist because of its aesthetic beauty. Like philosophy and natural science, it is a means for humankind to research natural and social questions. Thinking in a primitivist mode, he made a thirty-meter-long ink painting called *Primeval Chaos* using imaginary images to describe the process of the origins of life in the primordial period (Figure 9.38). More recently, he has been constructing pictures that symbolize the structure of the natural and human worlds. His new series, called the *Desiccation Series*, consists of four parts: *Main Line*, *Scan*, *Eclipse*, and *Stamp Collecting*. According to what he says, *Main Line* is a redescription of the structure of any air-dried natural object. *Scan* (Figure 9.39) is a description of the natural environment. *Eclipse*, filled with images from the news media, is condensed and shrunken history and time. *Stamp Collecting* (Figure 9.40) is an understanding of human communication and international relations.

Figure 9.36. Xu Bing, *A Mirror for Analyzing the World*. Installation, "China/Avant-Garde," February 1989

All five of these artists wish to transcend the level of psychological and personal feelings to make more universal statements. They have the potential for being more dangerous to the old artistic culture in China than the more openly critical artists because they seek to create a viable alternative to the old art. The new artistic styles they create, if successful, may replace the styles of the status quo.

Political pop. After the June 4 massacre, the socially critical side of avant-garde art could not be expressed directly and could not render the artists' thoughts as seriously as before. Work of this sort would be banned, so it could not be displayed publicly. Yet, in the face of political cataclysm, even if the work were shown it would seem weak. Therefore, many artists began painting with a cynical attitude. They chose popular images from society to make an art we call "political pop." Choosing themes from political propaganda pictures and advertisements, singing stars, and images from popular culture, their works appear very serious. But the viewer will

Figure 9.37. Xu Bing, *Ghosts Pounding the Wall*, 1991. Installation, Elvehem Museum of Art, University of Wisconsin, Madison.

Figure 9.38. Ren Jian, *Primeval Chaos*, 1987. Ink on polyester cloth, 150 × 3,000 cm. *Collection the artist*

spontaneously laugh after viewing the work, and in this laughter will feel a sense of scorn. One senses the artists' self-mockery, because they are unable to do anything about their own circumstances and environment. For example, Wang Guangyi exhibited *Mao Zedong, No. 1* at the China/Avant-Garde Exhibition, a work in which he rationalistically analyzed Mao Zedong (Figure 9.41). After Tiananmen, he painted a set called *Great Castigation* (Figure 9.42). The backgrounds of the paintings are Cultural Revolution images of workers, peasants, and soldiers. In the front are written "Coca-Cola," "Kodak," and other such commercial advertisements. This creates a strong sense of irony via the contrast between the political and the nonpolitical.[35]

Shu Qun inscribed Mao's political sayings on the covers of a fictitious "Collected Chinese Art" series, making a joke about the relationship between politics and art. In another ironic series, the four arithmetic operations, addition, subtraction, multiplication, and division, seem to be metaphors for China's political policy of the "Four Cardinal Princi-

[35]This phenomenon is similar to the slightly earlier Sots Art movement in the Soviet Union and was probably influenced by it.

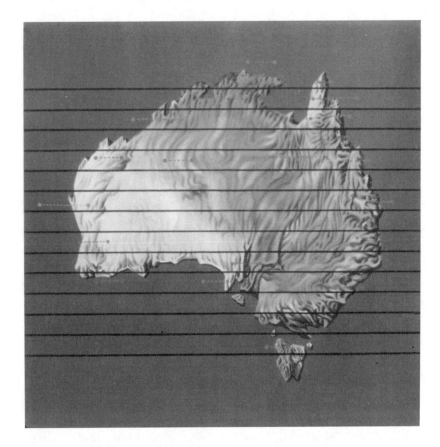

Figure 9.39. Ren Jian, from the *Scan* series, 1991. Oil on canvas, 100 × 100 cm. *Collection the artist*

ples" and thus comment on political inconsistency. Moreover, *The Subtraction Period, Cultural Pop Series* depicts a popular Chinese singing star, Cui Jian, and the lyrics to his songs. "I have absolutely nothing," "Solve it, solve it," and so forth, make people think about social and political problems (Figure 9.43).

Indeed, in the post–June 4 period, Mao Zedong and the Cultural Revolution were frequent subjects among avant-garde artists (Figure 9.44), a phenomenon similar to the sudden enthusiasm for Maoist relics and music on the part of China's youth in the early 1990s. This, obviously,

Figure 9.40. Ren Jian, from the *Stamp Collecting* series, 1991. Oil on canvas, 50 × 50 cm. *Collection the artist*

is not the result of an ideology that praises revolutionary history, but it does not praise contemporary society, either.

CONCLUSION

The introduction of Western-style art into China in the early twentieth century was fraught with ideological ramifications. For its proponents, it was an emblem of modernity and scientific progress. For its opponents, its challenge to traditional painting symbolized a threat to the foundations of Chinese culture. This irreconcilable conflict was tempered by the nation-

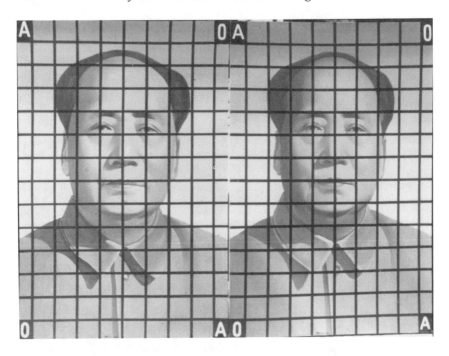

Figure 9.41. Wang Guangyi, *Mao Zedong No. 1*, 1989. Oil on canvas, dimensions unavailable. *Collection Song Wei*

alistic spirit of the anti-Japanese War, but reemerged during the 1950s, when Soviet painting became the standard for much of Chinese pictorial art. It was ultimately resolved by the anti-Rightist campaign of 1957, which silenced extremists on both sides, and by subsequent official policies, which promoted both quasi-traditional painting and realistic oil painting in a relatively even-handed manner. Broader and more nationalistic art policies in effect between 1958 and about 1964 allowed establishment of bureaucratic and critical structures that conferred social and material benefits on quasi-traditional painters, woodblock print makers, and oil painters. All forms of art suffered during the early years of the Cultural Revolution, but by 1972 had revived in a limited way. With the rehabilitation of rightists and other artists accused of political deviance in 1979, all three began developing in more pluralistic ways. More liberal cultural policies in effect between about 1961 and 1963 were revalidated.

Realistic oil painting, with its cosmopolitan cachet and its immediately

Figure 9.42. Wang Guangyi, *Great Castigation*, 1990. Oil on canvas. *Coca-Cola Company*

recognizable ideological efficacy, remained, and remains today, the most prestigious form of art in China. Its proponents in the 1980s, like those who promoted *guohua*, tried to strike a balance between the nationalistic, aestheticist goals first promoted in the early 1960s and the demands of a new commercial art. The merit of their work, as seen by many Chinese artists and critics, is grounded in a nationalism that often seems superficial to an outside observer. Opposed to both groups is the avant-garde, which has striven for cosmopolitan values linked neither to the dominant official style nor to the new markets its advocates seek.

The Chinese avant-garde art movement, which flourished from 1985 to 1989, was very much a product of its period. It emerged from the

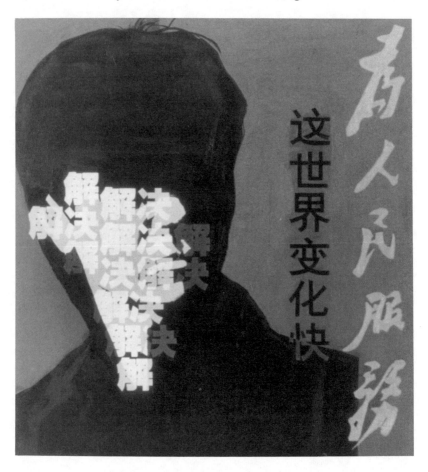

Figure 9.43. Shu Qun, *Age of Subtraction, Cultural Pop Series,* C, 1991. Oil on canvas, 130 × 120 cm. *Collection the artist*

intellectual engagements of the mid-1980s and has suffered as those concerns have been suppressed or transmuted by subsequent events. One might characterize the culture of the period as consisting of three different spheres: official culture, intellectual culture, and popular culture. Avant-garde art was a product of the second.

Particularly during the mid-1980s, as government attitudes encouraged intellectuals to contribute to society, the social and cultural influence of Chinese intellectuals increased. This is reflected in a great increase in activity in all cultural areas, ranging from universities to

Figure 9.44. Yu Youhan, *Untitled*, 1991. Oil on canvas, 118 × 166 cm. *Collection unknown*

newspapers to television networks. Moreover, at this time, many intellectuals felt a particularly strong responsibility to the public and believed that official and popular culture could be enlightened through their efforts. The ideas promoted by intellectuals in the mass media were generally not those of mainstream political propagandists, that is to say, of official culture, but the ideals of the intellectuals themselves. The latter is best exemplified by the production of television scripts like *River Elegy*, with its revisionist historical ideas, for public television. By this means, intellectual culture strongly influenced the culture of the public, and was generally treated with deference by officialdom.

Avant-garde art was created by a few young artists who were influenced by these ideas, but it had a disproportionate effect on the Chinese art world of the period. Even though most other artists did not understand its underlying philosophical ideas, they comprehended the importance of its emphasis on creative freedom and its attack on old arts policies. To a great degree, the avant-garde art movement was not about art; it concerned cultural attitudes and concepts that were bigger than the forms of art that contained them.

Since 1989, with the government's attacks on intellectual culture, the movement has weakened. Moreover, with increasing emphasis on the immediate economic benefits of any activity, official culture and popular culture have, at least temporarily, common priorities that are significantly different from those of most intellectuals.

The art world is now dominated by a concern for commercial success to the point that most other critical criteria have been discarded. Realists have, for various reasons, attained the greatest monetary success. With suppression of intellectual culture and of critics who publish analysis and opinions on avant-garde art, avant-garde artists have lost their most important audience. Indeed, the alternative of accommodating to the new commercialism or working in complete obscurity threatens their very survival as artists. The avant-garde artists, for whom critical recognition, not financial benefit, had been the only reward, found themselves with no public outlet for their works. The most prolific are now working abroad; many of those who remained at home exhibit only outside China.

Each generation of intellectuals since the early twentieth century has attempted, for a brief and extremely intense period, to reform Chinese culture. Every attempt to create a new Chinese cultural system, however, after working very hard for short-term progress, meets some insurmountable political or social obstacle, and stops. The avant-garde art movement, and even the intellectual trends from which it sprang, might suffer this same fate.

Our analysis leads us to conclude that events of the 1980s, while broadening the boundaries of acceptable art, did not overturn the idea of a single, official standard for Western-style art in China. Just as individuals today possess more personal freedom than they did in the 1970s, so artists are largely unrestricted in what they can produce for their personal pleasure. At every turn, however, they confront the twin challenges of a newly commodified society and an entrenched official art world. The immaturity of the Chinese art market; the weakness, or even absence, of an independent realm of art criticism in China; the few opportunities for non-profit exhibitions; and the limited and often ideological concerns of most Western champions of contemporary Chinese art combine to push avant-garde artists in directions that may conflict with their artistic and personal integrity. In spite of such pressures, the most serious artists continue to pursue what they believe to be high standards in their work and to exploit fully the rare chances they find to exhibit it.

10

The disintegration of the poetic "Berlin Wall"

SU WEI and WENDY LARSON

> Even the pigeon's whistle comes out a mature tune,
> It is past, that wild summer
> Think no more of that grim sweltering trial
> Structured memories in a dangerous swim . . .
> > "Qiu" (Autumn) (Bei Dao)

> Island under the palm trees, eyes closed,
> In a dream, shoulders quiver restlessly
> Then an azure coconut drops into the sea
> Silently splashes
> A patch of green moonlight . . .
> > "Ye" (Night) (Unknown)[1]

The two seemingly innocent poems cited above were focal points in the early 1980s' debate on Misty poetry (*menglongshi*). At the time of this controversy, China was experiencing a confusing cultural transition, and although the debate sometimes appeared to center on technical literary issues, it accelerated the collapse of orthodox, mainstream ideology throughout Chinese culture. This chapter locates this extreme cultural transformation in poetry and poetic theory, and shows how poets and their "schools" caught and exploited the exact nodes where general cultural meaning could be rejected, reformed, and reworked.

Misty poetry was recognized as a literary genre that through language undermined the Chinese ideological "Berlin Wall," a metaphor that was an appropriate mix of concrete and abstract, Chinese and Western images. The Chinese "Berlin Wall" held in, supported, and maintained

---

All translations from the Chinese are the authors' unless otherwise indicated.
[1]See *Shikan* (Poetry journal) (August 1980): 54.

Marxist literary ideology while it kept out "modernism" in the form of innovation in technique. In an age of computers, telephones, and media, the ideological wall that kept out change appeared anachronistically political.

Through the Misty poetry movement, poetry both reflected and created changes in the larger cultural domain. Yet as poetry continued to evolve after the Misty movement, changes within culture and the influence of Western postmodern aesthetics altered the cultural meaning of poetry and of poets, resulting in a change in audience. Although perhaps unanticipated by poets, this change in readership was possibly more profound than the change in poetry itself. The social position of poetry was bound up with its language and the way it could be interpreted by the general reader. By rejecting the language and overtly political context of officially sanctioned poetry, the so-called Misty poets broke with literary conventions established at Yanan in 1942. But they were quickly supplanted by poets who believed themselves part of the Information Age and who demanded a postmodern aesthetics of surface. Poetry became a kind of cult activity, written and read by the same people, and theorized about in such a way as to make it unavailable to the uninitiated.

Such a significant debate could be carried out in poetry because of poetry's central position within Chinese letters and intellectual culture. In traditional literary culture, fiction was noncanonical, but one mark of the literatus was his ability to write good poetry. In modern literature, although Liang Qichao and others proposed fiction as a means to national salvation, the famous short story and novel writers of the May Fourth era also all wrote, and were known for, poetry. Poetry continued to retain prestige throughout the contemporary period and was enhanced by Mao's own efforts, which were widely memorized and commonly displayed on walls and even postage stamps. No less an authority than Mao was actively involved in constructing postliberation poetic theory, and his traditional-style poetry and comments on theory and practice were published in the official *Shikan* (Poetry journal) in the 1950s and later. Many famous political figures, such as Chen Yi, Zhu De, Dong Biwu, and Ye Jianying, were poets who wrote and published in traditional styles.[2]

---

[2] See Bonnie S. McDougall, "Poems, Poets, and the *Poetry* 1976: An Exercise in the Typology of Modern Chinese Literature," *Contemporary China* 2, no. 4 (Winter 1978). McDougall points out that in poetry, "The persistence of traditional forms among Chinese radicals is remarkable" (109).

MISTY POETRY AND ITS SOCIAL CHALLENGE

The first "modern" Chinese poetry is often considered May Fourth poetry, which was written in Western metrical patterns or free verse and
contemptuous of the technical demands of traditional Chinese poetry.
One central goal of May Fourth poetry was to "reflect the living reality
of the present."[3] It was supplanted by the "revolutionary poetry" that
Mao advocated in 1942 after the publication of his *Talks at the Yanan
Forum on Literature and Art.*[4] Mao's *Talks* defined poetry as a political
tool and a "trumpet of the age" that should extol the revolution and its
leaders along with the "people," the workers, peasants, and soldiers.
Until the late 1970s, revolutionary poetry centered social and political
language and concerns as those most appropriate to the aesthetic experience. For example, the following lines from He Jingzhi's epic "Lei
Feng" extol the deep selfless feelings and acts of a commoner who is a
revolutionary at heart:

> Ah! Lei Feng . . .
> I am not
> alone
>> I am singing
>> the excitement of the hearts
>> of our hundreds of millions of people
> Look,
> hurrying after you!
> Studying you!
>> ——Our great land is full of footsteps!——
> Ten,
> A hundred,
> Ten million . . .
>> Lei Feng . . .
>> Lei Feng . . .
>> Lei Feng . . .
> Ah, Lei Feng
> You are we!
>> We
> are Lei Feng![5]

[3]Wen Yiduo's 1926 essay "The Form of Poetry" promoted the use of English patterns and
rhyme schemes. See Leo Ou-fan Lee, "Introduction," *The Red Azalea: Chinese Poetry
Since the Cultural Revolution,* ed. Edward Morin (Honolulu: University of Hawaii Press,
1990), xvi–xvii.
[4]Poets representing the "traditional revolutionary style" include Guo Xiaochuan and He
Jingzhi before the Cultural Revolution, and Li Ying and Lei Shuyan after.
[5]He Jingzhi, "Lei Feng zhige" (The song of Lei Feng), *Guangming ribao* (Guangming daily),

This style of poetry was the orthodoxy until after the Cultural Revolution, when it was attacked and overturned by the *Today* writers, a group of young poets (Bei Dao, Shu Ting, Gu Cheng, Yang Lian, Mang Ke, Jiang He et al.) who published the unofficial literary magazine *Jintian* (Today) and rapidly—in the two years from 1978 to 1980—became famous on the Chinese literary scene. The poetry published in *Today* replaced political ardor with a more obvious concern with aesthetics, or a reference to phenomena and emotions that could not be easily interpreted within past categories. Although, like May Fourth poetry, Misty poetry made use of symbolism and imagism, such techniques were not identical to those of the modern traditional vernacular poetry written by Hu Shi, Guo Moruo, or Wen Yiduo. To a much greater degree Misty poetry represented the "self," now redefined not as the origin of revolutionary emotions or the site through which revolutionary impulses will be channeled into action, but as a complex and often contradictory place for all kinds of emotions and beliefs that may not be "revolutionary."[6]

Selections from the poetry of two famous Misty poets, Bei Dao and Shu Ting, show why the debate on Misty poetry triggered a far-reaching social movement:

> Let me tell you, the world
> I—do—not—believe
>   "Huida" (The Answer) (Bei Dao)

> I, standing here
> substitute for one shot
> so that each time the sun rises
> let heavy shadows like a road
> cross the whole country
> . . .
> Perhaps one day
> the sun will become a withered garland,
> droop before
> tombstones of each undaunted fighter
> growing like a forest

March 5, 1977, trans. Richard Kraus. He Jingzhi, a poet and well-known cultural official in the early 1980s, was scriptwriter for "The White-haired Girl." He was appointed acting minister of culture in 1989.

[6]For a good introduction to Misty poetry that locates it historically, see William Tay, "Obscure Poetry: A Controversy in Post-Mao China," *After Mao: Chinese Literature and Society,* ed. Jeffrey C. Kinkley (Cambridge: Harvard University Press, 1985), 133–59; also in the same volume, Pan Yuan and Pan Jie, "The Unofficial Magazine *Today* and the Younger Generation's Ideals for a New Literature," 193–220.

Crows, night shards
disperse fragmented
"Jieju huo kaishi" (ending or beginning) (Bei Dao)

Each day I want to verdantly enter the lines of your verse
and each eve scarletly return to your side

. . .

The breeze you breathe moves me
under an expanse of moonlight ringing ding dong
"Hui changge de daiweihua" (The singing iris) (Shu Ting)[7]

In topic and language, both writers assume a stance radically different from revolutionary poetry of the past. In Bei Dao's poems the "individual" has emerged, detaching itself from existing social norms and standing openly to challenge the entire society. This individual has a strong sense of autonomy and, through the articulation of will and belief alone, can proclaim its significance. Images of shards, tombstones, and withered garlands belie the possibility of uncomplicated revolutionary fervor and describe a shattered reality.[8] Shu Ting's extreme lyricism centers on individual subjective experience and denies the significance of social context. The poem's voice glides in and out of natural imagery and language, equating the human body with common yet romanticized phenomena that deny history and class. Both poets reject the tradition of revolutionary poetry in favor of stark symbolic imagery.

Discussions in *Shikan* in 1980 and 1981 show that the poetry of Bei Dao and Shu Ting was often taken as representative of Misty poetry. These debates centered on the formal attributes of Misty poetry and on the question of whether a generation gap existed among poets and readers. The debate changed course when Sun Shaozhen, a professor at Fujian Teachers University, published his article "A New Aesthetic Principle Is Rising," in *Shikan* in March 1981. Sun turned the debate's focus toward an overarching discussion of the meaning of poetry and aes-

---

[7]For "The Answer" and "Ending or Beginning" see Ren Hongyuan, "Dui xifang xiandaizhuyi yu dongfang gudian shixue de shuangchong chaoyue" (The contemporary poetic tide: Double transcendence of Western modernism and the Eastern poetic classics); for "The Singing Iris" see Yu Cijiang, "Menglong shi yu disan dai shi: tuobianqi de shenke ludong" (Misty poetry and third-generation poetry: Deep change of rhyme and movement during the period of transformation), both in *Wenxue* (Literature), no. 5 (1988).

[8]Bonnie S. McDougall shows how Bei Dao's poetry "created an alternative literature to challenge the orthodoxy of the entire post-1949 period" (226). See "Bei Dao's Poetry: Revelation and Communication," *Modern Chinese Literature* 1, no. 2 (Spring 1985): 225–52.

thetics within Chinese society and showed that the main objection to Misty poetry was its rejection of the revolutionary social context and the resulting "flavor" of bourgeois liberalization.

The editorial department of *Shikan,* aware of the potentially explosive reaction that Sun's article might cause, wrote a long "Editor's Note" to introduce his thesis. Concluding that Chinese poetry was still largely embedded in Marxist aesthetics, the editors gently agreed with Sun that the main difficulty for Misty poets was that they confronted the "stubborn old inertia of aesthetic habit." Trying to walk the middle line, editors recognized that "sociology" and aesthetics should be distinguished, but also felt that young poets should learn from the past and not completely destroy "tradition." The theory of "self-expression" was one means through which to create the new, but the editors believed, with Sun, that "individual spirit should not be viewed as a hostile force against social spirit (the spirit of the times)."

Sun's article documents and explicates the influence of Western modernistic thinking on Chinese literature and society in the 1980s. Few went as far as Sun in analyzing the social meaning of Misty aesthetics. Sun organized his discussion around three salient aspects of the poetry and its debate: 1) the emergence of the self as a site of social challenge; 2) the alienation of the individual from society; 3) the new discourse of rebellion against tradition. Sun's analysis contributed to the perception that Misty poetry was a rebellion against a reified, authoritative "revolution," and was applauded in its role of destroyer of the old—represented in common parlance as *wa qiangjiao* (digging under the wall), thus helping tear down the Chinese Berlin Wall of poetry.[9]

In the early 1980s Chinese university and intellectual circles were beginning to buzz with excitement over long-forbidden Western theorists such as Sartre and Freud. As two concepts of modernist thought, existentialism and psychology were able to converge with the post–Cultural Revolution prevailing feeling of loss and despair. Taking as his reference point the loss of confidence in the Communist Party, a young worker named Pan Xiao published the article "Rensheng de lu, weishemma yue zou yue zhai?" (Why is the road of human life becoming narrower and

---

[9]Efforts by Chinese writers to redefine themselves and their works as part of global (Western) literary culture are documented in Wendy Larson and Richard Kraus, "China's Writers, the Nobel Prize, and the International Politics of Literature," *Australian Journal of Chinese Affairs,* no. 21 (January 1989): 143–60. As Larson and Kraus point out, Chinese writers who seek a "global" audience not only may gain access to resources such as trips abroad and prizes, but also disassociate themselves from Chinese Marxist literary policy.

narrower?) in the popular magazine *Zhongguo qingnian* (Chinese youth).[10] The article, which became a reference point in the prevailing atmosphere of social critique, expressed a generalized disillusionment with the direction of Chinese society at large.

Beijing's Democracy Wall Movement and other popular activities, such as the unofficial "Xinxin Art Exhibit," expressed the same social rebellion as that of the Misty poets. In their chapter in this book, Julia Andrews and Gao Minglu show how two post–Cultural Revolution schools of realistic painting, Scar painting and rustic realism, used humanistic concerns to criticize society. What was new about these paintings was not their realistic style, which was the orthodox style of painting throughout the Maoist period, but rather their negative and critical tone.

Although these events show wide recognition of the issues Misty poets approach, they had never been theorized—certainly not in a journal sanctioned by the Chinese Writers Association—until Sun published his article. One reason for this silence was the 1979 arrest of Wei Jingsheng.[11] Sun's article appeared to be a radical statement that squarely confronted and discussed something everyone knew but did not want to say: Chinese society was experiencing a breakdown of traditional social values. The resulting youthful rebellion against mainstream ideology was immediately condemned by Maoist literary theorists. At the same time that they attacked Sun's article, these critics also lashed out against the screenplay of *Kulian* (Bitter love). In these critiques, Sun's article eventually assumed the status of an "arch criminal" that represented the "three-rising" theory. The "three-rising" theory singled out three articles that used the term "rising" (*jueqi*) to applaud the emergence of a new aesthetics: Sun's article, Xie Mian's "Xinmin de jueqi" (The rising of a new people), and Xu Jingya's "Xin shiqun de jueqi" (The rising of new poetry groups).[12] All these articles imply that art stands outside politics, aesthetics occupies its own intellectual and emotional realm, art and literature must be judged by their own "internal" laws rather than political criteria, and thus artists, writers, and critics must have more autonomy in their work.[13]

[10]September 1979.

[11]An electrician at the Beijing Zoo arrested for advocating a fifth modernization, democracy. He was released in September 1993.

[12]Xie Mian is a professor at Beijing University, and Xu Jingya is a poet and theorist from northeast China.

[13]For explorations into the Chinese modernist movement and its backlash, see William

The affair that became known as the "Five Little Kites" (for the five participants) was instrumental in steering power away from conservative cultural officials and reassigning it to the modernists. The Kites debate centered on a book, *Xiandai xiaoshuo jiqiao chutan* (Initial investigation into the art of writing modern novels), published in 1981 by theorist and playwright Gao Xingjian, and letters about this book circulated among Wang Meng, Feng Jicai, Li Tuo, and Liu Xinwu.[14] Letters among Feng, Li, and Liu, which were published in *Shanghai wenxue* (Shanghai literature) in 1982 (no. 8), compared Gao's work to a kite: "It is as if a little kite suddenly appeared in an empty, lonely sky: how happy it makes you feel!" The kite symbolized a free-floating, whimsical spirit that would replace the wooden poetic models of the past. According to Li Tuo, party representatives in the Beijing Chinese Writers Association were concerned about the effects the correspondence would have on readers and attempted to delay its publication.[15] *Shanghai wenxue* did not heed the warning and published the letters under the title "Zhongguo xuyao 'xiandaipai'!" (Chinese literature needs "modernism"!).

As authorities feared, the letters helped modernist writing win legitimacy. However, because the letters were written casually between friends and did not set out systematically to develop or analyze, they were a theoretical step backward from the level reached by the "rising" schools. Liu Xinwu, for example, "poured cold water" onto the idea of modernism by emphasizing the necessity of drawing a distinction between the "universal law of literary development" and "literary laws of those in different places under different social systems." He criticized Feng Jicai and Li Tuo for affirming, generally and without distinction, both the content and the beauty of Western modernistic works.[16] Liu's cautious criticism did little to explicate modernistic texts or to explain why they had emerged, much less to support them. While Feng Jicai and

Tay, "Wang Meng, Stream-of-consciousness, and the Controversy over Modernism," *Modern Chinese Literature* 1, no. 1 (September 1984): 7–24; also Wendy Larson, "Realism, Modernism, and the Anti-'Spiritual Pollution' Campaign in China," *Modern China* 15, no. 1 (January 1989): 31–71.

[14]Gao Xingjian claimed that realistic techniques such as plot development, description of environment, creation of personality, and character development were out of date, and new "literary habits" such as stream-of-consciousness, fantasy, antilogic, and artistic abstraction should take over. However, he finds some "modernist" techniques, such as fantasy or symbolism, in the Chinese tradition, and points out that realism is not native to China. See Larson, "Realism, Modernism, . . . ", 56.

[15]Personal communication between Su Wei and Li Tuo.

[16]See *"Xuyao lengjing de sikao"* (Calm consideration required), *Shanghai wenxue* (Shanghai literature), no. 8 (1988): 88–96.

Li Tuo more clearly supported the new literature as something fresh and exciting, they did not develop a theory to explain it. To Feng, Chinese modernism was simply a kind of "modern Chinese literature with a revolutionary spirit." Feng defended a universalistic "independence" of formal technique while insisting that in content, Chinese modernism was different from that of the West. Li Tuo also claimed form as the most important aspect of Chinese modernism, thus implying that there could be a modernist form with a "Chinese" or a "revolutionary" content, implicitly denying that form is also a kind of ideology.

Critics were able to separate the contents of modernist literature from "decadent bourgeois ideology" and avoid official censure, but the result was a simplification of modernist literature's entry into China. It became merely a matter of formal innovation that did not carry ideological meaning. This conclusion was opposite that of Sun Shaozhen, who an-alyzed the *meaning* of modernist aesthetics within the Chinese social context.

Conceptual transformations in Chinese literary discourse were achieved only by inching ahead, explaining every word and probing every meaning, writing and working around official taboos to discuss the issues of aesthetics and literature. The form/content dichotomy was useful within this context because it allowed critics to maintain a stance of social concern while promoting new "styles," and in this way to pro-tect both the new literature and their own work from attack. When the "third generation"—or the post-Misty—writers came along, however, they discarded this carefully orchestrated "breakthrough" and the stale formula of form versus content.

MISTY POETRY AGES

I, on white paper
white paper—nothing at all
use three crayons
one draws a line
draw three lines

no ruler
lines twisted, askew

the adult says (very big):
Red blue yellow
are the three primary colors
three straight lines

symbolize three roads
I do not understand
(what's it about?)
and as I wish
draw three round circles

I want to draw really round, really round
   "San yuanse" (Three primary colors) (Che Qianzi)

The Misty poets "aged" very quickly in China's rapidly changing literary scene and soon were scorned by younger poets such as Che
Qianzi, quoted above. Now it was the turn of Misty poets to complain
of being unable to "understand" the new language and its younger generation. "Farewell to Bei Dao" became the new slogan of rebellion.
While the emotive, aestheticized, individualized, and psychologized poetry of Bei Dao, Mang Ke, Jiang He, Shu Ting, and others was still under attack by authorities as the "first wave" of the new poetry, a
"second wave," which branded the Misty poets as old-fashioned and
anachronistic, emerged.[17] The following poem, "Waike bingfang" (The
surgical ward) by Wang Xiaolong, became representative of the newer
poetry:

Even the geranium in the hall is crestfallen
Those who walk in here inevitably hang their heads
They trundle off to bed after dinner
Staring with one hundred percent sympathy at a body
That seems to lack something under a snow-white bandage
Later on they deliberately turn up the radio to a loud wah-wah
As they imagine they're the great Maradona
Or some fucking soccer ball kicked against the goalpost
Nobody comes this afternoon
That girl who brought one boy oranges and little smiles each afternoon
Won't be coming back anymore
Last night that boy
Took advantage of everyone's sleeping and stealthily died
This morning one old sparrow turned up to sob awhile
Now it hides under who-knows-what eave pondering a line of poetry
Nobody comes this afternoon
The nurse sits like a man with one knee to her bosom

---

[17]The "first generation" was the revolutionary poets after 1949. The "second generation"
was the post-Cultural Revolution Misty poets, also known as the "first wave." The "third
generation" was poets who emerged immediately after the Misty poets.

Writing a long letter that never comes to the last line
She flicks on the light and instantly the sky is black
After dark the mosquitoes' mouths loom especially large.
This world—if it had no mosquitoes—this world.
In spite of everything wouldn't be a bad place.[18]

Misty poems contained a social meaning, yet one concealed within a purposefully ambiguous language that consisted of a use of symbols and images much different from those of the revolutionary poets. The word "misty" speaks to the way in which readers understood their poetry as a deliberate attempt to effect an illusory and disfigured relationship between "image" and "subject," making a clear-cut meaning more difficult for the reader to determine. Criticized for writing about irrelevant matters, the Misty poets eventually came to represent a mournful yet tragic beauty, a kind of heavy splendor that was an artistic vehicle into which many complex individual emotions could be incorporated. Yet the social context was clear. In Misty poetry, the individual was a complicated thinking and feeling person, someone who could not unquestioningly accept society the way it was, but understood that society should and could be different. This subject, so clear and full of direction in revolutionary poetry, was murky and unsure in Misty poetry. Very quickly, however, as the poem above shows, the way in which Misty poets presented this subject became obsolete.

The third-generation poets labeled themselves "new age" (*xin shidai*) products of the information age. In China the Information Age indicates the introduction into the lives of upper-class citizens of such high technology as computers, fiber-optic communications, photocopiers, and fax machines. It also signifies the opening of market ties with the "outside world" and the resulting change in social and cultural behavior within China. As in capitalist, democratic modern societies, literature was partially deregulated, and the categories of commercial and experimental literature eventually became critical dichotomies. Critics accused commercial fiction—commercial poetry did not exist outside popular song lyrics—of promoting the "look toward money" mentality (*xiang qian kan*, a pun on the revolutionary slogan of the same pronunciation that means "look toward the future"), while others accused experimental

---

[18]Diego Armando Maradona is a famous Argentinean soccer player. Translated in *The Red Azalea: Chinese Poetry Since the Cultural Revolution*, ed. Edward Morin (Honolulu: University of Hawaii Press, 1990), 131.

literature of being irrelevant to the newly emerging market economy.[19] Theorists developed the notion of the "revolution in methodology" that resulted from new ideas in control, systems, and information.

To Che Qianzi, Wang Xiaolong, and others, the *Today* poets' passion appeared heavy and pretentious. The national references and social themes, while less transparent than those in revolutionary poetry, now seemed romantic and inappropriate to the Information Age. Meaning itself changed, favoring direct presentation and speed of interchange over emotive depth. Young poets questioned the meaning of poetry and the self and concluded that "poetry is poetry itself" and not adornment or metaphor, and "self is self itself" and not social meaning. New poets "discovered" that images can be part of mediocre as well as good poetry and questioned their elegance and depth. Rhetoric seemed to betray life. Thus the post-Misty poets began to abandon social theme and poetic image, advocating the "original meaning of the self and emotion" and the "original meaning of language and words." Yesterday's "poetic language" was disdained. Meaning resided only in language itself, not in the relationships between language and object, or object and object, implied in Misty poetry.

In desiring to restore life to its "original" state, post-Misty poets retheorized poetry as something basic and existing on its own internal principles. An entire theoretical vocabulary based on an inner-outer, natural-unnatural dichotomy became a way in which to imply a generalized corruption in all human—and especially language—areas. Poetry was supposed to cast off any "alien matters" imposed from "without." In the words of Han Dong, the representative writer of the Tamen (They) school, "Poetry stops at language. All matters and all things wait to be restored."[20] In "The Surgical Ward" life has nothing to do with beauty, ugliness, or overt meaning, but is a kind of disordered presentation. People eat, get sick, write letters, and die as they always have, but no significance can be attached to these actions, nor are there any real causal relationships between them or emotional ramifications because of them.

---

[19]For an analysis of pop music lyrics and postcolonialism, see Rey Chow, "Hong Kong 1990s: The Post-Colonial 'Chinese' City in Luo Dayou's Music," paper presented at the Woodrow Wilson Center's Urban China conference, May 1–4, 1992.

[20]Han Dong, " 'Tamen', ren yu shi" ("They," people and things) *Jintian* (Today), no. 1 (1992). To research contemporary Chinese poetry it is necessary to move beyond the officially published *Shikan*. The active poetry schools, groups, and publications are scattered around in places such as Sichuan, Guizhou, Xi'an, Lanzhou, Shanghai, Jinan, Nanjing, etc. The expatriate journals *Yi xian* (A line) and *Jiantian* are published in New York and Stockholm respectively.

People and acts assume the status of mosquitoes: not good, but not so bad either, mostly just flitting about for a while. Language must follow the disorder inherent in life.

As the concept of poetry changed, so did the role of the poet. Poetry was no longer the "war drum" or the "trumpet" of the age, nor the song or "self-life" of the Misty poets. Poetry could not be a means through which the individual "expressed" a deep and interior self that may possess social, national, and personal aspirations similar to those of his or her neighbor. With poetry as only poetry and language as only language, the reading and understanding of poetry became subjects for a small circle of poets, conducted in a salon. Thus the audience for poetry also altered as poetry's implied stance changed; it is often said that there are now more poets than readers. As many traditional characteristics of poetry—such as lyricism, beauty in language, or social relevance—disappeared, so did the position of poetry within art.

PLURALISM, SURFACE AESTHETICS, AND ARTISTIC AUTONOMY

Within a few years, the Chinese poetic world went through the modernist confirmation of self and the pursuit of the meaning and value of rebellion, to the postmodernist elimination of the relations between self and society and the questioning of meaning and its structure. Technology and the Information Age—available to a fraction of "cutting-edge" writers—partially caused the change, but the fast translation of theoretical texts by Fredric Jameson, Jacques Derrida, Michel Foucault, Julia Kristeva, and other poststructuralist writers in the West also formed the context in which modernism played a quick transitional role and was discarded. With its emotional depth and responsible social role, Misty poetry seemed to have inherited too many of the poetic conventions of revolutionary poetry to be functioning as a kind of ideology.

According to Jameson, postmodernism is the dominant cultural logic of late capitalism, not merely a style chosen from among many.[21] One of its characteristics is the "effacement of the older distinction between high and so-called mass culture" that causes the written text to lose its status as the premier art form.[22] While fiction may have lost ground,

[21]*Postmodernism, or the Cultural Logic of Late Capitalism* (Durham, N.C.: Duke University Press, 1991), 45–46.
[22]Ibid., 63.

in many cultures poetry has become virtually unread; to qualify as an intellectual one needs very little knowledge of poetry, yet "popular" knowledge implies some familiarity with song lyrics. Thus even more than fiction and certainly more than painting, postmodern culture forces poetry into the two poles of intellectual culture, on one hand, and popular song lyrics, on the other. Despite official homage to poetry in America as well as China, compared to fiction poetry has little general audience.

In Jameson's discussion of Andy Warhol, he points out the "emergence of a new kind of flatness or depthlessness, a new kind of superficiality in the most literal sense."[23] Both "Three Primary Colors" and "The Surgical Ward" exhibit this flatness, a lack of social or emotional depth that could verify the existence of a unified, active subject.[24] The critical passion of Bei Dao's "I—do—not—believe!" or Shu Ting's sensual linkage of the body, nature, and expression are totally missing. Oranges, the radio blaring, and Maradona all assume equal positions as aspects of the environment, no longer interpreted into emotion or action by a single person or a group.

At the end of 1986 *Shenzhen qingnian bao* (Shenzhen youth gazette) and the Anhui *Shige bao* (Poetry gazette) jointly organized a presentation entitled "The World of Chinese Poetry, 1986: A Great Exhibition of Modern Poetry Groups." Both journals simultaneously published the same poems. The schools represented included "Tamen" (They), with Han Dong and others; the "Boorish school" (Ben Han zhuyi), with Hu Dong, Wan Xia et al.; the "No-No school" (Feifei), with Zhou Lunyou, Lan Mao et al.; the "Modern Epic school" (Xiandai shishi), with Shi Guanghua, Liao Yiwu, Song Qu, Song Wei et al.; the "Behavior Image school" (Xingwei yixiang), with Che Qianzi, Liang Xiaobin et al.; and other schools such as "Totality" (Zhengti zhuyi) and "New Tradition" (Xin chuantong zhuyi).[25] The flourishing of a large number of small groups or "schools" shows both pluralism and the fragmentation of a larger overarching social meaning for poetry.

This was the first time that the new poets had spoken so openly, resulting in a critique and continuing investigation by conservative lit-

[23]Ibid., 9.

[24]In Jameson's discussion, film, video, and architecture are forms of culture that most clearly show postmodern aesthetics as the cultural logic of late capitalism.

[25]See Anhui *Shigebaou* (Poetry gazette), October 21, 1986, 1–3; *Shenzhen qingnian bao* (Shenzhen youth daily), October 21, 1986, 2–4, and October 24, 1986, 2–4. Also, Yu Cijiang, *"Menglong shi yu disan dai shi."*

erary authorities. The message of the new poets was radical in every sense, for it implied that all existing norms, in content, form, or otherwise, should be despised, and that any edifice—spiritual, emotional, or institutional—that implied a stable norm was gone. Thus although the Chinese Berlin Wall had disintegrated completely, another wall between poets and potential readers had been erected. Forming themselves into small groups and read largely by other poets, the new schools granted poetry an autonomy toward which the Misty poets had only gestured. Poetry was something for the informed reader, for someone who knew what it meant to write a certain kind of poetry and belong to a certain kind of school. Poetry was not political or social commentary, the delving into the self, or anything to do with communication between humans.

As in the West, when Chinese poetry reformulated its aesthetics away from depth toward surface, it lost its readers and became a specialized activity. As "The Surgical Ward" indicates, the deeply psychologized individual who perceives, interprets, and acts on that basis is gone. The representational postmodern "art" areas of video and, to some extent, television and film became popular cultural forms, popping in quick, informational images and sounds. Poetry likewise threw away the old forms of personal emotion, psychological depth, and social critique, but it became more arcane and specialized as a result. As in the case of painting, avant-garde poetry increasingly belonged to intellectual culture.

Built on the principles of lyricism and evolving out of songs, poetry may be inherently unable to adjust to postmodern aesthetics without losing so much of what identifies it as "poetry" to the general audience that they no longer wish to read it. Intellectual avant-garde poetry does not work well as general cultural critique or as a moment of lyrical pleasure for the nonspecialist reader. Aside from its role in song lyrics, even less can poetry fit into the commodified niche of popular fiction, painting, and film, and is thus isolated as a cult activity carried on by initiates for their own kind.

Part III

Urban associations

Introduction

ELIZABETH J. PERRY

The sudden transformation of most of the formerly Communist world raises the obvious question, Why not China? Instrumental as the Tiananmen protest of 1989 was in stimulating uprisings throughout Eastern Europe later that year, China continues to be ruled by a Leninist regime. Is this simply a case of revolution delayed, with China soon to follow in the footsteps of other failed Leninist systems?

In struggling to explain the amazing changes that have occurred elsewhere in the Communist world, scholars and journalists alike have been drawn to the concept of "civil society." According to their interpretation, urban citizens in Eastern Europe proved capable of overthrowing their discredited Leninist regimes because they had created an arena of *independent associational activity* free from state domination.[1] Conversely, the unrevolutionary outcome of the Chinese uprising is sometimes attributed to the weakness of civil society in contemporary China. Lacking the Catholic Church of Poland, the old democratic parties of Hungary, and the dissident intellectual circles of Czechoslovakia, China is portrayed as devoid of the institutional stage on which the revolutions of 1989 were played out elsewhere.[2]

This section examines public associations in urban China, with an eye toward exploring the existence or potentiality of a Chinese-style civil society. The chapters cover a diverse array of organizations: student clubs, labor unions, dissident legal institutes, and *qigong* associations. Despite their disparate empirical foci, however, the authors encounter a common frustration in trying to apply the European concept of "civil society." They find that the binary opposition between "state" and "society" implied by the term "civil society" obfuscates the peculiar blend

---

[1] Daniel Chirot, "What Happened in Eastern Europe in 1989?" in Jeffrey N. Wasserstrom and Elizabeth J. Perry, eds., *Political Protest and Popular Culture in Modern China: Learning from 1989* (Boulder: Westview, 1991).

[2] Joseph W. Esherick and Jeffrey N. Wasserstrom, "Acting Out Democracy," in Wasserstrom and Perry, *Political Protest and Popular Culture.*

of private, public, and state involvement that characterizes associational activity in contemporary China.

To be sure, the post-Mao economic reforms have seen an explosion of public associations. (See Chapter 6 by Shaoguang Wang.) Recent surveys count tens of thousands of new urban organizations. Some of these are for the purpose of leisure pursuits (e.g., fishing groups, chess clubs, amateur operatic troupes); some are organized around economic concerns (e.g., trade associations, chambers of commerce, labor unions); yet others are underground religious congregations (e.g., house-church Christians, Buddhist sectarians, folk Daoists); and still others have a clear political thrust (e.g., illegal parties with names like the Young Chinese Democratic Party).

Moreover, government authorities are anxious to gain control over these grass-roots organizations, viewing them as a potential challenge to their Leninist rule. Although the Chinese constitution guarantees its citizens freedom of association, a recent State Council directive makes clear that no social organization is considered legal unless it is duly registered and approved by the authorities. Thus a private religious gathering of house-church Christians is deemed illegal unless it has been preapproved by the Bureau of Religious Affairs of the local government and the names of everyone in attendance are forwarded to the Public Security Bureau.

Yet it is surprising how much associational activity occurs *despite* such regulations. The growing popularity of non-Communist sources of moral authority is suggested not only by the recent religious revival, but also by the tremendous resurgence of enthusiasm for what the Chinese call *qigong*—or traditional breathing, healing, and martial arts routines—discussed in Chapter 13 by Nancy Chen. Estimates place the number of *qigong* practitioners at more than 200 million, many of whom are affiliated with the thousands of *qigong* associations that have sprung up across the country. As Chen explains, *qigong* adepts—by relating the *qi* (or vital life force) in their bodies to the *qi* in the atmosphere—can escape to a personal universe beyond the control of the Chinese state. Furthermore, *qigong* practice also creates new communities—informal groups whose members address one another by terms of fictive kinship and whose ties are not necessarily based on the state-sanctioned work or residential units.

Significantly, however, Chen points out that there is a *range* of *qigong* associations, from popular revival movements led by charismatic masters to officially sanctioned bureaucratic organizations. Moreover, there is also considerable *overlap* among these entities. A *qigong* master may head a formally registered association while at the same time conducting a sideline business of illegally healing patients by special cures or training private students to continue a subversive regimen of practice.

This blurring of boundaries between state and society is not peculiar to *qigong*. Mark Sidel analyzes a similar phenomenon in Chapter 12 on dissident lawyer associations, finding that most of these "antistate" organizations actually grew out of state-dominated institutions. Even the most "autonomous" of these entities operated under protective umbrellas provided by state backers—who withdrew their support after the crackdown of June 4, 1989. The groups were organized along factional lines of patron-client networks, a further indication of "how closely tied to the state such groups were in a time of supposed rapid retreat from the state." And yet, despite these intimate links to the establishment, Sidel observes that "even where 'state' assistance was critical to the emergence of these groups, the motivation was in each case partially to challenge state orthodoxy."

Similarly, Jeffrey Wasserstrom and Liu Xinyong, writing about student associations, stress the fact that official organizations structured much of the protest movement of 1989. Thus students usually marched under banners of their school departments rather than under the banner of unofficial salons, study groups, or autonomous unions. In some cases, teachers actually ordered their students to participate in the marches. Eerily, the "new order" that the students created at Tiananmen Square mimicked the official bureaucratic order—with flags of Beijing universities situated near the center of the square and those of provincial campuses toward the periphery. As Wasserstrom and Liu observe, many student leaders of the protest had been active in officially sponsored campus clubs that long predated the uprising. Therefore, these authors conclude that such state-sanctioned experiences, as well as private friendships—more than the democracy salons made famous by adherents of a civil society perspective—were the crucial stepping-stones to Tiananmen.

In my chapter on worker associations, I also emphasize that the complex ties linking laborers—even in the act of protest—to the state apparatus make it awkward to consider these working-class groups an indication of an "autonomous" civil society. Moreover, the official trade unions, established in the 1950s by people who had led the Communist labor movement during the revolution, have often tried to carve out an independent role in the socialist system. Thus many union cadres were sympathetic to widespread labor unrest in 1956–57, and in 1989 official unions donated large sums of money to support the protesters in Tiananmen Square.

A simple state-society dichotomy proves of little help in explaining the labor activism of Chinese workers. Instead we find that society (like the state) consists of disparate—and often contradictory—elements. Even at the height of the Tiananmen uprising, Chinese urbanites were deeply divided. Many workers participated in the demonstrations, but they failed to form a close alliance with the students, in part because the two groups were demanding different things. Whereas students were calling for democracy and quickening the pace of reform, workers were complaining about corruption and inflation—which they often attributed to the post-Mao reforms. Most of the workers who joined the demonstrations were apparently permanent state employees who feared that the industrial reforms might "smash their iron rice bowls" and turn them into disprivileged temporary or contract workers. Indeed, divisions *among* workers—between permanent and temporary laborers, between older and younger workers, between workers from different native places—have been a hallmark of the Chinese labor movement from its nineteenth-century origins down to the present.

Familiar parochial ties—native place for workers, fictive kinship for *qigong* practitioners, personal friendships for students, factional allegiances for lawyers—thus continue to shape associational activity in contemporary China. In making sense of this phenomenon, a conventional Eurocentric view of civil society is of limited assistance. Like so many of our social science constructs, the concept of civil society was originally a product of the effort to explain the emergence and transformation of European capitalism. Thus there is a legitimate question as to its applicability to a country like China, where the economic trends characteristic of Europe never really took root.[3]

The dramatic resurgence of *qigong* is only one indication of the fact that presocialist practices—in an ever-changing manner—still exercise a tremendous hold over the Chinese popular imagination. (And not just the *popular* imagination; most of the aging top leaders, including eighty-nine-year-old Deng Xiaoping, are said to employ private *qigong* masters

---

[3]An elaboration of this argument can be found in Elizabeth J. Perry and Ellen V. Fuller, "China's Long March to Democracy," *World Policy Journal* (Fall 1991).

in a bid to defy the actuarial tables.) In any case, our Western social science habit of viewing state-society relations as a zero-sum game, in which society's gain is the state's loss, does not shed much light on a China where private ties, public associations, and state agents are so thoroughly intertwined.

11

Labor's battle for political space:
the role of worker associations in
contemporary China

ELIZABETH J. PERRY

When they first appeared on the Chinese political horizon some seventy years ago, labor unions immediately became an object of intense competition. Rival political parties as well as divided groups of workers battled among themselves to channel union activities in directions favorable to their particular agendas. This lent a special intensity to the unionization struggles of pre-1949 China that has already been captured, at least to some extent, by the secondary literature.[1]

Much less developed, however, is our understanding of labor politics after 1949. The general impression conveyed by the secondary literature is that unions under the People's Republic have been docile entities, completely under the thumb of the Chinese Communist Party (CCP).[2] This image is not entirely unfounded. The official trade unions, as so-called mass organizations established and operated according to strict criteria laid down by Beijing, have in fact usually toed the party line. Nevertheless, at critical junctures—the Hundred Flowers movement of 1956–57, the early Cultural Revolution of 1966–67, the popular uprising of 1989—official unions showed an inclination toward the autonomous

---

[1] Jean Chesneaux, *The Chinese Labor Movement, 1919–1927* (Stanford, Calif.: Stanford University Press, 1968); Ming K. Chan, "Labor and Empire: The Chinese Labor Movement in the Canton Delta, 1895–1927," Ph.D. diss., Stanford University, 1975; Lynda Shaffer, *Mao and the Workers: The Hunan Labor Movement, 1920–1923* (Armonk, NY: M. E. Sharpe, 1982); Gail Hershatter, *The Workers of Tianjin, 1900–1949* (Stanford: Stanford University Press, 1986); Emily Honig, *Sisters and Strangers: Women in the Shanghai Cotton Mills, 1919–1949* (Stanford, Calif.: Stanford University Press, 1986).
[2] See, e.g., Barry M. Richman, *Industrial Society in Communist China* (New York: Random House, 1969), 267–270.

articulation of workers' interests. And alongside these official unions have emerged independent unions willing to push even more forcefully for autonomous workers' rights.

These revealing moments of union ferment demonstrate that the Chinese labor movement, like labor movements elsewhere around the world, is an arena for heated conflict, not only between "state" and "society" but also *among* different state agents and societal elements. Government officials, factory cadres, and above all workers themselves have evidenced deep internal disagreements over the aims and functions of labor unions.

Labor historians have often viewed the fragmentation of a working class as a cause for concern. Disappointed by the failure of twentieth-century workers to live up to the exalted expectations raised by Karl Marx and Friedrich Engels, scholars have focused on fragmentation as an explanation for the lack of revolutionary action. Divided by gender, age, ethnicity, and skill, workers are depicted as having rarely acted in the cohesive, class-conscious fashion predicted by Communist visionaries. Contradictions between men and women, old and young, northern and southern European, black and white American, or skilled and unskilled have allegedly prevented workers from exhibiting the class-conscious party allegiances or revolutionary behaviors that might otherwise be expected of them.[3] In this view, intraclass divisions inhibit unionization and act as a brake on radical political transformation.

By contrast, my study of labor in pre-1949 Shanghai finds that the fragmentation of labor could itself provide a basis for politically influential working-class action, not only in support of one or another political party but even in the emergence of new political regimes.[4] Different segments of labor have linked up with state allies (sometimes through the intervention of factory management or gangster foremen) in such a way as to affect decisively the fate of both parties. In the Chinese case, fragmentation certainly did not imply passivity. Despite

[3]Richard Jules Oestreicher, *Solidarity and Fragmentation* (Urbana: University of Illinois Press, 1986); Charles F. Sabel, *Work and Politics: The Division of Labor in Industry* (Cambridge: Cambridge University Press, 1982); David M. Gordon, Richard Edwards, and Michael Reich, *Segmented Work, Divided Workers* (Cambridge: Cambridge University Press, 1982); Ira Katznelson, *City Trenches: Urban Politics and the Patterning of Class in the United States* (New York: Pantheon, 1981); Suzanne Berger and Michael J. Piore, *Dualism and Discontinuity in Industrial Societies* (Cambridge: Cambridge University Press, 1980).
[4]Elizabeth J. Perry, *Shanghai on Strike: The Politics of Chinese Labor* (Stanford, Calif.: Stanford University Press, 1993).

304   *Elizabeth J. Perry*

(and, in large part, because of) important distinctions along lines of native-place origin, age, gender, and skill, the Chinese working class has shown itself capable of effectual political action.

This chapter suggests that the activism of labor in contemporary China can also be linked to splits within the working class—splits that incline different sectors of labor to forge quite different alliances with powerholders. Unlike previous analyses of these divisions, I do not see them as artificially imposed by the Communist party-state.[5] Instead, I believe that they reflect a rich history of labor unrest that long predates the founding of the People's Republic of China (PRC). But these are also not "primordial" cleavages, immune to all change. The fissures that rend today's working class are equally a product of history and a reaction to contemporary circumstances—especially state industrial policies. The complex ties that link laborers, even when engaged in protest, to the state apparatus make it awkward to conceptualize labor associations as an indication of "civil society"—defined as the autonomy of individuals and groups in relation to the state. The familiar view of political space as the by-product of a zero-sum struggle between state and society is dispensed with here in favor of a messier, interwoven image. Yet this intertwining of labor and state does not render unionization efforts superfluous to a discussion of the potential for political transformation in contemporary China.

The turmoil of 1989 offered dramatic evidence of the important contribution of working-class organizations in the development of political protest. Autonomous unions sprang up in industrial cities across the country and captured special attention from scholars and journalists alike, but official unions also played a significant role in the process. To understand this Janus-faced phenomenon, rooted in social divisions as well as in state policies, a review of labor relations in the PRC is in order.

THE SOCIALIST INDUSTRIAL SYSTEM

Although it has been claimed that the Chinese working class was "remade" by the Communist state, many of the officials who developed

[5] Andrew G. Walder, *Communist Neo-traditionalism: Work and Authority in Chinese Industry* (Berkeley: University of California Press, 1986).

PRC labor policies in the 1950s and 1960s were themselves former activists in the labor movement. Chen Yun, chief architect of the socialist transformation of industry in the mid-1950s, had joined the Communist Party thirty years earlier while apprenticing at Shanghai's Commercial Press. The radical union at the press, of which Chen was an active member, was an outgrowth of a printers' guild that had preceded the Communist movement by years.[6] A skilled worker from the Jiangnan region of South China, Chen Yun was typical of many early adherents of the Communist labor movement in Shanghai. President Liu Shaoqi, whose formative education was in a work-study program geared toward factory labor, had undertaken his first political assignment as a labor organizer in Shanghai. Premier Zhou Enlai had directed the third, and successful, Shanghai workers' armed uprising of March 1927. Li Lisan, "anchorman" of trade union activities in the initial years of the People's Republic, had played a central role in Shanghai's historic May Thirtieth movement in 1925. Liu Changsheng, a leather worker in charge of Shanghai's Communist underground labor movement during the wartime and postwar periods, assumed the vice-chairmanship of the Shanghai Federation of Labor Unions after 1949. Zhang Qi, a skilled Jiangnan silk weaver who helped lead a major strike at his factory in 1934 as a member of Shanghai's underground Communist Youth League, became vice-chair of the Shanghai Federation of Trade Unions.

The new Communist regime provided the opportunity for these former labor organizers to play a key role in the formulation of national policy. Considering the importance of skilled workers in the revolutionary movement, it is not surprising that the pattern put in place after 1949 strongly emphasized security and welfare—issues dear to the hearts of artisans the world over.

Ironically, the artisan heritage was most visible in the sector of the industrial system that most exemplified the "new" socialist system: state-owned enterprises. It was these organizations that guaranteed permanent employment, high wages, and substantial welfare measures to their employees. (See Chapters 2 and 3.) Thanks to the perquisites it brought, a job in a state factory came to be known as an "iron rice bowl," in

---

[6]*Shangwu yinshuguan gonghuishi* (A history of unions at the Commercial Press) (Shanghai, n.d.), 1–2. On Chen Yun's role as "economic czar of new China," see Nicholas R. Lardy and Kenneth Lieberthal, eds., *Chen Yun's Strategy for China's Economic Development* (Armonk, NY: M. E. Sharpe, 1983).

contrast to the less durable and less desirable "earthen rice bowl" of the collective sector.[7]

The exclusivity and paternalism of the Communist enterprise were reminiscent of the artisan guild. One needed the introduction of friends or relatives to join these selective organizations, which offered lifetime benefits to their privileged members. Like its guild forerunner, the socialist factory also stipulated certain behavioral norms for its membership.[8] But whereas the traditional guild had relied on the authority of its patron deity to enforce these values, the new state enterprise claimed legitimacy from the Communist Party.

In each province and city, the special prerogatives of workers at state factories were overseen by the local federation of trade unions.[9] In Shanghai, the city's federation has been dominated by former activists in the Communist labor movement, most of whom rose from the ranks of Jiangnan artisans.

If the new Communist order embodied many of the priorities of the skilled artisans who designed it, the same was not true for excluded sectors of the labor force. Resentment against the benefits accruing to veteran workers at state enterprises was an important precipitant of the waves of labor unrest that have rolled across Chinese cities every decade since 1949.

THE EARLY 1950S

The initial years following the Communist victory of 1949 were turbulent ones for labor. Workers were hastily organized into official trade unions; by April 1950 the Shanghai municipal union already counted a membership of more than one million, for example.[10] Yet newly organized workers did not necessarily abandon their militant traditions in the process of incorporation into state-sponsored unions. In just the three summer months of 1949, the fledgling Shanghai union was burdened with more than two thousand labor disputes, most of which were protests over layoffs or wage cuts.[11]

[7]Martin King Whyte and William L. Parish, *Urban Life in Contemporary China* (Chicago: University of Chicago Press, 1984), 33.
[8]Walder, *Communist Neo-traditionalism,* chap. 4.
[9]Paul F. Harper, "The Party and Unions in Communist China," *China Quarterly,* no. 37 (January–March 1969): 105–6.
[10]*Shanghai jiefang yinian* (A year of liberated Shanghai) (Shanghai, 1950), 74.
[11]Shanghai Municipal Archives, #C1-2-26.

The disruption at the Shenxin Number Seven Cotton Mill in Shanghai illustrates the general pattern. In January 1950, some 700 temporary workers (out of 2,014 employees) stormed out of the factory to surround the general headquarters of the Shenxin textile company and demand redress for withheld wages. When these initiatives did not resolve the problem, the disappointed workers marched to the home of General Manager Rong Heqing. A group of the protesters, under the pretext of looking for cotton magnate Rong Yiren (later vice-president), broke into Rong Heqing's house and proceeded to confiscate, cook, and then consume chicken, ham, and cake. Having eaten without the company of Rong Yiren, they then marched to *his* home to continue the movable feast. Investigation by the Shanghai municipal trade union found that the local union at the Number Seven Cotton Mill had taken a passive stance during the incident, permitting former Kuomintang (KMT, the Nationalist Party) activists to assume a leading role in the disturbance. According to municipal authorities the event indicated a need to strengthen basic-level unions; a directive outlining the "Lesson of the Shenxin Seven Incident" was thus distributed to all subordinate unions to encourage closer adherence to party direction.[12]

The question of how far unions should go in promoting workers' interests was taken up in November 1951 in a speech by veteran labor leader Li Lisan, then serving as chairman of the national union. However, Li's eloquent support for workers' rights evoked sharp criticism of his alleged "economism" and "syndicalism," resulting in his abrupt dismissal from the union chairmanship.[13] Still the problem of labor unrest persisted. In a five-month period in 1952, Shanghai alone was beset by more than a thousand labor disputes.[14] To gain greater control over restive workers, the party appointed a new director of the All-China Federation of Trade Unions (ACFTU) in 1953. Director Lai Ruoyu's assignment, made easier by a rewritten ACFTU constitution stressing

[12]"Guanyu geji gonghui taolun he chuanda 'Shenqi shijian de jiaoxun' de tongzhi" (Directive concerning union discussion and dissemination of "Lesson of the Shenxin Seven Incident"), *Shanghai gongyun ziliao* (Materials on the Shanghai labor movement), no. 1 (March 15, 1953): 9–20.

[13]Li Jiaqi, "Wushi niandaichu pipan gonghui de 'jingjizhuyi,' 'gongtuanzhuyi,' jiqi zai Shanghai de yingxiang" (The early 1950s critique of "economism" and "syndicalism" and its influence in Shanghai), *Shanghai gongyunshi* (History of the Shanghai labor movement), no. 6 (1986): 1–7.

[14]Zhang Jinping, "Dadong yanchang shijian de zhenxiang" (The true face of the Dadong Tobacco Factory incident), internal circulation document, n.d., p. 34.

party leadership, was to exert tight top-down direction over the union apparatus.[15]

THE HUNDRED FLOWERS CAMPAIGN

Despite such efforts at containment, the Hundred Flowers campaign unleashed another, much larger wave of labor unrest.[16] Occurring on the heels of the socialization of industry, the strikes of 1956–57 reflected deep divisions among both laborers and state agents about the new order. The scale of the protest movement was truly remarkable. According to one, perhaps rough estimate by the party Central Committee, more than 10,000 labor strikes erupted across the country between October 1956 and March 1957.[17] More reliable statistics from the Shanghai municipal union document that more than 200 strikes occurred in that city in the spring of 1957.[18] To put these numbers in context, only 175 strikes took place in Shanghai during the tumultuous year of 1925—100 of which were in conjunction with the historic May Thirtieth movement.[19]

The strikes of the mid-1950s were instigated for the most part by "marginal" workers: temporary and contract laborers, workers in the service sector and at smaller-scale enterprises, apprentices, and others who failed to share in the privileges bestowed upon "skilled" veteran employees at state enterprises.[20] At the Taichang nail factory, for ex-

[15]Lee Lai To, *Trade Unions in China, 1949 to the Present* (Singapore: Singapore University Press, 1986), 82.

[16]Both Mao Zedong and Liu Shaoqi commented on the problem. See Mao's comments in *Communist China, 1955–1959: Policy Documents with Analysis* (Cambridge, Mass.: Harvard University Press, 1962), 278, 291–92; and in Roderick MacFarquhar, Timothy Cheek and Eugene Wu, eds., *The Secret Speeches of Chairman Mao* (Cambridge, Mass.: Harvard University Press, 1989), 122, 144; and for Liu's comments see *Joint Publications Research Service*, no. 41889, p. 58. Mao noted that "it is incorrect not to allow workers to strike" while Liu went so far as to propose that union and party officials participate in strikes to regain the workers' sympathy.

[17]*Zhongguo gongyun* (Chinese labor movement) no. 7 (1957). Reprinted in Yan Jiadong and Zhang Liangzhi, eds., *Shehuizhuyi gonghui xuexi wenjian xuanbian* (Compilation of study documents on socialist unions) (Beijing: Central Party History Publishing House, 1992), 176–83.

[18]Shanghai Municipal Archives, #C1-1-189; Qian Min and Zhang Jinping, "Guanyu 1957 nian Shanghai bufen gongchang naoshi de yanjiu" (A study of the disturbances at some Shanghai factories in 1957), February 5, 1990, p. 2.

[19]Shanghai Bureau of Social Affairs, ed., *Jin shiwunian lai Shanghai bagong yu tingye* (Strikes and lockouts in Shanghai in the past fifteen years) (Shanghai, 1934).

[20]François Gipouloux, *Les cent fleurs à l'usine* (Paris: L'école des hautes études en sciences sociales, 1986), 198–205. See also Lynn White, III, "Workers' Politics in Shanghai," *Journal of Asian Studies* 36, no. 1 (1976): 105–7. For examples of these disputes, see

ample, workers from rural backgrounds demanded that their dependents still living in the countryside receive the same benefits as workers from Shanghai whose dependents were living in the city. Barbers stationed at construction sites in the city demanded the same welfare provisions as the construction workers whose hair they were cutting.[21]

The disturbance at the Shanghai Fertilizer Factory in May 1957 illustrates the importance of these intraworker divisions. The previous summer, the factory had hired temporary workers, planning to advance them to the status of permanent employees after a three-month trial period. Because of contraction in production, however, a decision was made to fire these workers instead. Soon thereafter, when the union at the factory issued membership cards to regular employees, the discharged workers believed that access to a union card would facilitate permanent employee status. They thus demanded that the union issue them the cards. The union leaders refused to do so, pointing out that these workers had already lost their jobs. The angered temporary workers thereupon dragged the director and vice-director of the factory union down to the bank of the Huangpu River. After the cadres still refused to issue them union membership cards, the workers dunked the head of the union director into the polluted waters of the river. This continued for more than an hour, until the director's face was covered with mud and blood. At this point, the vice-director jumped into the river and attempted to swim off but was stopped by a barrage of stones. Only when the factory physician arrived on the scene to declare both cadres near death did the discharged workers finally release their captives to the authorities. Two days later, union and youth league leaders at the factory declared that if the party leadership considered this outrageous incident an example of contradictions *among* the people (which, as a *non*antagonistic contradiction, would not require serious punishment), then they would take matters into their own hands and repay violence with violence. The permanent workers expressed their hearty agreement with this declaration and began to stockpile weapons with which to kill the former temporary workers who had instigated the affair. The only sympathy these permanent employees evinced for the discharged laborers was a pledge

---

Xinwen ribao (News daily) (Shanghai), May 16, 1957, which describes a riot by apprentices at Shanghai's Lianyi Machine Factory, and *Xinwen ribao,* March 13 and April 27, 1957, which details a protest by hundreds of Shanghai bathhouse workers who were being repatriated to their native villages.

[21] Shanghai Municipal Archives, #C1-2-2407.

to take financial responsibility for the surviving dependents of the workers whom they intended to slay! This bloody scenario was averted when higher authorities, declaring the disturbance an *antagonistic* contradiction, intervened to handle the incident by arresting the ringleaders among the discharged workers.[22]

The protests of the mid-1950s created a real predicament for the trade unions. On the one hand, workers often criticized union cadres for being insensitive to their interests and sometimes targeted their struggles directly at the official unions. In several cases, independent workers' associations (known as *pingnan hui*, or "redress difficulties societies") were established, along with liaison committees and pickets to direct and carry out the struggle. Many disputes included a demand for disbursing the collective welfare fund, a pot of money under union control. Union directors who refused to comply were subjected to curses and in many cases beatings from enraged workers.[23] On the other hand, union cadres who were inclined to side with workers (as the director of the union at the Shanghai Knitting Factory) might well find themselves out of a job.[24]

These dilemmas generated another debate about the proper relationship between the labor movement and the ACFTU. Although unions had been in the business of protecting the interests of permanent state employees according to strict party-established guidelines, the liberalization of the Hundred Flowers period provided an opportunity for them to try to expand their operations. In May 1957, ACFTU director Lai Ruoyu criticized the unions for always siding with the Communist Party.[25] His aide, Wang Rong, took the lead in fighting for more union autonomy in the city of Shanghai.[26] Their challenge was short-lived, however. Both officials were replaced the following year in a major purge of trade union cadres charged with having advocated organizational independence.[27]

Lai Ruoyu was actually one of the most astute observers of the Chinese labor scene in 1957. His May speech had candidly acknowledged

[22]Ibid., #C1-2-2234.
[23]Ibid., #C1-2-2396.
[24]*Renmin ribao* (People's daily), May 9, 1957; *Gongren ribao* (Worker's daily), May 21, 1957.
[25]*Survey of China Mainland Press* (SCMP), no. 1535: 12; no. 1624: 41.
[26]Lee, *Trade Unions in China*, 83–85.
[27]Asia Labour Monitor, *Smashing the Iron Rice Bowl: Workers and Unions in China's Market Socialism* (Hong Kong, 1988), 28–29. At the same time, Chen Yun was criticized for having promoted union autonomy after a visit to Yugoslavia in which he witnessed firsthand the experiments in workplace democracy under way in that country.

that after the socialization of industry, unions had become useless in the eyes of many workers. Moreover, in a mode of analysis congruent with that of this paper, Lai noted that within the working class were serious divisions—between new and older workers, between locals and outsiders, and between ordinary workers and managerial staff. He pointed out that current policies were exacerbating these differences. New workers were promoted more rapidly than older workers because book-learning was valued above practical ability in tests for promotion. As a result, younger, better educated workers became arrogant and did not respect the seasoned skilled workers, while the older workers—the backbone of production—became resentful. Furthermore, newly established factories tended to hire workers from the Northeast or Shanghai who did not get along well with the local hires. In Lai's view, fissures such as these were fueling the labor protests of the day and demanded swift action from the trade unions.[28]

The unions' tentative efforts at enlarging the scope of their responsibilities ended in abject failure with the purge of Lai Ruoyu. So, too, did the gamble by excluded workers to improve their position. Despite the vociferous protests of that period, the gap between permanent state workers and temporary or contract laborers grew even greater in the years ahead—setting the stage for the factional violence of the Cultural Revolution.[29]

The GREAT PROLETARIAN CULTURAL REVOLUTION

In 1966–67, serious struggles again broke out in factories across the country. In Shanghai, the ranks of so-called conservative Scarlet Guards were filled with older state workers, predominantly from the Jiangnan region, experienced in the pre-1949 labor movement. Their leaders were largely former underground party labor organizers who hailed from the same region. The Revolutionary Rebels, by contrast, were mostly younger workers led in part by cadres sent down from the Subei area in the early 1950s. Among their constituents were more than a few "un-

---

[28]Lai Ruoyu, "Zhengdun gonghui de lingdao zuofeng, miqie yu qunzhong de lianxi, chong-fen fahui gonghui zai jiejue renmin neibu maodunzhong de taiojie zuoyong" (Overhaul the unions' leadership work style, intensify relations with the masses, thoroughly develop the mediating role of the unions in resolving contradictions among the people), reprinted in Yan and Zhang, eds., *Shehuizhuyi gonghui xuexi wenjian xuanbian*, 191–92.
[29]White, "Workers' Politics in Shanghai," 107–15.

skilled" contract and temporary workers.[30] As Lynn White has explained the motivations of disprivileged workers:

Unemployed and contract workers may not, at first, have been passionately excited about the errors of historians, the ideologies of novelists, or the philosophies of musicians—even though these issues concerned editorialists from the radical group that launched the Cultural Revolution in late 1965 and early 1966. Unemployed workers seem to have had some idea what political leaders they disliked, however. When men like Mayor Ts'ao Ti-chi'iu [of Shanghai], who had espoused the "worker-peasant system," were criticized for cultural policies, some enthusiasm was stirred within the lower proletariat.[31]

Factional strife was most intense at older factories where pre-1949 activists were numerous and obviously favored vis-à-vis younger workers. Such factories not only displayed glaring inequalities in labor treatment; they also boasted a glorious history of labor protest to which only the older workers could lay claim. As elder "revolutionary heroes" recounted their experiences at frequent factory roundtables, resentment between the generations was bound to grow. Take, for example, the case of the Shanghai Diesel Engine Factory—site of the city's bloodiest labor conflict in the summer of 1967. There one faction consisted largely of party members and "old conservatives" (*laobao*), while the opposing faction included a large number of young "petty thugs" (*xiao liumang*) and former KMT members (recruited when the factory was first founded by KMT notable T. V. Soong). The young thugs had formed their own gang—known as the "KO" organization because they scratched the initials "KO" onto their leather belts. Proud of their Western logo (perhaps a play on the word "okay"), these youngsters put up posters designed to infuriate their elders: "We can't help but feel ashamed that our half-month salary can buy only one pair of shoes!" "Our youthful spring has already lost its glory!" "Allow dance parties at once!" "Long live women!" The factory authorities dubbed this spontaneous workers' association the "KO counterrevolutionary clique," raising the curtain on factional battles that took eighteen lives and wounded hundreds of workers over the ensuing months.[32]

Subjected to repeated lectures by their elders about the revolutionary exploits of bygone days, younger workers had been longing for an opportunity to even the score. The Cultural Revolution offered them the

---

[30]Interviews conducted with former Shanghai Red Guards, May 25 and July 2, 1987.
[31]White, "Workers' Politics in Shanghai," 114–15.
[32]Chen Xianfa, *Minzu lei* (National tears) (Shanghai, 1988).

chance. Interestingly enough, however, the methods that young Revolutionary Rebels employed in their own struggles bore an uncanny resemblance to the protest repertoires of the previous generation.[33] It was probably no coincidence that the Shanghai Number Seventeen Cotton Mill, where Gang of Four member Wang Hongwen worked, had in the mid-1920s been the scene of labor violence strikingly similar in form to that of Cultural Revolution struggle sessions. In a 1925 incident at the factory, workers had tricked a hated foreman into attending a mass meeting at which he was publicly denounced. The hapless foreman was forced to kneel in front of the crowd with hands tied behind his back, dunce cap placed on his head, and a placard reading "Down with this traitor and running dog" hung across his chest. Photographs of the occasion were posted at the factory gate to serve as warning lest the unseated overseer ever try to resume his post.[34]

When radical workers adopted similar tactics during the Cultural Revolution, their targets were the older generation and the institutions (e.g., the Federation of Trade Unions) that symbolized its privileged position in the new Communist order. In Shanghai, the year 1967 saw a string of attacks by Wang Hongwen's Revolutionary Rebels against the former party underground labor organizers who then controlled the Shanghai Federation. The federation was accused—apparently with some justification—of serving as the "black backstage supporter" of the conservative Scarlet Guards. Zhang Qi, director of the federation and former secretary of the Shanghai party underground, was subjected to repeated humiliation in public struggle sessions. His hands were forced behind his back in the painful "jet plane" position, a dunce cap adorned his head, and a placard across his chest announced him as a "running dog" who had committed "revisionist crimes." In December, Zhang was imprisoned in the basement of the building of the federation that he had helped to create. By that point Wang Hongwen's Workers' General Headquarters—an amalgamation of radical labor associations—had already set up shop in the imposing building on the Bund.[35] Although

---

[33]On the importance of learned protest repertoires, see Charles Tilly, *The Contentious French* (Cambridge, MA: Belknap Press, 1986). This theme is creatively developed for Shanghai students in Jeffrey Wasserstrom, *Student Protest in Twentieth-Century China: The View from Shanghai* (Stanford, Calif.: Stanford University Press, 1991).

[34]Zhang Ben et al., "Shanghai guomian shiqichang gongren douzhengshi" (The history of labor struggles at Shanghai's Number Seventeen cotton mill), *Shanghai gongren yundong lishi ziliao* (Historical materials on the Shanghai labor movement) (1953): 61–70.

[35]Fan Wenxian, "Shanghai shi zonggonghui beiza jishi" (Annals of the assault on the

Zhang Qi survived the Cultural Revolution in remarkably good health, many of his colleagues were less fortunate. A recent listing of fatalities in radical assaults on the Shanghai Federation of Trade Unions illustrates the vulnerable position of former underground party organizers—most of whom were skilled craftspeople from Jiangnan.[36]

Divisions of age, native place, and occupation figured prominently in the factionalism of the Cultural Revolution. Moreover, the depth of these fissures is understandable only when interpreted in the light of a labor history stretching back into the pre-1949 era. Although nominally a "proletarian" movement, the Cultural Revolution did not result in notable improvements for workers. While the communitarian rhetoric may have seemed consonant with long-standing artisan values, the material sacrifice demanded by the Cultural Revolution was anything but popular with skilled workers whose privileged status had always been reflected in higher pay. In 1974–75, a wave of strikes and slowdowns swept across China's factories to demand bonuses and wage hikes, anathema as these were to the Maoist orthodoxy of the day. The most serious work stoppage, a series of strikes in Hangzhou, was resolved only when Deng Xiaoping went in person to assure the restive workers of an impending wage reform.[37]

THE 1980S

In the early 1980s, inspired by the success of Solidarity in Poland, workers throughout the country began to demand independent trade unions. During just the first two months of 1981, reports of strikes, slowdowns, and street demonstrations by workers demanding free trade unions came from Shanghai, Tianjin, Shaanxi, Wuhan, Chongqing, Xinjiang, Anshan, Nanchang, and Zhengzhou.[38] Fearful of a workers' rebellion, the central leadership responded by deleting the right to strike from the 1982 constitution.

Illegal though they were, strikes continued apace during the 1980s,

Shanghai Federation of Trade Unions), *Shanghai gongyun shiliao* (Historical materials on the Shanghai labor movement), no. 5 (1986): 1–6.

[36]"Zhengzheng tiegu chuiqing shi" (In appreciation of martyrdom), in ibid., 13–22.

[37]Lowell Dittmer, *China's Continuous Revolution* (Berkeley: University of California Press, 1987), 165–67.

[38]These incidents are summarized in Chen-chang Chiang, "The Role of the Trade Unions in Mainland China," *Issues and Studies* 26, no. 2 (February 1990): 92–94.

growing in frequency toward the end of the decade. According to the All-China Federation of Trade Unions, 129 strikes broke out in 1987— almost certainly an underestimate since other sources report more than a hundred strikes in Shenzhen alone. Strikers demanded workplace democracy, wage hikes, and improved management.[39] The next year saw more of the same.[40] In the first quarter of 1989, the Shanghai Federation of Trade Unions handled fifteen strikes, most of which concerned the allocation of bonuses or the grievances of workers idled by the restructuring of the economic reforms.[41] That January it was reported that thousands of People's Liberation Army (PLA) soldiers had been occupying the Daqing oil fields for several months to quell a labor stoppage demanding higher wages and better treatment. This was apparently the first time in the decade since the close of the Cultural Revolution that the military had been called upon to suppress labor unrest.[42]

Widespread worker protests were accompanied by general dissatisfaction with the official trade unions. In the spring of 1988, a national survey directed by the ACFTU found that more than 60 percent of the 640,000 respondents were seriously unhappy with the role played by the official unions. They complained that the unions served only to convey government decisions, collect membership dues, and convene recreational activities; seldom did they listen to workers' opinions.[43] Similarly, a survey conducted by the influential magazine *Liaowang* (Outlook) found that less than 15 percent of those queried would turn to their union for help when confronted with a "major" problem. On the other hand, when asked under what conditions they *would* turn to their union, 91 percent responded that they think of the union in times of illness, when trying to solve problems for colleagues or the elderly, or when they want to participate in union-sponsored recreational activities. In other words, the unions continued to perform social and welfare functions, but their political role as an advocate for workers' interests was regarded as virtually meaningless. Indeed, of the 40 cadres who responded to the *Liaowang* questionnaire, only one said that his major

[39] Asia Labour Monitor, *Smashing the Iron Rice Bowl*, 117.
[40] *Renmin ribao*, October 26, 1988, 1, 4; Foreign Broadcast Information Service *Daily Report* (hereafter FBIS), October 25, 1988, 21–22.
[41] Qian and Zhang, "Guanyu 1957 nian Shanghai bufen," 11–12.
[42] *Zhongbao* (Central report), January 13, 1989; *South China Morning Post*, January 12, 1989.
[43] Cited in Chiang, "The Role of Trade Unions," 84–85.

duties included taking part in political affairs and exercising "democratic management" in his work-unit.[44]

Disturbed by findings such as these and encouraged by the spirit of reform then sweeping the country, the ACFTU—as it had thirty years before—proposed that the official trade unions be permitted to act as autonomous entities charged with the protection of workers' interests and rights.[45] Along with this reformist proposal went a somewhat more tolerant attitude toward strikes. Henceforth, according to an ACFTU spokesman, "trade unions would support reasonable requests by workers."[46]

Repeated protests bespeak fundamental dissatisfaction with prevailing industrial relations, but the state has found it extremely difficult to reform a system around which so many embedded interests have coalesced. That many workers are in fact opposed to economic restructuring became evident during the demonstrations of 1989.

THE UPRISING OF 1989

Workers took to the streets in support of the student protesters in 1989, but not necessarily with the same objectives as their intellectual counterparts. The Beijing Workers Autonomous Union, which registered a membership of more than 20,000 workers, was one of the largest and most vocal of the many unofficial labor unions that sprang up alongside the student movement. Yet the Beijing Autonomous Union held "attitudes towards the party, the party's reformers, and the reforms of the 1980s, and even the student movement itself that are quite different from the more highly publicized views of China's students and intellectuals—and in many ways consciously opposed to them."[47] Whereas students were generally in favor of greater economic reform, workers—especially permanent employees in state enterprises—showed considerable hostility

---

[44]*Liaowang zhoukan* (Outlook weekly), no. 17 (April 25, 1988): 17.

[45]*Renmin ribao*, July 27, 1988, 1; *Gongren ribao*, August 3, 1988, 1.

[46]Chiang, "The Role of Trade Unions," 91. The tolerant attitude of unionists on the eve of the Tiananmen uprising is reflected in a collection of essays published in Shanghai: Guo Zhefeng and Zhang Liangzhi, eds., *Gonghui gongzuo "redian" tantao* (An investigation of union work "hot spots") (Shanghai, 1989). For the more conservative attitude that obtained after the June Fourth repression, see Yan Jiadong, *Shehuizhuyi gonghui gailun* (General discussion of socialist unions) (Beijing, 1992).

[47]Andrew G. Walder and Gong Xiaoxia, "Workers in the Beijing Democracy Movement: Reflections on the Brief History of the Beijing Workers' Autonomous Union," presented to the Berkeley China Seminar, November 15, 1990, 4.

toward the post-Mao economic restructuring. A slogan of the Beijing Autonomous Union put it this way: "The Third Plenum said get rich faster, but the people's pockets have not swelled, and cats black and white have gotten fatter."[48] The reforms were seen as responsible for the bureaucratic corruption that lay at the root of their own oppression:

We have carefully considered the exploitation of the workers. Marx's *Das Kapital* provided us with a method for understanding the character of our oppression. We deducted from the total value of output the workers' wages, welfare, medical welfare, the necessary social fund, equipment depreciation and reinvestment expenses. Surprisingly, we discovered that "civil servants" swallow all the remaining value produced by the people's blood and sweat! The total taken by them is really vast! How cruel! How typically Chinese! These bureaucrats use the people's hard earned money to build luxury villas all over the country (guarded by soldiers in so-called military areas), to buy luxury cars, to travel to foreign countries on so-called study tours (with their families and even baby sitters)! Their immoral and shameful deeds and crimes are too numerous to mention here.[49]

Ironic and cynical as the language was, its use of Marxist terminology was probably more than empty rhetoric. For workers with secure positions in a socialist industrial system, the prospect of an economic reform that might well threaten their rice bowl was anything but reassuring. Members of the Beijing Workers Autonomous Union were all regularly employed at one or another of the city's work-units; indeed, proof of employment was required to join the maverick union.[50] Likewise, in the more than two dozen other autonomous labor associations that sprang up in nineteen different provinces, "the leadership and membership were dominated by workers from large state owned industrial enterprises."[51] As an observer noted of those who marched in sympathy with the students at Tiananmen: "Most of the workers appeared to be skilled, including many from electronics factories."[52] Other eyewitnesses reported steelworkers, postal workers, technicians, machinists, and autoworkers among the ranks of the demonstrators.[53]

---

[48] Beijing Workers Autonomous Union handbill dated May 26, 1989; translated in ibid., 15–16.

[49] Mok Chiu Yu and J. Frank Harrison, eds., *Voices from Tiananmen Square* (Montreal: Black Rose Books, 1990), 109.

[50] Walder and Gong, "Workers in the Beijing Democracy Movement," 15.

[51] Ibid., 22.

[52] FBIS, May 17, 1989, 55.

[53] Han Minzhu, ed., *Cries for Democracy* (Princeton: Princeton University Press, 1990), 227.

To these favored "labor aristocrats," Marxist criticism was a powerful weapon in the struggle to cling to socialist securities. Although the reaction of skilled workers to the post-Mao reforms differed substantially from that of the students, the militance of both groups stemmed in no small measure from a quest to maintain their privileged position in the face of unsettling change. (On the students, see Chapter 14.) Worker activism issued, no doubt, not simply from concern for the students but also from fear that industrial reform might erase the prerogatives that distinguished them from unprotected contract and temporary laborers. Economic divisions within the work force thus continued to fuel labor militance. As Anita Chan characterizes the fissures that led to the Tiananmen protest, "dyads such as intellectuals/workers, state enterprise workers/foreign enterprise workers, workers in metropolitan areas/ workers in county towns, tenured workers/contract workers, workers on different shop floors within the same enterprises—and the list goes on— pointed fingers at each other in complaint that the others were receiving an unfairly large income."[54]

As in previous strike waves, official trade unions also made friendly gestures to the protesters. Pressured by the competition from autonomous unions, the ACFTU tried to assume a more active role in responding to working-class concerns. On May 1 (Labor Day), the president of the ACFTU conceded that government-sponsored unions "should fully support the workers in their fight against corruption."[55] Thanks to this encouragement, state workers became more involved in the public demonstrations. On May 17, as the hunger strike entered its fifth day,

millions of workers, peasants, and clerks from government organs, personnel from cultural and publishing circles and from the press took to the streets to show they supported and cared for the students. . . . Particularly noticeable were the marching columns of workers. They came from scores of enterprises such as the Capital Steel Corporation, the main factory of the Beijing Internal Combustion Engines, Beijing Lifting Machinery Factory, and the state-run Number 798 Factory.[56]

The next day the ACFTU took the bold step of donating 100,000 yuan for medical aid to students in the sixth day of their hunger strike. A spokesperson for the federation explained:

---

[54]Anita Chan, "Revolution or Corporatism? Workers and Trade Unions in Post-Mao China," *Australian Journal of Chinese Affairs*, no. 29 (January 1993).
[55]*China Daily*, May 1, 1989.
[56]FBIS, May 18, 1989, 49.

The vast number of students' . . . demands . . . have received widespread sympathy from the working masses. The ACFTU strongly urges the principal leading members of the party Central Committee and the State Council to make prompt arrangements for face-to-face dialogues with representatives of the students. . . . The vast number of workers are very worried about the current economic situation, which is very severe.[57]

That same day, the Shanghai Federation of Trade Unions added its voice in support of the movement: "Workers in the city have expressed universal concern and sympathy for the patriotism of students who are demanding democracy, rule of law, an end to corruption, checking inflation, and promoting reform. The municipal council of trade unions fully affirms this."[58]

But there were definite limits beyond which the official unions could not go. On May 20, a mass of workers gathered in front of the ACFTU offices to demand that the unions order a national strike.[59] Three days later, after the declaration of martial law, Beijing television announced:

In the last few days, there have been rumors in some localities saying that the All-China Federation of Trade Unions has called for a nationwide general strike. A spokesman for the Federation said that this is merely a rumor with ulterior motives. The spokesman emphatically pointed out that the ACFTU has recently stressed that the vast number of staff members and workers should firmly stay at their posts and properly carry out production work.[60]

By the end of the month, Ruan Chongwu, a former minister of public security, had been appointed to the post of labor minister. His brief was "to ensure that workers remain loyal to the party and government—and that they not take part in activities that challenge the regime."[61] Reported the Hong Kong press, "A top priority with Mr. Ruan and the restructured leadership of the trade unions federation will be to prevent unofficial unions from being organized."[62] The chastened ACFTU director put the matter bluntly: "no trade unions opposed to the party are allowed to be established."[63]

---

[57]Ibid., May 22, 1989, 80; reprinted in Michel Oksenberg, Lawrence R. Sullivan, and Marc Lambert, eds., *Beijing Spring, 1989: Confrontation and Conflict, The Basic Documents* (Armonk, N.Y.: M. E. Sharpe, 1990), 285–86.

[58]FBIS, May 22, 1989, 21.

[59]Ibid., 45.

[60]FBIS, May 23, 1989, 58. Whatever the ACFTU leadership may really have felt about a general strike, theirs was one of the last government or party units to express support for martial law. See FBIS, May 30, 1989, 9.

[61]FBIS, May 30, 1989, 9.

[62]Ibid.

[63]Ibid., July 26, 1989, 4.

One day before the tanks were called in to suppress the demonstrators at Tiananmen, the ACFTU director convened a meeting of the chairmen of the seventeen national industrial unions to enlist their support in combating the challenge of the autonomous unions. As Director Ni Zhifu framed the issue, "At present a tiny minority of people are misusing the name of workers' organizations, raising the banner of 'autonomous unions,' and spreading rumors; not only do they want the unions to escape from party leadership, but they seek to make the unions a political force to oppose the Communist Party and socialist system."[64] One week after the massacre, an open letter from the ACFTU to all workers and unions cadres called for "resolute struggle against so-called autonomous unions and other illegal organizations."[65]

IN THE AFTERMATH OF THE 1989 UPRISING

For obvious reasons, the state is anxious to gain control over grass-roots associations. A recent government survey in Jiangsu, which counted more than 10,000 unofficial (or "social") organizations in that province alone, advocated "particular efforts to solve the problems of social organizations that pursue political liberalization, that are excessive in number and poorly managed, and that engage in illegal operations."[66] Although the 1982 constitution guarantees Chinese citizens "freedom of association," a recent State Council regulation spells out the limitations: "No social organization, including societies, associations, federations, research units, foundations, cooperatives and chambers of commerce will be considered legal unless it is registered with the appropriate authorities."[67]

Even so, some evidence suggests that an underground labor organization lives on in the post-Tiananmen era.[68] Having experienced the satisfaction of unofficial trade unionism, some workers are evidently willing to risk severe sanctions to keep the movement alive. In late 1989, large-scale strikes and demonstrations broke out in the two medium-

---

[64]*Renmin ribao*, June 3, 1989.
[65]Ibid., June 12, 1989.
[66]FBIS, September 12, 1990, 50. I thank Robin Eckhardt for her research assistance on labor unrest since 1989.
[67]*China Daily*, November 1, 1989, 3.
[68]See, e.g., Sheryl WuDunn, "Secretly, Chinese Workers Press Their Cause," *New York Times*, August 14, 1989. Also see Daniel Kwan and Willy Wo-Lap Lam, "Government Takes Steps to Contain Labour Unrest," in *South China Morning Post*, May 20, 1992, 11, which refers to "underground trade unions" in cities from Beijing to Shenyang.

sized industrial cities of Luoyang, Henan, and Zhuzhou, Hunan, precipitated by unemployment and declining wages. A Chinese source noted that in both cases "underground labour unions—which played pivotal roles in demonstrations in Beijing, Chengdu and other cities last spring—have cropped up."[69] Two years later, the government was reported to have cracked down on underground labor organizations in Beijing, two of which (each with about 100 members) were modeled after Solidarity and were "believed to be responsible for several strikes in the capital, including one in a factory with a thousand workers."[70]

According to a confidential report by the ACFTU, during the two years following the suppression of the Tiananmen protests, more than fifty thousand workers engaged in strikes, slowdowns, rallies, petitions, and sit-ins to register dissatisfaction with the government's failure to guarantee a basic livelihood.[71] In January 1990, half a million workers in cities across China were said to have petitioned for permission to demonstrate against the deteriorating economic situation.[72] An internal document of the Ministry of Public Security calculated for 1990–91 a total of 523 "unapproved public rallies, marches, demonstrations and petitions involving ten or more people across the country, as well as incidents in which people collided with and surrounded local party and government departments."[73] For 1992, the Ministry of Public Security reported more than 540 cases of illegal demonstrations and assemblies and more than 480 strikes involving hundreds of thousands of workers.[74]

For the most part, labor unrest in the 1990s seems to consist of wildcat actions that erupt without significant organizational direction. A lumber company in Heilongjiang suffered a slowdown by more than a hundred workers who exploded in fury after three years of not being issued new shoes. A similar number of miners in Qinghai staged a sit-in at the local government office after several seriously ill retired workers

[69]*South China Morning Post*, March 9, 1990, 12.

[70]"Crackdown on 'Clandestine' Workers' Groups Noted," *South China Morning Post*, December 13, 1991, 1–15.

[71]FBIS, August 29, 1991, 31.

[72]*Far Eastern Economic Review*, January 18, 1990, 17.

[73]Lu Yan, "Public Security Ministry Reveals the 'Actual state of Stability'," *Zhengming* (Contention), no. 175 (May 1, 1992); translated in FBIS, May 12, 1992, 29.

[74]FBIS, March 10, 1993, 14–15. For reports of strikes in 1992 by Beijing sanitation workers and taxi drivers, see FBIS, August 11, 1992, 24–25; September 8, 1992, 31–32. A large-scale riot by discharged workers at a bankrupt knitting mill in Sichuan is reported in FBIS, April 6, 1993, 66–67.

were discharged from the hospital because the mining company had failed to pay their medical bills. Although the pretexts for these conflagrations may seem rather parochial, they could sometimes inspire a remarkably large reaction. In a coastal Zhejiang county, more than ten thousand workers from 110 enterprises protested en masse in support of a single woman worker who was apparently mistreated by her superior.[75]

A new labor union law, promulgated on April 3, 1992, to replace the previous law of 1950, stipulates that official unions must participate in the mediation of labor disputes that occur in their areas of jurisdiction, but guarantees them few resources with which to effect a resolution.[76] Moreover, the increased privatization and internationalization of the industrial economy has further hamstrung the official unions, since they have no authority in the growing nonstate and non-Chinese sector.[77]

Much of the recent labor strife has been concentrated in foreign-funded enterprises, where workers seldom enjoy union protection against managerial abuse.[78] At the Japanese-owned Mitsumi Electric Plant in the South China Special Economic Zone (SEZ) of Zhuhai, two thousand workers walked off the job in May 1993 to protest shabby treatment by Japanese overseers and to demand a wage hike. This was the fourth strike in two years at the Mitsumi plant, where most of the workers are women from North China.[79] In the northern port city of Tianjin, ten major strikes erupted at joint-venture and foreign-owned firms during the first nine months of 1993. Nine of the enterprises affected were South Korean; one was Japanese. According to a report in *Beijing Youth News*, more than twelve hundred workers at a South Korean shoe factory—mostly young women—went on strike and marched on the Tianjin Labor Bureau to lodge a complaint against maltreatment.

[75]FBIS, August 29, 1991, 31.
[76]*Renmin ribao*, April 9, 1992.
[77]This point was forcefully made by officials at the ACFTU during interviews conducted in Beijing in June 1992. The next year, concerned about the growing number of wildcat strikes, the party decreed that union branches should be set up in joint ventures and foreign-owned plants. Implementation is another matter, however.
[78]This is not to suggest that Chinese firms have been immune to protests. An extended strike involving hundreds of workers occurred at the Beijing Refrigerator Corporation in June 1993 to protest relocation of the factory to "a distant Beijing suburb where conditions are far worse" (FBIS, June 30, 1993, 28). In Shanxi, some ten thousand miners struck to demand a pay raise for the lunar new year (FBIS, March 3, 1993, 72).
[79]FBIS, May 13, 1993, 32–33; May 19, 1993, 42; May 25, 1993, 45. For a report of a strike at a Japanese-owned cannon factory in Zhuhai, see FBIS, April 15, 1993, 35–36.

Some months later, more than two hundred workers at a South Korean garment factory walked out. The newspaper reported:

Incidents of physical abuse of employees at both companies were reported, with South Korean executives at the shoe factory forcing women who worked too slowly to kneel down before them and kicking those who refused. At the garment factory, a South Korean injured a worker by kicking him. A woman employee who violated regulations was forced to eat seven cakes and seven eggs as punishment before being allowed to go home. . . . *The workers demanded to be allowed to set up a labor union.*[80]

In the SEZs of Shenzhen and Zhuhai, where official unions were barred from many foreign-owned firms, a total of 74 strikes involving nearly 10,000 workers occurred in the year and a half following the Tiananmen incident. The press noted, in a description remarkably reminiscent of pre-1949 patterns (see Chapter 15), that

workers from the outside have formed "regional gangs" which often create disturbances and could become a factor of social instability in the long run. For instance, 15 strikes took place in Longgang Town in Shenzhen, with eight of them instigated by Sichuan workers, three by Guangxi workers, two by workers from the south of the Chang Jiang, and two by Hunan workers.[81]

Familiar cleavages within the working class thus continue to structure styles of protest in contemporary China. As in the pre-Communist period, divisions along lines of native-place origin serve as a powerful catalyst for labor militance. Ethnographic evidence from a foreign-owned factory in Shenzhen confirms that

on the shopfloor, workers identify each other by province of origin and by the patron who brought them in. They may not know the names of workers they work with on the line, but they can tell right away this or that person is from Hubei or Sichuan and to whom they are related. . . . Many northern workers understand that their secondary status is due to the colonization of shopfloor management by Cantonese.[82]

In contrast to the permanent workers at state enterprises—for whom official unions provide some modicum of security, yet who strive for

---

[80]FBIS, September 28, 1993, 36–37. Emphasis added.

[81]*Mingbao*, January 30, 1991, 7; translated in FBIS, January 30, 1991, 67. Emphasis added.

[82]C. K. Lee, "Despotism and Nepotism: The Politics and Poetics of Production in South China's Capitalist Enclave," paper presented to the Regional Seminar of the Center for Chinese Studies on "Greater China," University of California, Berkeley, February 26–27, 1993, 15–16.

"Civsoc"?

independent unions to preserve their considerable rights—these less fortunate contract and temporary laborers turn to "regional gangs" (*bangkou*) for protection. The extraordinary labor mobility unleashed by the reforms of the 1980s (see Chapter 5) has encouraged the resurgence of presocialist forms of labor association. Supplanting the planned socialist city (described in Chapter 2) is a residential configuration based on regional origin that is eerily familiar from earlier days. In Beijing, for example, hundreds of thousands of migrant workers from Zhejiang Province have formed a "Zhejiang village" in the southern district of the capital.[83] As was true before 1949, today these native-place groupings are often linked, via gangsters, to secret societies (*banghui*) and organized crime.[84] A recent circular from the Ministry of Public Security calculates that China is currently home to "more than 1,830 underworld organizations, gangs and associations bearing the character of secret societies." The confidential report notes that in Guizhou's Guiyang Prefecture, secret societies have gained a foothold in factories, where they "agitate workers to go slow or go on strike and make unreasonable demands on the government."[85] The difference from the skilled workers so active in the uprising of 1989 is substantial, suggesting that intraclass divisions are not about to evaporate in some newfound horizontal solidarity among the Chinese working class.[86]

CONCLUSION

The popular protests of 1989 are correctly portrayed as affording "a glimpse of the political energies and mentalities that lie just beneath the surface of Chinese urban society, and that may play a much more important role in the country's near future."[87] But is it also correct to portray this recent activity as an entirely "new species of political pro-

[83]FBIS, November 16, 1992, 38.

[84]Cai Shaoqing and Peng Bangfu, "Dangdai Zhongguo heishehui wenti chutan" (Preliminary discussion of the underground problem in contemporary China), *Nanjing daxue xuebao* (Nanjing University Journal), no. 3 (1992), 143–67. On links between native-place associations and gangs in Republican China, see Emily Honig, *Creating Chinese Ethnicity: Subei People in Shanghai, 1850–1980* (New Haven: Yale University Press, 1992), 92ff.

[85]Guan Zhuan, "Secret Societies Rampant throughout Country," in *Zhengming*, no. 175 (May 1, 1992): 20–21; translated in FBIS, May 14, 1992, 29–30.

[86]On this point, I differ from the interpretation of Shaoguang Wang in his stimulating piece, "Deng Xiaoping's Reform and the Chinese Workers' Participation in the Protest Movement of 1989," *Research in Political Economy* 13.

[87]Andrew G. Walder, "Popular Protest in the Chinese Democracy Movement of 1989,"

test" that "does not fit the mold of worker activism in the Cultural Revolution and the mid-1970s, where factions of political leaders mobilized their local followers for political combat"?[88] I would suggest that Chinese labor activism has, for the better part of a century, been characterized by a complex blend of bottom-up initiatives and top-down mobilization. Working-class associations—whether directed by workers with links to the KMT or to the CCP, whether supportive or critical of gangster-controlled "yellow unions" during the Republican period or of the official Federation of Trade Unions under the People's Republic—have served as an arena of both contestation and cooperation between groups of laborers and would-be labor organizers. Just as we should not underplay the degree to which the factionalism of the Cultural Revolution reflected preexisting divisions within the working class itself, so we should not underestimate the extent to which contemporary labor protest is likely to feed into the projects of rival political leaders.

Rather than envision labor as a *solidary* expression of social interests poised to mount an opposition to the state, we should seek the roots of worker activism in a *segmented* labor force prepared to make common cause with responsive state agents.[89] Intralabor divisions today are certainly not identical with those in earlier periods. New socialist structures created new winners and losers while the experiences of the Hundred Flowers campaign, the Cultural Revolution, and the Tiananmen uprising provided new understandings of the possibilities and boundaries of labor activism. But Chinese labor remains no less fragmented than in the past. And its political struggles are likely to follow the lines of that fragmentation.

presented to the Regional China Seminar, University of California, Berkeley, April 27, 1991, 25.

[88]Walder and Gong, "Workers in the Beijing Democracy Movement," 3.

[89]Walder's pathbreaking *Communist Neo-Traditionalism* certainly does portray a divided work force, linked through clientelist ties to state agents. But his model attributes these divisions to state-imposed categories of "activist" and "non-activist" whereas I believe that such political distinctions may be better explained by more prosaic socioeconomic factors such as age, native-place origin, employment status, and the like.

12

Dissident and liberal legal scholars and
organizations in Beijing and the Chinese state in
the 1980s

MARK SIDEL

In the late 1970s and early 1980s, as legal development under Communist Party control emerged as a priority for the Chinese leadership,
virtually all of China's legal scholars and officials worked in—and found
their less formal networks through—elite, state-dominated urban legal
institutions such as the key law schools[1] and the primary party and
government agencies.[2] The state funded and controlled the administra-

The author had extensive contact with most of the individuals and organizations discussed
in this chapter while working in Beijing from 1988 to 1990, but the views expressed here
are his own and do not represent the views of any Chinese individuals or of the Ford
Foundation. The author is grateful to Elizabeth Perry and to several anonymous reviewers,
for comments on a draft of this essay; to several Chinese scholars who cannot be named,
for frank discussions; and to Bill Alford, Randy Edwards, Peter Geithner, and Jon Hecht,
for useful discussions of these issues.

[1] The Beijing University Faculty of Law, China People's University Faculty of Law, and the
Chinese University of Politics and Law are examples of such institutions in Beijing.
[2] The ministries of Justice, Public Security, State Security (an outgrowth of the Party Investigation Department and the Ministry of Public Security in the early 1980s), Civil
Affairs, the Supreme People's Court, the Supreme People's Procuratorate, various committees and offices of the National People's Congress and the State Council, and other
Beijing-based groups are examples of such government actors. On the party side the key
group—which directs the work of the state organizations above—was the Central Politics
and Law Leading Small Group (Zhongyang zhengfa lingdao xiaozu), headed during the
period under discussion by Qiao Shi and composed of senior (ministerial) representatives
from Civil Affairs, Justice, Public Security, State Security, Supreme People's Court, Supreme People's Procuratorate, the People's Liberation Army, and perhaps several others.
The Leading Small Group has had other names during its more than five decades of
existence, at times termed the Central Politics and Law Committee (Weiyuanhui) or Small
Group (Xiaozu). Its basic function—as the focal center for party control over domestic
security and legal functions and overall coordinator of the security and law apparatus—
has remained largely unchanged over the decades, although its day-to-day role in ordinary

tion of such urban institutions, but some of these fully state-controlled institutions (particularly the law schools and legal research institutes) have been ground in which new thought grew in the legal community and from which dissident legal scholars and their organizations emerged.

In the major Chinese cities, particularly Beijing and Shanghai, a group of largely young dissident legal scholars emerged in the mid-1980s from discussions within the law faculties, between younger academics and their counterparts in the ministries, in the National People's Congress (NPC) and other agencies, between young graduate students at the Institute of Law of the Chinese Academy of Social Sciences (CASS) and older academics, and through other networks. That process was aided by the extensive contact the Chinese academic legal community had in the late 1970s and early and mid-1980s with foreign law schools, legal scholars, and foreign legal thought.[3]

Initially, the institutional bases of Beijing's dissident and liberal legal scholars were much the same as those for an older, more conservative group of scholars and officials who sought, carefully, some revitalization of law in China after the Cultural Revolution. The younger, dissident legal scholars invariably began their careers under the protective umbrella of prominent, usually conservative, and well-protected urban state institutions. These included the Masses Publishing House under the Ministry of Public Security,[4] the Institute of Journalism in the Academy of Social Sciences and the *Chinese Legal Gazette* under the Ministry of

criminal and civil matters (and even in day-to-day formulation of legal policy) is likely more muted now than in the past.

[3]The influence of foreign study and contact on the thinking and development of Chinese legal scholars in the 1980s is a largely unexplored but key topic. Between 1983 and the Chinese political events of 1989 over a hundred young and middle-aged Chinese law teachers and researchers from a core set of key institutions in Beijing, Shanghai, Changchun, and Wuhan studied in American law schools with support from the Ford Foundation under the Chinese legal education exchange program, generally in graduate LL.M. programs or as visiting scholars. Others studied in Japan, Canada, Western Europe, Australia, and elsewhere in the United States. A significant number directly studied constitutional law, jurisprudence, and related fields, but even those whose work was largely limited to economic law, trade, and investment also certainly saw new models and a role for law far different from that with which they were familiar in China. This group of scholars who studied abroad returned to China to join the ranks of liberal legal scholars, more comfortable with the critiques of the dissident scholars and activists than an older generation and more accepting of divergent views on the role of law in rapidly changing societies.

[4]Yu Haocheng, director of the Masses Publishing House and later director of the Capital Iron and Steel Legal Research Institute, is the most prominent of the dissident legal scholars to emerge from the public security community.

Justice,[5] research groups under the State Council,[6] and the Chinese University of Politics and Law under the Ministry of Justice.[7]

In the mid-1980s and accelerating in 1988, China's dissident legal scholars began to move some of their activities out from the more highly controlled state institutions. This gradual shift came about for several reasons. China's dissident legal scholars became impatient with the limitations of the highly controlled urban state institutions. They became increasingly frustrated with limitations on the teaching they were allowed to engage in and the types of research that were rewarded, restrictions on the range of policy or theoretical options they were encouraged or allowed to suggest, and funding problems, among other issues. And with only the rarest exceptions, the highly controlled state institutions, including mainstream academic institutions, became impatient with the iconoclasm of or worried about perceived political "danger" from association with some of the younger, more radical scholars.

At the same time, political and economic "space" gradually opened up in the major cities, especially in 1988, in which dissident and liberal legal scholars could work out from under the traditional state institutions and into quasi-independent roles, either separately or under the far looser rubric of other state institutions.

Despite the general pattern outlined above, the circumstances under which individual scholars and groups of scholar-activists began to separate themselves from all-encompassing day-to-day state control varied dramatically between individuals and groups. After providing some context for the development of law, legal institutions, and legal scholarship in China after 1949, this chapter describes the formation, expansion, and decline of the groups of dissident legal scholars that sprang up in the mid-1980s, and especially in 1988.[8]

---

[5]Zhang Zonghou, later deputy director of the Capital Iron and Steel Legal Research Institute and discussed further later on, emerged from this background.

[6]Cao Siyuan, later director of the Stone Institute of Social Development and discussed further below, came out of the State Council.

[7]Several key members of the constitutional revision movement of 1988 and early 1989 and of the Beijing Social and Economic Sciences Research Institute, each discussed further below, came from faculty ranks at the Chinese University of Politics and Law.

[8]The author closely followed the development of these groups in 1988 and 1989. Two useful articles discussing this sector from the pre-Tiananmen Chinese press are Zhang Zonghou, "Let a Stagnant Pool Become a Mighty Stream: A Look at the Nongovernmental Research Institutes," *Guangming Daily*, October 23, 1988; and Huang Zhuanfang and Zhang Dehua, "No Longer Does No One Appreciate the Blooming Flowers: Notes from Interviews with Nongovernmental Social Science Research Institutes in the Capital," *People's Daily*, May 31, 1989. A later article, with a different tone, is "Determining the

LAW, LEGAL INSTITUTIONS, AND
LEGAL SCHOLARSHIP IN CHINA AFTER 1949

State control is the single key motif in the development of law, legal institutions, and legal scholarship in post-1949 China—and state control was the motivation for resistance by unorthodox, liberal, and dissident legal scholars when they began to formulate new ideas in the early and mid-1980s. As scholars of post-1949 Chinese law have shown, both before and after 1949 law and legal institutions were seen by the party leadership as a means of ensuring party control over society, and not an independent basis for authority or rulemaking.[9] Liberal and dissident legal scholarship emerged in the early and mid-1980s to establish law and legal institutions as an independent basis for authority separate from the party.

But the origins of that movement are in party control of the legal system. Thus the rhetoric of "legal construction" in the 1950s and early 1960s, and the building of legal institutions, followed a Soviet path in which the party and the state sought to institutionalize party dominance of society in functioning organizations that could attend to domestic security functions, or implement party political policy through state institutions, while freeing the party for more directly political and strategic work. The need for functioning organizations to attend to domestic security functions was fulfilled in the 1950s by the establishment and strengthening of the ministries of the Interior, Public Security, and Justice and of the Supreme People's Procuratorate and Supreme People's Court. These organizations, in turn, played a key role in implementing party political policy during the land reform and anticorruption campaigns of the early 1950s, and later drives against intellectuals and to promote agricultural collectivization, as well as punishment of criminal activity and other more professional aspects of legal work.

Those party-controlled institutions broke down during the Cultural

---

Nature of Zhao's Case, and the Disintegration of his Think Tanks," *Wen wei po* (Hong Kong), June 25, 1989 (translated in BBC *Summary of World Broadcasts*—The Far East, FE/0495/B2/1, June 29, 1989).

[9]See, for example, Jerome Cohen, *The Criminal Process in the People's Republic of China* (Cambridge, Mass.: Harvard University Press, 1973); Stanley Lubman, "Emerging Functions of Formal Law in the People's Republic of China," in Joint Economic Committee, *China's Economic Strategy* (Washington, D.C.: Government Printing Office, 1978); and essays by William Alford. The 1988–89 Chinese critique of the 1949–76 period is particularly stinging. See, for example, the articles in the tenth anniversary issue of *Faxue yanjiu* (Studies in law) (January–February 1989).

Revolution. Although the Cultural Revolution largely demolished the post-1949 legal institutions (except for the Ministry of Public Security, which emerged even more powerful), it did so in the name of intraparty struggle rather than to reduce party control. At no time in the Cultural Revolution—despite harsh criticisms of the legal institutions erected in the 1950s—was autonomy, separate authority, or any form of judicial independence proclaimed as the goal for the legal system.[10]

Legal scholarship, like institutions of legal control, had been under virtually complete state domination since 1949. Except for brief discussions of constitutional revision, the presumption of innocence and other questions during the Hundred Flowers period, legal scholarship focused almost entirely on technical questions of criminal and civil law between 1949 and 1965, and even those limited discussions were impossible during the Cultural Revolution.[11] Throughout this period little discussion took place within the scholarly community of a role for law apart from its function as the direct instrument of the state.

When the Cultural Revolution ended, party-dominated legal institutions were reestablished as party members and intellectuals began a fierce debate in 1977, 1978, and 1979 on the party's role.[12] The stage was set for the emergence of scholars and officials who advocated an autonomous—or at least more shielded—role for law and legal institutions.

By 1978 and 1979, when law schools and legal research institutes began to reopen with party encouragement, a somewhat less acquiescent attitude among a few recognized teachers, the infusion of hundreds of graduate students and young teachers into the system, and party support for at least some broader, more divergent thinking made a different

---

[10]On law in the Cultural Revolution, see Victor Li, *Law Without Lawyers* (Stanford: Stanford University Press).

[11]The battles over legal theory and the relationship between the party and law during the Hundred Flowers period deserve considerably more attention than they have received in the Western community analyzing law in China. Some of the most creative of China's liberal and dissident legal scholars in the 1980s, as in other fields, had their start either as critics during the Hundred Flowers campaign or as silent observers who learned much from the process.

[12]On this extraordinary time, see Yu Guangyuan and Hu Jiwei, eds., *Mengxing de shike—shiyijie sanzhong quanhi shizhounian jinian zhuanji* (A time of awakening: A special collection commemorating the tenth anniversary of the third plenum) (Beijing: Sino-Foreign Cultural Press, 1989), 17–31; Tao Jin, Zhang Yide, and Dai Qing, eds., *Zouchu xiandai mixin-guanyu zhenli biaozhun wenti de da bianlun* (Breaking out of modern superstition: The great debate on the issue of the criterion of truth) (Hong Kong: Joint Publishing Company, 1989); and recent work by Merle Goldman in *China Quarterly* and elsewhere.

scholarly atmosphere almost inevitable. The factors described above that gave rise to the intellectual growth of a group of dissident legal scholars, and the formation and then destruction of their organizations, are the direct result of state domination of the legal sector in the years before 1966, the devastation of the Cultural Revolution, and the reemergence of legal institutions, legal training, and legal scholarship after 1976.

The somewhat more open political and intellectual "space" that appeared in Beijing in 1988, and the political, intellectual, and scholarly factors discussed above allowed the formation of formal and informal groupings of dissident and liberal legal scholars in Beijing in early 1988. Between early 1988 and June 1989, these groups and the key individuals within them played key roles in the discussions, debates, and public events on which China focused until the events of early June 1989.

Beijing Social and Economic Sciences Research Institute. The role and influence of Chen Ziming and Wang Juntao's Social and Economic Sciences Research Institute (SERI) has been consistently overemphasized both by elements in the Chinese party and government (particularly Prime Minister Li Peng and Beijing Mayor Chen Xitong) and, ironically, by external groups such as Asia Watch.[13] But even a more realistic and measured view of SERI's influence on events in Beijing acknowledges that certain dissident legal scholars found their first and earliest experience in research and activist groups outside the more formal state sector in Chen Ziming and Wang Juntao's institute.[14]

The institute was founded in 1985, one of the first research and activist organizations to work consistently to maintain a Beijing-based presence fully outside the state sector. It did not base its work on law alone, but it was most certainly defiantly independent, and finding a new role for law in a more pluralist Chinese society was a key goal. Unlike the other nongovernmental associations of dissident and liberal legal scholars described here, the institute eschewed formal affiliation with a

---

[13]On the external side, see the extensive description of the institute in Robin Munro, "Rough Justice in Beijing: Punishing the 'Black Hands' of Tiananmen Square," *UCLA Pacific Basin Law Journal* 10, no. 77 (1991), which is based on the better-known Asia Watch report of January 27, 1991. Work by George Hicks and others also describes and analyzes the institute.

[14]Chen Xiaoping, a key figure in the "constitutional revision" movement of 1988 and 1989, was an active member of the SERI group. His role is described further in Munro, "Rough Justice in Beijing."

protective and protected state-run enterprise such as the Capital Iron and Steel Company, with a well-connected entrepreneurial enterprise such as the Stone Corporation, or with a well-protected grouping of the most senior intellectuals backed by some somewhat open party leaders, such as the Huaxia Academy.

The disavowal of protective links and the proud and defiant claim of independence is closely related to the institute's goals. For the most part, Chen Ziming's group did not see itself as a policy advisory body, like the Huaxia Institute of Legal Culture, or as a relatively scholarly group, such as the Huaxia group and the Capital Iron and Steel Legal Research Institute. It explicitly saw itself and presented itself to others (including foreign groups) as a relatively "radical" group of planners and theorists whose primary goal was independently to criticize old methods and to formulate new models. Independence, however tenuous (and June 3–4, 1989, proved just how tenuous) seemed the key underlying motif, both a strategy and a goal in itself.

Huaxia Institute of Legal Culture. This relatively small group of legal academics was centered among liberal, senior scholars at the Institute of Law in the Chinese Academy of Social Sciences[15] and was led by several Institute of Law scholars with work experience in or close ties to the General Office of the Central Committee during the days of Hu Yao-bang.[16] It operated under the protective umbrella of the Huaxia Academy, a formally independent grouping of senior scholars affiliated with the Academy of Social Sciences and universities who had the informal and protective sponsorship of Bo Yibo and other senior party leaders.[17]

From the beginning the institute's members intended that it serve as both a forum for intellectual discussion and a vehicle for policy-oriented law proposals to the party leadership. It was not a voice of "dissident"

---

[15]The Institute of Law and some of its senior and junior scholars have played key roles in contributing to theoretical creativity in the legal reform process. The highly critical and creative January–February 1989 issue of *Faxue yanjiu*, the scholarly journal of the institute, epitomizes its key, leading role at that time. Another, less startling example is Li Buyun, ed., *Zhongguo faxue—Guoqu, xianzai yu weilai* (Law in China: The past, present and future) (Nanjing: Nanjing University Press, 1988).

[16]Author interviews, Beijing, 1988, 1989, 1990, and 1991.

[17]Author interviews, Beijing, 1988, 1989, 1990, and 1991. Brief, official reports of the emergence of the Huaxia Academy (also called the Huaxia Research Institute) in 1987 stress its "nongovernmental" nature. An example is "Nongovernment Research Institute Set Up," *Xinhua General Overseas News Service*, January 10, 1987 (LEXIS/NEXIS Database, NEXIS Library, XINHUA File).

thought, but rather a channel from senior liberal intellectuals to senior, somewhat liberal party officials.[18]

In the run-up to Tiananmen, the Huaxia Academy and, in turn, the Huaxia Institute of Legal Culture did not clearly differ in viewpoint or activity from the Academy of Social Sciences or the Institute of Law, and membership greatly overlapped. This lack of divergence in viewpoint, political perspective, and activities prompted the few foreign observers of these developments in 1988 to question the rationale for the existence of what seemed to be merely a "less governmental" version of the Academy of Social Sciences and its Institute of Law.

To Huaxia Institute (and Institute of Law) members this was a diversionary question. In their view there were important differences between the institute, a creative but more controlled institution, and Huaxia, which was a far more flexible vehicle for discussion of key issues of legal history, culture, and theory.

Huaxia's ties to senior leaders and its nonconfrontational style have enabled a quasi-successor organization, the Dongfang Research Institute, to become virtually the sole "nongovernmental" research facility allowed to discuss potentially divergent legal perspectives in the few years since 1989. Dongfang, for example, was the vehicle identified by certain liberal and dissident legal scholars as early as the summer of 1990 for initial discussions on controversial legal and constitutional issues. And in August 1991 Dongfang sponsored perhaps the most lively discussion among legal scholars on constitutional law since 1989—a symposium that, because of its topic and content, could not be directly sponsored by the Institute of Law in the Chinese Academy of Social Sciences, whose liberal constitutional law scholars had organized the meeting. Like Huaxia, Dongfang had the protective support of one or two senior party leaders.

Capital Iron and Steel Legal Research Institute. Formed in August 1988, the Capital Iron and Steel Legal Research Institute had an unmistakably defiant theoretical approach and a seemingly unlikely state sponsor, the state-run Capital Iron and Steel Company. The irony of this key group is that it was both uncompromisingly "dissident" in substance and in tone

---

[18]Activities of the Huaxia Institute in 1988 and 1989 included, for example, an international conference on Chinese legal history and planning of scholarly activities in the areas of traditional legal culture and legal theory. In the political and cultural climate of late 1988 China, of course, such issues were already highly politicized.

and, at the same time, closely tied to what is regarded by many outside China as one of China's most important, state-run business bureaucracies. But during the period in which the Legal Research Institute was sponsored and founded, strong reformists held positions of significant authority at the Capital Iron and Steel Company, belying—at least at the top—its sometime image abroad as a stultifying state-run enterprise.

The key figure at the Capital Iron and Steel Legal Research Institute (and the senior theorist of the Chinese radical legal reform school) was Yu Haocheng, a senior legal scholar and publishing official in the Ministry of Public Security who was deposed in the Cultural Revolution and returned in the late 1970s to join Hu Yaobang's efforts to reinvigorate Chinese theory.

Known by 1978 for his uncompromising positions against Cultural Revolution abuses in the public security apparatus and his open, defiant criticisms of former Minister of Public Security Xie Fuzhi, Yu was plucked from the ministry by Hu Yaobang's staff in 1978 to attend the key four-month theoretical symposium that helped to build a political and theoretical base for the new reform policy of late 1978 and early 1979.[19]

Yu was an important participant in the struggle against remnant Maoism and Hua Guofeng loyalism in the Ministry of Public Security. He rapidly took leadership of the internal *(neibu)* ministry journal *Renmin gong'an* (People's public security) and in 1979 was named to head the ministry's press, the Masses Publishing House, an organization with national influence.

From the beginning Yu Haocheng directly used his institutional bases to argue for a new vision of democracy. In the late 1970s *Renmin gong'an* was so frank in its attacks on Maoism and the Hua legacy addressed to such key groups as police commanders and senior internal security cadres that senior party leaders ordered Yu to tone it down. Yu rapidly parted company with some of the other participants in the Hu

---

[19]The author is writing a longer study of Yu Haocheng and his key influence on post–Cultural Revolution Chinese jurisprudence. Much of the information in this discussion of Yu Haocheng comes from interviews with Professor Yu in Beijing in August 1991 and several short Chinese autobiographical accounts and interviews. See, for example, Yu Haocheng, "Ten Years of Theoretical Exploration," in Yu and Hu, eds., *A Time of Awakening*, 17–31; and the interview with Yu Haocheng in Tao et al., eds., *Breaking Out of Modern Superstition*, 172–85. The information on Yu Haocheng here is an abbreviated summary of a biographical article on him now in preparation by the author. An excellent discussion of the theoretical symposium is Merle Goldman's 1991 article in *China Quarterly*.

Yaobang theory meeting by arguing (long before it became fashionable among elite Beijing intellectuals) that political reform could not be made a stepchild of economic liberalization. His views were given national prominence through his use of the Masses Publishing House and of the Chinese Politics Society, which he also headed for a time.[20]

Forced out of the Masses Publishing House in the mid-1980s, Yu was given (or took) editorship of a sleepy ministry magazine for the general public entitled *Falu yu shenghuo* (Law and life). He transformed it into a reform platform, criticizing cadre excesses (including the excesses of Deng Liqun) while continuing to run standard "legal construction" articles.

For his various efforts Yu was turned out of the Masses Publishing House, removed from editorship of the law journal, and, in 1987, threatened with expulsion from the party. By then, he was already regarded as a key senior intellectual in theory circles, and his work brought him into contact with another radical reformer, Zhang Zonghou of the *Chinese Legal Gazette*.

Zhang Zonghou was in the first class of graduate students at the Academy of Social Sciences, entering in 1978 and graduating in 1981. He specialized in journalism. Despite (and to some degree because of) his lack of formal training in law, Zhang Zonghou emerged in the mid-1980s as perhaps the single most controversial figure in the Chinese legal world. Zhang took for himself the dangerous role of openly and completely rejecting the Soviet class-based, party-dominated, instrumentalist approach to law found in the work of the Stalinist legal theoretician Andrei Vishinskii, which has formed virtually the entire theoretical basis for Chinese law reform as it emerged in the late 1970s.[21]

---

[20]Many of Yu Haocheng's earlier articles have been collected in Editorial Group for the Collection on the Discussion of the Question of Rule by Law and Rule by Man, *Fazhi yu renzhi wenti taolunji* (Collection on the discussion of the question of rule by law and rule by man) (Beijing: Masses Publishing House, 1981); Yu Haocheng, *Woguo de minzhu zhengzhi yu fazhi jianshe* (Democracy, politics and legal construction in China) (Beijing: Masses Publishing House, 1982); and Yu Haocheng, *Minzhu fazhi shehuizhuyi* (Democracy, law, socialism) (Beijing: Masses Publishing House, 1985). Later articles were published in *Falu yu shenghuo* (Law and life), *Zhongguo faxue* (Law in China), and, for a fiery series of articles on constitutionalism and legal reform in 1988 and 1989, *Faxue* (Jurisprudence), published in Shanghai. In the heady days of 1988 and the first half of 1989, *Faxue* was the most active and daring of China's law journals.
[21]A representative work, largely an expanded collection of the articles on legal theory that shook the Chinese legal world in the mid-1980s, is *Faxue gengxinlun* (The renovation of law) (Kunming: Yunnan People's Press, January 1989). With one, very carefully arranged exception, Zhang was not permitted to publish in his own name for the first few years after the June 1989 events.

In Beijing in the late 1980s one was either for or against Zhang; there was no comfortable place in the middle. His battles with the conservative legal theory establishment (represented most directly by Professor Sun Guohua of People's University Faculty of Law in Beijing[22]) entranced and frightened Beijing's liberal legal establishment in the mid- and late 1980s.[23]

Emerging from the liberal Institute of Journalism in the early 1980s, Zhang found work in the editorial department of the *Chinese Legal Gazette*. Working at the house organ of the Soviet-inspired, deeply conservative Ministry of Justice may seem strange for someone who became an iconoclastic foe of Stalinist legal theory, but the professional and personal security of such positions was important and fertile ground from which dissident legal scholars could develop their own work and their organizations.

Zhang is a representative example of that process. Working at the *Chinese Legal Gazette* provided Zhang with the time, facilities, and contacts to begin his theoretical work and to push for specific reforms— such as a liberal press law. And it was also, in the early and mid-1980s, the only base from and channel through which an incessant critic of mainstream Chinese jurisprudence could attend the annual meetings of the Chinese Legal Theory Research Society (under the China Law Society) and other groups. Beijing- and Jilin-based liberal legal intellectuals returned to their campuses from such events stunned, fascinated, and sometimes frightened by the directness of the battles over theory between Zhang and Sun Guohua.[24]

---

[22]Sun Guohua's views (if perhaps not entirely his own words, and without being directly attributed to him) are represented in the single longest, most specific, and most comprehensive document attacking the academic work of liberal and dissident Chinese legal scholars (including Yu Haocheng and Zhang Zonghou), published in the internally circulated State Education Commission journal *Gaoxiao lilun cankao* (Higher education theory and reference). Zhong Ren (pseud.), "Several Theoretical Problems Requiring Clarification in the Legal Sphere," *Gaoxiao lilun cankao* (April 1991): 5–28.

[23]The directness of Zhang's rejection of the bases for Chinese law reform stunned both the liberal and conservative Chinese legal establishment. Many liberal academics and officials had hoped to work within the legal system (with "strengthening the imperfect legal system" and "using legality to construct democracy" as their state-formulated credos and mottos), but Zhang was suddenly, directly challenging them to reject the system and to rebuild it in a different image. The link between Zhang's critique and the politics (and political action) it might seem to require brought home to many liberal legal intellectuals the conflict between what they spent their days doing and what they truly believed about the party and the systems they were "strengthening" and "perfecting." Some responded by a form of academic denial in Beijing, thus the head shaking about Zhang's lack of formal legal training.

[24]For Chinese descriptions and analyses of some of these theoretical trends, see Wen

Zhang Zonghou became director of the editorial department of the *Chinese Legal Gazette* in 1987, but by early 1988 he was gone. In early 1988 he and Yu Haocheng were invited by the senior, reformist party secretary at the Capital Iron and Steel Company to form a legal research institute under the company's Research and Development Corporation. The Legal Research Institute was established in 1988.

The institute was to some degree a vehicle for research and presentation of views by Yu Haocheng, Zhang Zonghou, and their colleagues. Others, such as the well-known Zhang Xianyang, who had been expelled from the party in 1987, joined them.[25] As in most cases of the nongovernmental organizations in law, the footprints of the institute itself were much lighter than those of its key personnel, Yu and Zhang. Extensive research plans were drafted in 1988 in areas ranging from recent Chinese legal history to environmental law, but by early 1989 Yu, Zhang, and their colleagues were deep in the battles against "new authoritarianism"[26] and for constitutional revision.[27] Those were the political and theoretical battles riveting the Chinese legal world (and many intellectuals and others far beyond) in the key nine months before June 1989.

Yu Haocheng signed an early document calling for the release of political prisoners, and both he and Zhang Zonghou were allegedly active

Zhengbang et al., *Faxue biangelun* (The transformation of law) (Chongqing: Chongqing Publishing House, 1989), and He Qinhua, ed., *Dangdai Zhongguo faxue xin sichao* (New trends in jurisprudence in contemporary China) (Shanghai: Shanghai Academy of Social Sciences Press, 1991), especially 16–39.

[25]Zhang Xianyang has had a special ability to infuriate China's ideological and intellectual barons. A somewhat restrained example of his work, but among the better discussions of the development of political theory in China since 1978, is Su Shaozhi and Zhang Xianyang, eds., *Shiyijie sanzhong quanhui yilai Makesizhuyi zai Zhongguo de fazhan* (The development of Marxism in China since the third plenum of the eleventh central committee [December 1978]) (Beijing: People's Publishing House, 1988).

[26]The full context and contours of the debate over "new authoritarianism" in 1988 and early 1989 is unfortunately beyond the scope of this brief essay. One core collection of documents on the issue is Liu Jun and Li Lin, eds., *Xin chuanweizhuyi—Dui gaige lilun gangling de zhenglun* (New authoritarianism: The debate over the theoretical program for reform), partially translated in Rosen and Zou (eds.), "The Chinese Debate on the New Authoritarianism" (I and II), *Chinese Sociology and Anthropology* (Winter 1990–91 and Spring 1991). Yu Haocheng's scathing criticism of the theory, "Does China Need the New Authoritarianism?" is on 162–71; Zhang Zonghou's equally critical article, "New Authorities or the Authority of Law" is on 172–87. Yu and Zhang's critiques are unfortunately not included in the Rosen and Zou translation.

[27]One highly critical and representative statement of the constitutional revision movement of 1988 and early 1989 is Gong Xiangrui, "What Kind of Constitutional Theory Does China Need?" *Faxue* (April 1989). Gong is professor of law and political science at Beijing University.

in summoning intellectual support for students in Tiananmen Square and around the country. On orders from the Beijing Party Committee, the institute was closed at the end of April 1989, long before action was taken against the students and most other intellectuals.[28] Yu Haocheng was confined in a military facility outside Beijing from June 1989 through January 1991, then freed, but was not allowed to publish until 1992. What he wrote was then heavily criticized, and the journal in which he published was closed.[29] Zhang Zonghou was questioned but not arrested.

Yu Haocheng and Zhang Zonghou's institute was semi-autonomous in that it did not report directly to the Capital Iron and Steel Company and acted relatively independently in the active and complex Beijing politics of 1988 and the first half of 1989. It would be a mistake, however, to view such organizations as examples of any permanent new Chinese "civil society." When the authorities decided to close the institute it folded immediately, its staff reduced to minimum Capital Iron and Steel Company cadre salaries and urged to find new jobs. Paradoxically it was the protective support that Yu, Zhang, and their colleagues had received from the company's reformist party secretary, Zhou Guanwu, that enabled them to be as effective as they could be in their new organization—but that party secretary and his colleagues were, of course, still subject to party command, and ultimately the protective umbrella closed, as Yu Haocheng and Zhang Zonghou knew that it eventually would.[30]

Stone Institute of Social Development. Another key nongovernmental organization of legal scholars was the Stone Institute of Social Development, led by the now well-known legal reformer, drafter, and lobbyist Cao Siyuan.[31] After the Cultural Revolution, Cao emerged in Beijing

---

[28]See Willy Wo-Lap Lam, "Officials Move to Gag Top Scholar," *South China Morning Post*, April 24, 1989.

[29]According to a wire-service account, a "hard-hitting commentary by a dissident legal scholar, Yu Haocheng, warned that the Communist Party's power would be threatened unless it democratized" and the journal, *Future and Development*, was closed. See "China Shuts Pro-Democracy Journal," *International Herald Tribune*, December 13, 1992, 2.

[30]Zhou Guanwu's key reformist role at the Capital Iron and Steel Company has attracted relatively little attention in the Chinese press and even less abroad. One brief Chinese mention is in "China Names 20 Top Entrepreneurs," *Xinhua General Overseas News Service*, April 2, 1988 (LEXIS/NEXIS Database, NEXIS Library, XINHUA File).

[31]Much of the information in this section comes from extensive discussions with Cao and his full-time and part-time staff beginning in 1988 and through August 1991. See also

political and intellectual life as a graduate student at the Academy of Social Sciences, as did Zhang Zonghou. But he was considerably more an insider, a worker within institutions, than either Zhang Zonghou or Yu Haocheng.

Cao began his career after graduating from the Academy of Social Sciences by working at the State Council, the Central Committee, and Ma Hong's Research Center for Economic, Technological, and Social Development. He first came to prominence as the drafter and primary lobbyist for the Chinese bankruptcy law in the National People's Congress. (Yu and Zhang, on the other hand, never saw themselves or wished to work in such an institutional context.) Thus when, much later, Cao Siyuan turned to the Standing Committee of the NPC in late May 1989 in an attempt to overturn the declaration of martial law in Beijing, there were few members of the Standing Committee of the NPC who did not know Cao personally because they had been lobbied by him on the bankruptcy law and knew of his role as "China's first lobbyist."

After the extraordinary bankruptcy drafting and lobbying process of the mid-1980s, Cao turned directly to political reform and, more particularly, legislative reform, as his primary work. He began with a fierce commitment to market-oriented economic reform—a commitment so unbending that he may have been alone among recent political prisoners in writing poetry to the market while sitting in prison after Tiananmen.[32]

Like Yu Haocheng and Zhang Zonghou, Cao Siyuan eventually left the strictures of state-sector employment to found his own research institute, the Stone Institute of Social Development. Like the Capital Iron and Steel Legal Research Institute, Cao's group also had an institutional and political backer. For the Stone Institute, that was the reformist, entrepreneurial Stone Corporation and its chief, Wan Runnan.

After the institute was founded in 1988, Cao and his colleagues focused primarily on constitutional revision and legislative reform. Cao's work also concentrated more on the immediate and less on the theoretical than did that of Yu Haocheng and Zhang Zonghou. Besides calling for constitutional amendments to recognize and promote market-

Nicolas Howson's essay "Cao Siyuan: A Responsible Reformer Silenced," in *UCLA Pacific Basin Law Journal* (1990).

[32]The force of Cao's personality and his concentration are reflected in Andrew Nathan's brief, elegant profile of an inelegant and deeply committed man in *China's Crisis* (New York: Columbia University Press, 1990), 4–6. The poem was given to the author, the first foreigner to meet with Cao after his release from prison in May 1990.

oriented reform, Cao called for sessions of the NPC Standing Committee to be opened to citizens and broadcast on television, and for amendments to the constitution to remove the names of all individuals, recognize the market-oriented economic reforms, and include recognition of a presumption of innocence, among other changes.

Yu Haocheng and Zhang Zonghou are theoreticians who criticize from the outside. Cao was and remains very much an institutionalist. That is perhaps the most surprising aspect of this most remarkable individual, given the limitations he has seen—and the pain he has suffered—from some of China's most well-established and powerful institutions. But at the same time Cao's greatest single political victory for economic reform—the adoption of the bankruptcy law in 1987—came through the institutional process, and he clearly felt an affinity for using and reforming existing political institutions.

Yet the time came for Cao, as it had for the others, to leave the formal state sector. As with Yu and Zhang, the move gave Cao some greater freedom and time to pursue his own work. Also like Yu and Zhang, the change gave Cao a new master (in his case, Wan Runnan and the Stone Corporation) and thus strong motivation to raise the funds necessary to increase his autonomy.[33]

NONGOVERNMENTAL ORGANIZATIONS OF DISSIDENT LEGAL SCHOLARS AND THE RETREAT FROM THE STATE SECTOR IN CHINESE CITIES BEFORE TIANANMEN

Different tactics for change and routes to prison. If Yu Haocheng and Zhang Zonghou are representative of radical party theoreticians and some scholars, Cao Siyuan was—and remains, though now under different political circumstances—very much a "voice of the interests of young, high-tech entrepreneurs," as Carol Lee Hamrin has aptly put it.[34] And the institutional backing to these two groups reflects that distinction. According to Yu and Zhang's colleagues, the reformist party leadership of the Capital Iron and Steel Company actually wanted strong

---

[33]The author's initial contact with several of these people was at their request and in this regard.

[34]Carol Lee Hamrin, *China and the Challenge of the Future* (Boulder: Westview, 1990), 214. The key criticism of Wan Runnan and the Stone Corporation after the events of June 1989 is Ye Guang, "Whom Did Wan Runnan Want to Smash by Picking Up a 'Stone'?" *People's Daily*, August 17, 1989.

theoretical dissenters on their research staff in 1988 (though certainly not after June 1989). But Cao and his organization were far more the voice of economic interests and the political measures dictated by those interests—and, at least according to some of Cao's colleagues, that is precisely what the Stone Corporation wanted.

Thus in the great and confused movement that swept Beijing and much of urban China from April to June of 1989, the roles of these two "nongovernmental" organizations and their leaders were somewhat different. Cao Siyuan did not initially play a leading role in the intellectuals' movement of April and May, although he was a leader of the constitutional revision movement of late 1988 and early 1989 and Stone did play a role in the movement. But Cao certainly did not seem surprised by the size and strength of the movement or the rapidity with which it grew; it was a mark of Cao's elite and institutional connections that in 1988 he had been telling the Chinese and foreigners who would listen that 1989 would be a year of reckoning and intense conflict.

The declaration of martial law on May 19, 1989, threw Cao and his younger colleagues into feverish activity. Ever the institutionalist—albeit from a somewhat anti-institutionalist outpost—Cao turned to the National People's Congress, one of the institutions he knew best, in an ultimately ill-fated attempt to defeat martial law. Like the Capital Iron and Steel Legal Research Institute, Cao's Stone Institute of Social Development folded immediately under pressure when the attempt to reverse martial law failed.[35]

Yu Haocheng of the Capital Iron and Steel Legal Research Institute also landed in confinement, but through a different route. Yu was jailed for his theoretical activities, and not, like Cao Siyuan, for attempting to

[35]The effort landed Cao in an airport guesthouse commandeered by the Ministry of State Security, arrested by four men in a jeep at midday on June 3 while Cao was supposedly departing a grocery store carrying chickens. Cao was later transferred to the elite Qincheng Prison, questioned extensively, and released in May 1990 as part of that year's most favored nation status releases. On his release he wrote a complimentary and combative letter to his jailers and their employers, arguing that his initial imprisonment merely indicated the need for further political reform in China. The Stone Institute and its role in the events of late May and early June 1989 remained under investigation well into 1991; its papers were seized and retained by the security forces. In a final irony, after his release Cao obtained tacit government approval to found a new group, the "Siyuan Bankruptcy and Merger Consulting Firm," using the argument that he was now unemployable in the state sector. The firm has undertaken bankruptcy consultations in Hainan and South China, and published a newsletter implicitly criticizing the State Council's attempts to deal with interlocking debt and other problems in the state enterprise sector. Author interviews, Beijing, 1990.

manipulate one party-controlled institution (the Standing Committee of the NPC) against other party-controlled bodies. Yu Haocheng and Zhang Zonghou almost entirely eschewed institutional mechanisms as a road to more rapid political and economic reform—and thus while Cao Siyuan was imprisoned and his organization dissolved for an altogether too dangerous use of institutions (at least in the eyes of some in the party), Yu Haocheng and his group were forced to terminate activities for theoretical work challenging the very bases of such institutions and their power.

Bases of organization among the urban groups of dissident legal scholars. The nongovernmental organizations of dissident legal scholars (and other organizations, like Chen Ziming and Wang Juntao's SERI, of which they were a part) seem to have been organized largely along lines of political belief and were composed almost entirely of intellectuals based at the Academy of Social Sciences and urban universities.

But the power of urban, reformist economic interests in defining the associational motivations should not be underestimated, especially in cases such as the relationship between Cao Siyuan's Stone Institute of Social Development and Wan Runnan's Stone Corporation. There the sponsoring organization, the Stone Corporation, was openly assisting a high-profile research and advocacy group to promote political goals directly related to the Stone Group's economic interests. And at SERI, the link between promoting economic reform and advancing political reform was crucial to the rise and prominence of the organization itself.

The role of direct economic interest on the part of the sponsor as a key associational motivator is less clear for organizations such as the Huaxia Institute of Legal Culture and the Capital Iron and Steel Legal Research Institute, where more directly political interests played a more prominent role in bringing the scholars together. But economic motivations—at least among the reformist, market-oriented leaders of the Capital Iron and Steel Company who sponsored the Legal Research Institute—played a significant role in the ties to a large, state-run enterprise.

Factional identity was also an important bond of association for each of these organizations. To emphasize factional identity in the complex but fundamentally small world of Chinese politics in 1988 and early 1989 may be to stress how important political bonds and motivations were in the organization of these groups. In some sense the legal and other nongovernmental research and advocacy organizations became the research and advocacy arms of factions—factions of the state—although when stated so baldly the murkiness of Beijing politics is perhaps insufficiently reflected. For example, Cao Siyuan's Stone Institute and its sponsors in the Stone Corporation conducted research and advocated policy positions in tandem with—and arguably for—Zhao Ziyang's reformist staff led by Bao Tong in the Central Committee. That factional identification is but one further indication of how closely tied to the state such groups were at a time of supposed rapid retreat from the state.

Other groups were in some sense factions by themselves, because they refused some of the strong but informal linkages with party factions. Chen Ziming's SERI perhaps belongs in this category.[36] While Cao Siyuan's Stone Institute was clearly linked to a faction, and even Huaxia was relatively clearly linked to Central Committee staffers with similar affinities, SERI was as self-contained an organization and a faction in Beijing as was possible to achieve in the late 1980s.

Financing was a key problem for each of these institutions. Yu Haocheng and Zhang Zonghou's Capital Iron and Steel Legal Research Institute and Cao Siyuan's Stone Institute of Social Development were largely dependent on their sponsoring institutions (and the strong leaders there, primarily Zhou Guanwu and Wan Runnan) for much of their daily office needs, and those subsidies enabled most of their activities. The Capital Iron and Steel Company and the Stone Corporation each provided office space (in each case, and, by mutual agreement in each case, not in the company's headquarters), and each company also provided basic salaries for a small staff and basic office supplies. The Huaxia Institute of Legal Culture was a more threadbare operation, since it did not have a sponsor with the funds of a Capital or Stone, and seems to have relied more on resources available from the Institute of Law at the Academy of Social Sciences as well as the Huaxia Academy.

The dependence on funding from powerful corporate sponsors was viewed as a not unambiguous benefit by leaders of the Capital and Stone legal research groups. They worked to attract additional funds for conferences, research, and publications, both to expand activities and to gain some stronger measure of financial independence from generous

[36]Perhaps ironically, lack of truly strong ties to any faction—including the losing faction led by Zhao Ziyang and Bao Tong—may have eased the way for SERI to come under more severe criticism after June 1989. But SERI was a complex organization, and it would be a mistake to think of it as without any factional ties to party groups.

patrons. Events moved quickly in Beijing, however, and the run-up to Tiananmen was upon these groups as they were beginning to reach out to potential domestic and foreign funders.[37]

Creation by state initiative or by social initiative? Among the urban nongovernmental organizations of dissident legal scholars, a spectrum emerges of some that were clearly nonstate initiatives and others that were perhaps more closely related to state—or factional—initiative. SERI was as clearly a social initiative as was possible to find in Beijing in the late 1980s. Huaxia was more complicated, but is best explained as a "social," nonstate initiative of Beijing-based intellectuals with strong "statist" ties to Central Committee officials and staff. The Capital Iron and Steel group was a "social," nonstate initiative in its links between individual members, but its organizational emergence was due largely to state facilitation—little could be more "statist" than the Capital Iron and Steel Company and its party committee. What is key is that even where "state" assistance was critical to the emergence of these groups, the motivation was in each case partially to challenge state orthodoxy.

CITY DWELLERS AND THE LAW:
HOW MUCH SPACE FROM STATE INTRUSION?

The efforts of dissident legal scholars to carve out some freedom from state control in the realm of scholarship have taken place mostly in China's cities. Those efforts parallel and reemphasize the gradual process by which Chinese intellectuals have striven to create political and economic space somewhat more removed from state intrusion in the years since 1979.

But what of those in China's cities who are not intellectuals? Has law provided a useful means for creating any space of freedom from state control or intrusion for ordinary Chinese urban residents? The contributions of legal reform in post-Mao Chinese cities are most significant in shoring up and protecting the new modes of economic life that have

[37]The Huaxia Institute of Legal Culture received support from the Soros Foundation for a conference on legal history and legal culture in late 1988; that is the only foreign funding for any of these three groups of which the author is aware. Little domestic funding was available either beyond the sponsoring groups, although by late 1988 Yu, Zhang, and Cao had begun to cement links with some liberal legal scholars at Beijing and Jilin universities and to aim toward joint raising of state research funds. The events of 1989 disrupted and eventually ended that collaboration and those plans.

been introduced by economic reform. The party has stepped back from much day-to-day intrusion in the political realm, but law cannot be given significant credit for that worthy development.

In one sense there is undoubtably less state intrusion in the day-to-day lives of urban Chinese residents. Neither the public security bureaus nor the neighborhood committees dominate the lives of urban Chinese as closely as they did throughout the 1970s.

But it cannot be said that law was the means for that creation of space. Rather, the creation of some more autonomous space for China's urban citizens was the gradual, almost inevitable result of economic reform, including increases in urban incomes and improvements in housing stock, and of political decisions by the party to remove itself from the day-to-day lives of urban citizens. Only subsequently—more often as an afterthought—did law substantiate this new space from state intrusion. Even legal enactments intended to limit abuses by security forces and other state actors—such as the Criminal Procedure Law of 1979, or the Administrative Litigation Law enacted in 1989—fundamentally seek to solidify a modicum of political and economic space that had already been granted by the party, rather than to break new ground.

At the same time that the lives of urban Chinese are somewhat freer from state intrusion, state intrusion continues to occur in specific areas, and that intrusion is specifically legitimized and fortified by law. For example, the law continues to legitimize and to enable the state to intervene in political unrest, as the actions of the security forces during and after June 1989 clearly show. And the law—in its incentive, deterrence, and punishment forms—is a primary means of pressuring urban residents to control and limit fertility (although the decline in the strength of enforcement mechanisms also hinders this process). If anything, for urban Chinese, space free from state intrusion in the family planning process has shrunk rather than grown in the years since 1979.

The political potential of urban organizations of dissident legal scholars. Although the direct political potential of the urban organizations of dissident legal scholars is now negligible, the example set in 1988 and 1989 by the emergence of organizations of liberal and dissident scholars with more autonomy from the state is well remembered in China's urban centers.

Legal scholars in Beijing and other cities who joined or led these groups do not intend merely to replicate them when it is next possible to form quasi-autonomous groups with some distance from the state sector. The intention seems to be to learn from the experience of such groups and to find new ways of organizing, or, if the political climate allows, to find activities beyond research and criticism to engage in next time. In that sense the "test cases" filed by individuals such as Wang Meng, Dai Qing, Guo Luoji, and Chen Ziming were watched carefully in China—for if such actions are possible now, what may be possible when political controls loosen a bit?[38] The potential of these organizations to teach and to mold future developments is thus not obviated by their closure.

Do such organizations contribute to the "democratization" of China? In expanding the bounds of intellectual and political dialogue, leaders such as Yu Haocheng and Cao Siyuan clearly believe that they did. At the same time, the groups were quite limited. Their strength was in the urban centers, but, like the student movement of 1989, strength in the cities also implies limited appeal outside the cities and to such groups as the military. In China urban strength is unrepresentative of the country as a whole, as both scholars and students learned in 1989. Legal scholars who would work within such urban organizations do not now know whether they can transcend such limitations in the next stage, which they know will come.

---

[38]Outside China, William Alford has written on this process. See his "Double-edged Swords Cut Both Ways: Law and Legitimacy in the People's Republic of China," *Daedalus* (Spring 1993): 45–70. Not all scholars in China or observers outside agree with Alford's controversial conclusions on this important process.

13

◦▪▬◦▬◦▬◦▬◦▬◦▬◦▬◦▬◦▬◦▬◦▬◦▬◦▬◦▬◦▬◦▬◦▬◦▬▬◦▬◦▬◦▬◦▬◦▬◦▬◦▬◦▬◦▬◦▬◦

Urban spaces and experiences of *qigong*

NANCY N. CHEN

Cities, like dreams, are made of desires and fears . . . [1]

In the years following initiation of the post-Mao reforms, the popularity of *qigong* practice (traditional breathing and health exercises) and healing in the People's Republic of China (PRC) grew to such immense proportions that many referred to the phenomenon as *qigong re* (*qigong* fever). Heated discussions, vivid testimonies, and folklore about the miraculous powers of *qigong* spontaneously developed on buses, at work units (*danwei*), even on university campuses. The popularity of *qigong* was fueled by martial arts films and pulp novels, as well as by official bodies of medical science and research institutes. Chinese government estimates in 1990 placed the number of practitioners at 5 percent of the total population (about 60 million persons); more recent estimates raise the number to nearly 200 million.[2] But such figures cannot begin to capture the impact that the practice has had on personal experience and social groups. When I was in China in 1990 to conduct fieldwork in psychiatric hospitals, encounters with patients diagnosed with "*qigong* deviation" persuaded me to undertake ethnographic research outside mental institutions to contextualize the disorder that was rapidly filling urban clinics.[3] In contrast to confines where "abnormal" behavior was codified and countered with familiar structures of ordered treatment, I

This research was conducted with a graduate fellowship (1990–91) from the Committee for Scholarly Communication with the People's Republic of China.

[1]Italo Calvino, *Invisible Cities* (New York: Harcourt, Brace, Jovanovich, 1972), 44.
[2]Elizabeth J. Perry and Ellen V. Fuller, "China's Long March to Democracy," *World Policy Journal* (Fall 1991): 663–85.
[3]I discuss the phenomenon of "*qigong* deviation" elsewhere in the manuscript "Psychiatry and Popular Practice: Deviation and Mental Health in the People's Republic of China."

soon found myself in a social arena where trance, possession, and existence within otherworldly times and spaces were common practices of daily life.

The multifaceted practice of *qigong* in the contemporary urban setting can be at once a healing art, a daily regimen of exercise, and a spiritual revival. Whereas in imperial China modes of transmission were often familial and bases of organization frequently paralleled secret societies, the patterns of *qigong* association in the contemporary urban setting are distinct for the mental and emotional relief they provide from the physical landscape of the city. In place of urban anomie, there is a search for balance in one's life. Exercises in imagination and healing link one's body to the cosmos as an alternative to the alienation of life in the modern metropolis. Descriptions of Chinese cities and processes of urbanization usually focus on macro changes in economic and social conditions, but attention must also be directed to the everyday micro experiences of urban life.[4] The spaces created through *qigong* reflect intimate relations among practice, body, and landscape and imply alternative mentalities outside the prescribed order of the state.

An exploration of the consciousness of ordinary Chinese urbanites is germane to the debate over civil society. While categories of *gong* (public) and *si* (private) lend understanding to how the political and the personal are bounded in Chinese culture, it is important to note not only how these experiences are mutually constructed in the process of urbanization but also how individuals perceive or create such spheres. Such exploration is difficult, as our methodologies for analyzing cities are heavily steeped in a Western tradition of urbanization tied to capitalist development.[5] In the present reform period, when the Chinese socialist state is experimenting with free markets and private entrepreneurs, studies of the development of public-private spheres in capitalism suggest useful conceptual tools for viewing emergent relationships among the contemporary Chinese state, civil society, and everyday life. The meaning of *gong* implies public and state ownership. However institutions, work-units, and official associations are not the only public organizations found in contemporary China. In recent years nonstate associa-

---

[4]The literature on urbanization is vast. Greg Guilden's recent edited volume *Urbanizing China* (Westport, Ct.: Greenwood Press, 1992) discusses the political and economic conditions of contemporary urbanization.
[5]David Harvey's *Consciousness and the Urban Experience* (Baltimore: Johns Hopkins University Press, 1985) traces this process of urbanization in a capitalist context.

tions have expanded possibilities of public life to include the streets, common areas, and even open debates. Although the public sphere and civil society are useful constructs with which to understand city life, practices within these realms should also be examined.

As post-Mao urban spaces emerge from the structures of socialist planning to be more fluid in spatial and functional specialization (see Chapter 2), the practice of *qigong* also helps to negotiate former binary relations of rural-urban and public-private spheres into more meaningful spaces. Work units were developed as key sites of urban control during Maoist years. In the face of urban expansion or "sprawl" (documented by Barry Naughton) even these centers have come to accommodate popular practices. During the late 1980s *qigong* practice took place not only in parks but also in work-units. At the invitation of *danwei* officials, *qigong* masters held mass sessions including healing and altered states of consciousness. These *qigong* activities indicate how urban parks and work units could be simultaneously public sites and places of private experience. The inner experiences and social networks generated by such practices shape public arenas such as parks, gymnasiums, and buildings into zones of personal practice and cultivation. At the same time that individuals are aware of the physical landscape of the city, they are also producing mental spaces of an alternative order within this landscape.

URBAN PARKS: PUBLIC SPACES, POPULAR PLACES, AND PRIVATE SPHERES

"Bus Aria," a short story by Liu Xinwu (1990), describes a familiar experience for most Chinese city dwellers who ride the buses.

Lifeblood of the metropolis.

Anger. When you ride the bus it's hard to avoid. Waiting, bored. Damn bus won't come. When it finally does come, it often zooms right by without stopping, with that little "Express" or "Special" sign propped in the window. Or, you run up to the door and it slams in your face with a bang. Even if you manage to squeeze your way on, the ticket-seller pushes and shoves you from behind, as if you were nothing but a sack of potatoes. If she's feeling energetic, she'll make all kinds of trouble for you when she checks the tickets; if she's not in the mood, she won't trouble herself to sell you a ticket even if you want to buy one.

*   *   *

There's nothing more inaccessible than the human heart. It's extremely difficult to empathize with others.

But the desire to do so is a vital human attribute.

There's nothing easy about it.
It's hard to nurture this desire in everyone.
Life is a net.

* * *

The passengers on a bus are like a school of fish swimming from one knot in
the net to another. Their time on the bus may be spent lost in numbed reverie
or self absorption. To them, "bus driver" and "ticket-seller" are abstract concepts; even though the living, breathing ticket-seller is sitting before them, they
remain oblivious to the fact that she has a name, her own history, her own life
to lead, a family of her own, and that she experiences anger, grief and joy. . . .
Nobody has it easy on the bus.[6]

The emotional texture of city life is expressed in sentiments ranging from
anger to resignation or urban anomie. The bus is a microcosm of larger
social issues in urban China today, a metaphor found not only in literature but also in recent state-sponsored films such as *Good Morning,
Beijing* or official plays such as *On the Bus*.[7] Although buses are self-
contained units of common experience, they traverse streets filled with
dangerous intersections, traffic teeming with bicycles, and masses of humanity. Streets are noted for the chaos of urban life, in which violence
is rife and madness is easily observed (in individuals who dance in the
street only to be taken to mental hospitals). Floating populations (described in Chapter 5) of rural farmers, economic migrants, and tourists
gravitate to cities, making the streets even more unruly and difficult to
navigate. Occasionally islands of order appear where white-gloved traffic
police stand in the noxious fumes to direct buses, bikes, and cars. But
streets remain disorderly and fearfully fluid; in times of protest, the
streets become avenues of resistance (and suppression) where demonstrators block traffic and subvert the normal flow of directions and officialdom.

It is a long way from there to the parks, so I wish to convey a sense
of the Chinese urban landscape barely visible to individuals who jam
themselves into metal boxes on wheels sharing a square meter with thirteen other passengers. While less cramped than bus riders, bicyclists and
pedestrians face the dangers of collisions, the inhalation of pollution and
dust, and the wrath of the elements. For everyone who leaves the home

[6]Liu Xinwu, *Black Walls*, trans. Don Cohn (Hong Kong: Chinese University of Hong
Kong, Renditions, 1990). The story also notes that more than 8 million passengers ride
the buses in Beijing each day.
[7]The film was produced by the Beijing Youth Film Studio in 1990. The play, produced in
1990 by the Capital Theater, was highly acclaimed by party members.

the outside world (*wai*) remains treacherous and difficult to negotiate. Although the private sphere is certainly not without violence or terror, the streets and other places "outside" one's familiar gates of the city, unit, or home are often noted for their special dangers in Chinese urban folklore. While conducting fieldwork in the early 1990s I was often reminded to beware for my personal safety when going into the street. Informants would frequently complain that the streets have become too *luan* (chaotic) and then tell me to be careful of traffic accidents and *liumang* (hooligans).

This image of external turmoil and chaos was seized by the government officials during the post-Tiananmen period as cause to regulate and reestablish official order in the urban centers. A major sweep of city streets involved cleaning up remnants of damage as well as relocating to peripheral regions the mentally unstable and temporary workers who stayed in the streets. The official character of the capital became even more pronounced during the Asian Games in 1990. Long-awaited residential buildings along major streets were hastily constructed while old *hutong* facades were covered with fresh paint. Innumerable tourist hotels and shops targeted for foreign visitors opened instead to a largely domestic clientele. Street signs and traffic police appeared at key intersections, much to the surprise and annoyance of city dwellers. Instead of the familiar chaos of daily traffic, commuters faced a restrictive order of inconvenient stop signs and citations. Work-units, factories, free markets, parks, and especially the streets became key sites of repair and stepped-up surveillance in the pageantry of socialist modernization.

Upon entering an urban park, one immediately senses the relative tranquility and slower pace of activity. Grandparents stroll, sometimes while holding or pushing along young toddlers, lovers sit quietly in semi-seclusion on benches and rocks, old men with bird cages gather to smoke or chat, students practice English, groups of people exercise or dance together. While the parks are public spaces (*gong yuan*), these sites are also arenas where urban dwellers seek refuge and attain a semblance of privacy in anonymity from work or home. Although public arenas such as Tiananmen Square resonate with political meaning, parks commonly remain areas where nonpolitical activity can take place. Compared to the concrete streets or cramped quarters of the bus, urban parks provide natural surroundings, with trees and fresh air.

The history of public parks in Beijing is linked to the development of the People's Republic. Whereas sacred sites such as the Temple of

Heaven or the Forbidden City were once off-limits and intended for the imperial court, after 1949 these places were transformed into public gardens and places "for the people." In looking at sacred spaces in Beijing, Meyer notes the city is "an idea become visible in physical and architectural forms."[8] Temples provide an interface between heaven and earth where one can see a replication of the geometry of the universe and intuit an awareness of other worlds and mythic power. As Daoist and Buddhist temples rebuild and regain membership in the present reform era, urban parks constitute safe space not only because they are located on the sites of (some) former temples, but also because they provide areas where exercises of self-cultivation are socially accepted. The safety of these spaces varies as the day progresses. Upon evening twilight, these areas can also become danger zones of illicit activities. Public parks stand out not only as potential arenas of privacy but also as a reminder of the natural environment, a non-urban entity. Despite being planned by the government and bounded by fences and admission gates, the park remains a place where popular and personal healing can occur.

Qigong practice in urban parks takes place in all weather and seasons, primarily in the early mornings "when the air is better," alongside other martial arts and exercises. The weekday practitioners are present from 6 A.M. to 8 A.M., before working hours. There is a significant dropoff in the number of practitioners at 8 A.M., when workers return to official obligations at their work-units. Those who remain in the park after this time are usually retired or unemployed persons with chronic disorders. Most people cite health-related issues as the main reason for taking up the practice. Sunday mornings are prime time, as most individuals enjoy the whole day off.

The social topography of parks correlates with different regimens. Disco dancers and enthusiasts of tai ji and other martial arts also practice in the park, in addition to the babies in strollers and neighborhood members who visit in the mornings. Enthusiasts of all schools can be found in small groups or as individuals under trees. *Qigong* practitioners form "multiclass coalitions" whose members come from all ages, both sexes, diverse occupations, and a wide range of political backgrounds.[9] Membership is quite fluid and can take various forms: practice in official schools recognized by the state, followers of private masters, or

[8]Jeffrey F. Meyer, *The Dragons of Tienanmen: Beijing as Sacred City* (Columbia, S.C.: University of South Carolina Press, 1991).
[9]Perry and Fuller, "China's Long March to Democracy."

practice based on personal readings and instructions from popular literature. An individual might first practice in a large group and later move to a smaller group or private area for further practice. Official groups licensed with posted banners, membership rolls, and registered masters coexist with unofficial autonomous associations in which individuals gather together simply to exercise and socialize. Daily practice is common to all groups.

URBAN *QIGONG* ASSOCIATIONS

Urban parks contain a wide variety of practitioners, but experiences of *qigong* are not limited to parks. Individual and group performances can be found in numerous public venues—markets, work-units, train stations, even streets. Moreover, bookcarts and stands sell popular *qigong* novels or magazines throughout the city, a phenomenon that began in the mid-1980s. The following discussion will review the three main types of practice and then turn to the formation of urban *qigong* associations surrounding such practices. As with legal associations (examined in Chapter 12) and student groups (discussed in Chapter 14), there exist a multitude of official, state-initiated organizations as well as independent groups of practitioners. Despite ostensibly dichotomous oppositions between official and nongovernmental groups, in fact their operation and interaction strangely mirror one other. Membership can be eclectic, even overlapping, as practitioners can assume roles in more than one organization. Although the Chinese labor movement depended on long-standing fragmentation as a basis for agency (see Chapter 11), *qigong* associations are more fluid in their formation and alliances with official networks. Whereas legal, student, and labor associations all have discrete interests and membership, *qigong* associations are unique in their broad-based constituency.

Although there are innumerable forms and schools of *qigong*, there are three basic forms of practice—as martial art, as meditation practice, and as healing ritual. The first type of *qigong* as martial art is often referred to as "hard *qigong*" (*ying qigong*). Masters of this form carry out incredible feats such as breaking rocks with the force of *qi* in their hands or moving opponents ten feet away by concentrating their powers of *qi*. The second type, *qigong* practice as meditation, is found more commonly in the early morning in the park, where individuals stand in prescribed stances or sit in lotus position under trees. These practitioners believe that trees have special powers of *qi* that can revive the force of *qi* in their own bodies. Many individuals can be seen hugging trees, rubbing their bodies around the trunk of trees, dancing in circles around trees, or sitting quietly before a tree. The third type, *qigong* practice as healing ritual, poses the greatest threat to the state not only because of the immensely popular following that has grown since the early 1980s but also because of its growing resemblance to a spiritualist cult or millenarian movement. Individual masters of great charismatic authority visit the parks, instantly drawing waves of followers seeking relief or cures. Lineages and networks of followers emerge to reveal accumulations by such masters of political capital in *guanxi* (personal relations) and power.

The formation of *qigong* associations can be viewed in a continuum from officially sanctioned bureaucratic organizations to popular revitalistic movements headed by charismatic masters. While the basis of their organization depends partly upon the practice being promoted (exercise, meditation, or healing), it is primarily economic and political interests that determine the type of alliances that develop. The four main categories of *qigong* associations are: (1) official bodies that are formed by the state and administered by bureaucrats; (2) legitimate and public groups that have attained official recognition but retain some autonomy in membership and practice; (3) popular, informal groups that are autonomous and exist in a "gray zone" of activities not necessarily sanctioned by the state; and (4) underground associations that are officially condemned or denounced as dealing in "false" or "superstitious" practices. All these associations face similar issues regarding legitimacy, funding, and recruitment. Some associations interact on both an official level and an informal basis as members have multiple roles in various organizations. A *qigong* master, for example, may have a formally registered association while also, as sidelines, having patients seeking cures and training personal students to continue the lineage of knowledge.

Within the first category of official *qigong* associations are bureaucratic bodies such as the *qigong* Regulatory Bureau (established in 1989) and medical certification boards established for surveillance and regulation of the practice. These entities are responsible for defining "scientific" *qigong* and licensing *qigong* masters as officially recognized healers. State funded, their members consist primarily of medically oriented nonpractitioners. While such bureaucrats enjoy state sanction to define the boundaries of acceptable and rational practices, their legitimacy depends on countering and containing the popularity of masters whose bases of power exist outside official realms.

Members of public, registered *qigong* groups work closely with bureaucrats, with whom they share vested interests. The administrative bodies monitor public groups regularly, while such associations depend on legitimization by the official bureaucracy for both financial and symbolic support. In most major cities, municipal *qigong* associations perform a variety of functions: registering licensed masters and official practitioners, holding regular classes, receiving delegations of visiting *qigong* enthusiasts, and the like. These associations have regular monthly meetings and publications funded by membership and municipal appropriations. The Beijing *qigong* association, for example, has been in existence for over ten years and regularly promotes classes for local citizens and even foreigners.

Other officially recognized associations include research units devoted to the study of *qi* phenomena and promotion of the "scientific basis of *qi*." The units are usually located in medical institutes or physics departments of major universities such as Qinghua or Beijing University. While municipal associations are composed primarily of *qigong* masters and devoted practitioners, intellectuals collaborate with masters in experimental research on *teyi gongneng* (paranormal abilities) or special powers of healing. Whole congresses have been held solely on the phenomenon of *qi*.

The two types of associations discussed above are heavily dependent on the state, whereas the third type, popular, informal *qigong* associations, reveals a hidden economy whose existence is public but autonomous of state recognition. Funding is based entirely on voluntary, personal monies, and is independent of state sponsorship; membership is fluid with individuals often entering into multiple associations. Sometimes an informal group may spin off from an officially licensed class or *qigong* master. The possibilities for such associations are vast, and meetings take place in a variety of urban arenas—parks, work-units, temples, gymnasiums, even streets or apartments. The Thirteen Sisters, as the members of one such group call themselves, consist of women who range in age from the twenties to the sixties and meet every day to practice together. Often after a group trance of fits and movements, some members break into vigorous disco dancing or share morning snacks. The Thirteen Sisters also meet outside their regular practice site for picnics in other parks or visits in homes.

Another group that congregates daily at the base of a large tree refers to its members by kinship terms such as Elder Sister Zhang or Little Brother Tang. Many assume *qigong* pseudonyms culled from Buddhist classics or Daoist lore. When *qigong* masters appear, members respectfully part or crowd about the master to ask for healing or advice. Such informal gatherings constitute a "gray zone" of activity, especially at times of impromptu healing sessions. Individuals contribute specified membership dues for regular *qigong* instruction (ranging from as low as 20 yuan/month to 50 yuan/session) or donate voluntary amounts of money or gifts in exchange for healing sessions. Communications among members take various channels—word of mouth, printed flyers and signs affixed to public newsboards or street posts, or recommendation through friends.

Such popular and informal groups mushroomed between 1985 and 1990. Their proliferation was greatly aided by the official media, whose networks and major newspapers (*People's Daily, Guangming Daily, Beijing Evening News, Health News Daily, China Daily,* etc.) carried articles featuring the miraculous powers of *qigong*. This attention was viewed as encouragement by readers and practitioners. A vast offspring of popular monthly and weekly periodicals also flourished in this period. Articles focused on the sensational and phantasmagoric—a tree infused with special *qi* could heal various illnesses or induce trances; an individual once stricken with a chronic debilitating illness was now completely cured. Such narratives fueled the popular image of *qigong* masters as superhuman and capable of transmitting *qi* to heal individuals or throngs of people at once.

Before bans on large gatherings under post-Tiananmen martial law, it was common for hundreds, sometimes thousands, of people to gather in a mass healing session inside a crowded gym where a master would *fa qi* (send out *qi*) to the general audience. Members of the audience responded with uncharacteristic body movements of spontaneous twitching, shaking, even jumping, and dropped to the ground convulsing with the force of the *qi*. Others rocked back and forth in their chairs and laughed or cried uncontrollably. Such public events operated in a marginal zone; many practitioners claimed that because their exercises took place during leisure hours and were intended to promote healing, they were not at all dangerous.

By late 1990 the state regulatory bureau further enforced regulations concerning the strict licensing of masters and registration of practitioners. Such actions were carried out by public security in the name of social order to address the *luan* caused by "superstitious" activities. A fourth category of *qigong* associations, defined by the state bureaucracy, emerged in which "false" rather than "scientific" or "authentic" practice took place. Whereas previously people could move freely from group to group, they now had to submit to the watchful eye of the state or else risk being charged with illegal activity. Accordingly an underground network of communication, recruitment, and healing began to operate independently and even in defiance of the state bureaucracy. In 1990 Zhang Xiangyu, a female master in her thirties, was taken into custody by municipal authorities for "practicing and healing without a license."[10] Zhang was an intensely charismatic person with a wide following. Her disciples and individuals practiced *da ziran gong* (great universal *qigong*), a form marked by trance, possession, and speaking in tongues.

As mass trances and "communities of chaos" paradoxically bring personal order to people's bodies, the popularity of *qigong* transcends both public and private arenas.[11] The social body of healing thus involves a complex network of practitioners and masters who operate in both state and nongovernmental groups along with an accompanying array of scientists and bureaucrats who view the social phenomenon with varying degrees of dismay.

TRANSFORMATIONS:
URBAN BODIES AND ALTERED STATES

Encounters with *qigong* are both common and highly eclectic for cure-seeking individuals. Personal accounts of the miracles of *qigong* healing abound. University students who once felt weak and sickly talk of improving their constitution and concentration. Factory workers cite increased vigor after *qigong* practice. One elderly retiree in her sixties started dancing in response to questions about why she began. "You see this (pointing to her knee) . . . last year I was bedridden with pain because my arthritis was so bad. My master healed me and now I can move like a youth again because I practice every day." Even if they do not themselves practice, any urban dweller is likely to know someone who goes to parks or mass meetings in search of healing and longevity.

---

[10]*Shijie ribao* (World journal), August 27, 1990.
[11]Jean Comeroff and Ann Anagnost, Commentary from American Ethnological Society Meetings, Memphis, March 25, 1992.

The popularity of *qigong* has suddenly exploded for several reasons: charismatic masters, media coverage, and a general relaxation of control over leisure time under the post-Mao reforms (see Chapter 6). Above all, *qigong* is compelling to such a wide and diverse audience because it gives individuals the opportunity to experience their minds and bodies in a time and space outside the ordinary present. In the practice of *qigong* breathing, the body becomes a tool of imagination and desire. There is a longing to transcend the prescribed mentality of the state and the cramped spaces of urban life. Merleau-Ponty's multiple notions of the body as object, as experience, and as spatiality are useful for understanding how the body experiences *qigong* as a transformative process.[12] The mind-body is used as tool of perception not only to apprehend the world but also to create private mental spaces in a social setting. This spiritual or ecstatic body of energy, linked to the cosmological and natural environment, replaces the urban body. Urban constructs of parks, buildings, or streets give way to private experience.

This phenomenological transformation is often described as a blissful state of placing one's body in harmony with its surroundings and natural forces. Practitioners are told to relax (*fang song*) and through a litany of points along the body to relate the *qi* in their body to the *qi* in the atmosphere. Getting in touch with one's body through these traditional points of energy links the body to a universe outside the immediate urban surroundings of the Chinese state. These experiences illustrate what Kleinman terms the "somato-moral world" where "hidden transcripts" of identity and meaning are forged.[13] The self is rewritten as a personal being apart from, or disembodied from, the state. The linkages of the mind-body to a different source of power, that of a cosmological order, transgress familiar boundaries of the state. As a devoted practitioner once explained, "This city is laid out in the image of Buddha. This (park) location corresponds to the sacred *dan tian* [center of *qi* energy]. If you practice here, you will find yourself to be different than when in any other place." The individual enjoys a topography of the self where layers of meaning and images of power are personally inscribed, carrying imagination to new states of consciousness.[14]

[12]Maurice Merleau-Ponty, *The Phenomenology of Perception* (New York: Routledge and Kegan Paul, 1981).

[13]Arthur Kleinman and Joan Kleinman, "The Politics of Memory and the Memory of Alienation," paper presented at the annual meeting of the Association for Asian Studies, 1990.

[14]Michael Taussig, *The Nervous System* (London: Routledge, 1991).

The transformations of self, mind, and body in *qigong* entail a revision of one's understanding and relationship with the natural world. The individual body is not the only entity transformed by this experience. Where once associations such as work-units, schools, or neighborhood committees were the primary form of urban interaction, *qigong* networks create a new community of individuals from diverse backgrounds. Networks based on *guanxi* or familial relationships remain vital to everyday life but *qigong* associations encompass a new sense of urban humanism. As a middle-aged male worker commented with a broad smile, "I strive to do good in my everyday life. That's how *qigong* has changed me." Independent voluntary communities buttressed by such a broad base of alliances and meanings contain immense potential. Charismatic leaders and the popular image of *qigong* founded on media and healing narratives have created a sense of autonomous identity that is well entrenched in urban spaces and city life.

The unsettling nature of this process helps explain the state's response. The recent position of the Chinese socialist bureaucracy relative to *qigong* associations and masters indicates great concern over the revitalistic and political potential of such formations. Although *qigong* continues to be promoted by the state as a unique Chinese tradition, the social networks led by charismatic leaders present a latent danger. Popular *qigong* associations resonate with a long tradition of peasant uprisings and heterodox movements, such as the Boxers, who once practiced *qi* exercises to promote their visions of a utopian society.[15] Regulation and intervention by the Chinese socialist state blames society, an ironic turn of events since people take up *qigong* because of disenchantment with official ideology and policy. The state's presence is inserted into everyday life through surveillance of public arenas such as the parks. Categories of "official" versus "false" *qigong* are created to permit practitioners of "superstitious" activities to be taken into custody for questioning. Those who continue to practice in parks do so under red banners and white certificates of legitimately recognized schools of *qigong*. Witch hunts of masters are carried out in the name of fighting corruption. And boundaries of normality are reestablished through creating a medical disorder called *qigong* deviation.

Rather than think of civil society as "subaltern" or independent as-

---

[15]Susan Naquin, *Millenarian Rebellion in China: The Eight Trigrams Uprising of 1813* (New Haven: Yale University Press, 1976); Joseph Esherick, *Origins of the Boxer Uprising* (Berkeley: University of California Press, 1987).

sociations in opposition to the state, one should regard it as a more ambiguous relationship. Altered states refer not only to states of consciousness that shape certain experiences in *qigong*, but also to a refiguration of the state through *qigong* practice. Many party members and bureaucrats themselves have either received *qigong* healing treatment, or have been devoted practitioners. One such person remarked in 1990, "There were only two things that I believed in last year—the party and *qigong*. Now I just believe in *qigong*." While the Chinese socialist state tries to recapture control of center stage through surveillance, public censure, and imprisonment, the dimensions of time and space—two realms of power where *qigong* experience is mediated—remain contested.

As the Chinese socialist state adopts capitalist markets to stimulate the economy, time and space are becoming increasingly commodified. The bureaucracy attempts to harness the immense and unexplainable power of *qigong* by creating boundaries of legitimate scientific enterprise while appropriating its use for an officially mediated public sphere. *Qigong* practice is also being changed by such efforts. Some *qigong* masters are savvy entrepreneurs who subvert the system to create an even stronger base of power in monetary and political capital with commercialized courses and high prices for healing sessions. However the lag time between market forces, state policy, and effective enforcement creates the possibility for considerable autonomy and agency.

CONCLUSION: BREATHING SPACES

> Respiratory rhythm is a function of our awareness of our situation in the world.[16]

In the early dawn at the Temple of Heaven park about twenty practitioners can be observed at the stone altar in various states of *qi* meditation. Some sit in lotus position while others stand to concentrate on their breathing or lie on the stone in a trance. Nearby, thirty other practitioners dance beneath trees or consult with one another on the best forms of practice, masters, and daily regimens. Occasionally deep primal sounds disturb the morning stillness. A few individuals communicate by speaking in tongues. They all appear to be ordinary people whom one

[16]Georges Canguilhem, *Normality and Abnormality* (Reidel, 1978).

might encounter throughout the day—storekeepers, street sweepers, free-market merchants, students, nannies. While *qigong* practitioners are visibly situated in public parks, their alternative states of consciousness imply a withdrawal from the confines of city and the state. As city life becomes filled with market reforms that bring dream factories of commercial images, the desire to inject personal meanings into such realms becomes even more pervasive. *Qigong* practitioners rewrite their identity through healing practices in search of personal balance rather than state order.

Many practitioners and masters in the PRC look forward to an apocalyptic ending of the present regime in the formation of a Great Universe (*da ziran*). Within this yearning for utopian nature and cosmos are located important issues. The right to situate and define the individual body within an orthodox socialist state is being contested by an imagination that transcends official urban spaces. *Qigong* practice reveals how powerful and pervasive the Chinese tradition of healing and inner body cultivation can be. While remaining within the gates and walls of parks and city life, practitioners literally dissociate themselves from the state.

What is the Chinese socialist city, then, and what has happened to the urban landscape? The power to imagine and heal creates breathing space and the basis of autonomy in an urban environment. Personal identity transcends the city such that the public urban space where practice occurs is no longer either urban or public. Popular *qigong* creates a compelling and controversial base for the conversion of official spaces into sites of personal significance.

The practice of *qigong* can be found in urban contexts outside the PRC throughout Hong Kong, Taiwan, Japan, and even the United States and Europe. Transference of such practices is closely tied to transglobal processes whereby "Oriental" medicine is commodified within the paradigm of Western medical systems. Individual *qigong* masters traverse the globe to hold mass healing sessions, teach foreign students, and create a wider base of money and popularity. Such strategies follow capitalist notions of time and space where market values and commodification shape patterns of practice and association. By contrast the experience of *qigong* in China remains distinct—defined by an ever-watchful yet ambivalent state eager to harness the popularity and power of *qigong* to the mandates of science and socialist modernization.

14

Student associations and mass movements

JEFFREY N. WASSERSTROM and LIU XINYONG

Student-led mass movements have been a recurring feature of Chinese city life throughout the twentieth century. China's educated youth have repeatedly proved themselves remarkably adept both at transforming their shared grievances into coherent expressions of dissent and at winning the support of members of other urban groups. As a result, although the upheavals of 1989 were in many respects unprecedented and surprising, the popular movement of that year also needs to be seen as but one in a long series of struggles in which agitation on single college campuses has evolved into citywide protests affecting urban areas throughout the nation. Similarly, although the legitimacy crisis that those protests triggered showed some unique features—that the regime continued to wrestle with five years later—Deng Xiaoping and Li Peng are only the latest of many Chinese leaders who have had their power threatened by mass actions involving highly organized groups of students.

In an effort to shed light on the dynamics of this enduring feature of modern Chinese urban history, this chapter asks the following questions. What kinds of interpersonal ties made it possible in 1989 for students to organize themselves so effectively during the weeks immediately after the death of former General Secretary Hu Yaobang? Which preexisting groups and associations played the most important roles in preparing protest leaders for the parts they would play in the dramatic events that followed, including the student occupation of Beijing's Tiananmen Square? And to borrow a phrase that Frank Pieke uses as the title for his insightful ethnographic account of Beijing life just before and during the protests, what connection was there between "the ordinary and the

extraordinary" as regards patterns of campus life and student organizational behavior?[1]

Our answer to this last question is simple, and has important implications for the previous queries as well: the only way to make sense of
the *extraordinary* mobilization process that took place in the aftermath
of Hu's death is to see it as firmly rooted in *ordinary* patterns of campus
social life. Building upon knowledge of the 1989 protests derived from
published accounts, as well as from personal observation of Shanghai
events (in the case of Liu) and communications with foreign and Chinese
eyewitnesses to demonstrations that took place in Beijing and the provinces (in the case of Wasserstrom), we attempt to show that understanding the organizational dynamics of the movement requires looking
beyond the activities of explicitly political dissident groups, to the formal
and informal ties established through innocuous collective activities. In
short, the rise and effectiveness of the student protest associations of
1989 make sense only if these groups are viewed as part of a specific
urban social environment: that of the Chinese college campus.

Our insistence that patterns of daily life helped shape the protests of
1989 may seem little more than common sense to specialists who have
worked on labor or peasant movements. After all, for several decades, the
most illuminating studies of European food riots and factory strikes have
been done by historians and social scientists, ranging from E. P. Thompson and Michelle Perrot to Charles Tilly and William Sewell, who have
taken for granted that the ordinary and the extraordinary will always be
intimately connected.[2] And during the last twenty years or so, the field of
Asian studies has been enriched by studies that make similar assumptions.

[1] Frank N. Pieke, "The Ordinary and the Extraordinary: An Anthropological Study of
Chinese Reform and Political Protest," Ph.D. diss., University of California, Department
of Anthropology, 1992. The authors thank several eyewitnesses to the protests of 1989
who responded orally or in writing to our queries concerning the events they witnessed.
This group includes Gérémie Barmé, Craig Calhoun, Corinna-Barbara Francis, Norman
Kutcher, Kristen Parris, and Melissa Macauley, as well as several Chinese students and
an American teacher who have requested that we refrain from using their names. We are
also grateful to Elizabeth Perry and the other participants in the Woodrow Wilson Center
conference for their comments on an earlier draft of this chapter.
[2] E. P. Thompson, *The Making of the English Working Class* (New York: Vintage, 1966);
idem, *Customs in Common: Studies in Traditional Popular Culture* (New York: The
New Press, 1993); Michelle Perrot, *Workers on Strike: France, 1870–1891* (New Haven: Yale University Press, 1987); Charles Tilly, *The Contentious French* (Cambridge,
Mass.: Harvard University Press, 1986); William H. Sewell, Jr., *Work and Revolution:
The Language of Labor from the Old Regime to 1848* (Cambridge: Cambridge University
Press, 1980).

The books on peasant rebellion and labor unrest by the editor of this section are important cases in point, as are various publications by other participants in the Wilson Center workshop (such as David Strand, who wrote Chapter 15 in this volume, and Susan Naquin, who served as a commentator at the gathering) and the study of "hidden transcripts" of dissent by James Scott that Deborah Davis draws attention to in Chapter 1 of this volume.[3] All these scholars locate the deeds of the workers and peasants with whom they are concerned within particularized urban or rural settings. They assume that, to understand the history of social movements, we need to ask the following questions about the actors involved in popular protests: Which rituals gave meaning to their lives? How were they linked to one another through bonds associated with blood ties, common beliefs, residence patterns, workplace hierarchies, friendship networks, informal clubs, and the like? To what extent should their protests be understood as adaptations of or improvisations upon scripts associated with routine forms of group activity?

This concern with establishing connections between patterns of daily life and patterns of protest, which figures so prominently in case studies of peasant and labor unrest, remains a novelty in the literature on political struggles involving the *zhishifenzi* (a Chinese term for "intellectual" that includes college and university students). Rather than look for "hidden transcripts" or concentrate on quotidian social and economic relationships, analysts of campus activism have focused most intently on the psychological and ideological dimensions of social protest. Tactical and organizational decisions are typically left unexamined, explained as rational choices made by intelligent people aware of their options, or treated as fiats passed down by members of a small vanguard group connected to an explicitly political organization or party.[4] This is not the place to re-

[3] Elizabeth J. Perry, *Rebels and Revolutionaries in North China, 1845–1945* (Stanford: Stanford University Press, 1980); idem, *Shanghai on Strike* (Stanford, Calif.: Stanford University Press, 1993); David Strand, *Rickshaw Beijing: City People and Politics in the 1920s* (Berkeley: University of California Press, 1989); Susan Naquin, *Shantung Rebellion: The Wang Lun Uprising of 1774* (New Haven: Yale University Press, 1981); James Scott, *Domination and the Arts of Resistance* (New Haven: Yale University Press, 1990). For a careful discussion of a variety of other studies of Chinese rural unrest that fit into this category, see Daniel Little, *Understanding Peasant China: Case Studies in the Philosophy of Social Science* (New Haven: Yale University Press, 1989). Other important works on Chinese labor protest that pay close attention to patterns of daily life include Gail Hershatter, *The Workers of Tiajin* (Stanford, Calif.: Stanford University Press, 1986); and Emily Honig, *Sisters and Strangers: Women in the Shanghai Cotton Mills, 1919–1949* (Stanford, Calif.: Stanford University Press, 1986).

[4] Useful general overviews of the literature on student protest can be found in Donald Phillips, *Student Protest, 1960–1970* (New York: University Press of America, 1985); and

solve the question of why we find such different emphases in the literature on *zhishifenzi* as opposed to other kinds of protesters, but a couple of factors are worth mentioning in passing. One is that intelligentsia activists are more likely than rice rioters to leave detailed accounts justifying or explaining why they did what they did; another is that the scholars who study *zhishifenzi* protesters often personally identify with their subjects such that they become more comfortable using approaches associated with intellectual history and biography as opposed to cultural anthropology. Whatever the reason, in both China and the West, the social history of student activism has only recently begun to receive serious attention, and until very recently ethnographic approaches to campus unrest were extremely rare indeed.[5]

We first became interested in this phenomenon in the mid-1980s, when we were doing the background research for a piece on Shanghai student protests of the Republican era (1912–49). In surveying the extant scholarly literature on Chinese youth movements, we were struck by the fact that it was composed almost entirely of works that presented straightforward narratives of particular events, analyzed the ideas espoused by certain types of student activists, or tried to reconstruct the organizational activities of campus groups that were closely linked to one or another political party. Many of these works provided insight into the intellectual and political history of individual student movements, but significant pieces seemed to be missing from the general picture of Chinese campus activism they provided. In our article, which appeared in print (appropriately enough) at the beginning of 1989, we argued that in order to place events such as the May Fourth movement of 1919 and the December Ninth movement of 1935 into a more nuanced perspective, closer attention should be paid to the ways in which the highly organized nature of university daily life and patterns of student interaction facilitated and left their imprint on outbursts of collective action.[6] To illustrate this point, our attention concentrated on issues

Seymour Lipset and Philip Altbach, eds., *Students in Revolt* (Boston: Houghton Mifflin, 1969), which includes an important chapter on Chinese protests by John Israel.

[5]For citations relating to the Chinese case and further discussion of historiographic trends, see Jeffrey N. Wasserstrom, *Student Protests in Twentieth-Century China: The View from Shanghai* (Stanford, Calif.: Stanford University Press, 1991). For representative examples of PRC scholarship on the topic, see the translations on student activism included in Elizabeth J. Perry and Jeffrey N. Wasserstrom, eds., *Shanghai Social Movements, 1919–1949*, a special double issue of *Chinese Studies in History* 27, nos. 1–2 (Fall–Winter 1993–94).

[6]Jeffrey N. Wasserstrom and Liu Xinyong, "Student Protest and Student Life, Shanghai 1919–1949," *Social History* 14, no. 1 (1989): 1–30.

relating to mobilization, rather than to the vanguard roles of formally constituted political organizations in general, and to groups linked to the Nationalist and Communist parties in particular, which had already received sufficient notice. As important as these kinds of associations were, we claimed, other, less formal or less explicitly political groups (ranging from native-place societies to sports teams) often played equally or even more important roles in providing students with the skills and connections that they needed to stage effective collective protests.

The arguments concerning pre-1949 protests presented in our *Social History* article seem less novel now than they did when we began working on the piece in 1986, since several important studies of intelligentsia activism that highlight related themes have appeared since then. Thanks to these works by scholars such as Yeh Wen-hsin, Zhang Jishun, and Hans van de Ven, historians interested in the Republican era now have a much more nuanced picture than before of the social and political worlds in which Chinese students lived and took public action.[7] In addition, several important studies of post-1949 youth movements now exist that draw attention to the links between patterns of campus life and those of mass action.[8]

This said, the burgeoning literature on contemporary student activism continues to have some of the same shortcomings as the literature on Republican era activism that we critiqued in our *Social History* essay. This is because, with some important exceptions that are discussed in more detail below, studies of 1989 rarely address the centrally important social-historical question of how, precisely, students were able to mobilize themselves so rapidly and effectively for coherent large-scale group action. Only a few essays have been published thus far that focus directly

---

[7]Yeh Wen-hsin, *The Alienated Academy: Culture and Politics in Republican China, 1919–1937* (Cambridge, Mass.: Harvard University Press, 1990); Hans van de Ven, *From Friend to Comrade* (Berkeley: University of California Press, 1992); and Zhang Jishun, "Lun Shanghai zhengzhi yundongzhong de xuesheng qunti, 1925–1927 nian" (A discussion of student groups in Shanghai political movements, 1925–1927), translated in Perry and Wasserstrom, *Shanghai Social Movements*, 65–83. See also Ming K. Chan and Arif Dirlik, *Schools into Farms and Factories: Anarchists, the Guomindang, and the National Labor University in Shanghai, 1927–1932* (Durham, N.C.: Duke University Press, 1991).

[8]Two works of this sort that resonate particularly well with the arguments we present below are Corinna-Barbara Francis, "The Progress of Protest in China: The Student Movement of the Spring of 1989," *Asian Survey* 29, no. 1 (1990): 898–915; and Sebastian Heilman, *Die Gegen-Kulturrevolution in der VR China. Die Bewegung vom 5. April und der soziale Protest der siebziger Jahre* (The Countercultural Revolution in the PRC: The April Fifth Movement and the Grass Roots Protest of the 1970s) (Hamburg: Institut für Asienkunde, 1994). We are grateful to Dr. Heilman for bringing the latter to our attention when it was still a work in progress, and for providing us with several unpublished English-language essays that expand upon discussions in his book.

on the organizational dynamics of the student movement, and in these works (as in most of the many general narrative accounts of the events of 1989 by journalists, participants, and scholars that have appeared) most of the discussion centers on the activities of a handful of highly visible *shetuan* (associations), such as Beijing University's famous Min-zhu Shalong (Democracy Salon) and the Beijing Autonomous Students Association (BASU). Only rarely do commentators note that the protests of 1989 broke out at a time when (as Shaoguang Wang points out in Chapter 6) a plethora of clubs and interest groups without explicitly political agendas were being formed in cities (and schools) throughout the country. These works also tend to have little or nothing to say about the role that officially sponsored organizations, such as campus branches of the Communist Youth League (CYL), may have played in laying the organizational groundwork for the protests of 1989.

What emerges, in other words, is a vision of student mobilization that might, for heuristic purposes, be called a "salon-centered" one, which overstresses the importance of certain actors and particular kinds of organizations and underemphasizes patterns of daily life. This chapter draws on new data provided primarily by interviews and observation, as well as the discussions of a few specialists (such as political scientist Corinna-Barbara Francis, sociologist Craig Calhoun, and anthropologist Frank Pieke) whose works on 1989 have highlighted the connections between ordinary practices and protest activities, to sketch out and defend a different view of the mobilization process. Before describing this alternative approach in any more detail, however, it is worth taking some time to examine the empirical and theoretical attractions of a salon-centered style of analysis, since these are by no means inconsiderable.

THE SALON-CENTERED APPROACH

One of the great attractions of a salon-centered approach is that the only student organizations about which data are readily available are officially sanctioned campus associations and explicitly political dissident groups, since the former are discussed in official publications and the latter can be studied through wall posters and other texts from the movement itself, as well as through memoirs by protest leaders such as Li Lu.[9] In part simply because of the paucity of information con-

[9]See, for example, Han Minzhu, ed., *Cries for Democracy* (Princeton: Princeton University Press, 1990), esp. 135–37, 299–300; Shen Tong and Marianne Yeh, *Almost a Revolution* (Boston: Houghton-Mifflin, 1990); Li Lu, *Moving the Mountain* (London: Macmillan,

cerning other kinds of campus *shetuan*, most scholarly discussions of contemporary student associational life have focused on one or the other of these two types of organizations. In the case of government-sanctioned groups, writers such as Stanley Rosen have carefully documented the process by which students of the Dengist era have become increasingly alienated from the CYL and officially sponsored school unions.[10] In the case of dissident *shetuan*, scholars such as Josephine M. T. Khu and Woei Lien Chong have analyzed the organizational dynamics, composition, and ideological stances of several of the most important explicitly political groups to which one or more of the most prominent participants in the protests of 1989 belonged.[11]

These two groups of studies shed considerable light on the crisis of 1989. Most significantly, Rosen described shifts in student attitudes toward the Chinese Communist Party (CCP), and Khu and Chong, among others, indicate that students who became leaders of groups such as the BASU after the movement began were often the same people who had previously played central roles in campus salons. Unfortunately, when taken together, their studies can all too easily leave the impression that the late 1980s saw the emergence of a new breed of student leader, who seemingly came from nowhere to organize salons that filled the vacuum

1990); and Human Rights in China, *Children of the Dragon: The Story of Tiananmen Square* (New York: Macmillan, 1990), especially 46–67. For an excellent general overview of many relevant primary sources, see Helmut Martin, *China's Democracy Movement 1989: A Selected Bibliography of Chinese Source Materials* (Cologne: Bundesinstitut für ostwissenschaftliche und internationale Studien, 1990).

[10]The most important of these for our purposes is Stanley Rosen, "Students and the State in China: The Crisis in Ideology and Organization," in Arthur Rosenbaum, ed., *State and Society in China: The Consequences of Reform* (Boulder, Colo.: Westview Press, 1992), 167–91, the footnotes to which direct readers to his earlier essays on related topics. Additional comments on the CYL's declining prestige in the 1980s can be found in Hsi-sheng Ch'i, *Politics of Disillusionment: The Chinese Communist Party under Deng Xiaoping, 1978–1989* (Armonk, N.Y.: M. E. Sharpe, 1991), 146–50. During the protests of 1986, this process of alienation was obvious to anyone who read campus wall posters, since many of these referred to the leaders of official campus groups as "running dogs" who had no interest in democracy. The authors saw wall posters of this sort in Shanghai, and comparable Hangzhou texts were described in a personal communication from Kristen Parris to Jeffrey Wasserstrom, August 24, 1992.

[11]Woei Lien Chong, "Petitioners, Popperians, and Hunger Strikers: The Uncoordinated Efforts of the 1989 Chinese Democratic Movement," in Tony Saich, ed., *The Chinese People's Movement: Perspectives on Spring 1989* (Armonk, N.Y.: M. E. Sharpe, 1990), 106–25; Josephine M. T. Khu, "Student Organization in the Movement," in Roger Des Forges, Luo Ning, and Wu Yenbo, eds., *Chinese Democracy and the Crisis of 1989: Chinese and American Reflections* (Albany: State University of New York Press, 1993), 161–76; Luo Qiping et al., "The 1989 Pro-Democracy Movement: Student Organizations and Strategies" (trans. Fons Lamboo), *China Information* 5, no. 2 (1990): 30–43, esp. 30.

created by the declining prestige of official student groups, and then after Hu's death naturally and logically shifted from founding campus-based dissident associations to establishing and directing citywide protest leagues.

Although this idealized image of the mobilization process is problematic in ways discussed in detail below, the main assumptions underlying it are firmly grounded in empirical evidence. As Rosen's work shows, public opinion polls and other sources (including CYL publications by authors who were undoubtedly displeased by the implications of their findings) demonstrate that official campus groups did indeed suffer a significant loss of legitimacy in the 1980s. And equally persuasive (though more anecdotal) evidence supports the notion that the leading figures in the protests of 1989 were often the same people who had previously been involved in explicitly political campus *shetuan*. That Wang Dan was a founding member of both Beijing University's Minzhu Shalong and the BASU is well known; Shen Tong's autobiography includes an account of the author playing leading roles in, first, a dissident *shetuan* known as the "Olympic Institute" and, later, a more broadly based protest group known as the "Dialogue Delegation"; and Liu Gang (a veteran of the 1986–87 protests and one of the more influential graduate students involved in the 1989 struggle) was a key figure in the world of Beijing campus salons.[12]

Autobiographical accounts by Tong Boqiao and Li Lu show, moreover, that Beijing dissident *shetuan* were not the only ones that provided training for future movement leaders. Tong describes a Hunan Normal University group that shared the same name as, but was not directly tied to, the Democracy Salon at Beijing University. According to Tong, this provincial Minzhu Shalong was a "tightly organized" association whose members included many of the students who "went on to become core leaders" of the local protest movement.[13] Li Lu's memoir also refers to a provincial group with a familiar name. He writes that, more than a year before he traveled to Beijing's Tiananmen Square and became Chai

---

[12] The activities of all of these figures are discussed in George Black and Robin Munro, *Black Hands of Beijing: Lives of Defiance in China's Democracy Movement* (New York: John Wiley and Sons, 1993), 140–41 and passim, as well as in Shen and Yeh, *Almost a Revolution*. The former work, which focuses primarily on figures such as Wang Juntao who first became politically involved in the late 1970s, is particularly useful when it comes to tracing the connections between different generations of dissident intellectuals.

[13] Tong Boqiao, comp. and Robin Munro, ed., *Anthems of Defeat: Crackdown in Hunan Province, 1989–92* (New York: Asia Watch, 1992), 4.

Ling's deputy, he was a central figure in a Nanjing University salon known as the "Olympic Institute," a group that appears to have had no direct connection with Shen Tong's *shetuan,* beyond the fact that members of each were admirers of the European society of that name whose founders included Albert Einstein.[14]

In addition to the continuities relating to personnel that emerge from materials such as memoirs, even a cursory examination of the documents circulated by dissident students before and after the founding of groups such as the BASU indicates that ideological ties also linked salons to protest leagues. Many of the phrases and arguments found in the proclamations that protest leagues issued between the end of April and the beginning of June were strikingly like those that had appeared previously in speeches, wall posters, and magazine articles associated with salon-type organizations. This kind of continuity is stressed in a *Far Eastern Economic Review* report on the rise of the student movement entitled "From Salon to Street."[15]

An additional attraction of a salon-centered approach to 1989 is that it fits so well with much of the literature on comparative student movements. Most notably, it suggests that Frank Pinner's work on West European protests after World War II can be easily applied to the Chinese case. Pinner claims that, in the case of European campuses of the 1950s and 1960s, it is useful to distinguish between the different political roles played by *socializing organizations* (such as fraternities and school councils), whose main goals were to prepare youths for preestablished occupational and social roles that awaited them upon graduation, and *transgressive organizations* (such as militant student trade unions and protest leagues), whose members were interested in challenging the status quo and creating new roles for themselves in public life. While Pinner is quick to admit that members of socializing organizations sometimes ended up taking part in radical movements, he insists that in most cases they served as a conservative force, a brake on militant student activism. According to his arguments, the groups that provide student movements with their core activists tend to be transgressive organizations, the category in which the Chinese salons of the late 1980s clearly belong.[16]

---

[14]Li, *Moving the Mountain.*

[15]Louise de Rosario, "From Salon to Street," *Far Eastern Economic Review,* May 4, 1989, 11–12.

[16]Frank A. Pinner, "Tradition and Transgression: Western European Students in the Postwar World," *Daedalus* 97, no. 1 (Winter 1968): 137–55, esp. p. 142. Scholars interested in American student activism have seldom discussed the issue in such a direct fashion,

Another kind of theoretical support for a salon-centered approach can be found in several recent discussions of modern China that relate popular upheaval to a strengthening of "civil society," an expanding "public sphere," or some combination of the two. The question of whether and how these terms should be applied to any period in China's past is a subject of intense debate within the field, and a subject that has received considerable attention in discussions among Wilson Center workshop participants, before, during, and since the May 1992 gathering. There is still little consensus within the China field on this issue, and even those who are most convinced of the analytical or heuristic value of the terms in question continue to define the concepts in widely varying ways, invoking the names of theorists as diverse as Jean-Jacques Rousseau, Antonio Gramsci, and Jurgen Habermas to support their positions.[17] Nonetheless, at the broadest level of generalization, there is considerable agreement, at least in some quarters, that the reformist policies of the 1980s should be seen as having helped to create a situation in which the urban public sphere expanded and civil society was strengthened. Working from this premise, some scholars have claimed that the increase in political space available for autonomous (i.e., non–state-controlled) forms of organizational, commercial, artistic, and intellectual activities played an important role in making the protests of 1989 possible and

but their narratives often suggest the same kind of situation. The scholarly and popular literature on the topic is filled with cases in which one sees a small band of dedicated activists belonging to an unofficial and explicitly political organization (such as Students for a Democratic Society—SDS) successfully mobilizing large numbers of previously uncommitted students for action; see, e.g., Todd Gitlin, *The Sixties: Years of Hope, Days of Rage* (New York: Bantam, 1987). Members of other types of campus groups (such as fraternities, school councils, sports teams, and the Reserve Officers Training Corps—ROTC) are shown either remaining uninvolved or playing active roles in trying to discredit or disrupt radical protests. For cases in point, see William Friedland and Harry Edwards, "Confrontation at Cornell," in Alexander DeConde, *Student Activism: Town and Gown in Historical Perspective* (New York: Charles Scribner's Sons, 1971), 318–36; Robert P. Cohen, "Revolt of the Depression Generation: America's First Mass Student Protest Movement, 1929–1940," Ph.D. diss., University of California, Berkeley, 1987, 156–57, 316–18; and Helen Lefkowitz Horowitz, *Campus Life: Undergraduate Cultures from the End of the Eighteenth Century to the Present* (New York: Knopf, 1987), 169 and 239. There were, of course, exceptions to this pattern in the United States; as some of these same works indicate (see, e.g., Cohen, "Revolt," 309) some members of socializing groups became leading activists in the 1930s and 1960s. Nonetheless, Pinner's ideas appear to work as well for the American case as they do for the European one.

[17]Perhaps the best way to get a sense of the competing definitions being advanced, and to understand what is at stake in the debate over these concepts, is to read the contributions to Philip Huang, ed., *Symposium: "Public Sphere"/"Civil Society" in China?* a special issue of *Modern China* 19, no. 2 (1993).

shaping the course these protests took.[18] Since salons were quintessentially "civil" organizations that often sponsored events described as
"public" forums, it should come as no surprise that campus *shetuan* of
this sort are often mentioned in discussions of the issue.

Yet another attraction of a salon-centered approach to 1989 is that it
suits the image that some protesters tried to project of themselves as
participants in a "New May Fourth movement" that would carry forth
a tradition of enlightened political engagement dating back seventy
years. The activities of salon-type groups of the May Fourth era have
been carefully documented by CCP historians in a multivolume work
devoted to this subject, and several recent essays by Western analysts
highlight the parallels between the groups discussed in that collection
and those that have emerged in the contemporary era.[19] In a chapter
written for another conference volume, for example, Wilson Center
workshop participant Martin K. Whyte claims that, in the late 1980s,
"a large number of 'cultural salons' sprang up in which intellectuals,
students, and others debated the problems of China's cultural tradition,
much as their May Fourth–era predecessors had done."[20]

If a salon-centered approach has all these attractions, why do we find
it so problematic? The reason is that, if one looks more closely at the
basic assumptions, empirical data, theoretical connections, and historical
parallels alluded to above, they all start to seem less convincing. In addition, our previous studies of Chinese students of earlier eras have made
us wary of both attempts to draw sharp lines of demarcation between
campus groups that serve "transgressive" and "socializing" functions

---

[18]Elizabeth J. Perry and Ellen Fuller, "China's Long March to Democracy," *World Policy Journal* (Fall 1991): 663–85; Tu Wei-ming, "Intellectual Effervescence in China," *Daedalus* 121, no. 2 (Spring 1992): 251–92; Craig Calhoun, "Tiananmen, Television and the Public Sphere: Internationalization of Culture and the Beijing Spring," *Public Culture* 2, no. 1 (Fall 1989): 54–71; David Kelley, "Emergent Civil Society and the Intellectuals in China," in Robert P. Miller, ed., *The Development of Civil Society in Communist Systems* (London: Allen and Unwin, 1992); Lawrence Sullivan, "The Emergence of Civil Society in China, Spring 1989," in Saich, ed., *The Chinese People's Movement*, 126–44; Tang Tsou, "The Tiananmen Tragedy: The State-Society Relationship, Choices, and Mechanisms in Historical Perspective," in Brantley Womack, ed., *Contemporary Chinese Politics in Historical Perspective* (Cambridge: Cambridge University Press, 1991), 265–328.

[19]*Wusi shiqi de shetuan* (Social organizations of the May Fourth era), 4 vols. (Beijing: Shenghuo-Dushu-Xinzhi sanlian shudian, 1979). Effective use of these materials has been made in several works by scholars based outside China, including most recently Arif Dirlik, *The Origins of Chinese Communism* (New York: Oxford University Press, 1989), and van de Ven, *From Friend to Comrade*.

[20]Martin K. Whyte, "Urban China: A Civil Society in the Making?" in Rosenbaum, *State and Society in China*, 77–101.

and models for explaining youth mobilization strategies that focus exclusively on associations with explicitly political purposes.

In light of the efforts contemporary students have made to link their protests to those of 1919, a consideration of May Fourth–era campus life seems an appropriate place to start our discussion of these last two points. Transgressive *shetuan* certainly played a central role in the 1918 protests demanding an end to secret negotiations between Chinese ministers and Japanese officials that set the stage for the May Fourth movement proper, as well as in the much larger demonstrations against the Treaty of Versailles and the "Three Traitorous Officials" that took place in 1919 itself. However, in both these struggles, less overtly political student groups also figured prominently. For example, provincial native-place associations (*tongxianghui*), to which most or perhaps all Chinese youths studying in Japan belonged, played crucial organizational roles in the 1918 protests, which began in Tokyo and then spread to several Chinese cities. A year later, when the May Fourth movement came to Shanghai, the local chapter of the Chinese Boy Scouts shifted rapidly from functioning as a quintessentially *socializing* association to one that took on protest tasks such as providing teams of march monitors for demonstrations and rallies.[21]

The situation was much the same during the May Thirtieth movement of 1925, during which even activists at radical Shanghai University found that joining explicitly political associations was not enough. If you wanted to "get anything done," according to one former student organizer, you also had to join other kinds of groups, such as native-place societies.[22] The same was true during the December Ninth movement of 1935, since (at least according to one former participant interviewed in the 1980s) not only *tongxianghui* but also other types of socializing groups even less often thought of as helping to further radical causes (such as sports teams) played central roles in that struggle. Our informant claims that Fudan's Guangdong *tongxianghui* emerged as a core group in the protests of both 1935 and 1936, thanks largely to the popularity of one of its members, who was both an underground Communist organizer and a player on the school's highly successful volleyball

[21]On the 1918 protests, see Hu Hou, "Ji wusi yundong qianhou liuri xuesheng de aiguo yundong" (A record of the patriotic activities of Chinese students in Japan before and after the May Fourth movement), in *Wusi yundong huiyilu* (Memoirs of the May Fourth movement) (Beijing: Chinese Academy of Social Science, 1979), III: 457–59; on the Boy Scouts and May Fourth, see Wasserstrom, *Student Protests*, 82–83.
[22]Zhong Fuguang, cited in Wasserstrom and Liu, "Student Protest," 13.

team, which happened to be composed almost exclusively of students from the Guangzhou region. When things got rough in a post–December Ninth protest at the Shanghai train station, the activist recalled, it was only natural that the volleyball team (which he described as being composed of big youths used to working together as a group) took charge of running interference between the demonstrators and the police.[23] Memoirs recounting antigovernment protests of the 1940s are filled with comparable instances in which the activities of transgressive and socializing groups overlapped during the growth of student movements. Just as the leaders of radical movements of the 1920s often benefited from the prestige, skills, and interpersonal connections they had acquired as activists in both politically oriented study societies and *tongxianghui*, their counterparts of the Civil War era (1945–49) were often linked to a range of campus *shetuan*, from religious fellowships to underground Communist cells.[24]

CIVIL SOCIETY AND THE PUBLIC SPHERE

The preceding discussion raises doubts about the usefulness of Pinner's categories for understanding Chinese student activism, but it does not necessarily call into question the assumptions relating to "civil society" and the "public sphere" referred to above. After all, the kinds of campus groups that Pinner labels socializing groups, such as native-place societies and religious fellowships, were often as autonomous of the state as radical study societies. In fact, scholars such as David Strand and William Rowe, who have recently argued persuasively that late Imperial and early Republican Chinese society and politics were more open and fluid in certain ways than was previously thought, have highlighted the existence and expanded influence of groups based on ties such as native place in their portrayal of a growing (although still fragile) civil society and an expanded (although still restricted) public sphere.[25] And while

[23]In order to encourage candor, these and other Chinese interview subjects were assured that their anonymity would be protected.
[24]For details and relevant citations, see Wasserstrom and Liu, "Student Protest," 8–11; and Wasserstrom, *Student Protests*, 139–41.
[25]David Strand, " 'Civil Society' and 'Public Sphere' in Modern China: A Perspective on Popular Movements in Beijing, 1919–1989," *Duke Working Papers in Asian/Pacific Studies* (Durham, N.C.: Asian/Pacific Studies Institute, 1990), a revised version of which appears in Des Forges et al., *Chinese Democracy*, 53–85, under the title "Civil Society and Public Sphere in Modern Chinese History"; William Rowe, *Hankow: Commerce and Society in a Chinese City, 1796–1889* (Stanford, Calif.: Stanford University Press,

religious groups have received little attention in this literature, they figure centrally in discussions of the role that rejuvenated civil societies played in fostering the transformation of various East European countries in the late 1980s.[26]

The history of student protest in China does, however, make me wary of at least two general features of at least some treatments of 1989 that rely on notions of civil society and the public sphere. First, although those who take seriously the work of the great theorists of civil society (a list that includes Gramsci, as well as Rousseau and Habermas) need not do so, many of those who have applied this concept to contemporary China pay too little attention to the variations in civil societies and public spheres of differing cultures and differing time periods. Primarily concerned with highlighting certain processes (the development of capitalism and democratic political institutions) that (in the West) have accompanied an increase in the power of society vis-à-vis the state, the literature on Chinese civil society often gives the impression that all that is important is quantifying the number, scope, and influence of two groups: those controlled by the regime and those operating with some degree of autonomy. Measuring the size of the public sphere and assessing the power of civil society associations thus takes priority over figuring out how flesh-and-blood actors in a given context organize themselves for action and use the political space available to them.

Some China specialists interested in the concepts have stressed that different countries are likely to have different civil societies, and that public spheres may be dissimilar in various lands. Elizabeth Perry and Ellen Fuller's recent essay on the topic is an important case in point. Their piece highlights the unusually important role that mass movements have played (and are likely to continue to play) in the development of Chinese civil society. The authors also draw attention to the Taylor-Chatterjee interchange on civil society, in which the latter stresses contrasts between the Western and third world situations.[27]

Exceptions such as this article aside, however, the variable content and form of civil societies and public spheres has received too little at-

---

1984); idem, *Hankow: Conflict and Community in a Chinese City, 1796–1895* (Stanford, Calif.: Stanford University Press, 1989); idem, "The Public Sphere in Modern China," *Modern China* 16, no. 3 (July 1990): 309–29.

[26]See, for example, Sabrina P. Ramet, *Social Currents in Eastern Europe: The Sources and Meaning of the Great Transformation* (Durham: Duke University Press, 1991), 42–52 and 133–72.

[27]Perry and Fuller, "China's Long March to Democracy."

tention. Thus one finds comparative discussions of Eastern Europe and China in the late 1980s that contrast the strength of civil society in the former with its weakness in the latter, without looking closely at qualitative differences between the traditions of, say, Polish clerics and Chinese entrepreneurs (two groups associated with the carving out of public spheres for autonomous action in their respective lands). This culturally and historically flattened approach to civil society, and the assumptions associated with it concerning the inevitable connection between capitalism and democratization, is important not only because of its influence on Western China specialists but also because of its impact on Chinese dissidents themselves. A speech given in the early 1990s by Wan Runnan, who is both president of the Stone Corporation and a leader of Minzhen (Federation for a Democratic China), illustrates this point. Speaking at Berkeley's China Forum, Wan's topic was the "development of the private sector in China and its relationship with the establishment of a civil society." He began by noting that "civil society was totally wiped out" during the "first years of totalitarian rule by the Chinese communists," then proceeded to make the following statement:

Now as we all know, democracy is to a large degree based upon the existence of a very exuberant civil society, *gongmin shehui*. I recently talked with Yu Yingshi at Princeton University and he delved into this lack of civil society in China, which in his opinion is the major difference between Chinese and Western society.[28]

If Wan used this statement as a starting point for exploration and went on to provide evidence to support his assumptions, we would not single it out for criticism. Unfortunately, as has happened too often in the discourse on 1989, the statement was left to stand on its own as though it was axiomatic. Wan felt no need to defend the assumption that the more vibrant the civil society and market economy of a given land, the more democratic its political institutions would be. This assumption is troubling for several reasons and open to question on a variety of grounds. Nevertheless what is of the greatest concern here is that this assumption infers that civil society can be understood in quantitative terms—that an equation can be formulated and solved without reference to qualitative issues, such as the institutions, traditions, and symbols that make a particular society tick.[29]

[28]Wan Runnan, "Capitalism and Democracy in China (I)," *China Forum Newsletter* 2, no. 2 (February 1992): 1–4.
[29]For discussion of other kinds of problems with or ambiguities in the Chinese studies

The problem with this idea is that, as one of us argues in an article on 1989 co-written with Joseph Esherick, the Chinese and European cases are qualitatively as well as quantatively different with regard to civil society institutions. For example, that piece emphasizes that even some of the most hierarchically constituted European social organizations often have democratic traditions relating to the selection of leaders. This is true of the Catholic Church, in which the pope (for all his power) is still elected.[30] Rather than delve more deeply into East European contrasts here, however, we would like to underscore the need to eschew a quantitative vision of civil society by looking briefly at the problems such an approach engenders with respect to historical analogies between the 1980s and the warlord era.[31]

The years immediately preceding the protest movement of 1989 were undeniably, like those that preceded the struggles of 1919 and 1925, ones in which a wide variety of student associations were formed.[32] It is likewise undeniable that the months leading up to the June 4 massacre were ones in which members of other urban groups were engaged in a flurry of organizational activity, as chapters in this volume by Shaoguang

discourse on "civil society," see Frederic Wakeman, Jr., "The Civil Society and Public Sphere Debate: Western Reflections on Chinese Political Culture," in Huang, *Symposium*, 108–38. Different perspectives on the issue that should also be taken into account are provided by other pieces that appear in the same *Modern China* forum: William T. Rowe, "The Problem of 'Civil Society' in Late Imperial China" (139–57), and Mary B. Rankin, "Some Observations on a Chinese Public Sphere" (158–82), are, in part at least, intended as responses to Wakeman's critique; whereas Heath B. Chamberlain, "On the Search for Civil Society in China" (199–215), expands on some of the critical themes Wakeman raises.

[30]Joseph W. Esherick and Jeffrey N. Wasserstrom, "Acting Out Democracy: Political Theater in Modern China," in Jeffrey N. Wasserstrom and Elizabeth J. Perry, eds., *Popular Protest and Political Culture in Modern China*, 2d ed. (Boulder, Colo.: Westview Press, 1994), 32–69.

[31]For a valuable survey of recent Eastern European events, see Daniel Chirot, "What Happened in Eastern Europe in 1989?" in Wasserstrom and Perry, *Popular Protest,* 218–45. For discussions of specific issues related to civil society, see the sources Chirot cites on page 243, as well as various chapters in Miller, *Development.*

[32]The CYL was well aware of the growing importance of unofficial youth clubs and societies during the mid-1980s. In response, it tried to shift its attention away from strictly political concerns and focus as well on the social and cultural needs of youths. City branches of the CYL tried to create new roles for themselves, either as supervisory agencies that would keep track of and oversee the activities of the new *shetuan,* or as founders of competing dance clubs, teahouses, and recreation societies. Jin Guohua, "Lun qingnian shao qunti" (A discussion of small groups formed by youth), in Wang Min et al., eds., *Qingnian yu qingniangongzuo yanjiu wenji* (Collected articles on youth and youth work) (Shanghai: Shanghai qingnian guanli ganbu xueyuan, 1986), 44–55; Ch'i, *Politics of Disillusionment,* 149–50; authors' discussions with Shanghai CYL leaders during the 1980s.

Wang, Elizabeth Perry, Nancy Chen, Mark Sidel, and others demonstrate. These facts are certainly worth mentioning, and the search for "sprouts of civil society" in these two eras is by no means a pointless one, since newly formed *shetuan* clearly played key roles in shaping the mass movements of 1919, 1925, and 1989. The problem with simply stating these things and then moving on is that to do so obscures key differences between the civil society organizing of the warlord and Dengist eras—differences that have important ramifications where the evolution of movements carried out in the name of democracy are concerned. One of the most significant of these differences has to do with class boundaries. The campus organizations formed in the 1980s tended to be based on a single class. Exceptions to this were groups whose members included both people active in private enterprises like the Stone Corporation and people affiliated with universities. But the "multiclass" nature of some of these groups was ambiguous at best, since many of the entrepreneurs involved were also *zhishifenzi* in the broader sense of the Chinese term.[33] Like the legal associations and labor unions that Mark Sidel and Elizabeth Perry describe in their chapters, but unlike the *qigong* groups that interest Nancy Chen, campus groups seldom established connections between intellectuals and workers.

The situation was very different in the warlord era. Some of the pre–May Fourth equivalents of the democracy salons of the 1980s were popular lecture corps whose main reason for being was to bring students into contact with workers and peasants.[34] Many of the leaders of the May Thirtieth movement, meanwhile, came to their participation in protest mass actions via campus associations that had been involved in helping workers set up laborers' clubs and unions. It is also worth noting

[33]Michael Bonin and Yves Chèvrier, "The Intellectual and the State," *China Quarterly*, no. 127 (September 1991): 569–93. Wan Runnan ("Capitalism and Democracy in China") highlights the significance of the fact that an entrepreneur such as himself rather than an intellectual is head of one of the main dissident organizations attempting to attain the goals of the 1989 protests. But as various other China specialists have noted, despite Wan's status as a former head of the Stone Corporation and a current leader of Minzhen, he is in an important sense still a *zhishifenzi*.

[34]Admittedly, there was an elitism inherent in these groups, since they were intended to go to the masses in the traditional role of intellectuals imparting knowledge to the *laobaixing* (common people). Nonetheless, the simple fact that they made concerted and organized efforts to reach out even to those living in villages that were far removed from their campuses is significant, as Mark Selden stresses in his essay "The Social Origins and Limits of the Democratic Movement," in Des Forges et al., eds., *Chinese Democracy*, 107–31.

that campus *tongxianghui* often had close ties to citywide native-place leagues (*huiguan*), which established networks between members of all social classes from a given place of origin.[35]

If we want to understand the differing kinds of difficulties that student activists of the 1980s and their counterparts of the warlord era had in forging links with members of other classes, it seems sensible to start with contrasts in the types of civil societies in which they were operating. It seems sensible, that is, if one does not begin with the assumption that civil society is civil society is civil society. That assumption also preempts the asking of various related questions for which we do not have ready answers, but which we feel are worth exploring. For example, how might the differing civil society traditions in the two eras help explain why no major May Fourth–era student protest league leaders were female, while in 1989 (although most high-profile student leaders were once again male) Chai Ling emerged as one of the most prominent figures involved in the occupation of Tiananmen Square?[36]

A related feature of the discourse on civil society and 1989 that troubles us has to do with the hegemonic power of rituals and cultural norms associated with the state. Although there is no reason for those who take Rousseau, Gramsci, or Habermas seriously to do so, many of those who have applied their concepts to China assume that groups operating autonomously from the state apparatus will be relatively unaffected by official social and cultural orthodoxies, especially if such groups think of themselves as espousing ideologies that are counterhegemonic. By this line of reasoning, since salons and autonomous student unions were civil society institutions whose members were committed to democratic ideals different from those of the CCP, we can assume that they would have little in common with official organizations in terms of structure and function. Our own reading of events such as the May Fourth movement leads us to think that this assumption greatly underestimates the power hegemonic patterns of behavior have to structure social and cultural life, even in the midst of movements for radical change.

[35]For background information on these groups, see Bryna Goodman, "New Culture, Old Habits: Native-Place Organization and the May Fourth Movement," in Frederic Wakeman, Jr., and Yeh Wen-hsin, eds., *Shanghai Sojourners* (Berkeley: Institute of East Asian Studies, 1992), 76–107.

[36]We have yet to see much discussion of the role that female leaders and women's groups played in the recent changes in Eastern Europe, but certainly there too it is worth asking about the significance of gender in "democratic" civil society traditions.

STUDENT ORGANIZING AND THE STATE

Participants in the May Fourth movement have been portrayed (with some justification) as "radical iconoclasts"—people who saw themselves as rebelling against the whole Confucian order in a desperate attempt to create a truly "new" China. New Culture movement rhetoric attacked a wide range of values the activists associated with "Chinese tradition." Thus the promotion of social-status hierarchies, subordination of women, love of bureaucratization, and the tendency to be suspicious of individuality and free thought, which radical intellectuals of the day linked to Confucianism, all came under attack. When May Fourth protest activities began in 1919, many participants in this struggle had been steeped in the ideas of the New Culture movement, and many leaders of the new student protest unions were veterans of study societies and popular lecture associations formed to search for and propagate ideologies (ranging from anarchism to Social Darwinism) conceived of as radically unorthodox. Since so many of their core participants were self-professed opponents of the traditional order, and had strong ties to groups that were part of a nascent civil society and had been operating within an expanding public sphere of popular action and debate, one would expect the protest leagues and work teams that grew up in the aftermath of the May Fourth movement to have little in common with organs of the Chinese state.

Ironically, however, as we have argued elsewhere, the mass movement that developed in 1919 was organized along quite "traditional" lines.[37] The boycotting of Japanese goods was enforced in large part by *shirentuan* (groups of ten), which bore more than a passing resemblance to the smallest collectivity in that most "Confucian" and bureaucratized of social control structures, the *baojia* mutual responsibility system.[38] Student *shirentuan*, like those organized by other protesters, had designated leaders, as well as other officers with special responsibilities, and (in theory at least) were incorporated into larger groups of one hundred

---

[37]Wasserstrom, *Student Protests*, 57–60 and passim.

[38]One can argue that the *baojia* system is actually more Legalist than Confucian in nature, or at least a synthetic creation (the suspiciousness of the former combined with the interest in social relations and hierarchies of the latter). Whatever its actual philosophical underpinnings, however, it was certainly a part of the general structure that New Culture movement activists meant when they wrote of the "Confucian" cultural tradition. We are grateful to Melissa Macauley for comments on an earlier draft concerning this point.

(ten *shirentuan*) and one thousand (one hundred *shirentuan*) run by still more elaborate bureaucracies.

The *shirentuan* were not, moreover, the only Republican era protest groups that resembled state organs, for the dissident unions formed by educated youths had many features (security forces, propaganda bureaus, carefully spelled out hierarchies) reminiscent of the official associations (Western treaty-port as well as Chinese) to which the student activists had been exposed. Resemblances to formal government structures can play a crucial role in empowering protest leagues, since by their very existence such groups call into question the legitimacy of the status quo by raising doubts about the ruling regime's monopoly on authority. Nonetheless, there is a dark side to this phenomenon where democratization and related issues are concerned, for in the process of (consciously or unconsciously) imitating official organizations, protest groups often internalize some of the less appealing features of the orders they oppose.[39]

This was certainly true during the May Fourth movement, in which, to return to the example of gender, the distribution of power between men and women within protest leagues was far from equal. Little detailed information on this matter is available, but the lack of female students in positions of high leadership is a key piece of evidence. One other sign of the persistence of traditional role casting, despite New Culture movement calls for an end to Confucian subordination of women, is that (as far as we have been able to tell) the most important assignment given to the women's branch of the local student union in Shanghai in 1919 was to sew special caps for protesters to don at rallies.[40]

Writings on 1989 have made it clear that the protest leagues that spearheaded this "New May Fourth movement" were plagued by some of the same problems as the organizations of the party-state they challenged. Most non-CCP works on 1989 highlight positive features of the protest movement, praising the students for their commitment to nonviolence and their interest in new ideas. These same works also point out that the political decision-making process carried out in the open

[39]For an extended discussion of the tendency for Republican-era student protesters to improvise on official forms, which draws on the work of social theorists such as Charles Tilly and Clifford Geertz, see Wasserstrom, *Student Protests*, 65–71, 90–94, and 283–93.

[40]Ibid., 63–64.

spaces of Tiananmen Square was much more inclusive and egalitarian than that practiced in the Great Hall of the People. As valid as these points are, however, even sympathetic observers and analysts have noted that the political community and the alternative government created in the square also had their dark sides. Foreign eyewitnesses have accused specific student leaders of behaving too much like the CCP officials whose actions the youths condemned, charging the youths with everything from mishandling funds to using security guards to keep themselves aloof from ordinary members of their constituency, to creating their own personality cults.[41] Documents such as the June Second Hunger Strike Proclamation show, moreover, that even at the height of the movement, some dissidents were concerned that the protesters were falling into familiar traps of enforced orthodoxies of opinion, bureaucratization, and the like.[42] The failure of the protesters to form effective multiclass organizations, while perhaps partly attributable to the single-class nature of so many pre-movement civil society associations (a point alluded to above) must also be seen as due in part to student internalization of hegemonic ideas relating to social status hierarchies.[43] Similarly, in 1989 as in 1919, radical iconoclasts fell into traditional patterns regarding issues of gender and power.[44]

[41]Sample critiques of the movement that highlight one or more of these themes include: Sarah Lubman, "The Myth of Tiananmen: The Students Preached Democracy but They Didn't Practice It," *Washington Post*, July 30, 1989; Jane Macartney, "The Students: Heroes, Pawns, or Power-Brokers," in George Hicks, *The Broken Mirror: China After Tiananmen* (London: Longman, 1990), 3–23; Anita Chan, "The Social Origins and Consequences of the Tiananmen Crisis," in David S. G. Goodman and Gerald Segal, eds., *China in the Nineties: Crisis Management and Beyond* (Oxford: Clarendon Press; 1991), 105–30; and various chapters in Wasserstrom and Perry, *Popular Protest.*

[42]For a translation of this important document, see Han, *Cries,* 349–54. The most insightful discussions to date of the critiques of the movement by Chinese dissidents have been by Gérémie Barmé. See, e.g., his comments on figures such as Liu Xiaobo in "Traveling Heavy: The Intellectual Baggage of the Chinese Diaspora," *Problems of Communism* (January–April 1991): 94–114, as well as various introductory sections and translations in his and Linda Javin's tour de force anthology, *New Ghosts, Old Dreams: Chinese Rebel Voices* (New York: Random House, 1992). Liu Xiaobo continues to be one of the most interesting and controversial critical voices within the dissident camp; see, e.g., his "That Holy Word, Revolution," in Wasserstrom and Perry, *Popular Protest,* 309–24.

[43]For more extensive comments on this point, see Elizabeth J. Perry, "Casting a Chinese 'Democracy' Movement: The Roles of Students, Workers, and Entrepreneurs," in Wasserstrom and Perry, *Popular Protest,* 74–92.

[44]Much more research needs to be done on both the May Fourth and contemporary student movements where gender-related issues are concerned. Preliminary discussions of 1989 that have touched on such issues suggest, however, that many gender iniquities were replicated within the movement, even though a few women (such as Chai Ling and Wang Wen) rose to such prominent positions within dissident leagues and one of the struggle's

OFFICIAL ORGANIZATIONS

Lastly, the most basic (and most important) problem with a salon-centered approach is that official organizations, individuals enmeshed in the state apparatus, and activities carried out in the private sphere all played extremely significant roles in the evolution of the protests of 1989. Discussions of civil society and the public sphere direct our attention away from these topics, but their significance was stressed continually in discussions with eyewitnesses to the protests. The need to look closely at the activities of officially constituted organizations and remember the significance of connections (such as those forged by friendship) and events (such as secret meetings) that took place outside the "public sphere" is also stressed in some of the best published accounts of the protests of 1989.

The work unit. As officially constituted parts of the CCP's social welfare and social control systems, work units and smaller equivalent groups (such as the individual workshops into which a factory *danwei* is divided) can hardly be considered "civil" organizations. Nor can meetings that are held in work-unit rooms and are led by work-unit leaders be classified as ideal "public" gatherings, since not only are *danwei*s created by the state but they are also institutions that function in contemporary China as equivalents to the oldest of Chinese "private" sphere units, paternalistic lineages.[45] Nonetheless, when workers in the capital took part in the May demonstrations, they did so not as individuals or members of "autonomous" unions but as members of *danwei* delegations, which were usually organized with either the direct support or the passive approval of work-group leaders, and which were generally led onto the streets by people carrying flags emblazoned with the name of the unit.[46]

prominent symbols (the Goddess of Democracy) took a female form. For some preliminary comments on this topic, see Lee Feigon, "Gender and the Chinese Student Movement," in Wasserstrom and Perry, *Popular Protest*, 125–35.

[45]Lu Feng, "The Unit," in Barmé and Javin, *New Ghosts, Old Dreams*, 132–33. The following discussion of the work unit and the protest movement owes much to personal communications on the topic with Corinna-Barbara Francis, Melissa Macauley, and Kristen Parris. Written works that draw attention to the crucial role work units play in contemporary Chinese protest movements include Pieke, "The Ordinary and the Extraordinary"; and Sebastian Heilman, "The Social Context of Mobilization in China: Factions, Work Units, and Activists during the April Fifth Movement in 1976" (unpublished manuscript cited with author's permission).

[46]Frank Niming, "Learning How to Protest," in Saich, ed., *Chinese People's Movement,*

Obvious ironies emerge from an officially constituted contemporary equivalent of the paternalistic lineages of old playing a central role in an iconoclastic democracy movement. Nevertheless, for our purposes, the main point is that the pattern of labor mobilization described above had parallels within the student community. There were some differences, to be sure. From the beginning of the movement, there were more student than worker protesters who eschewed the protection and partial anonymity that *danwei* affiliation provided, and chose instead to draw attention to themselves as individuals or personally identify themselves as members of dissident associations. In addition, administrators (the campus equivalents of labor *danwei* leaders) often took little role in mobilizing youths to take to the streets. The fact remains, however, that when university students marched together in large groups behind banners identifying themselves with a collective entity, the name on the flag was much more likely to be that of a department or school (student equivalents of worker *danwei*s) than that of a salon, study group, or even autonomous union.[47] Similarly, while many wall posters carried the names or pseudonyms of individual authors, others carried the names of departments, schools, or sets of campuses.[48] Nor should the importance of permission given by *danwei* authorities be written off altogether in the student case, since some of the most active university campuses were those at which high-ranking officials acted in ways that could be interpreted as indicating limited support for the movement, such as using the excuse of illness to exempt themselves from carrying out official policies aimed at repressing the struggle. In some cases, campus officials or professorial authority figures showed their support in more direct ways. For example, at one point in 1989, Fudan University vans transported a group of retired faculty members to join a march, and at an-

---

83–105, cites several reasons that worker participation tended to take this form, including the fact that it was safer to join a march as part of a delegation than as an individual worker. The author also probes the significance of such behavior, noting, for example, that it made the protest marches structurally similar to state-sponsored demonstrations.

[47] The photograph of a Fudan group following p. 318 of Wasserstrom, *Student Protests*, illustrates this tendency.

[48] Han, *Cries*, includes wall posters signed by "Faculty and Students of Universities in the Xi'an Area" (97–103); "Graduate Students at Beijing Normal University" (112–14); and "Some Beijing University Teachers" (262–64). In 1986, many of the posters we saw at Fudan and Tongji universities were issued in the names of departments, and several informants described the same thing as happening in 1989. It is also interesting to note that pseudonymous authors sometimes described themselves as simply "a student" or "a teacher" of a specific department or school; see Han, *Cries*, 95 and 170.

other point that same school's vice presidents visited demonstrators in the heart of the city.[49]

The imprint of official organizing principles shows through in other features of the student movement. For example, when youths from middle schools joined the demonstrations of April and May, they were often explicitly directed to join specific protest events by their *banzhuren* or "head teachers" (the authority figures who serve as the equivalents of unit leaders for specific groups of teenage students). Divided into *ban* (classes) and marching behind campus flags, middle school student protest brigades took much the same form as those typically seen in officially sanctioned demonstrations held on the dates of revolutionary anniversaries.[50]

Official organizational patterns also shaped the alternative order that protesting students created at Tiananmen Square. The division of student flags at the square showed that, at least at the symbolic level, there were parallels relating to political geography as well as collective identification between the authorities and the protesters. The flags of Beijing universities tended to be near the center of the square, while those of provincial campuses were arrayed nearer the periphery. In addition, although there was not a complete match between distance from the center and distance from the capital, there was a good deal of correlation between official relations and those between student groups: youths from provinces generally thought of as "friendly" to each other set up camp near one another.[51]

Student associations. Along with providing the basic building blocks for protest mobilization and a model for mass gatherings, associations and organizational structures devised by or linked to the state also played a part in preparing individual students to take on leadership roles. Cor-

[49]Personal communication with an anonymous source.

[50]Gérémie Barmé, personal communication with Jeffrey Wasserstrom. For the role that middle-school *ban* play in student social life and CCP social control strategies, see Susan Shirk, *Competitive Comrades: Career Incentives and Student Strategies in China* (Berkeley: University of California Press, 1982), 36–39, a section that also contains some discussion of *banzhuren*. Her comments on the *ban* as an all-encompassing unit of identification is relevant for those interested in Chinese university campuses as well, as are her discussions of the selection and roles of class officers (97–104). There are some differences between the two levels of educational institutions, but we have yet to find an equally detailed work on the topic that focuses on colleges.

[51]Here once again, we are indebted to Gérémie Barmé for sharing with us his observations of the square.

inna-Barbara Francis, who was at Beijing University during the protests of 1988, draws attention to this point in an article that appeared in *Asian Survey*:

> In an ironic twist, the students' ability to organize themselves so effectively, to maintain a high level of discipline, and to maneuver politically with the government owes a great deal to the training and skills developed by students in school. Throughout their student careers, and particularly in the university, students are taught to organize and be organized, to lead others and be led. The plethora of [official] student organizations in the university . . . provides students with rich organizational experience and skills.[52]

In April and May 1989 university class monitors (*banzhang*) in at least two cities could be seen putting the propaganda skills that they had gained as messengers for school officials to a new use—that of spreading the word concerning demonstration plans and the like.[53]

Thus salon-related activities were not the only ones that helped prepare protest leaders for leadership roles. In fact, groups that were part of the official system inadvertently provided dissenters with important skills and organizational models. There are, moreover, clear historical precedents for this situation. In our previous work on Republican Shanghai, we highlight the irony (which some Westerners noted at the time) that foreign-run schools and civic institutions often inadvertently helped prepare youths to lead anti-imperialist movements.[54] In a similar vein, Tom Gold notes that, even though the leaders of the Democracy Wall movement were harsh critics of ideas they associated with the Cultural Revolution, their Red Guard experiences played a crucial role in teaching them how to "organize on their own, for their own ends."[55] Hu Ping, who participated in protests of the Democracy Wall era before gaining prominence in dissident circles within the United States through his involvement with the journal *Zhongguo zhichun* (China's spring) and the organization Minlian (Democratic Alliance), draws attention to a similar phenomenon in his autobiographical writings. He notes that his childhood was that of a *"sanhao xuesheng"* (triply good student), who not only studied hard but also served the state (and in the process honed his leadership skills) by taking on of-

[52]Francis, "The Progress of Protest," 915.
[53]Calhoun, "The Beijing Spring, 1989," *Dissent* (Fall 1989): 435–47; Kristen Parris, personal communication.
[54]Wasserstrom, *Student Protests*, 79–83.
[55]Gold, "Youth and the State," *China Quarterly*, no. 127 (September 1991): 594–612, esp. p. 603.

ficial posts within his classes and the Young Pioneers groups to which he belonged.[56]

To return to the present, not enough hard data are available to piece together a detailed picture of the experiences in official groups that helped prepare individual leaders of the 1989 movement to rise to prominence and (in many cases) act effectively once in charge. Some interesting anecdotal evidence relating to salon organizers that has received little attention thus far takes on new meaning in light of the above discussion. For example, we learn from Shen Tong's autobiography that his career as a politicized college student involved with groups such as the Olympic Institute was preceded by a post within the official Beijing University Student Association. Placed "in charge of public affairs and liaison" activities in that organization, which as a student he had come to think of as responsible primarily for sponsoring "very dull lectures," he had tried to jazz up its image by organizing a fashion show. Still earlier in his autobiography, we read of a much younger Shen Tong, who served as a "team leader of the Young Pioneers" and was proud that this special rank ensured that he would be one of the first in his class to see the new Mao Mausoleum. Shen also notes that he served briefly as a class monitor while in middle school.[57]

A close examination of the pre-1989 political careers of other prominent activists suggests, moreover, that Shen Tong's life story is far from atypical. For example, before becoming a national symbol of dissent, Wuer Kaixi had been a member of his middle school student council, and Li Lu was involved in at least one officially sponsored campus government organization early in his college career.[58] Somewhat older dissidents involved in the 1989 protests, such as Liu Gang and Wang Juntao, also seem to have moved easily between the worlds of official and unofficial campus associations. Liu was a prominent figure in campus CYL groups before his emergence as a protest leader in 1986 and his activism as a salon organizer in 1989, and Wang Juntao held important positions in "state" youth movement circles before moving into "civil" society ones.[59]

---

[56]Hu Ping, "Xie zai shiji zhijiao, yigeren de jingyan yu sikao de chenshu (liu)" (Writing at the cross-point of a century—A statement of personal experiences and thoughts, VI"), *China Spring*, no. 2 (1992): 64–66.

[57]Shen and Yeh, *Almost a Revolution*, 41, 58, 132, and 148.

[58]Li, *Moving the Mountain*; Wuer Kaixi interview translated in Yu Mok Chiu and J. Frank Harrison, eds., *Voices from Tiananmen Square* (New York: Black Rose, 1990), 155.

[59]Conversations with informants.

The preceding anecdotes all concern people who were involved in Beijing events, but the same pattern of official organizations helping to prepare activists to take leading roles in protest groups also appears if we turn our gaze away from Tiananmen Square. In Hangzhou, for example, local students who took charge of spreading the news of Beijing occurrences often brought to this task experience gained through participation in authorized activities. The organizers of an underground newspaper used "the skills and connections they had acquired through participation in the official student union and the official campus newspaper," and one of the key people involved setting up a Hangzhou school's unofficial broadcasting center had previously been active in running the school's official broadcasting system.[60]

The case of student activism in Shanghai, the city we know best, is also revealing in this regard, for the organizational and personnel overlaps there between the world of officially sanctioned organizations and dissident salons in the late 1980s were striking, to say the least. The case of Fudan University's Dajia Salon is a telling case in point. This group, which was one of the city's most famous campus-based *shetuan* and a center for dissident activity, enjoyed considerable support from high-ranking officials within the Fudan administration, including Party Secretary Lin Ke and Vice President Wang Youlan.[61] Before the protest of 1989 broke out, many famous Chinese scholars and dissidents came to the Dajia Salon to lecture, and the organization sponsored a series of forums on controversial issues related to political reform.

The Dajia Salon was also part of a larger organization known as the Fudan Student Center for Science and Technology Consulting, to which a number of other "unofficial" or quasi-official student groups (including an independent bookstore) belonged. The center was founded in 1984 and quickly gained a national reputation as a local clearinghouse for reformist and dissident activity. Not surprisingly, in 1989 people involved in its operations played important roles in the protests that took place in Shanghai. What may be surprising, at least to those who expect to see sharp fissures between transgressive and socializing activities, is that according to a 1988 study, more than half the center's personnel belonged to the CCP, and a high percentage of its members held cadre posts above the departmental level. Pan Haobo, the first general manager

---

[60]Kristen Parris, personal communication.
[61]Zhang Deming and Zhang Xiaolin, *Zhongguo daxuesheng* (Chinese university students) (Beijing: Zhongguo Wenlian Press, 1988), 53.

of this "autonomous" organization, was a CYL official and a party member, and the second person to hold this post, Yu Shu, was also a cadre who had significant clout within Fudan's official bureaucratic apparatus.[62] One final point worth making about Shanghai campus politics is that throughout the 1980s official student organizations and salons frequently cosponsored public events, including lecture series that were part of the "*wenhuare*" (cultural fever) that many regard as having helped to set the stage for the 1989 protests.

If, as we have suggested, looking only to "civil" as opposed to "state" organizations causes significant problems, so too can focusing exclusively upon the "public" as opposed to "private" sphere. The case of intra-*danwei* meetings has already suggested one way in which privately held meetings contributed to the mobilization process, but there are other cases in point. For example, both Chinese and Western eyewitnesses frequently refer to the role that informal discussions among roommates played in the development of the movement. These same informants also stress that personal friendships and other ties established and cemented in private settings played a crucial part in the mobilization process, a phenomenon alluded to in several published accounts as well. And personal connections and knowledge carried over from private realms of activity influenced the leadership selection process as well.[63]

One way to get a better feel for the role that activities taking place in private and public spheres played in the movement's growth is to focus on the political geography of two key spaces: individual university campuses and Tiananmen Square itself. It is tempting in both cases to stress the "public" character of these locales. Chinese universities—like campuses elsewhere in the world—have always had a number of areas (dining halls, lawns, walkways) that seem custom-made for open exchanges of opinion. Moreover, during the late 1980s the space available to those interested in public political action expanded, thanks to the opening on some campuses of coffeehouses and other informal gathering places designed to encourage conversation.[64] During the height of the movement,

[62]Ibid., 62, 80–82, and 93.

[63]Calhoun, "Beijing Spring," stresses the importance of friendships in the spread of the movement; Li's *Moving the Mountain* illustrates the importance of personal connections among leaders of dissident groups, as well as of those between the leaders of Nanjing University's official and unofficial associations. In addition, the power that Feng Congde and Chai Ling exercised within the Beijing movement was based in part at least on the fact that they were married to each other.

[64]Craig Calhoun, "The Ideology of Intellectuals and the Chinese Student Protest Movement of 1989," *Praxis International* 10, nos. 1–2 (1989): 131–60, esp. p. 139.

moreover, the open areas near bulletin boards were used as communal centers for debate and the exchange of news. The case for stressing the public character of Tiananmen at the time of the movement seems even stronger, for during the mass occupation of 1989 it seemed that the people had finally succeeded (at least for a time) in making this central gathering place the kind of space the CCP had always claimed it to be— a truly public square.

If there is much to be said for stressing the public character of both these locales, however, it is also important to remember their private dimensions and to keep in mind that limits were put on who could gain access to these new centers of "open" politics. The importance of informal meetings held within the private spaces of university campuses (especially dorm rooms) has already been mentioned above, but even formal gatherings (such as those sponsored by salons) were often held clandestinely. Salons may have helped expand the scope of public political discourse within universities, but until the movement was fully under way they were frequently forced to do this in a furtive and limited manner.[65] In the case of Shanghai and perhaps other cities as well, it is not too much of a stretch to say, in fact, that the most important of all centers for radical political discourse before Hu Yaobang's death were the informal and essentially private "dormitory salons" that groups of students established on an ad hoc basis in their rooms.

After the movement began, open arenas for debate became increasingly important, but even then the political geography of campuses (which are bounded by walls and entered primarily through a few gates, and serve in some ways as microcosms of larger urban environments described in Chapter 2) made gathering places inside university compounds peculiar "public" spaces. In our *Social History* essay on protests of the Republican era, we drew attention to the ways in which the "all-encompassing nature of university life"—i.e., the tendency for Chinese students to sleep, eat, and study within close proximity of one another— facilitated rapid mobilization in times of political crisis, and our observations during the protest waves of 1986–87 (which both of us witnessed) and 1989 (which one of us observed) have convinced us that the same holds equally true for the Communist period.[66] The structure

---

[65]The authors are grateful to Melissa Macauley for bringing this to their attention.
[66]Wasserstrom, *Student Protests*, 136–39; see also Wasserstrom and Liu, "Student Protest." In December 1986 we watched with great interest as Fudan University's students were swept into the movement. The process began with a delegation from nearby Tongji

of university life and the nature of campus architecture also means, however, that students are often cut off from those who are not connected in some way with academia. Thus, even when salon meetings were held in open spaces, people from non-university *danweis* who wanted to listen to invited speakers or take part in discussions had to pass through gates at which they might be asked to show some form of identification. After protests begin, moreover, officials can take simple steps to keep students from leaving particular universities. These steps have never been wholly effective, since campus walls are notoriously easy to climb, and they clearly did not work well in 1989. Nonetheless, the fact that access to university grounds is routinely subjected to some sort of scrutiny, and that in times of crisis the authorities typically turn to stricter (if still imperfect) methods of control, suggests that seeing any part of a campus as a fully "public" space is problematic.

In the case of Tiananmen Square, the students themselves tried to privatize what seems at first to have been a space made fully public by the protests. As various journalists noted at the time, the alternative order that students created at the square was never a completely open one. At least in theory, a series of concentric circles emanated out from the leadership, and gaining access to each more central area required presentation of a student card or identification badge. Several eyewitnesses have emphasized to us that this system never operated as smoothly as some news reports suggested and that "security" at the square was often a fairly hodge-podge affair.[67] Nevertheless, attempts were made to limit access to certain group discussions. These attempts were defended in terms of the need to protect the movement from the scheming of paid agitators and the prying eyes of informers sent by the regime, and some fears related to such activities were certainly justified. But there was also an elitist character to some "protective" measures, and the effect (if not always the intention) of these tactics was to keep students and workers at arm's length from each other.

University, which was one of the schools that took a vanguard role in the 1986 protests, marching through one of Fudan's gates and proceeding through the campus common areas during the lunch hour. Hearing that something was going on, students drifted out of dining halls until, by the time the marchers reached the other main gate, a considerable crowd had gathered to read the banners and listen to the Tongji youth calling on their Fudan counterparts to join them on the streets the following day in downtown Shanghai.

[67] Personal communications with Norman Kutcher and others. For a description of events that captures both the anarchic and bureaucratized features of the movement, see Luo et al., "The 1989 Pro-Democracy Movement," esp. p. 30.

CONCLUSION

Where does all this leave us? Having drawn attention to the problems caused by taking a salon-centered approach to the subject at hand, we must admit that we have nothing equally coherent to put in its place. But at this point it is probably advisable simply to cast our investigative nets as widely as possible, paying attention to what was going on in official as well as unofficial associations and looking at the middle school (and perhaps even primary school) experiences of student protest leaders as well as at their collegiate activism.

Moreover, the effort begun by others to apply concepts of "civil society" and "public sphere" to the Chinese case in a more nuanced way should continue. Meetings held by salons and other associations at least partially autonomous of state control before Hu Yaobang's death certainly influenced some features of the movement, most notably perhaps the language some student protesters used when writing for the domestic intelligentsia audience and speaking to foreign correspondents. The movement also drew some of its inspiration and symbolism from the invigorated (and increasingly "public") urban culture of the late 1980s, a culture in which rock songs by counterculture figures like Cui Jian and television productions like *He shang* (River elegy), as well as articles by journalists critical of official policies, had important political implications.[68] It is misleading, however, to use these phenomena as a basis for portraying the Chinese upheavals of 1989 as closely following patterns described by Rousseau or Habermas, which are rooted firmly in Western history and are reflective of Western utopian and dystopian fantasies. The case of student associations suggests, in other words, that if notions of "civil society" and "public sphere" are to retain some heuristic value and be used (as we still think they can) to highlight differences between the East European and Chinese experiences in 1989, they will have to be used with a great deal more caution and attention to cultural nuances than has often been the case thus far.

If this essay has been successful, it will have generated new types of questions rather than provided clear-cut answers. It will also have dem-

[68]The authors are grateful to Craig Calhoun for personal communications that helped them put this issue in perspective. See also his comments in "Ideology of Intellectuals," 139. A more nuanced discussion of "public sphere" issues can be found in Calhoun's book on the Chinese protests of 1989, *Neither Gods nor Emperors* (Berkeley: University of California Press, 1995); the authors are grateful to him for sharing this work with them when it was still in draft form.

onstrated that those of us concerned with China's future course should combine our interest in formal ideologies of "democracy" with closer inspection of how power is divided along lines of class and gender within dissident movements. Most of all, it will have indicated that we should temper our fascination with self-conscious iconoclasm with an appreciation of the power of hegemonic traditions and patterns of behavior.

What implications for the future does a move away from salon-centered explanatory models hold? What difference does the preceding discussion make, when it comes to trying to assess the likelihood that China will adopt a more open form of governance in the next several years or perhaps decades? The alternative picture of movement politics we have sketched out would seem to provide grounds for both optimism and pessimism. On the bright side, this picture suggests that the regime's efforts to prevent large-scale popular protests from taking place in the future are likely to prove ineffectual in the long run. The authorities have directed much of their attention thus far to arresting individual ringleaders and driving dissident associations underground. But in the process they have left in place many of the groups and associations that proved to be key organizational building blocks in the protests of 1989, and which could easily serve (again inadvertently) as leadership training grounds for the next generation of student leaders.

On the other hand, our picture of movement politics indicates that a resurgence of mass activism will not necessarily guarantee a shift toward a genuinely open form of politics, even if the next movement (or the movement after that) succeeds in overthrowing the regime in power. Although ability to appropriate official forms of behavior has long been a source of strength for protesters in various parts of the world, the Chinese events of 1989 illustrated once again how easy it is for revolutionaries to replicate within their own organizations the less savory features of the regimes they challenge. If meaningful change is to come to China, the next generation of protesters will not only have to prove themselves the equals of their predecessors when it comes to courage and commitment; they will also have to pay closer attention to combining a longing for popular sovereignty with an interest in developing democratic forms of practice. The key to success may thus lie in developing strategies that will allow them to make use of preexisting official networks and systems, without becoming ensnared in the bureaucratic and elitist character of these structures.

15

Conclusion:
Historical perspectives

DAVID STRAND

The preceding chapters highlight issues of autonomy and community against a backdrop of dramatic urban economic growth and more limited, but still significant, political change. They explore the degree to which residents of large cities such as Beijing, Shanghai, and Guangzhou, as well as smaller urban centers, manage their own lives as individuals or members of groups. They also consider the presence or emergence of a collective dimension to urban life beneath, alongside, or beyond the control mechanisms associated with the current Communist regime. In terms of size, technology, and administrative presence, late twentieth-century Chinese cities differ markedly from their late Imperial and Republican predecessors. They are many times larger, wired for sight, sound, and mechanical reproduction, and heavily bureaucratized. Still, the recent and more distant histories of Chinese cities provide a record of individuals, groups, and government grappling with comparable fundamental issues of urban life: social order, livelihood, cultural representation, and the role of state power. A review of precedent may suggest ways in which past practice has narrowed or broadened the strategies and structures available to city dwellers today.

OVERCOMING SOCIAL FRAGMENTATION

When the Communists took over in China in 1949, the cities were in difficult straits. Inflation, unemployment, a breakdown of public services, crime, and social distress of all kinds were manifest. A visitor to Shanghai in the autumn of 1948 reported "the near-complete demoral-

394

ization of people of all sorts and [a] prevailing feeling of cynicism and despair."[1] To be sure, much of the disorder was due to years of war against the Japanese and between the Communists and the Nationalists. But the failure of cities to cope with the admittedly severe challenges of the mid-twentieth century also seemed rooted in their constitutional inability to manage their own affairs. For example, Kenneth Lieberthal's study of Tianjin during the Communist transition offers a portrait of a deeply divided city with little sense of community or common purpose.[2] Characterizing the city as "a bifurcated society" of mutually exclusive traditional and modern components, Lieberthal observes that many residents were newcomers to the city and many more relied on "traditional modes of thought" with the result that "few of the inhabitants perceived the city as a whole." Tianjin "resembled a multi-cellular organism: it required complex forms of cooperation in order to function, but at the same time permitted cell walls to screen out all but the bare essentials that each minuscule part required from the whole."[3] Given this one-dimensional economic interdependence, he concludes that "there was very little civic consciousness [and] very little concern with events and problems that fell outside one's own social web."[4]

Terms like "bifurcation" and "cellular" suggest deep barriers separating people on the basis of occupation, residence, subethnicity (the locality or region one hailed from originally), and degree of urbanness or ruralness. The implication is that the Communists after 1949 took divided cities and remade them in ways that reinforced this sense of separateness (the rise of work-unit [*danwei*]–based living) and unified city people under Communist supervision. Autonomy of a parochial type was exchanged for a managed sense of community. Several chapters in this volume emphasize the importance of the *danwei* system in reordering city life in ways that localized, "miniaturized" (Chapter 2), and "froze" (Chapter 7) urban society. Today's cities, in contrast, offer residents the larger, more open stages of marketplace and public square as possible sites for less regimented, more fluid activity.

If Chinese cities have begun to look rather like they used to in terms of bustling markets, jarring divisions based on class and culture, and a

[1]A. Doak Barnett, *China on the Eve of Communist Takeover* (New York: Praeger, 1961), 82.

[2]Kenneth Lieberthal, *Revolution and Tradition in Tientsin, 1949–1952* (Stanford, Calif.: Stanford University Press, 1980).

[3]Ibid., 27.

[4]Ibid., 181.

general tendency toward social disorder, this may be simply a return to the normal "chaos of the living city" temporarily held at bay by state socialism.[5] As Gaubatz observes in Chapter 2, the Maoist "generalized model of urban organization" has receded in favor of the "specialization" or diversity that is more typical of city life everywhere. We may also be seeing a return to some older patterns of urban life and development in evidence before the midcentury rupture, patterns suppressed, but not erased, by Communist ideology and organization.

During the late Imperial period (c. 1550—c. 1920), most Chinese cities were command posts of empire given to minimal administrative intervention in community affairs.[6] The reluctance of the state to invest in an administrative presence, beyond a light dusting of officials, left cities and other communities partly free to govern themselves. In an extreme but telling example, the commercial city of Hankou, with a population of about one million in the nineteenth century, had a dozen officials and no more than a thousand lesser functionaries like private secretaries and tax collectors.[7] At the citywide level and below, autonomy flourished because elites had the wherewithal to raise militia, feed the poor, and repair city walls. The state, for reasons of economy and ideological self-confidence, permitted and even encouraged these initiatives. China's urban tradition included formal subservience to state power that fell short of slavish devotion or continuous supervision. By the nineteenth century this tacit partnership between state and society had resulted in cities where "many if not most urban services" had become the responsibility of guilds and other corporate entities.[8] Degree-holding literati, or "gentry," and merchants managed and financed an impressive catalog of ventures including, by one accounting, "schools, academies, city walls, granaries, bridges, ferry docks, hydraulic systems, orphanages, temples to state sanctioned gods, shrines to local figures, even Buddhist monasteries."[9] But this informal cooperation did not produce permanent mu-

---

[5]See Charles Tilly's meditation on the naturalness of urban disorder in "The Chaos of the Living City," in Tilly, ed., *An Urban World* (Boston: Little, Brown, 1974).

[6]William T. Rowe, "Urban Policy in China," *Problems of Communism* 33 (November–October 1984): 75.

[7]William T. Rowe, *Hankow: Conflict and Community in a Chinese City* (Stanford, Calif.: Stanford University Press, 1989), 29.

[8]G. W. Skinner, "Introduction: Urban Social Structure in Ch'ing China," in Skinner, ed., *The City in Late Imperial China* (Stanford: Stanford University Press, 1977), 548.

[9]Timothy Brook, "Family Continuity and Cultural Hegemony: The Gentry of Ningbo, 1368–1911," in Joseph W. Esherick and Mary Backus Rankin, *Chinese Local Elites and Patterns of Dominance* (Berkeley: University of California Press, 1990), 46.

nicipal institutions. City residents in China managed to "govern themselves without having noticeable governmental institutions."[10]

Chinese cities favored informal over formal unity and "intermittent" over continuous leadership.[11] This responsiveness to crises on the part of elites, and those they led and dominated, lessened the costs of the kind of social fragmentation Lieberthal cites as a debilitating feature of 1940s Tianjin. Fragmentation was both a structural condition and a phase in a cycle of group interaction. This processual or cyclical aspect to urban life makes any snapshot view of the late Imperial Chinese city partial and misleading. As a case in point, the nineteenth-century Taiwanese port city of Lugang was periodically torn by conflict (exemplified by a boisterous, often bloody annual rock fight involving rival surname groups) and served by the collaborative efforts of merchant guilds and local officials in meeting charitable and defense needs. The resulting social scene "consisted of overlapping groups, each recruited on a different principle and each acting in a different sphere."[12] This imbricated social structure, according to Donald DeGlopper, supported a functioning "urban community" capable of fostering "civic confederations."[13] Divisions abounded, based on the hometowns or home villages (*tongxiang*) of urban migrants, lineage, occupation, neighborhood, and having or not having an official degree or status. But this fragmentation was softened by overlapping group affiliations (merchants from different localities belonging to the same guild) and counterbalanced by a willingness to rally around government or nongovernmental initiatives. "The scale of urban societal activism continually expanded. Projects begun on a neighborhood or subcommunal basis, such as fire brigades and benevolent halls, over time were integrated and systematized at the municipal level."[14] Socially rooted and organizationally light, citywide governing bodies built, repaired, and restored urban infrastructure and kept the peace in the years and seasons when such action was deemed necessary. In this regard, local society, including the urban part of it, was as thrifty with public or collective resources as the Chinese state.

[10]Lawrence W. Crissman, "The Segmentary Structure of Urban Overseas Chinese Communities," *Man* 2, no. 2 (June 1967): 200.

[11]G. W. Skinner, "Introduction: Urban Social Structure in Ch'ing China," in Skinner, *The City in Late Imperial China*, 522.

[12]Donald R. DeGlopper, "Social Structure in a Nineteenth-Century Taiwanese Port City," in Skinner, *The City in Late Imperial China*, 650.

[13]Ibid., 633.

[14]Rowe, *Hankow*, 184.

CONTROL AND AUTONOMY

In this common spirit of social and political parsimony, state and society were normally self-limiting. By modern standards they did not demand much of each other. Late Imperial scholar-officials were well aware of this balance or, more precisely, tension between control and autonomy.[15] They saw the problem of how much should be done and by whom through the lens of the long-standing debate over centralization (*junxian*) and decentralization, or "feudalism" (*fengjian*). Following the *junxian* tradition, the Chinese state worried about the possibility of locally based rebellion or defiance.[16] As one *junxian* partisan put it, allowing local power to develop would mean "the tail is too big to wag" (*weida budiao*).[17] As a result, positions as magistrates were, by a rule of "avoidance," staffed by strangers to an area so that officials would be less likely to strike up alliances with local people against the center. At the same time, the state, including Confucian reformers with *fengjian* sympathies interested in strengthening the state, assumed that under the right conditions local energies could be mobilized to serve the higher interests of empire. They "called for infusing the centralized bureaucratic system with the feudal system's proclivity toward local self-government."[18] For example, an institution like the community covenant or compact (*xiangyue*) authored by philosopher Zhu Xi in the twelfth century as an autonomous local body could later be incorporated into the decimal (ten-family) mutual guarantee system (*baojia*) by the sixteenth-century reformer Lu Kun without violating the general thrust of Zhu's proposal.[19] Zhu Xi's brand of autonomy and Lu Kun's vision of a more centralized polity assumed a common moral framework unifying commoners, the literati, and the state, an assumption that was based in fact as well as Confucian fancy. A Chinese way of life organized around the

---

[15]Philip A. Kuhn, "Local Self-Government Under the Republic: Problems of Control, Autonomy, and Mobilization," in Frederic Wakeman, Jr., and Carolyn Grant, eds., *Conflict and Control in Late Imperial China* (Berkeley: University of California Press, 1975).

[16]Timothy Brook notes that "the state's anxiety about local autonomy" limited the range of local projects the state was willing to permit. Brook, "Family Continuity and Cultural Hegemony," 43.

[17]Min Tu-Ki, *National Polity and Local Power: The Transformation of Late Imperial China*, ed. by Philip A. Kuhn and Timothy Brook (Cambridge, Mass.: Harvard University Press, 1989), 103.

[18]Ibid., 112. Min observes that there were at least three camps: *junxian* advocates, *fengjian* advocates, and scholar-officials who sought a middle ground of the sort reflected in this notion of "infusion" (111–12).

[19]Kuhn, "Local Self-Government," 261.

ritual practices (*li*) associated with weddings, funerals, and the like really did extend, as the cliché put it, from the emperor and "the princes and nobles and greater and lesser officials down to the common people" and across the realm from city to countryside.[20]

Paradoxically, local autonomy was both an obstacle to state power and an inspiration to a certain kind of statist. Reformers were excited by the prospect of turning local activism to larger purposes. It was true that some of the initiatives taken independently by local elites to address a community problem were colored by resentment of outside bureaucratic interference.[21] Locals who paid the bills might reasonably wish to control things on their own. In some cases, like the sponsorship of temples, clear separation between official and unofficial patronage might emerge to underline more open tensions between state and society.[22] In moments of crisis, for even a good Confucian "*local* defense, not defense of the dynasty or the imperial system, . . . took priority in the scheme of loyalties."[23] Those who appeared to defy the state might win broad community approval and be "lionized as a local hero" as was the reward of Ge Cheng, the leader of a weavers' protest against new taxes in Xuzhou in 1601. "When [Ge] made his way to the local prison, over ten thousand [fellow] townsmen expressed their gratitude to him by lining his route with offerings of food and wine."[24] Ge's popularity stemmed largely from his willingness to take personal responsibility for what was essentially a communitywide movement.[25] As a result, the state in its ideological teachings might express the wish for a more cellular, less imbricated society in which "each one attend[s] to his own profession,

---

[20]See Myron Cohen's interesting discussion of this issue of cultural unity in his essay "Being Chinese: The Peripheralization of Traditional Identity," in *Daedalus* 120, no. 2 (Spring 1991), especially pp. 117–19.

[21]Mary B. Rankin, "The Origins of a Chinese Public Sphere: Local Elites and Community Affairs in the Late Imperial Period," *Etudes chinoises* 9, no. 2 (Fall 1990): 30.

[22]James L. Watson, "Standardizing the Gods: The Promotion of T'ien Hou (Empress of Heaven) Along the South China Coast, 960–1960," in David Johnson, Andrew J. Nathan, and Evelyn S. Rawski, eds., *Popular Culture in Late Imperial China* (Berkeley: University of California Press, 1985), 301. Watson stresses that in this case, in Taiwan, the actual "unpopularity of official temples" was a result of the arrival of the Qing state long after settlers from the mainland had established themselves without official assistance.

[23]Rowe, *Hankow*, 257.

[24]Tsing Yuan, "Urban Riots and Disturbances," in Jonathan D. Spence and John E. Wills, Jr., eds., *From Ming to Ch'ing: Conquest, Region, and Continuity in Seventeenth-Century China* (New Haven: Yale University Press, 1979), 290.

[25]Paolo Santangelo, "Urban Society in Late Imperial Suzhou," in Linda C. Johnson, *Cities of Jiangnan in Late Imperial China* (Albany: State University of New York Press, 1993), 103.

so that the minds of the people may be fixed, and each one remain[s] quiet and contented in his own sphere."[26] The Chinese state would have to await the advent of communism and the *danwei* even to approach that degree of closely bounded "surveillance and social control" (Naughton). In this regard, state Confucianism, and successor ideologies like state communism, invariably found the city an untidy and potentially subversive place.

Localism of the more vocal and open sort in China was analogous to liberal efforts in the West to check the state.[27] But Chinese reformers, including those of the *fengjian* persuasion, and local elites also saw the impulse to act locally as compatible with thinking imperially, and supporting a stronger, more intrusive state. As a result, local organizations and arrangements attempted to embody the doubleness of control and autonomy rather than articulate the tension in a juridical or openly confrontational form.

Even when confrontations came, they tended to retain these alloyed elements of control and autonomy. Susumu Fuma notes, in his study of a sixteenth-century tax riot in Hangzhou, how the control-oriented *bao-jia* system was turned in an instant by city dwellers (*shimin*) into the organizing principle of their rebellion.[28] When rioters in 1582 seized control of the city, neighborhood by neighborhood, they counted and grouped households by tens as the government and tradition had taught them to do. The government's template of control became the protesters' instrument of resistance. As Wasserstrom points out in Chapter 14 on student protest, this "hegemony of the rituals and cultural norms of the state" has been a recurring feature of "antistate" resistance down to the practice of counting out supporters, or subjects, by groups of ten (*shi-rentuan*). This feature of the Chinese tradition makes it difficult to gauge the strength of systems of state control in cities. Recruiting local people as agents of control means granting them resources like status and symbols that can, in a moment, be turned against higher authorities. Autonomy appears not so much the opposite of control as its mirror image.

The Hangzhou riot, as it happened, was directed against literati priv-

---

[26]Victor H. Mair, "Language and Ideology in the Written Popularizations of the *Sacred Edict*," in Johnson et al., *Popular Culture*, 353. The passage is a nineteenth-century commentary on the 1670 list of maxims issued by the Kangxi emperor.
[27]Marie-Claire Bergère, *The Golden Age of the Chinese Bourgeoisie* (Cambridge: Cambridge University Press, 1989), 204.
[28]Fuma, "Late Ming Urban Reform and the Popular Uprising in Hangzhou," in Johnson, *Cities of Jiangnan*.

ileges of tax and corvée exemption. These privileges were spread out over a considerable proportion of the population who stood as clients to powerful, degree-holding patrons. But most urban residents were excluded from privilege and dragooned into serving their social betters. What was at stake in sixteenth-century Hangzhou is analogous to the all-important Communist state–bestowed residency (*hukou*) privileges stressed by Solinger in Chapter 5 in this volume on fixed and "floating" city residents. In a sign of statist sentiments, the Hangzhou rioters demanded more, not less, bureaucratic intervention in the city's affairs in the form of direct government policing. This would exempt them from the hated burden of standing corvée guard duty outside the homes of the great families. The Hangzhou uprising, like the 1989 democracy protests, was not a community-based rebellion against the state so much as an attack on the corruption of a politically privileged social elite. Although they exhibited considerable independence of mind and freedom of maneuver, rioters demanded justice not freedom, control not autonomy. They also felt free to use the rhetoric and institutions of social order to make their disorderly political statement. Since no permanent municipal institutions or rights emerged from these late Ming conflicts, it was a relatively simple matter for the stronger, successor Qing regime to stamp out such outbursts.[29]

CRACKS IN THE URBAN-RURAL CONTINUUM

The 1582 Hangzhou tax riot is also interesting because of the light it sheds on the relationship between urban and rural culture. F. W. Mote has observed that the conventional Western assumption of profound division between city and countryside does not apply in the Chinese case, where a "continuum" between the two rather than a gap was the rule.[30] As Fuma points out, the ingenious argument made by Ding Shiqing, the leader of the Hangzhou tax revolt, emphasized this notion by demanding that city property be taxed at the same low rates as those applied to agricultural land. Even though they understood the economic absurdity of equating of urban and rural real estate, officials were hard put to dismiss the point. Rhetorically, city and village were one. But, especially

[29]For this point and further analysis of sixteenth- and seventeenth-century urban disorders, see Tsing Yuan, "Urban Riots and Disturbances."
[30]F. W. Mote, "The Transformation of Nanking," in Skinner, *The City in Late Imperial China.*

beginning with the late Ming commercial revolution and continuing into the Qing, the material foundation of a distinctively urban way of life and a less than seamless connection to the countryside was established. An urban bias became detectable in some elite-led relief programs.[31] The literati could parlay the cultural and social advantages of city living into marginally better odds at achieving an official career.[32] And if the rural base of the civilization continued to exert influence on urban culture through the medium of Confucian ideology, the economically vital cities now began to dispatch urban culture into the hinterland in a systematic and insistent fashion.[33]

Urban places were above all scenes of intense competition for money, privilege, and pleasure beyond the immediate control of government officials.[34] The entry of large numbers of vagrants (*liumin*), comparable to today's "floating population" (*liudong renkou*) studied by Solinger, into late Ming cities added a further impression of a breakdown of social order in the countryside and rising urban turmoil.[35] This cutthroat environment pushed city dwellers to consider strategies that might help them cope. Beyond the obvious ones related to money-making, urbanites armed themselves with new religious beliefs that "valorize[d] work as a vehicle of self-improvement and self-cultivation" analogous to the West's Calvinist ethic.[36] Other believers in persecuted religious sects like the White Lotus found in lightly governed big cities, including Beijing, the freedom to establish extensive networks of the faithful and halls for worship.[37] As Chen's discussion of contemporary *qigong* practitioners in Chapter 13 bears out, a turbulent urban setting can both stimulate and provide sanctuary for this kind of individual and group religious response.

Out of this intense competition and the occasional riot or rock fight emerged a social consensus constructed with an awareness of threats of rebels, pirates, famine, flood, and revenue-hungry officials (insiders act-

---

[31]In Shaoxing in the late Qing, efforts to aid victims of rice shortages were concentrated in urban areas. James H. Cole, *Shaohsing: Competition and Cooperation in Nineteenth-Century China* (Tucson: University of Arizona Press, 1986), 55.

[32]Ibid., 176.

[33]Evelyn Rawski, "Economic and Social Foundations of Late Imperial Culture," in Johnson et al., *Popular Culture*, 5.

[34]Judith A. Berling, "Religion and Popular Culture: The Management of Moral Capital in *The Romance of the Three Teachings*," in Johnson et al., *Popular Culture*, 193–94.

[35]Harriet T. Zurndorfer, *Change and Continuity in Chinese Local History: The Development of Hui-chou Prefecture 800 to 1800* (Leiden: E. J. Brill, 1989), 113.

[36]Ibid.

[37]Susan Naquin, "The Transmission of White Lotus Sectarianism in Late Imperial China," in Johnson et al., *Popular Culture*, 269.

ing as outsiders) outside the walls and common problems within. In the most successful cases, this consensus, expressed in Confucian terms, "could include opium racketeers and brothel-keepers as well as classical literati, casual laborers and beggars as well as propertied merchants and shopkeepers. In the end, the only social elements it failed to include (or to co-opt) were those who actively sought to escape or deny it," like sectarian rebels.[38]

Despite the emerging power of the city as a cultural and economic force beyond its walls, the countercurrents supported by a self-consciously agrarian empire and a mobile elite remained in force. Linking both urban and rural China was the continued presence not only of a single Imperial government for the great cities and the villages alike but a social elite that was " 'amphibious'—equally at home in town and countryside."[39] The balance between state and society and between city and countryside was managed by an elite with a complex "portfolio" of official and unofficial, gentry and commercial, and urban and rural connections.[40] Perhaps one feature in today's China that exacerbates urban-rural difference is the fact that the mass of the mobile population (Solinger's "floaters") is more "amphibious" than elites fixed by urban privilege and position. As a result, the contemporary urban political order may be relentless in the defense of privilege and repression of outsiders, instead of open to the need to expand public services to cope with the new poverty that accompanies the new wealth. A relative absence of charity and philanthropic initiative is one of the more striking differences between Chinese cities now and those in the past. Personal and group mobility does not seem to be matched by an expansiveness of moral vision or community feeling.

PUBLIC SPHERES AND INNER ARENAS

The nineteenth- and early twentieth-century transition from the early modern to the modern city threw into doubt the workability of the old formula of light government, intermittently active elites, and attentive

---

[38]Rowe, *Hankow*, 347.

[39]William T. Rowe, "Success Stories: Lineage and Elite Status in Hanyang County, Hubei, c. 1368–1949," in Esherick and Rankin, *Chinese Local Elites*, 81.

[40]The term "portfolio" is used by Rowe to emphasize the diversity of elite interests and backgrounds (ibid.). The elite itself was highly stratified in degrees from the *jinshi* at the top to the *shengyuan* near the bottom. These status distinctions led to intra-elite conflict and variation in the configuration of elite power. For example, a *shengyuan* who might be a marginal, even dissident figure in the city might have a counterpart in a more rural area who played the dominant role. See the discussion in Cole, *Shaohsing*, 18–20.

and occasionally violent, but normally passive, crowds and groups. Internal rebellion, external threat, and the rise of modern commerce, culture, and industry encouraged government expansion, legal formality, and public and popular mobilization.

When the Qing began its final sequence of collapse and reform leading up to the 1911 Revolution, Chinese cities were in many ways well positioned to achieve municipal and other kinds of autonomy. In addition to their tradition of self-management, cities offered legal and customary protections for private property, extensive social organization led by merchant and craft guilds, and a distinctive urban culture in which individual cities had recognized personalities of their own.[41] As Mary Rankin has shown, gentry and merchant activists took advantage of these assets first to consolidate a "local managerial public sphere" of community projects like those discussed above and then to inflate a more directly political realm of public opinion.[42] The social indispensability of the gentry-merchant elite in managing local affairs gave them the standing to criticize the state and address the range of problems that plagued China after Qing prohibitions against overt political activity were neutralized.[43] The precedents offered by local elite activism in the management of public (*gong*) affairs made the emergence of a modern arena of debate and protest less a violent break with the past than a continuation of civic action by other means.[44]

Of course, in promoting this new politics, activists relied heavily on imported notions of "self-government" (*zizhi*) and citizenship. But this did not mean that new civic initiatives were necessarily narrowed and isolated by their foreign and elite origins. For one thing, the *junxian/fengjian* discourse encouraged reformers to combine "an affirmation of the [*fengjian*] system, taking local autonomy as the basic principle of reform, with Western parliamentary thought."[45] In addition, China's

[41]See Rowe's *Hankow* and the first volume of his two-volume study of the city, *Hankow: Commerce and Society in a Chinese City, 1796–1889* (Stanford, Calif.: Stanford University Press, 1984).

[42]Mary Rankin, "The Origins of a Chinese Public Sphere," and her book *Elite Activism and Political Transformation in China* (Stanford, Calif.: Stanford University Press, 1986).

[43]Ibid.

[44]The question of the existence or nature of a public sphere in late Imperial and Republican history has stimulated a rather intense debate. See David Strand, "Protest in Beijing: Civil Society and Public Sphere in China," *Problems of Communism* 34, no. 3 (May–June 1990), and essays by Frederic Wakeman, William T. Rowe, and Mary B. Rankin in a special "Symposium: 'Public Sphere'/'Civil Society' in China?" *Modern China* 19, no. 2 (April 1993).

[45]Min, *National Polity and Local Power*, 116.

merely "semi-colonial" experience is germane. Indigenous elites and their social connections facilitated ties between new public arenas and the corporate structure of urban life. In a recent study of Indian public life in Surat under colonialism, Douglas Haynes distinguishes between the "very narrow arena of politics . . . the *civic* arena" defined by British law and rhetoric and the city's *"inner* political arenas" characterized by "idioms of precolonial origin" stressing "such values as the importance of social reputation and duty to family, caste, neighborhood, or religious grouping."[46] While the emergent Chinese public realm was undoubtedly weaker in terms of rule of law and formal institutional support, its long-standing inner connections to lineage, native place, and occupational bodies made the public acts of revolution and reform more intelligible to the broader, still traditionally minded population.

This bridging function from "inner" arenas of lineage, guild, and native place to public realms of discourse and action was as much a matter of the mechanics of social influence as it was a case of ideological resonance between old and new meanings of "public." The Chinese cultural ethos stressing the social nature of identity urges careful attention to the intricacies and potentialities of relationships. This might mean looking to one's own in the city in an exclusive and parochial sense. Coteries of intellectuals, gangs of workers, and lodges of religious sect members banded together in this fashion. The choice of exclusivity did not necessarily hamper efforts to cope with change and new opportunities. Some relatively exclusive bodies, like lineage trusts (*tang*), functioned as "an analogue of the business corporation" by husbanding capital to promote industrial projects like salt mining.[47] Alternatively, one might scout out new or latent relationships of moral and material promise. In his novel of intellectual life in the 1930s, *Weicheng* (Besieged city), Qian Zhong-shu lampoons the reflexive quest for such connections in the suggestion by one young man on the make in Shanghai that he and a perceived romantic rival were "suitors-in-arms" (*tongqing*): "if you study with another gentleman, you call him your fellow student (*tongshi xiongdi*). If you are at school together, you are classmates (*tongxue*). If you have

---

[46]Douglas Haynes, *Rhetoric and Ritual in Colonial India: The Shaping of a Public Culture in Surat City, 1852–1928* (Berkeley: University of California Press, 1991), 15.

[47]Madeline Zelin, "The Rise and Fall of the Fu-Rong Salt-Yard Elite: Merchant Dominance in Late Qing China," in Esherick and Rankin, *Chinese Local Elites,* 91. In fact, these *tang* might be relatively *inclusive* in gathering in a wide circle of kin. William T. Rowe also makes this point with regard to the economic role of lineages ("Success Stories," in ibid., 65–66).

the same sweetheart, you are *tongqing*."[48] The satire underlines the real, open, and overlapping nature of such affiliations in an urban context where classmates might unite to do business or politics as well as compete against one another for the affections of a woman. (And as it happens, in the novel, with Miss Xu set to marry another, the *tongqing* connection becomes a way of recouping social capital left from a misfired love affair.)

Of all of these shared or common (*tong*) identities, common locality or native place (*tongxiang*) was among the most important and supple. Urbanization in late Imperial and early Republican China was carried out in a socially organized fashion by sojourners who found in their common locality ties a powerful remedy for their vulnerable status as strangers in the city.[49] In fact, localism's very portability might make it stronger outside one's immediate locale. As Chapters 11 and 14 on workers and students, respectively, show, the forging of *tongxiang*-based connections is one of the most persistent and effective social strategies employed by urban Chinese. In the later Imperial period, cities like Beijing and Shanghai were the repositories of these feelings of solidarity by mobile literati, merchants, and laborers. All manner of relationships, including student-teacher, employer-worker, and master-apprentice, could be enclosed within and supported by localist identities.[50] When a prominent lineage from the Ningbo and Shaoxing area sought to revive the solidarity of its immigrant members in Shanghai, it organized in 1919 "The Ning-Shao All-Shanghai Association for Strengthening Our Lineage."[51] Lineage loyalties were placed in the flexible context of localist ties (and the shared experience of doing business in Shanghai).

The notion of many competing localisms might suggest simple fragmentation. But the parochial character of this kind of clubbing together is belied by the flexibility of these *tongxiang* or sojourner ties. The frame or unit of one's native place might be a county, prefecture, or province.[52] One need not have met one's fellow native until one arrived at a *huiguan* (provincial hostel) in an alien city for the tie to be operative. In many cases, grouping by locality was the first step to cross-locality alliances among merchants, politicians, and students. For example, in the early

---

[48]Qian Zhongshu, *Weicheng* (Besieged city) (Hong Kong: Wenjiao chubanshe, 1981), 114.
[49]Rawski, "Economic and Social Foundations," 9.
[50]Skinner, *The City in Late Imperial China*, 541.
[51]Cole, *Shaohsing*, 155–56.
[52]Ibid., 541–42.

1920s a group of eight students at the National Art Institute in Beijing decided to form a painting society (*huashe*). They all happened to hail from Shandong province. As one of the group later recalled:

The year I enrolled at school [1923], the eight of us fellow-provincials from Shandong, picked by Yuan Zhongyi, established a painting society. Since Yuan Zhongyi was the oldest among the eight of us, the society's affairs were managed by him. At that time Wang Xuetao was also studying at the school. At first he studied western painting. Afterwards, owing to his ardently patriotic painting, he switched over to the national style (*guohuaxi*). He was a native of Chengan county, Hebei. Everyone had great respect for him, and because of that we recruited this non-Shandongese to participate . . . , giving rise to the name "Nine Friends Painting Society."[53]

For this one small society, the matrix formed by school and provincial affiliation made organizing a simple matter. Notions of friendship and patriotism made the *tongxiang* core readily, though self-consciously, expandable.

The quest for common ties was at once restricted and exclusive as it pertained to the core group of supporters and more open as "intramural competition" stimulated the formation of larger federations and associations.[54] In Hankou, where extensive commercial connections had drawn in migrants from many parts of China, the city's multiethnic character and common problems fighting flood, fire, and disorder bred an "unusual cultural tolerance" rather than mutual hostility.[55] As Bryna Goodman has shown in the case of early Republican Shanghai, "native-place networks were vital links in the extraordinary merging of student, business, and worker concerns and in the formation of the 'united front' effort that characterized" the May Fourth movement.[56] Wasserstrom's essay, and his earlier research, underlines the ongoing importance of native-place ties in Shanghai and other cities.[57]

[53]Xu Peixia as told to Wang Dawei, "Yi 'Jiuyou huashe' " (Recalling the "Nine Friends Painting Society"), in Zhang Changbing and Ning Yuhuan, eds., *Jinghua fengwu* (Styles and customs of the capital) (Shanghai: Shanghai shudian chubanshe, 1992), 138.

[54]Jeffrey Wasserstrom, *Student Protests in Twentieth-Century China: The View from Shanghai* (Stanford, Calif.: Stanford University Press, 1991), 131–32. Vera Schwarcz makes a similar point about the positive contribution of provincial ties to student mobilization during the May Fourth movement in 1919 in *The Chinese Enlightenment: Intellectuals and the Legacy of the May Fourth Movement of 1919* (Berkeley: University of California Press, 1986), 70.

[55]Rowe, *Hankow* (1989), 27.

[56]Goodman, "New Culture, Old Habits: Native-Place Organization and the May Fourth Movement," in Frederic Wakeman, Jr., and Wen-hsin Yeh, *Shanghai Sojourners* (Berkeley: Institute of East Asian Studies, 1992), 96–97.

[57]See also Wasserstrom, *Student Protests in Twentieth-Century China*, 127–45.

THE OTHER CHINA

The new or newly developing cities of China's littoral, the so-called treaty ports, introduced radically new ideas and technologies to China in the late nineteenth century. Neon-lit and filled with novelties like electric power stations, streetcars, and cinemas, coastal cities made indelible impressions on Chinese who approached them from the interior and the countryside.[58] Their capacity to shock and disorient was notorious. As late as the 1920s a writer from the hinterland mistook the opening elevator in the lobby of his Shanghai hotel for what he thought was his disappointingly small room.[59] For the turn-of-the-century author Wu Woyao, Shanghai evoked "the smell of money . . . swirling crowds . . . rackets, kidnapping, and gambling . . . a shelter for sinners and swindlers."[60] These cities were dynamic mixers of people but, like their sixteenth-century predecessors, were also morally suspect for that reason. The cautionary statement of a 1928 Shanghai police report gave the conventional assessment: "We have found that along the banks of the Hu, Chinese and foreign residents mix together in great numbers. Their style of life has been traditionally frivolous and flashy. There is mutual competition for profit, owing to the convenience of communications and the crass materialism."[61] A Chinese visitor to Shanghai in 1892 listed the city's seven "modern" developments as "brothels, theatres, restaurants, tea-houses, opium dens, opera houses, and horse carriages."[62] That many of these treaty port disorders were Chinese, rather than foreign, and traditional, rather than modern, in origin was less important than "demoralization" by association or "mixing."[63] Over time coastal urbanization had complex cultural ramifications ranging from the heightened popularity of old-fashioned novels and theatrical pro-

[58]Lucian Pye, "Foreword," in Christopher Howe, *Shanghai: Revolution and Development in an Asian Metropolis* (Cambridge: Cambridge University Press, 1981), xv.
[59]Perry Link, "Traditional-Style Popular Urban Fiction in the Teens and Twenties," in Merle Goldman, ed., *Modern Chinese Literature in the May Fourth Era* (Cambridge, Mass.: Harvard University Press, 1977), 346.
[60]Cited and discussed in Milena Dolezelova-Velingerova, "Narrative Modes in Late Qing Novels," in Dolezelova-Velingerova, ed., *The Chinese Novel and the Turn of the Century* (Toronto: University of Toronto Press, 1980), 66–67.
[61]Cited in Frederic Wakeman, Jr., "Policing Modern Shanghai," *China Quarterly*, no. 115 (September 1988): 408.
[62]Leung Yuen-sang, *The Shanghai Taotai: Linkage Man in a Changing Society, 1843–90* (Honolulu: University of Hawaii, 1990), 102.
[63]Ibid.

ductions to the popular introduction of the toothbrush.[64] Change concealed continuity (the enduring merchant guild basis of new chambers of commerce) and vice versa (*tongxiang* societies put to partisan political use).

The social structure of the treaty ports included multiple worlds and communities.[65] One of the most obvious divisions issued from imperialist appropriation of Chinese territory. Foreign control of large sections of cities like Shanghai and Tianjin created "states within the state."[66] Affronts to insurgent Chinese national feeling, these foreign settlements were partly under the control of Chinese interests including criminal bodies like the Qing Bang (Green Gang).[67] In a typical move of this kind, the Green Gang reached agreement in 1925 with Shanghai's Frenchtown authorities to help regulate crime in return for protection of its illegal interests in areas like the opium trade.[68] Foreign institutions could be likewise bent to the purposes of Chinese employees. For example, foreign-owned banks in the treaty ports were staffed mostly with Chinese hired by the "comprador," or agent charged with standing between foreigners and the Chinese banking public. The Shanghai branch building of the Hongkong and Shanghai Banking Corporation was clearly divided into separate Western and Chinese units. As a result, for the Chinese banking customer "the visual impact would be overwhelmingly Chinese."[69] As a matter of procedures, the Chinese section functioned as a "bank within a bank," dependent on foreign managers for "authenticating signatures" and yet independent enough in business dealings to create considerable confusion as to who was responsible for loan defaults or the occasional spectacular cases of fraud and embezzlement.[70] For Chinese bankers themselves in these circumstances, being at once both inside and outside a foreign bank that

---

[64]Perry Link on the popularity of "butterfly fiction"; Olga Lang on the rise of the toothbrush (*Chinese Family and Society* [New Haven: Yale University Press, 1946], 96).

[65]Frederic Wakeman, Jr., and Wen-hsin Yeh, "Introduction," in Wakeman and Yeh, *Shanghai Sojourners*, 13.

[66]Marie-Claire Bergère, " 'The Other China': Shanghai from 1919 to 1949," in Howe, *Shanghai*, 7.

[67]Wakeman, "Policing Modern Shanghai," 413–18.

[68]Nicholas R. Clifford, *Spoilt Children of Empire: Westerners in Shanghai and the Chinese Revolution of the 1920s* (Hanover, N.H.: University Press of New England, 1991), 153. The French officials also received bribes for their trouble.

[69]Frank H. H. King, *The History of the Hongkong and Shanghai Banking Corporation* (Cambridge: Cambridge University Press, 1988), III: 351.

[70]Ibid.

looked Chinese, and sometimes in point of practice was, suggested a degree of ambiguity that might either confuse or stimulate those caught
up in such contradictory social positions. Other foreign enterprises, like
the Swedish Match Company, included similar Chinese employee-
managed reconfigurations of business practice within the form supplied
by the Western firm.[71]

Negotiating these multiple roles and identities was part and parcel of
urban life in what Marie-Claire Bergère has termed "the Other China"
of the treaty port cities.[72] Visual, social, and moral ambiguity earned the
new metropolises the opprobrium of many critics of this seemingly "un-
Chinese" creation.[73] However, as Bergère argues, the treaty ports also
"gave the hitherto fettered forces of traditional Chinese society (such as
tradesmen, contractors, dissenting writers or rebellious students) a
chance to blossom out."[74] Merchants who, because of personal inclination or occupational status, did not assimilate into the Confucian social order had the chance to create their own domain. Experience in
trade had schooled them to the value of openness to the outside world
as contrasted with the more insular prejudices of bureaucratic, agrarian
China.[75] Their pieces of the fragmented urban social structure might be
assembled in a new composite order by business leaders, politicians, foreign capitalists, or gangsters.

Ironically, cities that advertised the importance, even ascendance of
law, treaties, constitutions, and rational procedure, were not governed
in these terms themselves. Perhaps Shanghai was the paramount example
in China of a modern city run on the basis of connection, brute force,
and illegality. In these cities where rule of men, not law, prevailed, urban
China's long-standing informal approach to governance continued, albeit in a caricature of its former moral self. Long-gowned gangsters took
their place beside long-gowned and Western-clothed gentlemen. At one
level the contest for Shanghai was between foreign imperialists and the
Chinese government. At another, the men of the foreigners' Shanghai
Club competed and colluded with the men of the Green Gang in a duel

[71]Sherman Cochran, "Three Roads into Shanghai's Market: Japanese, Western, and Chinese Companies in the Match Trade, 1895–1937," in Wakeman and Yeh, *Shanghai
Sojourners,* 54.
[72]Bergère, " 'The Other China.' "
[73]Ibid., 3.
[74]Ibid., 13.
[75]Ibid., 2. As early as 1873 some residents of Hankou thought foreign ambassadors should
be allowed to have interviews with the emperor. Rowe, *Hankow* (1989), 28.

of rival fraternal organizations.[76] On an issue-by-issue basis the results of this kind of combat were by no means preordained.[77]

In this urban world of many "worlds" the broker or mediator was crucial to getting things done. This might be articulated in vertical fashion between city and regime (the latter in settled, national, or international form, or as an invading warlord), among equals, or between groups whose relative status was unclear or contested. In the late 1920s and early 1930s, Shanghai was "run," as much as any one person could manage the feat, by gangster Du Yuesheng. Du held an honorary post as a French police detective, was after 1924 boss of the Green Gang, posed as a "gangster philanthropist," and took advantage of the protection offered by Portuguese citizenship.[78] His career illustrated how national, legal, and social contradictions could be efficiently resolved in the actions of one person who had mastered every possible connection and affiliation.[79] As Perry indicates, gangster networks are reappearing in Chinese cities, especially among workers left unprotected by the existing *danwei* and the state enterprise system. The growing role for labor brokers discussed by Solinger is an example of how informal networks are coming to displace the kind of institutional channels that had long served to limit the gray region of fixers and mediators essential to such *sub rosa* systems.

THE REACH OF URBAN SOCIETY

From the turn of the century, the habits and skills associated with citizenship continued to be acquired and exercised by widening circles of urban residents.[80] Nationalism and interest politics were the principal engines of the expansion. The movement toward a more open, participatory politics developed beyond the elitist scope of late Qing local activism. The continued weakness of formal institutions, including the

[76]See Clifford's account of the Shanghai Club's cultural role in shaping Shanghai's foreign community.

[77]See Tim Wright on the limits of imperialist power in Shanghai in "Shanghai Imperialists versus Rickshaw Racketeers: The Defeat of the 1934 Rickshaw Reforms," *Modern China* 17, no. 1 (January 1991): 76–111.

[78]Wakeman, "Policing Modern Shanghai," 417–18, and Clifford, *Spoilt Children*, 64 and 152.

[79]Brian G. Martin, " 'The Pact with the Devil': The Relationship between the Green Gang and the Shanghai French Concession Authorities, 1925–1935," in Wakeman and Yeh, *Shanghai Sojourners*.

[80]Keith Schoppa, *Chinese Elites and Political Change: Zhejiang Province in the Early Twentieth Century* (Cambridge, Mass.: Harvard University Press, 1982).

state, and the strength of patron-client relations of old and new vintage made for a complex blend of network and mass politics.

Many attempts at creating new institutions were carried out under the rubric of "local self-government" (*difang zizhi*), also translatable as "local autonomy."[81] Cities, neighborhoods, schools, and labor unions readily appropriated the idea.[82] The notion, introduced via Japan in the late nineteenth century, followed the line of thinking of the *fengjian* school in that self-government was supposed to strengthen the state by promoting local activism.[83] As late Qing reformers had imagined the process, "From a foundation in self-governing localities, a new order was to be constructed in ascending stages—from the county, to the province, to the empire as a whole."[84] In the tradition of earlier literati projects, self-government was also to begin with the cultivation of one's character against the corrupting influences of the world. (Reformer Huang Zunxian's injunction was: "What I demand of you is to govern your own persons; and to govern your own localities.")[85]

While ascending in this fashion, the value attached to state recognition of local endeavors made groups bent on local autonomy receptive to government control and regulation. Perhaps the best example of how this process worked in the late Qing and early Republican period is the professional association (*fatuan*). Formed shortly after 1900, these chambers of commerce, bankers' associations, and lawyers' associations were chartered by the government in the hope of winning their loyalty. It was an effort by "official rule" (*guanzhi*) to co-opt "elite proponents of self-rule (*zizhi*)."[86] Judged from this angle, this process of group formation was clearly statist, except for the fact that *fatuan* status helped consolidate elite control over local affairs in ways often detrimental to central control. As Susan Mann has suggested, the *fatuan* strategy of giving power to merchants, say, as a means of taking control of local communities is inexplicable except as part of a long tradition of ideologically dependent self-regulation and civic activism.[87] This tradition of

---

[81]Bergère, *The Golden Age*, 51–52.
[82]David Strand, *Rickshaw Beijing: City People and Politics in the 1920s* (Berkeley: University of California Press, 1989), 178–81.
[83]Kuhn, "Local Self-Government," 270.
[84]Ibid.
[85]Cited and discussed in ibid.
[86]Schoppa, *Chinese Elites and Political Change*, 34.
[87]Susan Mann, *Local Merchants and the Chinese Bureaucracy, 1750–1950* (Stanford, Calif.: Stanford University Press, 1987), 152–55.

"dependent autonomy" continued into the twentieth century and gave associational life the same, peculiar double edge exhibited by *xiangyue*, *baojia*, and the less formal (but more potent) structures of elite activism in the centuries preceding. In Chapter 12, on legal activists, Sidel reports on legal societies that mix "state initiative" and "social initiative" and so exhibit comparably complex variations on the themes of dependence and autonomy. Chapter 4, on social and political change in the town of Xinji, explores comparable ambiguities in the relationship between the state as regulatory agent and new private merchant associations and finds more dependence than autonomy.

Self-government in the Republican period put a new ideological edge on the ascending curve of social organization in the city. Association building and the *fatuan* phenomenon pointed to concrete and immediate ways of joining legal status to local power. Many observers, from students and workers to intellectuals, politicians, and business people, at first assumed that the modern China that was emerging in the cities carried with it a social and political structure that was democratic and republican in some fundamental sense. In his 1919 essay "A Great Alliance of the Popular Masses" (*Minzhong di da lianhe*), Mao Zedong imagined a new political community made up of locality clubs, guilds, labor unions, student federations, and professional associations, all rising from local society toward some larger national unity.[88] Mao shared the iconoclasm of his generation and naturally was disinclined to credit the past as contributor to the new politics of the May Fourth movement. But his insistence on the need for a broad union of diverse groups also drew on the traditional ideal of social consensus and a kind of social, community-based "united front." Social fragmentation was overcome by a national mobilization that aimed at something more than intermittent leadership.

Traditional social patterns might facilitate or inhibit these larger scales of organization. Whereas *tongxiang* ties helped students organize on a larger scale, locality differences often proved divisive for workers.[89] As a new study of Shanghai labor politics suggests, "The politics of [native]

---

[88]Mao, "Minzhong di da lianhe" (A great alliance of the masses), in *Mao Zedong ji* (The collected works) (Tokyo: Sososha, 1983), vol. 1, originally published in *Xiangjiang pinglun* (The Xiang River review) July 21; July 28; August 4, 1919. An English translation and commentary by Stuart R. Schram can be found in *China Quarterly*, no. 49 (January–March 1972): 76–105.

[89]Wasserstrom, *Student Protests*, 132.

place was ... a two-edged sword that both opened possibilities and set boundaries to the development of collective action."[90] Modern associations like chambers of commerce and labor unions were often built on the basis of merchant or craft guild practice and organization. This could facilitate rapid mobilization and give social stability to these new societies and associations. At the same time, formalizing what had been informal and chartering what had been extralegal could create conflicts over leadership, control, and funding issues. For women employed in Shanghai textile factories, sworn sisterhoods (*jiemei hui*) based on home village and gender offered immediate protection against harassment.[91] But only by overcoming their own subethnic divisions could they turn these sisterhoods to the project of union activity by the 1940s.[92] *Tongxiang* solidarities played a comparable, fragmenting role among workers in Tianjin, as Lieberthal argues and more recent research has confirmed.[93] When autonomy at one level required subordination of members and member groups, conflict might erupt. Chamber of commerce and union federation leaders battled dissident guild members and work groups over the issues of whether and how such incorporation would take place.[94] As Perry suggests in her essay, the kind of intense factional struggles typical of contemporary worker politics was well established as a pattern early in the century.

In Republican cities balance among social forces, many newly mobilized, became more elusive and collision more common. Under the pressure to organize, not all "inner arenas" turned out to be as supportive of civic action as others. New political vehicles like mass parties lacked the self-limiting instincts of the Imperial regime and its local elite allies. The old bogey of localism emerged in the *junxian* fear of fledgling national organizations like the Communist Party that they would be undermined by "local cliques."[95] The stage was set for bitter and bloody

[90]Elizabeth J. Perry, *Shanghai on Strike: The Politics of Chinese Labor* (Stanford, Calif.: Stanford University Press, 1993), 30.
[91]Emily Honig, *Sisters and Strangers; Women in the Shanghai Cotton Mills, 1919–1949* (Stanford, Calif.: Stanford University Press, 1987).
[92]Ibid.
[93]Gail Hershatter, *The Workers of Tianjin, 1900–1949* (Stanford, Calif.: Stanford University Press, 1986).
[94]Strand, *Rickshaw Beijing*, chaps. 5, 7, and 10, for examples of merchant and worker conflict of this kind.
[95]Hans J. van de Ven, *From Friend to Comrade: The Founding of the Chinese Communist Party, 1920–1927* (Berkeley: University of California Press, 1991), 224.

conflict over who would dominate the cities. The cost to dreams of local autonomy would be dear.

But in 1919 activists like Mao were transfixed by the spectacle of an insurgent and elastic society stretching from parochial interests (Mao recognized that particular interests could be a limiting factor in achieving greater cooperation among groups) to broad-based union and beyond. In the aftermath of the May Fourth movement, many Chinese attempted to realize such unions in the form of "citizen assemblies" (*guomin dahui*) held at the local, provincial, or national level to supplant or replace corrupted Republican institutions. One Shanghai-based manifesto, by a federation of "all circles" (*gejie*) representing students, merchants, workers, and other *jie*, proposed a national *guomin dahui* made up of one elected representative from each county convened at a place from which armed men could be banned.[96] Such assemblies never progressed beyond local protest meetings. For all their rhetorical appeal and social support, these local representations of the nation could not grasp the state power encamped outside cities or on the march along the rail lines that linked them. Nor was the late Imperial option of "nongovernmental" management as attractive in an era when social and economic problems seemed to demand direct state intervention. How could one be "thrifty" with resources in the face of poverty and backwardness? The richness of Chinese cities in terms of old and new cultural and economic practices could not conceal the desperate poverty of many city residents in their courtyard slums, squatter shacks, or factory tenements. During the Republican era, every major urban center developed slum areas spurred or enlarged by forces including rapid industrialization, the arrival of war and famine refugees, and expulsion of the poor from other quarters of the city by government fiat.[97] In Shanghai in the 1930s nearly 100,000 people lived "in horrifyingly insalubrious conditions in shanties made of mud and straw."[98] In addition, the rise of coastal cities to world standards of production and discourse made the real and perceived gap between city and village ever more striking and politically explosive. Against the weight of these urban and

---

[96]*Yishi bao* (Social welfare) (Beijing), August 18, 1920, 3.

[97]Hu Zhenghao, "Pinmin ku yu penghu qu" (Slums and slum areas), in Xin Ping, Hu Zhenghao, and Li Xuechang, eds., *Minguo shehui daguan* (An omnibus of Republican society) (Fuzhou: Fujian chubanshe, 1991), 530–33.

[98]Christian Henriot, *Shanghai 1927–1937: Municipal Power, Locality, and Modernization* (Berkeley: University of California Press, 1993), 221.

societal crises, the tension between control and autonomy was still operative but the old balance between central and local and official and informal power was disappearing.

One might have expected the powerful economic forces shaping cities like Shanghai to create the conditions for a social and political breakthrough by a new urban elite, led by the captains of industry, finance, and commerce. The industrialization of Chinese cities produced a bourgeoisie connected to the merchant tradition but possessed of vastly greater resources. But as Bergère has pointed out, the strength of class-based and class-led urban society suffered, paradoxically, from the weakness of the state.[99] This governmental inconstancy and unreliability had been evident decades earlier when urban residents appeared ripe for state-led formalization and regularization of city services. Instead of achieving a new partnership with willing social forces, officials misappropriated tax monies or spent them to benefit the few, rather than build broad public support.[100]

Then, during the bourgeoisie's "golden age" in the 1920s, when Shanghai elites appeared well positioned to develop beyond locality to national prominence, the state proved insufficiently powerful to be worth capturing or influencing. As Bergère argues from a comparative perspective:

The emergence of an autonomous society tends to naturally limit the interventions of State power, and the defense of the individual—or local—liberties encourages a measure of pluralism. But after 1911, the very disintegration of the Chinese State checked the development of an anti-government opposition of the kind that provided the basis for the revolutionary character of the Russian bourgeoisie at the end of the eighteenth century and of the Russian bourgeoisie a hundred years later.[101]

Instead there were ironic gestures toward the local assertion of a national role for these new urban forces. For example, in 1923 a Shanghai federation of groups and associations, led by the local chamber of commerce, in exasperation declared itself the government of China.[102] For all the money and social connections this formal body represented, it had no more luck in reforming the state than did the more modest rallies and pronouncements common throughout urban China in the 1920s. As

---

[99]Bergère, *The Golden Age.*
[100]Rowe, *Hankow* (1989), 182.
[101]Bergère, *The Golden Age,* 240.
[102]Ibid., 224–25.

W.en-hsin Yeh has argued in her study of the reformist Shanghai publication *Shenghuo* (Life), advocates for radical change "pinned [their] hopes on the capacity of the modernizing state" to act strongly in social and cultural matters and were sorely disappointed.[103]

On a more practical level, local elites like the Shanghai bourgeoisie were willing to cede rule at the higher levels to autocratic individuals or parties in exchange for retention of power within their own bailiwicks. Federalist schemes for the country, though seriously and energetically proposed, came to naught.[104] Ambitious plans for national change generally stalled at the local level. The impressive record of municipal administration in Chinese-controlled Shanghai during the late 1920s and early 1930s uncovered by Christian Henriot stands out as a fascinating exception to what has long been assumed to be the rule of failure by city governments.[105] The resulting social retreat in the face of government's failure to advance in a constructive fashion was consistent with a traditional tendency to adopt a purely defensive strategy when it came to local interests.[106] On the one hand, the nationalization of politics, economics, and culture from the late nineteenth century on had stimulated more "proactive" strategies.[107] On the other, the absence of a reliable state undermined the rationality of such attempts to extend the reach of society.

POPULAR AND MASS URBAN CULTURE

The unsettled institutional legacy of the Republican revolution was reflected in the divided, complex state of urban culture. The combination of cosmopolitan and nativist, elite and popular currents that, Kraus sug-

[103]Wen-Hsin Yeh, "Progressive Journalism and Shanghai's Petty Urbanites: Zou Taofen and the Shenghuo Enterprise, 1926–1945," in Wakeman and Yeh, *Shanghai Sojourners,* 216.

[104]Arthur Waldron, "Warlordism Versus Federalism: The Revival of a Debate?" *China Quarterly,* no. 121 (March 1990).

[105]Henriot suggests that these successes in areas like city planning and public health were due to the presence of unusually talented officials and to the desire by the Nationalist government in Nanjing to make Shanghai a showcase suitable for supporting the argument that all of Shanghai should be under Chinese control. Henriot, *Shanghai, 1927–1937,* 234–35.

[106]Pye, "Foreword," xiii–xiv.

[107]See Madeline Zelin's discussion of the shift by Sichuan salt dealers in the late nineteenth century from a purely local strategy to defend their business interests to an effort to cultivate official ties in Beijing ("The Rise and Fall," 101). The term "proactive" is Charles Tilly's. See his *From Mobilization to Revolution* (Reading, Mass.: Addison-Wesley, 1977).

gests in Chapter 7, divides today's cities was powerfully evident then as well. Cities hosted brave new worlds of social experimentation and cultural iconoclasm, comparable to the more recent Misty poets (Chapter 10) and the artistic avant-garde (Chapter 9), while popular culture developed in directions that showed strong continuities with the past. May Fourth activists less catholic in their sympathies than Mao were hostile to anything that looked like Confucianism and suspicious of all existing social arrangements.[108] Their "study societies" (*xueshe*) declared themselves at war with the urban social order in ways that prefigured or embodied a radical, Marxian critique. In an antiurban gesture some of these student "homes" or communes in the city were called "new villages" dedicated to a wholly different way of life.[109] The key concept for many of these groups was "autonomy" in the sense of "self-realization" (*zijue*).[110] Like the networks of artists discussed by Andrews and Gao in Chapter 9, group support was crucial in sustaining cultural experimentation in an often hostile or indifferent environment. The mixed blessing of aggressive state patronage (the "velvet prison" described by Pickowicz in Chapter 8) for new art forms like film and oil painting lay some decades ahead.

As with the case of self-government initiatives, the Republican emphasis on personal cultivation resonated with the past. And for all the novelty of study society ideology and practice, the form itself can be seen as growing out of the literati tradition of poetry clubs and the more overtly political groups sponsored by late Qing reformers like Kang Youwei and Liang Qichao.[111] One of the biggest differences had to do with the perception and reality of cultural context. In the Confucian world, small groups and even single individuals could expect the right idea or gesture to achieve resonance far beyond group or locality. If contemporary urban culture was as corrupt, divided, and moribund as many radicals believed, then example alone was unlikely to achieve much. It was here that nationalism's potential for quickly fabricating such a positive context was so apparent and seductive. But for this substitution of

---

[108]Van de Ven, *From Friend to Comrade*, 43.

[109]Arlif Dirlik, *The Origins of Chinese Communism* (Oxford: Oxford University Press, 1989), 181.

[110]Schwarcz, *The Chinese Enlightenment*, 26.

[111]Discussed in van de Ven, *From Friend to Comrade*, 38–39. Kang and Liang's Self-strengthening Study Society (Qiang xuehui), founded in the closing decade of the nineteenth century, had an official patron. Later *xuehui* were more openly independent.

ideology for culture to work, popular culture with all its contradictions would have to be transformed into a more regimented kind of "mass culture."[112]

In fact, through the 1940s urban culture remained eclectic and popular. Nationalism had a handmade rather than machined feel to it, emerging as it did from the little assemblies of school, shop, and factory. This was partly because no single place or institution monopolized citizenship as a role or idea. Study societies and their "homes" as well as locality inns, merchant and craft guild halls, bathhouses, restaurants, teahouses, brothels, public parks, pavilions, and temples renting out space for meetings formed a network of locations for an expanded public sphere of debate and discussion. Bigger meetings could be accommodated by renting out cinemas or theaters. New public buildings like chamber of commerce headquarters often had auditoria (*huitang*) inside them for large gatherings.[113] New *tongxianghui* buildings included large rooms for meetings and lectures.[114] "Sports stadiums attached to missionary schools, another imported form of architecture, also provided venues for the new politics."[115] The largest assemblies met outdoors in newly appropriated public spaces like the area outside Tiananmen in Beijing. City walls offered almost unlimited "billboard" space for commercial advertisements and political messages in the form of posters as well as slogans scrawled in chalk. Leaflets were handed out on street corners, pitched from moving cars, and thrown from drumtowers and theater balconies. To the marketplaces and hiding places exploited by late Imperial antitax protesters and religious dissidents, and the hostels, guild halls, homes, and teahouses favored by the gentry and merchant elite, the Republican city added a range of new assembly points and converted old ones to new uses. New media like newspapers but also radio and open-air speech making conveyed opinion and polemics to large audiences.

Relative ease of communication gave Chinese cities an air of volatility commented on by a Beijing writer in 1924 in an editorial entitled "Student Upheaval and Currency Prices":

[112]Leo Ou-fan Lee and Andrew Nathan, "The Beginnings of Mass Culture: Journalism and Fiction in the Late Ch'ing and Beyond," in Johnson et al., *Popular Culture,* 360.

[113]Joseph W. Esherick and Jeffrey N. Wasserstrom, "Acting Out Democracy: Political Theater in Modern China," *Journal of Asian Studies* 49, no. 4 (November 1990): 852.

[114]Goodman, "New Culture, Old Habits," 77.

[115]Ibid.

China's boundaries are vast, communications organs are incomplete, and trade back and forth is extremely inconvenient. However, socially there often develops a special kind of phenomenon in which in a moment something will spread from place A to place B. And then, in the blink of an eye, it spreads over the whole country, almost like a kind of plague. . . . For example, Beijing often has student upheavals and then the provinces respond like an echo. School A attacks its president and School B assaults its teachers and then the whole body of teachers and students is accusing each other and fighting for power.[116]

The editorialist went on to argue that currency and financial panic spread the same way, from place to place, city to city, and with the same chaotic results. Then, as now, shared and overlapping spheres of exchange and discourse gave urban China an amplified, unpredictable presence in national economic and political life.

It would be hard to imagine a view or idea not conveyed during the "golden age" of public opinion in the Republican city. Social Darwinists, Confucianists, anarchists, Manchu rights activists, feminists, Buddhists, Christians, anti-Christians, labor unionists, liberals, Fascists, federalists, and Communists all had their innings in the realm of press conference, manifesto, tract, and rally. Much of this speech was direct and critical in the sense of being based on argument and appeals to some higher value.[117] But the Chinese public sphere was also heavily ritualized both in the old sense of relying on the deployment of high-status individuals to make a point, through a kind of "social speech," and in a new sense of political symbolism derived from the May Fourth style of protest politics.[118] The social and ideological coherence of the gentry-merchant activist gave way to what must have seemed at times a Babel of political and cultural idioms. The inner arenas of guild, work group, school, temple, lineage, and *tongxiang* society themselves became politicized in ways that suggested chaos, not consensus. For their part, the regimes of the period, whether of the early Republic, the warlords, the Nationalists, or the insurgent Communists, "never developed a mechanism to connect this new open politics of speeches and meetings to the 'real' politics of governing."[119]

The extensive nature of the periodical press, the growing popularity

---

[116]*Yishi bao*, June 29, 1924, p. 7.

[117]And therefore corresponding to the public sphere as defined for the European case by Jurgen Habermas, in his *The Structural Transformation of the Public Sphere: An Inquiry into a Category of Bourgeois Society* (Cambridge, Mass.: MIT Press, 1989).

[118]See Esherick and Wasserstrom's discussion of the complex roots of twentieth-century China's "political theater."

[119]Esherick and Wasserstrom, "Acting Out Democracy," 853.

of photography, and ability of city residents to fix local events in the dramatic national narratives of the day gave urban culture an archival quality. Cities and city dwellers exhibited a powerful sense of memory. When the novelist Lao She took up residence in Jinan in 1930, he noted in his walks the marks of Japanese cannon fire on the city gates left by the May Third incident of 1928. Inspired to write a novel based on the attack, Lao She later recalled that "many people were able to supply me with materials, including photographs that they had preserved."[120] This capacity to preserve history keyed to bullet holes and "national humiliation" days like May 3 was joined to an "altered . . . sense of space and time" in which newspaper and novel reading, moviegoing, and the witnessing of the public spectacles of revolution and reaction allowed urban Chinese to see their city "as part of a nation [and] the nation as a fragile entity in a threatening world."[121]

City-based authors and audiences also reflected the divisions and contradictions in urban society. As Perry Link has noted, the market for popular fiction among an increasingly literate urban population helped meet the "psychological needs of urban dwellers" disturbed and intrigued by shifting manners and mores.[122] On the one hand, some magazines showcased the work ethic and the advantages of small families in helping urbanites achieve social mobility.[123] On the other, the traditional messages of popular or "butterfly" fiction told in stories of "talent meets beauty" and "knights-errant" helped "keep Westernization at arm's length and to 'protest' against deviations from proper values."[124] Anticipating the issues raised in Chapter 6 on the contested nature of leisure time, personal energies spent on private pursuits became matters of public debate.[125]

Divided cities gave birth to "divided selves" as represented in warring literary tendencies toward the "serious and flippant, harshly realistic and harmlessly escapist, conscientious and degenerate, elitist and popular."[126]

---

[120]Lao She, "Wo zenma xie 'Daming hu' " (How I wrote Lake Daming), in Hu Xieqing, ed., *Lao She shenghuo yu chuangzuo zishu* (An account of Lao She's life and creative work in his own words) (Hong Kong: Sanlian shudian, 1981), 31. The manuscript was later lost in a Japanese bombing attack.
[121]Lee and Nathan, "The Beginnings of Mass Culture," 393.
[122]Link, "Traditional-Style Popular Urban Fiction," 329.
[123]Yeh, "Progressive Journalism," 200–1, 205.
[124]Ibid., 345.
[125]Yeh, "Progressive Journalism," 202–3.
[126]Lee and Nathan, citing the work of Perry Link, "The Beginnings of Mass Culture," 388.

Over time, these divisions took root in radically different tastes and attitudes among different social classes.[127] Urban intellectuals, before many decamped to join the Communists in the hinterland, tried to imagine the China that lay beyond city walls and limits. One of the great themes of city-based political and social rhetoric was the putative gap between city and village. The old Confucian ability to elide urban-rural differences by asserting with confidence that their essential identity was lost as "urban intellectuals replaced the landed literati and speculated on the peasant mind as if the villages were on another planet."[128] When communism returned from its rural sojourn to run the country and manage the cities, rural and rural-minded cadres returned the favor with the "antiurban biases" discussed by Naughton in Chapter 3 on urban economic development.

CHINA'S URBAN NEXUS

In a recent work on the social and cultural bases of political change in the Soviet Union, Moshe Lewin stresses the importance of the twentieth-century shift from an "agrarian nexus" to an urban one.[129] Before 1930, Russian cities were merely the "semiurban branch of the rural world" marked by very low levels of education and culture ("half the cities had no library of any kind and 95 percent had no institutions of higher education") and a near-peasant way of life for most "urban" inhabitants.[130] Massive urbanization from the 1930s on, propelled by Stalinist forced collectivization and industrialization, created a society of "poorly collectivized peasants . . . flanked by millions of poorly urbanized ones" all ruled by "rural or semi-rural" bureaucrats.[131] Then, in the course of the decades to follow, city living, even in an aggressively statist context, allowed the recuperation of a more independent "civil society." In the shadow of Stalinist structures, both bureaucratic and architectural (Moscow's seven monumental skyscraper "beauties" come to mind), "urban microworlds" or "social microforms" emerged based on circles of family, friends, colleagues, and neighbors. In the process life was partly privatized and the state was partly "socialized" or "softened." In more

---

[127]Ibid.
[128]Ibid., 394.
[129]Moshe Lewin, *The Gorbachev Phenomenon: A Historical Interpretation* (Berkeley: University of California Press, 1991).
[130]Ibid., 20.
[131]Ibid., 24.

general, comparative terms, Lewin concludes, "Social disparities, social strife, and social chasms do not prevent an aggregate, a social system, from forming and impinging upon all its parts. . . . Even a loose imbrication is still an interconnected system."[132]

By comparison, although Russia and the Soviet Union were decades ahead in the creation of state socialism, China's cities were fully urban in the sixteenth century. This urban world was constructed on the basis of a "loose imbrication" of "social microforms" tightened periodically through gentry and merchant leadership. Thanks to China's "amphibian" elites this urbanity could emerge without severing cultural ties with the rural population. In the first half of this century Chinese cities grew around a cluster of modern architectural and institutional forms including factories, banks, universities, cinemas, libraries, museums, and hotels, while, by and large, preserving key elements of the older order like *huiguan*, temples, markets, theaters, and city walls.[133]

Most city walls and most of this older architectural and institutional legacy failed to survive intact or at all the construction of socialism. Chinese cities, like their Russian counterparts, today face a comparable project of physical rebuilding and social recuperation. A long and deep tradition of social interaction in urban environments will surely comprise a significant precedent and resource. This is despite the fact that, as Naughton points out, the socialist preference for industrialization with a minimum of urban amenities and culture vitiated the pre-1949 traditions. On the political front, if China's democratic tradition is largely one of movements and false starts rather than institutions, the prospects for a direct turn to democracy in the cities is problematic. However, if China's societal tradition is rooted in informal networks and social microforms, society itself is far more resilient and capable of regeneration in forms ranging from democracy salons and think tanks to gangster organizations, independent labor unions, and poetry clubs.

More specifically, contemporary Chinese cities in historical perspective still represent major tests of the control and autonomy, *junxian* and *fengjian* tension. Cities cannot manage their affairs anywhere in the world without state intervention and coordination. This has been generally apparent to Chinese city residents since the late nineteenth century

---

[132]Ibid., 6.

[133]See, for example, Chen Jiang, "Congwu daoyou di bowuguan shiye" (Museums from scratch), and Wan Shaoyuan, "Shiren zhumu di tushuguan shiye" (Libraries in the public eye), in Xin Ping et al., *Minguo shehui daguan*, 950–59.

(as it was to Hangzhou tax protesters in the sixteenth). The problem has been how to intervene and where to put Chinese society's prodigious capacity for self-management. Shue's study of Xinji shows a complex, emerging relationship between a more limited, but still heavily staffed, regulatory state and new corporate entities that are neither in the state nor really outside state control. The obvious solution—self-government—has been tried without success, but without ever fading entirely from the imaginations of urbanites and officials. Instead, energies have flowed into the *sub rosa* realm of networking, punctuated by the occasional protest or riot. The floating population as described by Solinger presents a rich field for both network and direct action strategies. Others, like entrepreneurs, who are relatively free from state patronage and *danwei* restrictions, for the most part appear to prefer networking to formal representation.

If autonomy is conceived of in Lewin's sense as informal, emergent, and embedded in urbanism, however, greater autonomy for individuals, groups, and communities in Chinese cities is likely to be more a matter of formal recognition than adding something entirely new. Based on historical precedent, the steps from state control to popular upheaval and from state initiative to social initiative can be made in a moment. Constructing or reconstructing a balanced, constitutional relationship between state and society is likely to be a much knottier problem. One lasting contribution of communism has been a level of oppression sufficient to bring the state close enough even for local society to grasp it firmly. Whether the tail will now wag the dog remains to be seen. As Shue argues, the state has not yet released its grip on social life. As Chapters 6, 13, and others show, there is now too much independent and semi-independent social life for the state to grasp.

One of the reasons central authorities regard urban autonomy in its various manifestations as deviant behavior is that they have the old fear of localism without the *fengjian* faith that it will all work out in the end. This helps explain the state effort, recounted by Wang, to prevent cross-*danwei* affiliations by various social groups. "Imbrication" in Lewin's terms, a long-standing urban tradition in China, threatens the eventual emergence of new social "united fronts" of a formal and self-governing nature. Of course, *fengjian* reformers were typically too busy with local projects to care much about regime survival; they showed "a deep concern for the welfare of the people and emphasized the historical necessity of a system rather than its contribution to the stability of a dynasty."[134] This kind of indifference to the "Imperial" center is likely to be provocative to a state sensitive to late Qing analogies to its own mixed record of decadence and development.

Localism in both its fixed and portable forms continues to be a key means by which city dwellers in China have turned strangers into allies and neighbors into adversaries. Localism is likely to expand to fit the larger urban community under conditions of maximum mobility and common purpose. As Gaubatz observes, there are plenty of basic urban problems that require a communitywide perspective to achieve a solution. But the potential for constructing community can be subverted by broad prejudice, like that held before and after 1949 in Shanghai against residents from north of the Yangzi River (the subethnic Subei people) by residents from south of the river.[135] Prejudices against rural immigrants as "animals" recounted by Solinger are hardly encouraging on this score. Community can also be undermined by the state's refusal to permit participation in citywide governance, an obstacle that seems likely to remain in place for the immediate future.

As Bergère has pointed out, where autonomy and localism meet the outside world, as they have historically in the coastal areas, the makings of a peculiarly aggressive and provocative urbanism are at hand. "The Other China" has lost little of its controversial character in the last hundred years. As the treaty port experience suggested, the maddening complexity of the boxed (worlds within worlds and states within states) and imbricated structures of these cities has made it difficult for Chinese states this century to perch atop them.[136] As Gaubatz indicates, the regime has sought to replicate to a degree the treaty port pattern spatial isolation of Western-style enterprises and entertainments. But the creative power of these zones and these cities in the realms of economy, culture, and politics has been unrivaled and will prove difficult to isolate or contain. Coastal cities in this century have been powerful centers for the diffusion of social, cultural, and political models to the rest of the country, from cinemas in provincial capitals to newspapers and maga-

[134]Min, *National Polity and Local Power*, 99.
[135]Honig, "Pride and Prejudice: Subei People in Contemporary Shanghai," in Perry Link, Richard Madsen, and Paul G. Pickowicz, *Unofficial China: Popular Culture and Thought in the People's Republic* (Boulder, Colo.: Westview, 1989).
[136]Lewin imagines an urban or rural nexus as something a state can try to "perch" on (*The Gorbachev Phenomenon*, 15).

zines in county seats and cigarettes and communism everywhere else.[137]
The "suburban industrialization" described by Naughton is yet another
example of this kind of influence.

Finally, popular culture, as distinguished (though not entirely separate) from official, elite, or high culture, is an integral part of the Chinese
urban tradition. Whether this meant coping with the onset of a money
economy in the sixteenth century or the rise of modernity in its various
guises in the twentieth, city residents as worshipers, readers, and viewers
have often confounded their elite and official critics by revering the
wrong god or reading the wrong book. Chen's essay on *qigong* demonstrates how pervasive and influential popular responses to urban crises
can be. Pickowicz and Wang indicate the power of consumers of popular
culture to welcome sexually explicit films and novels in defiance of state
efforts to ban or regulate such materials. The urban populace has also
participated voluntarily in the opening of culture to include a conception
of self (understood as individual, family, or group) permanently placed
in the wider realms of nation and world. Even if commodification of
culture replaces ideological regimentation, this popular dimension promises a return to its pre-Communist state of unpredictability.

[137]For the diffusion of big city material culture to provincial capitals and county seats see
Lang, *Chinese Family and Society*, 78.

Editors and contributors

EDITORS

DEBORAH S. DAVIS, professor and chair in the Department of Sociology at Yale University, is the author of *Long Lives: Chinese Elderly and the Communist Revolution*. She has also coedited, with Ezra Vogel, *Chinese Society on the Eve of Tiananmen* and, with Stevan Harrell, *Chinese Families in the Post-Mao Era*.

RICHARD KRAUS is professor and chair of the Political Science Department at the University of Oregon. His books include *Class Conflict in Chinese Socialism; Pianos and Politics in China: Middle Class Ambitions and the Struggle over Western Music;* and *Brushes with Power: Modern Politics and the Chinese Art of Calligraphy*.

BARRY NAUGHTON, an economist, is an associate professor at the Graduate School of International Relations and Pacific Studies of the University of California, San Diego. He is the author of many articles on the Chinese economy and of the book *Growing Out of the Plan: Chinese Economic Reform, 1978–1993*.

ELIZABETH J. PERRY is a professor in the Department of Political Science at the University of California, Berkeley. Her books include *Shanghai on Strike: The Politics of Chinese Labor* and *Popular Protest and Political Culture in Modern China*.

CONTRIBUTORS

JULIA F. ANDREWS is an associate professor in the Department of History of Art at the Ohio State University.

NANCY N. CHEN is an assistant professor in the Department of Anthropology at the University of California, Santa Cruz.

GAO MINGLU, formerly a critic at *Meishu*, served as head of the *China/ Avant-Garde* curatorial committee. Since 1991, he has worked on contemporary art, art history, and art theory at the Ohio State University, Harvard University, and currently the University of Chicago.

PIPER RAE GAUBATZ is an assistant professor in the Department of Geology and Geography at the University of Massachusetts at Amherst.

WENDY LARSON is associate professor of Chinese language and literature at the University of Oregon.

LIU XINYONG is in the Department of Social Science at Syracuse University.

PAUL G. PICKOWICZ is professor of history at the University of California, San Diego.

VIVIENNE SHUE is professor of government at Cornell University.

MARK SIDEL is program officer for the Asia Program of the Ford Foundation in Bangkok.

DOROTHY J. SOLINGER is a professor in the Department of Politics and Society of the School of Social Sciences at the University of California, Irvine.

DAVID STRAND is a professor in the Department of Political Science at Dickinson College.

SU WEI is researcher at the Princeton China Initiative in Princeton, New Jersey.

SHAOGUANG WANG is an assistant professor in the Department of Political Science at Yale University.

JEFFREY N. WASSERSTROM is an associate professor in the Department of History at Indiana University.

Index